D0226398

LF

THE POLITICS
OF URBAN DEVELOPMENT

STUDIES IN
GOVERNMENT AND PUBLIC POLICY

THE POLITICS
OF URBAN
DEVELOPMENT

Edited by
CLARENCE N. STONE
and
HEYWOOD T. SANDERS

UNIVERSITY PRESS OF KANSAS

ALBRIGHT COLLEGE LIBRARY

To Norton E. Long,
who understands the nature of urban political inquiry

© 1987 by the University Press of Kansas
All rights reserved

Published by the University Press of Kansas (Lawrence, Kansas
66045), which was organized by the Kansas Board of Regents and
is operated and funded by Emporia State University, Fort Hays
State University, Kansas State University, Pittsburg State
University, the University of Kansas, and Wichita State University

Library of Congress Cataloging-in-Publication Data
The Politics of urban development.
(Studies in government and public policy)
Includes bibliographies and index.
1. Municipal government—United States. 2. Urban
policy—United States. I. Stone, Clarence N.
(Clarence Nathan), 1935–   . II. Sanders,
Heywood T., 1948–   . III. Series.
JS341.P65 1987   320.973   87-13311
ISBN 0-7006-0332-8
ISBN 0-7006-0333-6 (pbk.)

British Library Cataloguing in Publication Data is available.

Printed in the United States of America
10 9 8 7 6 5 4 3 2 1

352
P769

212833

Contents

14.45

Part 2
Conflict and Conflict Management

Conclusion

Acknowledgments

Any book represents the efforts of many people. An edited book is no exception. Quite the contrary, it represents the efforts of an extraordinarily large number of people. Although we cannot name individually all who have helped to bring this book to fruition, we would like to single out those who have read all or part of this manuscript and have offered us many useful comments and suggestions: Bryan D. Jones, Dennis R. Judd, Norton E. Long, Hilary Sanders, Michael P. Smith, Mary N. Stone, and Todd Swanstrom. In addition to contributing to this volume, Jameson W. Doig has offered much useful advice. At the University Press of Kansas, the staff has excelled in offering encouragement, timely assistance, and unstinting goodwill. That errors of omission and commission and infelicities of language remain is, however, the sole responsibility of the editors. To the contributors to this volume, the editors wish to offer thanks not only for the substance of their chapters but also for their willingness to pull together and keep on schedule in the face of the many demands of contemporary academic life.

Clarence N. Stone
Silver Spring, Maryland

Heywood T. Sanders
San Antonio, Texas

vii

INTRODUCTION

1

The Study of
the Politics of Urban Development

Clarence N. Stone

In the past quarter-century the study of urban politics has shifted from a predominant concern with political culture and ethos to a growing interest in political economy, especially the political economy of urban development. Along with this shift, students of urban affairs have become increasingly conscious of a centralizing economy. As cities strive for economic growth, they find that important decisions about location are often in the hands of large national and international corporations. Few major businesses are strictly local; most are linked to national or even to world markets.

Just as huge enterprises with large domains hold sway in the private sector, big government dominates the public sector. National policies provide much of the framework within which local governments operate. The national government is not only the dominant partner in our federal system; it is also a major influence on the economy. National policies strongly encourage some investment decisions but discourage others.

Urban scholars appropriately have come to recognize that cities are shaped by forces beyond their boundaries. While local officials enjoy considerable formal autonomy, they must respond to external inducements and to penalties beyond their influence. To a large extent, they must play by rules they have not made. Thus, much recent analysis has come to center on the national political economy and how cities are constrained by that context.

There are competing ideas about the city and the national political economy, but one of the most influential is put forward by Paul Peterson. In his *City Limits,*[1] Peterson argues that the city is analogous to a business firm. Peterson maintains that cities, like businesses, seek to maximize the economic return on the resources they control. For cities these resources consist mainly of controls over land use. Peterson contends that in making

3

decisions about land use, cities are limited by the necessity of competing economically. As competitors in a market economy, cities are driven to make the development policies that will most enhance their economic position.

John Mollenkopf offers, not so much a direct challenge to Peterson, as a substantial amendment.[2] Mollenkopf discards the notion of a neutrally operating market and invites us to consider the ways in which national policy decisions have tilted the market process toward greater suburbanization within metropolitan areas and have facilitated regional growth in the Sun Belt at the expense of the Frost Belt. National policies on taxes and capital expenditures, as well as more direct forms of subsidy, confer enormous advantages on some locations and give direction and intensity to the processes through which development occurs. In Mollenkopf's account, these consequences of national policy are not necessarily intended. Instead, they are side effects that come from the jockeying by national political entrepreneurs seeking partisan advantage in the game of coalition building.

Just as Mollenkopf challenges the notion of a neutral market as the allocator of locational advantages, others challenge the notion of a neutral political process.[3] They see the formation of alliances against a background of class and factional struggle. Whereas Peterson talks about a unitary city interest in economic growth, class analysis focuses on the conflicts that pervade development policy. Any given decision, they remind us, may be less concerned with the general welfare than with group or class advantage.[4] Struggle and contradiction, they argue, are built into a capitalist order.

From this quick overview of major schools of thought, several conclusions emerge. Clearly, cities are engaged in economic competition. Clearly, market processes are shaped by national-policy decisions, sometimes intentionally, sometimes inadvertently. Clearly, the costs and benefits of economic growth and change are not uniformly distributed—consequently, class and factional struggle are often evident and are always latent even when they are not manifest. But what else needs to be said? Is there some element of urban-development politics that the existing schools of thought neglect?

The contributors to this volume answer yes. They provide evidence that local government officials make genuine choices, albeit within structural boundaries. Local decision makers do not simply follow the imperatives that emanate from the national political economy; they must also interpret those imperatives, apply them to local conditions, and act on them within the constraints of the political arrangements they build and maintain. Operating from that view, the contributors to this volume subscribe to the view that urban politics still matters. Collectively, their chapters aim to increase awareness of local political practices and how they make a difference.

One of the intellectual challenges that contemporary students of urban development policy face is that of how best to talk about political choice and structural context. Some refer to this as the problem of agency and structure. Others see it as a matter of describing the nature of political autonomy in a complex society. Several contributors to this volume, perhaps most explicitly Stephen Elkin, in his chapter on Dallas, look at the interplay between structural constraint and political choice as a working out of the division of labor between the state (as embodied in the machinery of government at all levels) and the market (in which private ownership prevails). Choice enters into the creation of a set of arrangements whereby accommodation is reached between the wielders of state power and the wielders of market power. Put another way, local politics matters, but it is shaped by the political-economy context.

In the chapters ahead, as we look at a variety of cities and in some cases their development experience across considerable time, we can expect certain continuities. Those who control investment capital are bound to be important actors, along with those who control public authority. These two sets of actors must reach an accommodation. We can also expect differences— variations in how that accommodation is reached. Several contributors explore those variations and the factors that contribute to them.

My task in this opening essay is to place this volume within a body of relevant literature. Of necessity, I must be selective. Since this volume itself is built around the dual theme that local politics matters and that politics is shaped by the division of labor between state and market, I have chosen to focus on the process of coalition building in the local community. How the governing coalition is constituted and what kind of accommodation it represents are centrally important questions. For that reason, in the pages ahead, I give special attention to the importance of political processes.

In many ways this volume can be considered an alternative to Peterson's *City Limits*: it departs in particular from his notion that a unitary interest guides the making of development policy. Peterson's book is enormously influential and is full of insights, especially about the federal system. But by operating deductively to conclude that a local jurisdiction has a unitary interest in favorable development, Peterson takes much of the politics out of city politics. This volume aims to put it back in by talking descriptively and conceptually about the politics of development. That politics has to do centrally with a city's governing coalition. Let me make a preliminary explanation.

There is no objective conception of the public interest to which a community's decision makers are subordinate. They do not simply ask how they can efficiently serve the interest of the community. They may have a general notion of what is good for the community, but the realization of that idea entails a set of operational procedures and arrangements that are themselves very powerful shapers of policy. That is why, in the general study of public policy, implementation should never be treated as something distinct from policy making. Thus, the city's governing coalition is the agent through which conceptions of the interest of the whole community are mediated.

As most students of policy implementation are keenly aware, consensus over general goals often breaks down as the process moves from formal adoption to actual implementation. At that stage, hidden costs rise to the surface, and the stakes in *how* policy is carried out and *by whom* come to the forefront. Conflict emerges, and the struggle may center on the governing coalition—that is, on which interests compose that coalition and by what rules they play. At the execution stage the question of what is good development policy cannot be separated from issues about the means by which that policy is made.

In this opening essay, I start with a description of urban development as an area of inquiry and then attempt to show, through various intellectual traditions, what grounds there are for deeming local politics to be important in its own right. Politics, of course, does not occur in a vacuum. This survey of the literature also gives attention to the structural context within which development policy is made. Here the issue is whether there is a single, overriding economic imperative in which the force of market competition dictates what is to happen, or whether there are multiple imperatives, some of which are political. Winning elections and gaining useful forms of cooperation are, after all, at the center of governing responsibilities in a democratic system. That these responsibilities can be met in more than one way is what political choice is about. That these choices are not trivial is what is meant by the phrase "politics matters."

DEVELOPMENT POLITICS AS AN AREA OF INQUIRY

Urban development *policy* can be defined as consisting of those practices fostered by public authority that contribute to the shaping of the local community through control of land use and investments in physical structure. What falls into the category of urban development is at some point a matter of judgment. Since virtually anything that local government does has at least a remote effect on land use, it seems appropriate to talk about activities that have a reasonably direct and appreciable impact. Even so, the question of directness and size of impact remains as one of judgment. My aim, though, is one, not of precise delineation, but of identifying a general area of inquiry. Zoning; transportation and other infrastructure investments; convention centers and exhibit halls; tax abatements or, inversely, allocations of the revenue burden; development bonds; governmental subsidy of business activities; the use of eminent domain to assemble parcels of land

for resale or leasing; social and amenities requirements attached to development permissions—all are widely recognized examples of development policy.
Even such practices as selective law enforcement can have an effect, for example, on whether a given area becomes or remains a vice district or assumes
a more wholesome character.

The use of the word *development* is itself in need of some clarification.
First, since policy makers generally do not start with a clean slate on land
use, their efforts are more accurately described as reshaping the local community than simply as shaping it. And what I have termed "development
policy" might more strictly be termed "redevelopment policy." Still, as the
term "development policy" is already in use, we have decided to stay with it.

Given the influence of Paul Peterson's book *City Limits* in this area, I
offer a further clarification. Peterson defines development policies as "those
that contribute to the economic well-being of the city."[5] That particular
definition seems to assume the very point that is at issue. To what extent
and in which ways do various projects contribute to well-being? As we shall
see later in chapters on various cities, people may disagree about the impact of a given policy. Some projects that are promoted as economically
beneficial represent risky investments. More than a few grandiose schemes
have failed to reach fruition, or when completed, they have fallen short of
expectations. Even where there are clear and measurable short-term benefits, the long-term consequences may be very much in doubt. Take, for
example, the case of casino development in Atlantic City. A recent analysis
indicates that immediate gains in jobs and tax base should be weighed against
increased costs of services and infrastructure, foregone development alternatives, and the limited capacity of city residents to take advantage of Atlantic City's particular form of economic growth.[6] Development projects often
have hidden costs in the form of unintended consequences. And if development changes the quality of urban life, that change is likely to have long-
term implications for economic well-being. Because quality of life in a community affects the attractiveness of an area as an investment site, economic
well-being cannot be neatly separated from other aspects of the urban condition.

Not only are there questions about the net long-term effects of various
policies, but it is also important to remember that *net* effects are quite different from *uniform* effects. Development is rarely just a matter of adding
to what is already there. It is also a matter of changing and transforming,
and the beneficiaries and defenders of established uses may be quite different from the beneficiaries and defenders of new uses. Even when economic
change increases land value, expands employment, and opens up new investment opportunities, some people end up by losing. Increased land values
mean higher taxes or rents for those on fixed incomes. New job opportunities
may be filled by suburban dwellers, thus by-passing an underemployed city

work force while building pressure for expanded transportation routes through older neighborhoods. High-rise development may discourage the street trade that many small retailers depend upon. Why should a city government embrace policies that help some people while neglecting or harming others? That question may be more pressing politically than are questions about overall economic results. Particular impacts are likely to be clearer and more urgently felt than something as general as the net long-term effect. Yet, city officials cannot be completely inattentive to net long-term effect, clouded by uncertainty though it may be.

To Peterson, this means that development politics is a matter of promoting the most productive use of land. Certainly, cities cannot ignore their competitive economic relationship with other localities, and land is the main commodity that they have to wage the competitive battle with. The inadequacy of this line of argument is what it ignores, the varied and particular interests of those who live, work, and invest in the urban community. City residents are not stockholders whose economic positions go up or down in unison as land-use decisions prove to be shrewd or not so shrewd. The very nature of land is such that it heightens concern with particular interests. The competitive economic struggle goes on within cities as well as between them, and it is made all the more intense by the fact that what happens on one parcel of land affects the surrounding parcels. Locational character cannot be segmented so that there will be no spillover effects from one parcel to another. At the same time, gains and losses are particular to location. If a given area becomes a prime investment location, huge speculative gains are possible for those who hold or can acquire property in requisite-sized blocs. Similarly, disinvestment in a given area—whether because of racial prejudice, environmental deterioration, a shift in the character of the economy, or something else—can harm property holders in that area, while others may be largely unaffected. Land is not a public good, nor is it so pure in its private character that it lacks spillover effects.

What is the significance of this point for Peterson's argument? It is, to paraphrase the National Rifle Association, that cities don't make development decisions; people do. And the people have neither uniform material interests in the decisions that are made nor a common understanding of the risks involved in and the probable consequences of those decisions. The politics of urban development is thus interwoven with a high potential for conflict. Coalition building on behalf of a program is therefore not a simple matter of rallying support from among the indifferent. Instead, it is a complicated task of bringing together the people whose particular interests are served, allaying the concerns or isolating those whose particular interests are threatened, and presenting one's actions as being consistent with the good of at least a majority. Development policy is thus imbued with issues about who benefits and who bears the cost. Peterson is aware of these issues, but he separates them conceptually from development policy, and his analysis never puts them together again.

There are, then, several ways in which the viewpoint set forth here differs from the one offered by Paul Peterson. Instead of focusing on the unitary interest of the city as a corporate entity, this volume suggests that it is more appropriate to consider the pervasiveness of conflict over land use and how that conflict is interwoven with opportunities for particular benefits and protection of organizational domain. Whereas Peterson's analysis concerns the economic position of the city in a competitive process, I think it is important to remember that cities are also places in which people live and seek social as well as physical shelter.[7] Land therefore has use value, in a qualitative sense; and its use value as a place of residence or as a neighborhood setting to one group may come into conflict with its commodity value to another group that is more concerned about speculative profits or investment opportunities.[8] And the city is a sufficiently complex entity to make even calculations about commodity value and investment consequences uncertain. There is no scarcity of positions from which conflicting judgments can be made about how the future of the city can best be served.

CITY DEVELOPMENT AND ORGANIZATIONAL THEORY: PARALLELS IN ANALYSIS

The emphasis here on conflict, in contrast with Peterson's reliance on the notion of a unitary interest, points to a difference in intellectual traditions. In treating the city as an entity bent upon maximizing its economic productivity, Peterson joins those who view organizations as instruments for the efficient pursuit of goals.[9] In taking a different tack, by focusing on coalition building and conflict management, I align myself with an alternative tradition, the natural-systems tradition in organizational analysis.[10] This latter tradition is not inattentive to the fact that organizations are goal-directed, but it treats the members and subunits of organizations as entities with wants and needs that may be separate from the goals of the larger organizational system in which they are located.[11] That business firms are engaged in economic competition does not eliminate internal conflict or remove the tendency to make special accommodations to well-placed individuals and subunits within the organization. Officials in business firms thus are heavily engaged in the political task of coalition building, of bringing into existence a "prevailing coalition."[12] On close examination, it turns out that at the operational level, business firms don't have a single goal; they have a series of goals. It is likely that all goals must be satisfied to some degree, but none is likely to be maximized.[13] How various operational goals are to be blended is a matter of judgment, about which there is no natural harmony. As Graham Allison observes, "priorities and perceptions are shaped by positions."[14]

The concrete behavior of the business firm grows out of the way in which these differences are surmounted—that is, by how the "prevailing coalition" is put together and maintained. The same surely is the case with cities. It seems likely, then, that the development-policy actions of cities are rooted in the political arrangements by which coalitions of actors are brought together and achieve cooperation. It is therefore not enough to look at the competitive economic position of cities; one must look at internal political relationships as well. The fact that entities are engaged in economic competition does not eliminate their political character.

Even when there is agreement on an overall objective (e.g., maximizing profits or promoting growth), that in itself is no guarantee that individuals will exert themselves on behalf of the interest of the whole. The free-rider problem and the game of "odd man out" stand as barriers to cooperation on behalf of a common good.[15] For that reason, organizations often make use of selective incentives or side payments to see that needed actions are performed. The ability and willingness to offer such individual compensations may arguably be an essential feature of effective leadership.

The role of side payments in facilitating cooperation opens up the issue of the dual character of authority. Let us digress for a moment. Because spontaneous and uncoordinated actions of individuals do not automatically cumulate into the common good, there is ground for creating and maintaining a system of authority.[16] Hence, one face of authority is the capacity to induce coordinated action on behalf of the common good. But there is another, a less benign, face of authority. It can be used to routinize the domination of one element of society over its other elements.[17]

The point, as so forcefully made by Robert Michels, is that those in authority inevitably possess a degree of discretion and that discretion may be used to fortify the power they have and perhaps even expand the privileges they and their allies enjoy.[18] Political authority thus can be used to further personal or factional aims: this is the second face of authority. While authority is something distinct from the naked power of domination, it still can be abused, and that is as true in the development area as in any other policy area. We need to keep both faces of authority in mind.

The common good is something that doesn't just happen. It is something that must be brought into being, albeit imperfectly, by a set of political actors. However defined, the common good is mediated through the agency of political leadership. In the case of organizations, the needs of the organization as a whole, Gouldner argues, are "mediated and shaped by powerful individuals."[19] Those who control the levers of organizational power act on the basis of their perceptions and their felt needs, and their actions may diverge from some other observer's assessment of the organization and its needs. Here we confront the central dilemma of politics. In order to be able to advance the common good, some set of actors must be endowed with a capacity to act on behalf of that aim, but those who are endowed with authority may use their capacity in pursuance of a partial view of the common good.

Even where a development coalition is at one point acting within the bounds of what appears to be a policy consensus, this conception of the common good can fall out of favor as conditions change.[20] The common good is not a fixed program to which all agree. It changes over time and may be perceived differently by different constituencies. As programs are made concrete in the process of implementation, they are fashioned by the value trade-offs and the tactical concessions to "realism" that this process represents.[21] For this reason, any policy, no matter how sincerely put forward as being in the public interest, is inescapably shaped by those who carry it out: it is shaped by their interests, their perceptions, their mode of operation, and their particular form of interdependence with one another. Talk of a unitary interest confuses an abstraction with concrete reality; it also shows a lack of appreciation for the difficulty of separating means and ends.[22]

Let us now return to side payments and the furtherance of a general policy. Like coercive acts, side payments can be justified as being necessary expedients for promoting a community's well-being. Patronage, for example, can be useful in achieving needed cooperation. However, the system of patronage can, as in the case of machine politics, become an end in itself. And as Robert Caro documents in his detailed account of the career of Robert Moses, erstwhile reformers may themselves become deeply enmeshed in arrangements to maintain personal power and privilege.[23] Caro shows how Moses made various decisions—about the location of bridges and expressways, about funding arrangements, and about facilitating automotive traffic to the disregard of New York's mass-transit system—in order to generate resources and build alliances that would protect his administrative empire. Whether those were the best decisions for the community can be questioned. Certainly Caro suggests that they were not, that a variety of alternative decisions could have been made that were more supportive of neighborhood stabilization, environmental quality, and mass transit. As the example of Robert Moses illustrates, much that is done in the area of development is more closely linked to the building of coalitions of political support than it is to the furtherance of the community's economic well-being. This is not to suggest that public concerns had no role. Rather, it is to argue that often the connection of policy to economic well-being is less clear and less direct than is the connection of policy to the interests of a coalition of actors who have substantial development concerns.[24]

STRUCTURAL DETERMINISM
VERSUS POLITICAL AUTONOMY

The discussion of the city as a corporate entity engaged in maximizing its economic productivity versus the city as an arena of coalition building is closely related to another debate, that of structural determinism versus political autonomy. That cities are engaged in economic competition is indisputable. Economic competition, particularly as encouraged by the mobility of capital, has to be part of the policy calculus that public officials do. Few would dispute that. The debate is not over whether economic competition is a major constraint on the making of development policy—clearly it is. The debate is over whether the economic imperative is a single, overriding imperative, or whether there are multiple "imperatives" that public officials must balance.[25]

First, consider those who regard profit-driven markets as especially powerful instruments. Whether they be ideologically right, center, or left, they see a single overriding economic imperative. For Edward Banfield, on the right, market imperatives are a reason for discarding hope and compassion as elements of policy making.[26] Ignoring market imperatives only leads to frustration and dissatisfaction. For Paul Peterson, in the center, economic competition among cities is a fundamental fact of federalism and, given a consequent propensity of cities to avoid redistributive policies favoring the poor, a good reason to turn welfare responsibilities over to the national government.[27] For David Harvey, on the left, the power of market-driven decisions is ground for seeking revolutionary change—that is, basic system transformation. Banfield takes the market as given.[28] Peterson sees the market as something to be respected but also to be by-passed where appropriate. Harvey regards it as something to be worked against. But in each case, the market is the central force in city development policy.

What about those who see the city as an arena of multiple imperatives? Do they represent a return to pluralism, a revival of the group approach to politics? Is that what coalition building is about? Not at all. The study of urban politics has undergone a fundamental shift, and there is no going back to pluralism.

A quick review is in order. When Dahl and his colleagues presented their pluralist version of urban politics, they focused almost exclusively on characteristics that are internal to groups and their members. The external world is a source of stimuli to group action but is not a shaper of group capacity and power. According to the pluralist view, groups respond to issues in proportion to the immediacy of the impact that those issues have on the lives of members of the group.[29] Variations in intensity of interest lead to variations in political effort. For those whose career is politics or administrative service in the public sector, career interests stimulate them to develop their skills and apply the resources at their command in pursuit of political influence. But most people most of the time are content to engage in purely private activities. Nelson Polsby has assured us: "If a man's major life work is in banking, the pluralist presumes he will spend his time at the bank, and not in manipulating community decisions."[30] To be sure, pluralists acknowledged that groups vary in resources such as size, cohesion, organization, and wealth; but they contended that no group has a monopoly on resources, and no group devotes all of its resources to politics. According to pluralist analysis, groups make heightened use of resources only on occasional issues of great concern. Hence, pluralists believe that resources are widely dispersed and are only sporadically applied to politics. Differences in the political use of resources account for differences in influence. Aaron Wildavsky says that "the prizes in politics go to the interested and active."[31]

The social characteristics of groups—such things as the time available to members, membership skills in organization and persuasion, and exposure to cosmopolitan norms—have a bearing on political activity. Or, Dahl has suggested, political action is partly a matter of variations in alternative opportunities. For those who are discriminated against in private life, politics may prove to be an attractive channel of mobility and influence.[32]

Whether talking about the impact of policy or about motivations based on socialization, the pluralist frame of reference was inward to groups and their members more than outward (except as a source of stimuli) to the context in which groups operate. Moreover, pluralists gave little attention to barriers in the way of participation. It was natural for them, therefore, to talk about political activity as a recourse for responding to discrimination in the private sector. In Jeffrey Henig's characterization, pluralism assumes a "frictionless transition from interests to interest group."[33] And Dahl, in fact, talked about the openness and accessibility of "pluralistic systems."[34]

Times have changed, and new ideas have gained ascendancy. Pluralist assumptions have been confronted by the free-rider problem as a barrier to collective action and by an array of historical evidence to the effect that some groups are better equipped than others with resources and opportunities to act on behalf of political aims. Increasingly, attention has shifted to the political-economy context in which group struggle occurs.

Structural Marxism, perhaps more than any other body of thought, has led the way in focusing attention on the larger context that sets the terms on which groups contend with one another. And it is Marxism that is most emphatic in talking about society as an arena of conflict. Marxism was thus better able to explain the intense conflict of the 1960s than was either pluralist political science or its close relative, Parsonian sociology. Further, Marxism provided a ready explanation for the fiscal strains that engulfed so many cities in the 1970s. James O'Connor's *The Fiscal Crisis of the State,* which appeared shortly before New York's near bankruptcy, seemed to many to be a prophetic account of the underlying contradictions of modern capitalism, as manifested in cities.[35] According to O'Connor, the state must facilitate capital accumulation through serving the profit-seeking needs of business while at the same time trying to maintain social harmony. Both demands—for capital accumulation and for social harmony—he argues, cannot be met without overspending and throwing the system into crisis.

Structural Marxism has, however, come under criticism for being excessively abstract and for being so general as to explain almost any policy outcome. The capital-accumulation and social-harmony or legitimation functions, for example, are so broad as to include just about everything. One response to the generality of Marxian class analysis is to temper expectations about general theoretical explanation and to focus on the historically specific, but without ignoring continuities in context. Allen Whitt observes: "Specific events and actions are important and variable, not mere epiphenomenal reflections of deep historical principles. To focus on the structural principles alone is to see only the tent, and to miss the circus going on inside."[36]

Such a concern with specific events and actions guides Martin Shefter's recent analysis of fiscal crises in New York City over time.[37] Shefter combines a concern with structural imperatives and a concern with the historically specific choices of political leaders. Like Elkin, Shefter looks at the evolving character of urban regimes. Shefter treats the imperatives surrounding public officials in a highly concrete manner, talking about the need to win votes and to maintain civil order, while at the same time being able to raise revenue, maintain the city's credit, and promote the health of the city's economy. Shefter explains that the word *imperative* should be used cautiously. He observes that what political leaders are surrounded by "are not imperatives in the sense that public officials cannot but heed them, but the penalty of failing to do so can be severe."[38] Furthermore, because there are multiple imperatives, public officials are subjected to a treacherous pattern of cross pressures. In addition, the policy solutions that work at one time "may be insufficient later, as changes in the broader economic and political systems of which the city is a part alter."[39] Yet, while local officials are buffeted by many forces they cannot control and may not foresee, they nevertheless are the architects of their own responses to the structural constraints and changing conditions in which city politics is embedded. As Shefter explains, the way local officials meet these imperatives and challenges "is shaped by the composition of the political coalitions they depend on for support and the structure of political organizations and institutions in their city."[40] Shefter suggests that because coalitions and the arrangements on which they rest are not easily changed, political crises and realignments can be expected periodically, as incumbent coalitions prove incapable of devising satisfactory responses to changing conditions. In New York City this has led to a cycle of political crisis and reform.

The political instability that Shefter calls our attention to is, on the surface, consonant with pluralism and the fluidity of group alignments. Yet Shefter is not talking about the kind of fluidity and issue-by-issue reconstituting of coalitions that pluralists envisaged. Not only are the coalitions he talks about relatively stable except in the long run, coalitions come together as arrangements for coping with enduring constraints. It is the necessity of responding to these constraints that makes appropriate the use of the term *imperatives*. So, whereas pluralism looked mainly inward—that is, to the social psychology of groups, to what group members care about, and to how directly and immediately policies affect group members—contemporary analysis looks mainly outward—to the context that groups operate within.

What is that context? Even though the specifics of the context may change, we still need to be mindful of its durable features, especially the division of labor between market and state.[41] Because of this division, Elkin argues, public officials are forced to resolve the tension between popular control and economic productivity; and because the resolution is imperfect, this tension remains a source of political uncertainty. Liberal democracy grants wide freedom to the holders of capital; it also provides substantial opportunity for discontented groups to challenge those who wield public authority. Political autonomy is therefore not a matter of creating a world of one's own choosing. Instead, it is a matter of putting together arrangements that can hold in check the tension between what Charles Lindblom calls the "privileged position of business,"[42] which is characteristic of capitalism, and the equality of citizens in voting rights and civil liberties, which is the foundation of popular control. The position of business can clash with the principle of popular control. Significantly, Shefter concludes his study of New York City with the query Can cities be democratically governed? And he answers, "Only partially": political arrangements are shaped and reshaped by the need for city officials to "retain the confidence of the capital markets as well as the support of a majority of their city's voters."[43]

If the same structural constraints are found in all cities, what is at issue? Development politics is in part about variations in the arrangements through which a governing coalition is put together and how it copes with those not included. Development politics is also in part about policies themselves and how they are understood in public discourse. Development projects are almost always defended as being in the public interest, and opposition is often stated in the same terms.[44] Yet a law of indeterminacy prevails: a community cannot know in concrete terms what the public interest is, independent of political activity. Participants pursue what is most immediate and real to themselves. But as governing arrangements are put together, maintained, and modified, perception of what is immediate, as well as understandings of what is real, change. The process of governing, opposing, and compromising in the face of multiple imperatives alters the participants' understanding of what is at stake in development policy and how that policy should be handled. Deliberation occurs, but it occurs in a context of making adjustments among imperatives—political as well as economic. Understandings do change: understandings about the riskiness of large and costly projects, about the appropriateness of various forms of subsidy, and, above all, about the interdependence of various elements of the community. To talk about coalition formation and conflict management is not to reduce policy making to those activities but to suggest that the understanding of development policy that guides a set of decision makers will be influenced by the political arrangements that surround the process of deliberation. Development politics is about the substance of policies, political arrangements, and connections between the two.

CONCLUSION

This book differs from Peterson's influential *City Limits* and from structural Marxism in a particular way: it operates from a different paradigm—a regime paradigm.[45] Structural constraints are real, but they are mediated through the political arrangements that enable a prevailing coalition to govern a community. This book is therefore in no way intended to deny that cities are limited by the structure of their situation. But as the chapters that follow make clear, settings vary, and what community actors make of these settings varies as understandings change from one time and governing coalition to another.

Some readers may respond that the beauty of *City Limits* is that it explains much with a few simple assumptions about utility maximization. There is no doubt that deductive models are powerful tools of analysis, but Philip Abrams cautions that such models tend to absorb rather than to explain history.[46] An exclusive focus on structural requirements obscures the range of efforts, strategies, and value choices that community actors make in meeting those requirements.

Operating from a regime paradigm, the ensuing chapters do two things. First, they convey some of the variety of time and place that characterize development politics. Second, they give some sense of why this variety is significant in political study. They point to value choices that are implicit in efforts to shape policy by one set of arrangements rather than another. Struggle is therefore very much a part of the development picture they paint.

A regime paradigm, as exemplified in the ensuing chapters, then, runs counter to Peterson's deductive model in significant ways. As Thomas Kuhn argues, paradigms compete less on the basis of which commands the strongest support in a body of evidence and more on the basis of the issues they raise.[47] Paradigmatic debates are not over who has the best evidence; they are over who has the best questions. Perhaps the main question in *City Limits* is one about which level of government is most suited to make redistributive policy; and the answer, based on the fact of economic competition among states and localities, is the national government. In making that argument forcefully, Peterson's paradigm employs the notion of a unitary interest of the city, an overriding interest in economic productivity. This idea about a unitary interest guides inquiry. It precludes a set of questions about why one development strategy rather than another is employed and therefore suggests no need to look for conflict. Furthermore, it provides no invitation to probe the policy strategies that a community pursues. If the typical development strategy is one that relies on a trickle-down effect to benefit the general public, the notion of a unitary interest provides no basis for questioning that choice or how it came about. Issues of equity are by-passed, and political study is left without any critical role to play. A regime paradigm, on the other hand, invites us to ask how a governing coalition is held together and what difference that makes in a city's development agenda. Instead of policy making being a matter of a community's unitary interest, regime theory treats policy as a product of the struggle over a community's political arrangements. Eventually that form of analysis leads us to ask about alternative arrangements and the policies they might have generated. As I hope to show in the concluding chapter, after a range of regimes has been considered, questions of equity surround the particular form that development policy takes.

The contributors to this volume bring a variety of perspectives to bear on these issues. For those who might want greater uniformity, I urge them to read Philip Abrams's caution about modern scholarship's being "captivated by the possibilities of imposing elegant conceptual schemes on the vast untidiness of history."[48] For those who fear that this untidiness will be overwhelming, I offer the themes below to guide them through the following accounts of the many-sided nature of development politics.

First, politics matters. Cities are not mere economic units in a competitive market. The contributors to this volume make this assertion concrete, showing how politics is an integral part of the formation of development policy.

Second, politics is shaped profoundly by the interrelationship between state and market. The politics of urban development is not a free-floating activity, shaped only by the creative ingenuity and personal preferences of its major actors. They perform within a structure, and the basic feature of that structure is the division of labor between state and market. The latter, for many years, has been misleadingly called "the private sector." There is little about the economy that is genuinely private. Most property, of course, is not publicly owned, but investment decisions have a profound social and public impact. Development policy is understandably, then, very much a matter in which business and government are jointly engaged. Government does not ignore business, and business is an integral part of political life in urban communities. Politics takes place within these circumstances.

Third, since politics matters, we need appropriate and realistic criteria by which policies and political practices can be judged. To say that politics matters is not to suggest that all is well. Politics can be organized around the distribution of patronage, the protection of privilege, the substitution of show for substance, the favoring of factional interests, or the perpetuation of unfairness. So, our claim that politics matters is not the final point in an argument. Rather, it is the first step in recognizing a responsibility— a responsibility to identify and work for good political practice. More I will not attempt to say at this stage. In the concluding essay, I will return to this question of evaluative criteria. This is little-explored territory, but territory for which I will nevertheless attempt to offer some guideposts.

A PERSONAL POSTSCRIPT ON STUDYING POLITICS

Perhaps it is in order to say something about why neither this introductory essay nor the contributed chapters to this volume follow very closely, if at all, the usual canons of behavioral-science writing. Speaking for myself, sometime ago I became unenamored of behavioral science and its limited capacity to expand understanding. I say this in opposition neither to generalization nor to empirical observation. But students of urban politics, especially, should know by now that most generalizations are suspect unless they are put into a context (and often that context needs to be quite particular). Put another way, most outcomes have multiple causes that are never easy to sort out. Contexts and the salience of various causal forces change, confounding our efforts to amass a body of scientific knowledge that can be replicated through repeated observations. That humankind is reflective and can change behavior accordingly is another complicating factor.

In political science, parsimony is always at war with the importance of context and with the capacity of humankind to analyze context and to take some hand in altering social conditions. As scholars, how should we respond to such a situation? Parsimony cannot be our exclusive goal. One possibility is to engage in the observation of events in the manner of historians. This is an appropriate form of study, particularly when, as here, the concern is with a variety of experiences. Yet this book is not celebrating variety for the sake of variety. All of us engage in a search for general tendencies, but we can do so in a way that is sensitive to the importance of particular context. How, then, do we choose among ways of talking about the general and the particular? My preference is first for acknowledging that what is important about political-science generalizations is not their capacity to lead us to a set of firmly established and continuously replicatable findings. The political world is too complex and changeable for that. As I hope to show in the concluding essay, what is important is that generalizations be about issues that are normatively significant, that they lead us to investigate and reflect on something we care about politically.

This does not mean that empirical observation is irrelevant. Far from it. Lest I be accused of being indifferent to questions of evidence, let me say a word about different uses of evidence. The notion of behavioral science invites us to formulate hypotheses that can be tested by relatively unambiguous forms of evidence—ideally, a variety of observers agree about what the evidence means and about its capacity to support and disconfirm a given statement. In political science (and perhaps other social sciences as well), the ideal is seldom met to a degree that results in stable and universally subscribed-to bodies of findings. Instead, there is an ongoing process of refinement, contextual qualification, and reformulation, often accompanied by debate about the adequacy and meaning of various findings as evidence. Perhaps this is a genuinely worthy enterprise; perhaps not. One consequence may be to draw students into a search for more and more narrowly drawn statements for which the problem of unambiguous evidence is less serious. This is akin to the infamous "knowing more and more about less and less."

There is, however, a counterforce at work. Many political scientists, perhaps most, don't worship at the altar of knowledge for knowledge's sake. They want to know about things that are politically significant, and they therefore are drawn, even if fearfully, to big questions. These questions, however, tend not to lend themselves to findings based on unambiguous forms of evidence. Most political scientists seek some kind of intermediate position and give lip service at least to the Mertonian call for middle-range theory.

The problem, however, is not simply one of narrow versus broad statements. Broad statements tend to get caught up in competing formulations of a problem or issue. This is somewhat related to the competing scientific paradigms that Kuhn talks about. At that level, evidence is not unambiguous. The debate over competing formulations is unlike the process of testing hypotheses under laboratory conditions in which the experimenters agree on the nature of the evidence that is being examined. It is more akin to an adversarial legal proceeding in which contending sides argue about the appropriateness of various legal doctrines as well as the soundness of evidence. Or consider the debate among historians about the frontier thesis or about an economic interpretation of the Constitutional Convention. The debate is not a straight confirm/disconfirm application of evidence; it is an argument about the adequacy of an interpretation to capture what is important in an event or in a historical era. Evidence is not necessarily conclusive; judgment is involved in determining what the evidence means and how important it is in the overall picture. Any historical interpretation is something of an abstraction from reality, a selective reporting done in the service of telling what is important. It is subject to dispute on the ground that there is contradictory evidence and also on the ground that it hides rather than reveals what is important. Both, but especially the latter, can be a matter of judgment about which there is no universal agreement. But the absence of universal agreement does not make the issue any less important.

This book therefore has kinship with the discipline of history. It is about a matter of interpretation. It puts forward a conceptualization of urban development at odds with the influential one offered by Paul Peterson. The case that it argues in a variety of forms is that the city is a diverse community, seeking its common interest in a search that is mediated through the regime, or "prevailing coalition." In concrete and specific terms, there is no interest of the whole community that the governing coalition knows about and pursues apart from the governing coalition's own character and composition. Development policy thus grows out of the "prevailing coalition" and its relationship to the populace and to the controllers of private investment.

That is the case to be argued. The readers can now weigh the argument and evidence in the ensuing chapters, each of which begins with an introduction by the editors. The chapters are arranged in two parts. The first set treats the character of urban regimes, and the second set focuses on conflict and strategies for managing it. The book concludes with two chapters, one summing up the findings from Parts 1 and 2, the other outlining some directions for future research.

NOTES

1. Paul E. Peterson, *City Limits* (Chicago: University of Chicago Press, 1981).
2. John H. Mollenkopf, *The Contested City* (Princeton, N.J.: Princeton University Press, 1983).
3. See, e.g., Susan S. Fainstein et al., *Restructuring the City* (New York: Longman, 1983); Michael P. Smith, ed., *Cities in Transformation*, Urban Affairs Annual Reviews, vol. 26 (Beverly Hills, Calif.: Sage Publications, 1984); and J. Allen Whitt, *Urban Elites and Mass Transportation* (Princeton, N.J.: Princeton University Press, 1982).
4. In particular, see Harvey Molotch, "The City as a Growth Machine," *American Journal of Sociology* 82 (Sept. 1976): 309–31.
5. Peterson, *City Limits*, p. 131.
6. George Sternlieb and James W. Hughes, *The Atlantic City Gamble* (Cambridge, Mass.: Harvard University Press, 1983).

7. See Richard Child Hill, "Market, State and Community," *Urban Affairs Quarterly* 19 (Sept. 1983): 5–20.

8. David Harvey, *Social Justice and the City* (Baltimore, Md.: John Hopkins University Press, 1973); and Manuel Castells, *The City and the Grassroots* (Berkeley: University of California Press, 1983).

9. For the origins of this tradition see Alvin W. Gouldner, "Organizational Analysis," in *Sociology Today,* ed. Robert K. Merton et al. (New York: Basic Books, 1959).

10. Ibid.

11. James G. March, "The Business Firm as a Political Coalition," *Journal of Politics* 24 (Nov. 1962): 662–78.

12. Graham T. Allison, *Essence of Decision* (Boston, Mass.: Little, Brown, 1971), p. 76.

13. March, "Business Firm as a Political Coalition."

14. Allison, *Essence of Decision,* p. 146.

15. Mancur Olson, *The Logic of Collective Action* (Cambridge, Mass.: Harvard University Press, 1971); and Eugene C. Bardach, *The Implementation Game* (Cambridge, Mass.: MIT Press, 1977), pp. 163–67.

16. Yves Simon, *A General Theory of Authority* (Notre Dame, Ind.: University of Notre Dame Press, 1962, 1980).

17. Richard E. Flatham, *The Practice of Political Authority* (Chicago: University of Chicago Press, 1980), pp. 1–2.

18. Robert Michels, *Political Parties* (New York: Dover Publications, 1959).

19. Alvin W. Gouldner, *Patterns of Industrial Bureaucracy* (New York: Free Press, 1954), p. 98.

20. See Michael N. Danielson and Jameson W. Doig, *New York: The Politics of Urban Regional Development* (Berkeley: University of California Press, 1982), pp. 310–11.

21. Clarence N. Stone, 'Efficiency versus Social Learning," *Policy Studies Review* 4 (Feb. 1985): 484–96.

22. On the inseparability of means and ends see David Braybrooke and Charles E. Lindblom, *A Strategy of Decision* (New York: Free Press, 1970); and Stephen L. Elkin, "Economic and Political Rationality," *Polity* 18 (Winter 1985): 253–71.

23. Robert A. Caro, *The Power Broker* (New York: Alfred A. Knopf, 1974).

24. See especially Molotch, "The City as a Growth Machine."

25. For a regional perspective on this issue see Danielson and Doig, *New York.*

26. Edward C. Banfield, *The Unheavenly City Revisited* (Boston, Mass.: Little, Brown, 1974).

27. Peterson, *City Limits.*

28. Harvey, *Social Justice and the City.*

29. Robert A. Dahl, *Who Governs?* (New Haven, Conn.: Yale University Press, 1961), p. 297.

30. Nelson Polsby, *Community Power and Political Theory: A Further Look at Evidence and Inference* 2d rev. ed. (New Haven, Conn.: Yale University Press, 1980), p. 117.

31. Aaron Wildavsky, *Leadership in a Small Town* (Totowa, N.J.: Bedminster Press, 1964), p. 337.

32. Dahl, *Who Governs?* pp. 293–96.

33. Jeffrey Henig, *Neighborhood Mobilization* (New Brunswick, N.J.: Rutgers University Press, 1982), p. 13.

34. Dahl, *Who Governs?* pp. 91–93.

35. James O'Connor, *The Fiscal Crisis of the State* (New York: St. Martin's Press, 1973).

36. Allen Whitt, "Structural Fetishism in the New Urban Theory," in *Cities in Transformation,* p. 77.

37. Martin Shefter, *Political Crisis/Fiscal Crisis* (New York: Basic Books, 1985).

38. Ibid., p. 4.

39. Ibid., p. 220. On the importance of national policies for the durability of local coalitions see Mollenkopf, *Contested City.*

40. Shefter, *Political Crisis/Fiscal Crisis,* p. 220.

41. Stephen L. Elkin, "Twentieth Century Urban Regimes," *Journal of Urban Affairs* 7 (Spring 1985): 11–28.

42. Charles E. Lindblom, *Politics and Markets* (New York: Basic Books, 1977).

43. Shefter, *Political Crisis/Fiscal Crisis,* p. 235.

44. Henig, *Neighborhood Mobilization,* p. 211.

45. Parentage of the regime paradigm belongs to Stephen L. Elkin, "Cities without Power: The Transformation of American Urban Regimes," in *National Resources and Urban Policy,* ed. Douglas Ashford (New York: Methuen, 1980), pp. 265–93.

46. Philip Abrams, *Historical Sociology* (Ithaca, N.Y.: Cornell University Press, 1982), p. 142.

47. Thomas Kuhn, *The Structure of Scientific Revolutions,* 2d ed. (Chicago: University of Chicago Press, 1970).

48. Abrams, *Historical Sociology,* p. 11.

PART 1

THE CHARACTER OF URBAN REGIMES

212833

ALBRIGHT COLLEGE LIBRARY

2

State and Market in City Politics: Or, The "Real" Dallas

Stephen L. Elkin

In this opening chapter of Part 1, Stephen Elkin develops the regime concept by describing how major business interests in Dallas organized themselves and the city's politics to promote their collective interests in economic growth. Patronage opportunities and particularistic development interests were largely foreclosed by a set of institutional arrangements at the heart of the good-government reform program. Nonpartisan at-large elections, council-manager government, and blue-ribbon candidacies provided a context within which a growth agenda could be promoted with minimum distraction from the career aspirations of elected politicians or the profit seeking of individual business firms. For a time, Dallas approximated the elite-dominated low-intensity politics of development that Paul Peterson has described. But as Elkin points out, that was only for a time. A policy focused on downtown-centered development does not necessarily enjoy priority among minority and neighborhood groups. As those groups have mobilized and as the city's political structure has altered, development politics has also modified.

Elkin reminds us, however, that the politics of development is not simply a matter of following the election returns. From a political-economy perspective, the issue is one of bringing into accommodation the principle of the popular control of elected officials and the community's need for private investment activity. Diversifying participation in electoral politics does not alter development policy in any simple or direct way. Instead, it leads to a reconstitution of the urban regime. In Elkin's characterization, the pure entrepreneurial regime in Dallas gave way to a more complex regime. However, it remains a regime in which the career of professional politician is not encour-

25

aged and in which it is not easy to make challenges to business-backed policies.

City politics is shaped by the division of labor between the state and the market, on the one hand, and the concomitant powers given to city governments, on the other. This division is the product of a historical and ongoing struggle about how we shall govern ourselves. The phrase "division of labor" is a summary term for the resolution of numerous particular contests in a variety of arenas. The cumulative result of these contests has been a political-economic order in which all levels and types of governments operate in a context in which many of the most important social decisions are made by private actors who can only be cajoled and enjoined, not commanded. What has come to be known as Dillon's rule, as well as its surrounding legal-constitutional interpretation, continues to give concrete meaning to this division of labor as it applies to cities.

By the early twentieth century it was well established that cities were public corporations which had only those powers that state governments granted to them, such powers to be strictly interpreted. This was the burden of the views of the nineteenth-century jurist John Dillon, and his interpretation was widely accepted by the courts. Popular control in cities was only to concern matters that had not already been settled by defining the city as a public corporation with specific and limited powers. The fundamental result of this definition of the city's place in the national political economy was that the political life of cities has been substantially shaped by a concern with maintaining and stimulating economic vitality. If public officials were to do their jobs, they would have to induce economic performance from those who control productive assets in the city, and more ambitiously, they would have to attract new asset holders. Among other things, payrolls and bond repayments require it. Public officials and city businessmen would then be drawn into extensive links with one another. But the nature of these links differs with the character and organization of both the business community and the political leadership of the city. Particularly important is how public officials, both elected and appointed, pursue political careers.

Politics in Dallas is a particularly illuminating example of how the links between public officials and businessmen have been constructed, how they have evolved over time, and how extensive they can be. Dallas city politics is also instructive for how the type of careers available to local officials can make them deeply attentive to the concerns of the leading businessmen of the city.

After the creation of the city-manager system, the politics of Dallas falls into two parts, which may be termed the "pure" and the "complex" entrepreneurial political economy. The first characterized the politics of the city from the late 1930s until approximately the mid 1970s. The second has taken shape since that time, and while not all of its outlines are clear, much can be discerned. In the pure entrepreneurial variant, public officials and business leaders shared a strong community of interest, and their discussions essentially defined the subject matter of local politics. They were not so much in coalition—which implies parties with distinct and at least partly competing interests—but were joined in a community of interests that centered on the creation of a local business climate that would facilitate the rapid economic growth of the city. The key to understanding this political economy is the political arrangements that leading businessmen set in motion early on. These resulted in public officials who would of their own volition pursue policies of city expansion that were fully compatible with the broad purposes of leading businessmen. In the complex entrepreneurial variant, the political arrangements that business leaders set in motion are weaker, but there are still strong links between public officials and business interests. These links are, however, more like those of a coalition. Both political patterns can be characterized as entrepreneurial since in each the concerns of businessmen to organize city politics around growth have largely succeeded. In both, extensive links between businessmen and public officials are crucial for understanding the general pattern of politics.[1]

THE "PURE" ENTREPRENEURIAL
POLITICAL ECONOMY

From the late 1930s until the mid 1970s the broad purpose of city politics in Dallas was clear to anyone who paid attention to local affairs. The purpose was to promote the growth of the city, particularly its economic growth. There was none of the baroque complexity of the contemporary politics of Chicago or even that of Philadelphia. What is striking is simply that the voices that were heard with any force loudly proclaimed Dallas to be a businessman's city. It was necessary to run it in businesslike ways, they said, and in a manner that was attractive to those who would conduct its business affairs. The politics of St. Louis or Boston is not fundamentally different; land interests and public officials would like to be able to concentrate on making the city grow. However, they need to take account of much else, including, not trivially, how they or their favorites are going to get elected. The key to the pure entrepreneurial political economy of Dallas was that public officials and local business leaders were relatively undistracted in the pursuit of city growth.

To understand this relatively pure entrepreneurial political economy, it is necessary to focus on the following dimensions of urban political economies: the manner and extent to which the natural alliance between businessmen and public officials is organized; the extent to which the local bureaucracy is autonomous from the alliance and from politicians who are anxious to use local resources and personnel to improve their electoral prospects; and the manner in which the electorate is organized.[2] My principal attention will be given to the alliance between businessmen and officials, since once this is understood, the nature of the other dimensions is easily seen.

THE ALLIANCE BETWEEN BUSINESSMEN AND PUBLIC OFFICIALS

The links between public officials and business leaders were extensive and well developed. They were in evidence in the full range of city affairs, from specific civic projects to bolstering up the city-manager form of government, from guiding the capital-works agenda through approval to affecting the outcome of elections. The extensiveness of the links is suggested by the fact that for a substantial portion of the period of the pure entrepreneurial political economy, leading business figures were also the principal elected officials.

Much more than is true in the case of older cities, the alliance was dominated by business figures. This did not mean that businessmen merely gave orders and officials carried them out, in a kind of crude Marxist fantasy of the capitalist state at work. Still, public officials did not have the independent basis of support characteristic of their counterparts in many cities. More important, public officials, both elected and appointed, had views in common with leading businessmen. But it was *business* views that were shared, not vice versa. Why this was so and how it came about form the crucial step in understanding the pure entrepreneurial political economy.

The place to begin is with the extensive efforts that business leaders made to ensure that elected officials would share their views on what they considered a fundamental aspect of local politics—namely, the protection of the council-manager system and, with it, Dallas' reputation as an honest and efficient city. From 1907 to 1931 Dallas was governed under a commission form of government, which had come into being largely as a result of efforts to find a form of government that would run in a businesslike manner. By the late twenties, however, the city government was thought to be dominated by officials who were pursuing personal political ambitions in a way that was no longer suitable for economic progress.[3] Many of those who had previously supported the commission form of government now switched their allegiance to the city-manager system. Most visible in this shift was the owner of the most important newspaper in the city, G. B. Dealey, whose newspaper paid for research into the experience of the council-manager form of government in other cities and ran a series of articles advocating its virtues for Dallas. The efforts of local civic worthies in behalf of the council-manager system resulted in the creation of the Citizens Charter Association (CCA). To sell the city-manager system to the electorate, the CCA orchestrated a campaign that included hiring a professional director and clerical staff and creating neighborhood organizations. These efforts were crowned with success in 1930 when the citizenry voted in a council-manager form of government.

From the beginning, leading local business figures viewed the city-manager system as a form of government that would best suit their concerns. Local business leaders were willing to see that some sustained effort was made to recruit candidates for office who would be committed to the perpetuation of a local government that was efficient, professional, and administered by experts. This commitment to the city-manager system was at the core of a more general judgment that Dallas would best prosper under honest professional government. New investment would more likely come to the city if investors knew that they did not have to engage in corrupt negotiations with public officials for whom politics was a livelihood.

In addition to looking toward an honest and professional city government to promote the economic growth of the city, business leaders also saw the importance of fiscal restraint. A city government that kept its revenue demands to a minimum would also be a city government that would have high bond ratings and would have little trouble in raising money in the bond market. In turn, this would enhance the city's reputation as a good place to do business. The city would be seen as capable of providing the necessary infrastructure without imposing a heavy tax burden on business enterprises. Beyond the commitment to fiscal restraint, leading businessmen also believed that a lively civic and cultural climate was necessary if Dallas was to grow. The city needed to be attractive as a place to live in for those who would manage its new and expanded firms.

Beyond a concern for making Dallas an honest and efficient place that would be attractive to new investment, the business elite wanted Dallas to expand its land area and wanted the necessary infrastructure to be available for such expansion to occur. This meant a policy of aggressive annexation and a steady expansion of capital investment as new areas opened up. It also meant solving the water problem, because Dallas, in common with many cities of the Southwest, did not have enough water at hand to expand very far.

In understanding this commitment to growth on the part of leading businessmen, it will be helpful to specify in some detail just who they were. First, there were bankers. The commitment of the banks to a growing Dallas is easy to see. A bigger city meant more business for them. This was true not only because of increased deposits and loans but also because expansion meant that their own investments would prosper. In addition, a growing city meant more city funds to be put into their coffers. But the motives were not only monetary; the heads of the banks had a good deal of civic pride. This was their city, and they wanted it to be a great one. To be head of a bank in a modest provincial city was one thing; to be a bank president in a great city was quite another.

The motives of the other involved business leaders were not very different. They ranged from downtown merchants to heads of the big corporations that were doing business in the city, as well as a few developers. Perhaps most important was the head of the local morning newspaper, G. B. Dealey, whose commitment to preserving the city-manager system was widely evident. The most important point about these business leaders, including the bankers, is that they were engaged in trying to establish a set of rules within which city growth would occur. Their commitment was to the rules, from which they fully expected to benefit, rather than to political arrangements that would further their particular interests on an individual basis.

Business leaders were also well organized for a variety of charitable purposes. A local system of moving through various levels of responsibilities for local charitable works evolved, known locally as "working through the chairs." Those who wished to rise to the top of the business community were expected to spend time on charitable functions, working their way up through the various levels of responsibility for money raising and organization. This system increased the degree of contact among businessmen and tended to promote a common outlook on city problems. These organizational links were added to a relative homogeneity of background among business leaders during this period. They tended to be Texas men and to be Southern Baptist by religious conviction. The overall result was to make for a relatively cohesive business community that was in a position to act with some impact in city affairs.

The Citizens Charter Association was the principal means by which leading businessmen sought to ensure that elected officials would share their views on the importance of city growth and how it was to be fostered. The association only supported candidates who were committed to the continuation of the council-manager system. This was a more serious issue during the early days of the system, when its continuation was in doubt. Later on, the pertinent question was more likely to be whether a prospective candidate showed any signs of wishing to pursue the allure of political life in a full-time way. What the association wanted was amateurs who would be happy to leave the day-to-day running of the city to the city manager and his staff. Full-time politicians would seek and require independent bases of support in the electorate, whether through party organization or through personal followings, and would thus likely be independent of businessmen's counsel. The ideal elected officials would be business executives who would take time out from their principal careers. If full-time businessmen could not be found, then other people who were sympathetic to clean honest growth-oriented government would do as long as they, too, saw politics as an avocation. Middle-class women, in the days before women's liberation, nicely fit the bill. If appropriate candidates could be found and elected, appointed officials, especially the city manager, would then be appointed by and broadly responsive to the right sort of people. These appointed officials might then be expected to be attentive to the concerns of the business elite. An additional advantage of part-time nonprofessional politicians is that they are less likely to be drawn to expensive ways of running a city, and it was such demands on the city fisc that leading businessmen wished to avoid.

In all these efforts, the CCA and therefore the business elite proved to be eminently successful. Business leaders, when they came to discuss city affairs with elected officials, were largely engaged in intramural discussions. They faced officials who had no independent political base from which to dissent and, in general, were dealing with people who did not find the pleasures of politics so alluring that they wished to trade in their present careers for full-time political activity. Moreover, when business leaders came to discuss city affairs with the city manager and his staff, they were dealing with someone whose elected bosses were not inclined to push him in directions that would make it difficult for him to listen sympathetically to business concerns.

The sources of the CCA's success are not difficult to discern. Consider the case of George Allen, a black candidate for city council who ran twice for the city council, in 1963 and 1965, without the endorsement of the CCA, and lost both times. In the 1963 race he spent about $6,000, of which about $4,600 came out of his own pocket. He was endorsed by two slating organizations, but neither of them had any money to give to him. In 1965, the slating organizations did manage to come up with a little money, but most of the financing came from a loan that he took out. This race cost him about $9,600. By one estimate, it would have taken about seven times that amount to have been elected.[4]

This points to the economies of scale that the CCA was able to reap. Because it advertised its slate as a single package, some publicity could be given to each candidate at a far-lower price than it would cost any candidate who was running alone. Put differently, without the endorsement of a slating organization that could raise on the order of $75,000 to $100,000, no candidate had a serious chance at office unless he or she either could manage to raise something like this sum personally or was possessed of substantial popularity before the campaign began.

In 1968, Allen was appointed to one of the new seats that were created by the expansion of the city council.[5] He was, at that point, the preferred candidate of the black leadership of the city. This endorsement by the black leadership and his appointment to the city council paved the way for his endorsement by the CCA. This time there was no runoff election; in the two previous elections he had not even managed to get that far. He was subsequently reelected twice, all with the CCA's endorsement.[6]

Evidence of the CCA's prowess in getting its candidates elected can be seen by looking at its rate of success between 1959 and 1973. According to one calculation, the organization endorsed seventy-five candidates during this period, sixty-four of whom were elected, making for a success rate of 85 percent. The organization was far from invincible, but it surely must be counted as successful, especially because its candidates during this period always held at least a two-thirds majority on the council.[7] Perhaps the high point of the CCA's strength was in 1955, when its ticket ran unopposed. The turnout in the election was remarkably low, 2.5 percent of the registered voters. In general, the voter turnout was modest at best during this period. This, in part, reflected the perceived dominance of the CCA and the lack of attractive alternative candidates. Whatever the reasons, the low turnout worked to the advantage of the association, because the turnout was highest in the more affluent districts of the city where the CCA's strength was greatest. This increased the organizational advantages that it held against possible competing slating organizations.

At its high point, the CCA had a vice-president for each council district and a twenty-one-member committee to seek out and screen candidates for each district. The nominations of each district committee were then passed on to a city nominating committee, which, in consultation with the executive committee of the organization, made up the slate. CCA-endorsed candidates did not need to raise any money on their own, which in an at-large system, as noted, can be a substantial burden. In 1971, for example, the CCA raised about $70,000 in addition to incurring debts on the order of $14,500. None of its candidates reported any source of money other than CCA support. In addition to campaign financing, the CCA also organized all the publicity for the candidates and went so far as to do the filings required of each candidate under the campaign law.[8] The association was also able to enforce a policy of supporting candidates for only two terms. In this way, the CCA itself, not particular elected officials, was the preeminent electoral force.

Thus, at its height, the CCA operated as an extension of the business elite. This did not mean, however, that, except for the mayor, leading business figures were themselves active in lining up candidates and organizing campaigns. For the most part, this was left to others, those who had every reason of their own to select candidates who would prove to be sympathetic to the particular projects that leading businessmen were interested in and who were otherwise committed to maintaining the essential features of the probusiness climate. By the mid 1960s this was even more the case, because those who were active in CCA affairs had begun to understand the need to bring into the organization a wide variety of local citizens, including prominent blacks and other minorities. The concerns of the CCA might be best reflected by saying that it still wished to recruit "responsible" candidates, by which it meant ones who were committed to the council-manager system and to a growing and efficiently run Dallas, but was willing to entertain the idea that a variety of people might fit this description. Still, the head of the CCA in the mid 1960s testified that in general, the organization was looking for business people, "because we thought it was a business job."[9] He went on to note that in any case, probably only business or professional people could afford to hold office, because only they could give the necessary time without the need to earn a salary.

From the point of view of the business elite, this expansion apparently did not occasion any anxiety. If anything, had the effort not been interrupted by the coming of single-member districts, it might well have strengthened the CCA and accordingly made more secure the alliance between the business elite and public officials who were committed to an expanding Dallas.[10] Altogether, the dominance of the CCA in the electoral arena and the continuation of the city-manager system ensured that holding office on the city council was not a way to make a career; it was a grace note to a career that had already been made.

Among elected public officials, the mayor was the most important figure, being the principal link between elected officials, the city manager, and business leaders. This was reflected in the fact that leading businessmen were more anxious that he be one of them than was the case with ordinary council members. Their efforts took the form of seeing that a person of substantial business standing ran for mayor under the CCA banner, and by and large they succeeded.[11] The other crucial public official in Dallas was, of course, the city manager.[12] His elected bosses, the council members, were themselves unlikely to have views very different from those of the leading businessmen, and in particular, they would be unlikely to press on him the competing concerns of neighborhoods, ethnic and racial groups, or, indeed, any other concerns that would make it difficult for the manager to respond to leading business interests. In effect, he could consult his professional training and his career ambitions, and these might reasonably lead him to views that were not markedly different from those of the business elite. Since Dallas businessmen were anxious that the city government be run honestly and efficiently and were by and large drawn to the latest techniques in management, they were likely to give the manager free rein. Beyond that, there was certainly little in the training of city managers that made them insensitive to the claims of promoting city growth. Perhaps as important, a manager's own career ambitions might reasonably lead to favoring the rapid growth of the city. After all, it would be good for his career to preside over a booming city in which he might, in any case, continue to live because there were no bigger cities in which to pursue his career as manager. Most important, however, is the consequence of the division of labor between state and market, as it is manifest in cities. Given a long time horizon and a concern for professional reputation, the city manager, even more than elected officials, might be expected to understand the need to encourage business activity. Perhaps the most suggestive evidence in this regard is that one of Dallas' early managers became head of one of the city's banks and that another, a later, manager became an executive in a leading business firm in the city.

The nature of the alliance between business leaders and public officials is best suggested by taking a brief look at the decisions on capital works that were undertaken by the city and other major decisions of this sort. The overwhelming portion of capital works in Dallas are financed through a regular bond program that has been approved by Dallas voters. This in itself is significant, because it effectively institutionalizes the business leadership's commitment to low taxes and puts the system on a pay-as-you-go basis. In addition, because capital works are a crucial part of the expenditures of any city, this mode of financing means that those who are most influential in shaping the bond program have significant influence over the budget of the city. Business leaders who wish for a fiscally conservative city then can concentrate on the capital-works program and thereby can convince bond buyers and bond-rating agencies that the city has not unduly strained its resources.

Now to some degree, business leaders could, as noted, rely on public officials who shared their views. But the links between city officials and the business community could not be limited to campaigns for office. Because the capital works must be approved by voters, the crucial question becomes how the bond campaigns were organized. Typically the mayor approached a leading business figure and asked him to head up the bond campaign. The latter, in turn, undertook to raise the money necessary to explain and otherwise support the city's proposals to the voters. The actual vehicle for raising the money for the campaign was and still is an organization called the Dallas Citizens Council (DCC), another businessmen's organization, which drew on the same pool as the CCA. The system was described by one of the participants: "The chairman of the bond drive is picked by the mayor who checks with leading businessmen to see if the money to run the campaign will be available with a campaign headed by a person he has in mind. The businessmen raise the money. It takes about $250,000 [this is 1982] per campaign to pay for the public relations firm, advertising, brochures, speaker's kits and so on."

The DCC was formed in 1937 by Robert Lee Thornton, president of the Mercantile Bank and subsequently mayor of the city.[13] His experience in raising money for the Texas Centennial, which he had headed, convinced him of the need for better ways of undertaking this task and, in general, of organizing business leaders in support of community projects. To this end, Thornton envisioned what he thought of as an "organization of bosses"— that is, a group of top executives in the city who were in a position to commit resources and, in general, to say yes or no on their own account. This vision grew to fruition in the Dallas Citizens Council.

No very elaborate theory of influence is required here. If, indeed, public officials harbored any inclinations that were strongly at variance with those of leading businessmen, they would likely reconsider them in the light of the business elite's crucial role in the bond campaign. Some discriminations are, however, required here. There is no reason to think that business leaders were interested in the full range of capital projects, from street repairs on up. It is much more likely that their concerns were limited to pushing for a few major projects, which they were either anxious to see passed or about which they had strong objections. Beyond that, it is reasonable to suppose they only cared that the proposed projects would not negatively affect the city's bond ratings.

The DCC's role was not confined to capital projects connected to votes on bonds. There was a variety of other capital projects that could not be handled through the bond program. These included projects that involved cooperation with other authorities, as well as those which voters might find objectionable. In addition, there were also projects that involved city resources but were not capital works and that also either required cooperation with other authorities or were particularly delicate and might not flourish if they became the subject of public scrutiny. The kinds of decisions that were at issue here range from ensuring that Dallas had an adequate water supply,[14] to problems of school desegregation, to building a new library downtown for the city. The existence of a businessmen's organization that was able to raise money and other resources meant that when public officials needed to take action in these matters, they had help at hand in laying the groundwork for the projects, in carrying on delicate negotiations, and generally in pushing the project to completion.[15] In this context, public officials could be expected to tailor their views to what they supposed leading businessmen would find acceptable.

This was a two-way street, however. Public officials not only approached business leaders; leading businessmen, of course, had their own projects, and the DCC was the principal vehicle for promoting them. Once again the fact of being able to raise money and to deploy other resources made public officials more likely to listen attentively. This was not so much a case of business bringing pressure to bear, but that, given the resources at their command, they could in fact probably bring the project to fruition. There was therefore little reason to resist the initiative.

What is crucial to understand here is that the core of the pure entrepreneurial political economy was *not* a business elite that was giving orders to public officials whether elected or appointed. Especially as the city grew more complex, it is doubtful that business leaders were inclined to take the time and effort to hammer out agreements on the full range of city matters, quite apart from the difficulties of mastering the relevant information. To think of leading business figures in effect planning for the city and passing on the results of their contemplation is to misunderstand the nature of the alliance. These business leaders were, after all, business executives, bankers, and merchants first and foremost.

The heart of the entrepreneurial political economy was, rather, that the business elite was instrumental in helping to create and maintain a political system in which those who held elected and appointed office did not have to be told what to do. They would be drawn of their own volition to particular projects and to general ways of looking at the city that were compatible with the inclinations of business leaders. They were to act in ways that, if the members of the business elite had time and authority, they might be drawn to themselves. The officials were often, in fact, leading businessmen themselves, or, if not, they were most often people with business backgrounds. Equally important, if they were elected officials, they had no strong incentive to look at matters in ways that would bring them into conflict with leading business figures. They were part-time officials who had no need or opportunity to build independent political followings and whose election depended on an organization that was strongly supported by business leaders. To which we need only add that the city manager was in a position to act in accordance with the highest standards of his profession. The manager knew what sorts of projects and policies the business elite would be sympathetic to, and by and large these were things that he would likely pursue on his own. The key to the compatibility of views between business leaders and officials was not the direct exercise of influence on particular decisions; it was the structural arrangements that the business leadership was largely responsible for putting in place and maintaining.

The degree to which business and politics were closely intertwined in Dallas is nicely captured by the remarks of one of the former mayors of Dallas who commented: "if this were a strong mayor system, I would never have run. That would have meant isolating myself from my company. But any mayor of Dallas really works for nothing. I could continue to work in politics and stay with my company because it was obvious that I had to make a living somehow. I could still be a businessman."

One aspect of the alliance between leading businessmen and public officials remains to be mentioned. In effect, leading businessmen contrived a situation in which, if all cooperated, all would be better off. They would all prosper from adhering to general rules that produced honest, low-tax, and professional government. There was, however, an alternative possibility. A stream of public decisions that conferred special advantages on those who were able to extract them also beckoned, and this tack promised immediate benefits. The temptation was simply for each to try to stuff his pockets by working to promote public decisions that would be of direct personal benefit. The situation was akin to the group provision of a public good and had the attendant problems of "prisoner's dilemma" games.[16] If each person can trust the others to make the necessary moves, all will benefit in the long run. But each person has an incentive to make other moves that promise immediate benefit. If all, or at least a significant number, act on such incentives, all the participants will lose. In the case at issue, an effort to seek favors by corrupting the officials promised immediate benefits. The cumulation of such efforts, however, would be the demise of professional, honest, low-tax government.

The most likely source of such corruption were those who were concerned with development matters, for whom decisions about zoning changes and infrastructure were crucial to success. Many factors explain why development interests did not succeed in corrupting the city-manager system, but three stand out. First, the business elite was both cohesive enough and was itself not directly tied to particular projects so that it could enforce some sort of discipline. In effect, its members could provide the public good on their own because they were in a position to develop sufficient trust.

In addition, the abundance of open land, which was facilitated by rapid annexation, lessened the need for corruption.[17] There simply were fewer forces at work making officials hesitant to grant at least the necessary zoning provisions. Finally, development interests in fact found that public officials were receptive to whatever pace of development they could sustain. The institutional arrangements that the business elite was instrumental in putting into place meant that public officials were in a position to be sympathetic to a wide range of development proposals. Developers had little need to attempt to corrupt officials; and even though the business elite was not dominated by land interests, the latter had every reason to be happy with the arrangements. They, too, could prosper nicely.

BUREAUCRACY AND ELECTORATE

The analysis of the other two dimensions of the pure entrepreneurial political economy follows directly from what has already been said about the alliance between the businessmen elite and public officials. The central fact about the Dallas bureaucracy is that it was and still is highly professionalized. Appointments were made according to civil-service procedures and according to professional criteria, not as a reward for political service, and the principal administrators were in a position to act for the most part according to professional judgment. Partly, the character of the bureaucracy stemmed from the fact of the city's having a city-manager system. But more important, since legal formalities may be overridden, were two things. First, elected officials had little incentive to interfere with the day-to-day running of the city, because they were not engaged in building political careers. And second, business leaders wanted a well-administered city and understood this to mean that the manager and his staff had to be allowed considerable autonomy. The leaders also believed that the manager shared their views about how the city should be made to grow. In the case of both elected officials and business leaders it was also generally understood that attempting to extract personal favors or using bureaucratic largesse to advance political careers would make it more difficult to attract competent managers and skilled city administrators. The autonomy of the manager and his staff remained, however, within well-understood, if broad, boundaries, which were the purposes shared by the business elite and elected officials about how to promote the vigorous growth of the city and the need for fiscal constraint.

The central point about the organization of appeals to the electorate is that there was no serious organizational alternative to the CCA, and therefore any electoral challenge to the alliance between business leaders and public officials was effectively precluded. Other slating organizations came and went or, if they stayed, lacked resources. Neighborhood organizations were too weak to provide an organizational basis for a political career, even if the at-large voting system had not effectively made a career rooted in neighborhood appeals very difficult. As for organizations of municipal employees, which provide a source of organizational support in many cities, Dallas' city workers were not engaged in collective bargaining, much less in direct political activity.[18]

The CCA did not, in fact, set its face against accommodating those people who were not themselves local businessmen but who still wished to hold office, as long as they were willing to be attentive to the basic purposes of the alliance. So, over time, the association sponsored both black and brown candidates who could show that they had wide support. Those who were excluded were simply those who wished to pursue independent political careers or who had doubts about how the alliance was trying to create a greater Dallas. Spokesmen for the poor, minorities, the working class, neighborhood interests, or any other groups with views that might complicate the business of creating an attractive expansionary climate faced substantial difficulties. The voting data suggest that when candidates did emerge to challenge the CCA, many black voters at least were drawn to their support. In the period from 1959 to 1973, when the CCA-endorsed candidates won sixty-four out of seventy-five races, a majority of black voters in the principal black wards (except for one case) voted for the challengers who won the other eleven races. In a 1963 race, in which a candidate for the city council ran in strong opposition to the CCA and the DCC, she received nearly 70 percent of the black vote in these wards.[19]

Of course, occasionally those who had independent local reputations could break through the barriers, but they did not find enough allies in local politics to cause more than occasional unease. Beyond such possible challenges, the CCA could simply count on those voters for whom an expanding Dallas, low taxes, and efficient government were desirable. These included middle-class homeowners and those who were in a position to take advantage of expanding white-collar job opportunities. In general, a low voter turnout meant that many of the interests that composed the political system of the city were virtually excluded from the electoral arena and local politics generally.

It only needs to be added that in attempting to organize the electorate, those who were contending for office did not, and in reality could not, rely on a stream of benefits such as jobs, contracts, and favorable decisions generated from past or prospective control of the city bureaucracy. The manner of building the type of political following that is characteristic of patronage politics in many other cities was not important in Dallas. In part, this was simply because the council-manager system itself prohibits elected officials from intervening in the day-to-day decision making of the city and in personnel matters. An electoral politics that protected the integrity of the city-manager system thus served to preclude patronage as a political base.

The outlines of the pure entrepreneurial political economy have now been presented. Organized businessmen were able to create and foster a political system that was directed at promoting a greater Dallas. This was done, not by corrupting the system, but by excluding "politics," by which was meant the pulling and hauling of various neighborhood and other interests and of politicians who spoke for these interests and who could act to further their own pocketbooks and their political careers. Instead, the aims were to professionalize the city bureaucracy and to see that the day-to-day matters of the city were dealt with honestly and efficiently.

It was under the "pure" entrepreneurial political economy that Dallas took on its present physical shape. The great expansion to the north was started, and flourishing middle-class neighborhoods were created. Similarly, after a slump during the early 1970s, the central business district (CBD) exploded into life as the commercial space of the city was dramatically expanded. The pure entrepreneurial political economy brought together civic pride, civic efficiency, and business expansion. In this fashion, it was quintessentially American: morally edifying, economically efficient, and, for some, personally enriching.

THE COMPLEX ENTREPRENEURIAL
POLITICAL ECONOMY

Dallas is now a largely built-up city, confined more or less to its present boundaries and competing in a larger metropolitan region with suburban locations and with nearby Fort Worth. The fact that Dallas' land area is mostly filled in is in part a testimony to the efficiency of the pure entrepreneurial political economy. Increasingly, city growth will depend on rearranging land use. This will be true regardless of whether it is a matter of investment by those who are already located in the city or of attracting new investment. One important result is that progrowth activities will increasingly result in direct, tangible, and significant costs to substantial portions of the local citizenry. The most important result is likely to be the improvement of transportation flows within the city, particularly between the middle-class districts north of the downtown area and the CBD. Both new roads and fixed-rail schemes will impose substantial costs on significant numbers of city residents.

Responses to these costs in the form of community organization must be seen in the context of a variety of gentrification efforts in neighborhoods within striking distance of the CBD. Gentrification has brought in its trail a modest level of neighborhood organization where almost none existed before. Now a variety of neighborhood associations are at work protesting new traffic patterns or trying to ease the path of gentrification by having housing inspections enforced or simply by protesting new development in areas from which development will remove low-income citizens—in short, the usual concerns of citizen associations.

In addition to the physical and economic changes in Dallas, the political arrangements that business leaders set in motion, which were crucial for explaining the views held in common by public officials and businessmen, have now altered significantly. Three changes are of particular note: the change in the electoral system to a mixed single-member/at-large form; the demise of the CCA; and the weakening of the DCC.

Single-member districts grew out of a suit that was brought by a black candidate for office, who argued that the at-large system effectively discriminated against blacks. The electoral system that emerged from the suit was to have an eleven-member city council, eight of whom were to be elected from districts and three of whom, including the mayor, were to be elected at large. The suit was one of many in federal district courts that made similar arguments, and as in other cases, the courts agreed. As in many other cities, council for the defeated candidate was provided by the poverty-law program that was supported by OEO funds—in this case, Dallas Legal Services. In Dallas, the alteration of the electoral system was almost certainly the largest change that was fostered by the various social programs of the period. Other funds, for the most part, went into the coordination of existing social-welfare programs, but the poverty-law program ended up helping to engineer a significant change in the political arrangements of the city.

Of the several reasons for the demise of the CCA, the increasing fragmentation of the business community was one. Probably more important was the onset of single-member districts, which significantly reduced the comparative advantage of the money that business leaders could raise and the organization that they could bring to bear. At present, there is no single dominant slating organization at work in Dallas elections, and thus the change from the electoral situation under the pure entrepreneurial variant is considerable.

The DCC has not disappeared, but it has changed, and the changes have somewhat weakened its impact on city affairs. Its principal impact as an organization was on specific projects and on the bond program, in which it served as the principal vehicle for raising money for leading business figures. Its impact on the bond program has continued. The principal weakening has occurred in the realm of specific projects. The DCC is now probably somewhat less capable both of carrying out specific projects proposed by public officials and of proposing its own. The sources of the weakening are simply that the organization is no longer a small group of elite businessmen who, on their own, are able to say yes or no. It is now a larger organization which has a paid staff to facilitate coordination.

Lying behind the demise of the CCA and the weakening of the DCC are significant changes in the business community of Dallas. The kinds of business leaders who were actively concerned with city affairs in the pure entrepreneurial variant are still in evidence. Their concerns remain the same; that is, they wish to see that an attractive climate for business investment is maintained. To this end they still work to see that the city-manager system remains, that cultural facilities attractive to middle and top business managers are provided, that housing suitable for the professional classes is widely available, and that suitable schools can be found. But these business leaders, who are themselves largely not directly concerned with land-use matters, have now been joined by a significant number of developers and others who are concerned with development and redevelopment projects and whose concerns, while they overlap those of leading businessmen, also differ. These developers also wish to see a local political order that will facilitate investment, but for them this largely means a city government that will ease changes in land use and will provide the infrastructure necessary for new development. These developers are, more broadly, less interested in honest, efficient government than in government that facilitates good development opportunities.

Not only have major developers become more important in Dallas politics, but the local business elite has itself become more complex. Dallas has grown enormously, and the number of leading businessmen has expanded. More-over, they do not now come mostly from the same background (some even come from the Northeast), and their business success is as likely to be tied to markets outside of Dallas as to anything going on inside of it. Dallas, in short, is experiencing what many scholars have said is char-acteristic of older cities. Some idea of the extent of the change is sug-gested by the fact that in 1960, 69 percent of the corporate headquarters in Dallas were those of local firms. Throughout the 1960s, 33 percent of the new headquarters that located in the city came from outside the state, but in the period 1970–76, the figure rose to 92 percent.[20] The result is simply that it is harder for leading businessmen to organize themselves.

The crucial point in all this is that as Dallas has evolved into a major city with its business executives and banks conducting business nationally and internationally, the question that increasingly presses on them is what incentive they have to remain or take an active interest in city affairs. The business leaders who founded and ran the CCA and the DCC during the period of the pure entrepreneurial political economy had strong material and civic reasons to devote themselves to city affairs. They were engaged in making a city that would make them rich and proud and would provide a style of living that suited their tastes. The present generation of business executives is as likely as not to have other interests. The city is already at-tractive; its government is not corrupt. Moreover, they are as likely as not to seek to advance their careers in the national business arena and to seek entertainment outside of the city. In short, they are no longer as tied to the city as their predecessors were, and they could plausibly pay little atten-tion to city affairs.[21]

With all these changes in the business elite, it is important to note that candidates for mayor at least can still run as *businessmen*. This is perhaps the most suggestive point of all. Business leaders are widely believed, not only in their own circles but outside as well, to have a rightful, indeed prom-inent, place in the running of the city. That has continued. It is no longer possible for business elites to think that they do not need to explain their claims publicly, that if they come out for a candidate or a project that ought to be enough. But even with the need to argue and struggle in a more public fashion, they need not dress up as politicians who are trying to build political followings. Their claim is that the city's well-being depends on them and therefore that their views ought to carry considerable weight. In this, they are still widely believed.

The full implications of the expansion in neighborhood organization, of alterations in the political arrangements that were earlier created by business leaders, and of the increased fragmentation of the business elite are not yet clear. The shape of the political economy, particularly of the organization of the bureaucracy and electorate, is still emerging. But the implications for the broad character of the relationship between business interests and public officials can be discerned. And because, as the discussion of the pure entrepreneurial political economy suggests, much follows from that relationship, it will be useful to confine our attention to it.

Even in the context of more politically difficult land-use strategies for promoting city growth and of changes in the political arrangements, public officials are still drawn to policies that promote the economic growth of the city. They are thus drawn into extensive links with business figures who share these purposes and whose cooperation is in any case required in order to pursue them. These links are, inevitably, different from those that existed under the pure entrepreneurial political economy. They are, in fact, more complex, not least because public officials are now themselves more diverse in their incentives and business interests are more fragmented. On balance, the relationship is one in which public officials play a stronger role than they did previously. This is partly because business interests are, in fact, more fragmented and partly because the problems are more complex and business executives lack the time to act as civic statesmen, thinking through proposals. In general, the relationship between public officials and business is more like a coalition than like the alliance that was characteristic of the pure entrepreneurial political economy.

First, consider elected officials, starting with those who are elected at large, notably the mayor. Contests for these three seats still draw significant financial support from leading business figures and increasingly from development interests. The reasons are not hard to find. The mayor, although formally just another member of the city council with the same powers as other members, is the most visible elected official. He is, moreover, more influential in city decisions than are ordinary councillors, because he spends more time at it. This is partly because he represents the city in all sorts of negotiations and on public occasions. But even more importantly, it stems from the fact that he is the principal link between elected officials and the city manager. His acquiescence, at least, and, more probably, his active support are required for pursuing progrowth policies. Not surprisingly, this key role is reflected in the amount of money spent on mayoral campaigns.

The size of expenditures in recent campaigns for the mayor's office reflects not only the importance of the office but also a decrease in the ease with which someone who is sympathetic to the concerns of the business elite can be elected to office. In retrospect, the turning point seems to have occurred in the early 1980s. The last several races have required the spending of a good deal of money and have been more hotly contested than hitherto had been the case. For example, in the race for mayor in 1983, the candidate who was most sympathetic to keeping intact the existing arrangements to promote the economic advancement of the city spent on the order of $1 million to defeat a candidate who represented much that the alliance between officials and leading businessmen found objectionable. In the next race, the challenger, a hardware-store owner who has served on the city council and has been active in city affairs for many years, raised $20,000, whereas the incumbent, who had raised large sums in the previous election, again did so, this time spending about $400,000. The turnout was low, about 15 percent of the registered voters, and the race was much closer than expected, with the incumbent getting just over 50 percent of the vote and the principal challenger just over 45 percent. The most striking feature of the voting is the decline in support of the incumbent in the north Dallas neighborhoods, whose support is crucial if the alliance between business leaders and public officials who are committed to reworking the land patterns of Dallas is to continue. But the feeling among local observers was that supporters of the incumbent had underestimated the appeal of the challenger and had done little to see that voters who were sympathetic to their candidate turned out at the polls, because they considered the outcome of the race to be a foregone conclusion.[22]

The central point in all this is that while the mayor is very much a public figure on whom the competing pressures will fall and is by no means a creature of businessmen, he is typically a leading business figure himself, and his principal financial backers in the election are business executives and developers. It would, therefore, be surprising if he were inclined to take any other tack than one directed at promoting the growth of the city and at facilitating changes in the pattern of land use.

The situation is much the same for the other members of the city council who are elected at large. If they are not themselves leading business figures, they still draw their principal backing from the same sources as the mayor does and for much the same reasons. But the council members who are elected in single-member districts present a more complicated story.

Single-member districts have substantially reduced the importance of money in getting elected. Candidates who are widely known in their districts now have some chance to get elected even if they are short on funds. Almost as important, the Dallas media, which at the height of the pure entrepreneurial political economy constituted a relatively quiet element that was largely supportive of local businessmen and city officials, have now altered dramatically. Gone are the days of Mr. Dealey, visits of prospective candidates to his office, and his active role in the DCC. Dallas is now one of the few cities with two newspapers that really compete. In addition, there are now several local magazines that pay some attention to Dallas affairs. The result is that organized business interests and their allies among public officials can no longer depend on the favorable coverage that Dealey afforded. Quite the contrary, for now the incentives in a competitive system are to ferret out evidence of unfairness, incompetence, and the like. Indeed, like many other cities, Dallas now has a city magazine that covers local affairs and that appears to define its mission as bringing to public light what it understands to be the real workings of city politics.

The corollary is that it is now possible for ambitious local politicians to think that they can make up for lack of money with astute publicity. At least one feature of a local politics that can support a full-time political career is now in place—namely, the ability to develop an independent reputation. While possible before, this was probably restricted to those who were most adept at the arts of public promotion. Now there are reporters and media persons of various types who have incentives to seek out those who look as though they might make a good local news story. One member of the city council, reflecting hope as much as reality, suggested the extent of the change in this fashion: "In the past, councilors were more or less rubber stamps. But now with single-member districts, we can ask more questions. We can point to the votes in the districts that elected us. We can't as easily be shut up or beaten in election. We have the votes." In short, the recruitment process is no longer controlled, and there is now evidence, for example, of a variety of minority politicians who are starting to build careers around the single-member districts and the possibilities of media attention.

These changes, however, have not meant that those who hold seats in single-member districts have proven to be a substantial barrier to progrowth strategies. The reason is not hard to find, because a crucial ingredient is missing. Only those who expect to make full-time political careers would make substantial investments in trying to build up political followings. Resistance to growth strategies, particularly in the context in which they mean changes in land use, is most likely to come from citizens who are adversely affected by the new commercial developments—roads and the like. To be sure, any elected official from the affected area will pay some attention to such discontent, but usually, only those who see articulating the discontent as being crucial to a long-term political career will devote sustained energy to the matter. The part-time politician and the person who, for whatever reason, cannot build a political career are less likely to do so. Elected officials in Dallas lack such incentives.

Crucial here is a 1981 amendment to the City Charter, which set a limit of three terms for holding office on the city council. When this is added to the fact that members of the city council are still paid only $50 per council meeting, the incentives to invest much in trying to build up a political following by responding to citizen discontent about development projects or, in general, by not acting to facilitate growth strategies do not seem very large. As a consequence, even though the variety of neighborhood, racial, and other interests that go into making up a city political order now find it easier to gain expression, they are far from having elected officials who will give them significant voice.

Among those who hold and seek office in single-member districts, there is some difference in the extent to which those from more affluent districts and those from poor and minority districts resist progrowth strategies. Those from the former are most likely to be enthusiastic, because their constituents are most likely to be the beneficiaries, reaping a larger, more vibrant city with better job opportunities for those with high educational attainment and suffering few direct costs from redevelopment. There is every reason to suppose that such support will continue as long as progrowth policies do not push up against the tax rate. Dallas still has no income tax, and its property taxes are still low by the standards of the rest of the country. The policy of financing capital investment almost entirely by bonds continues. If tax rates were to rise significantly, development strategies might well be attacked. The last time a significant tax rise was proposed, there was a major uproar, accompanied by law suits.[23]

In poor and minority districts, residents and, hence, council members are more suspicious of growth strategies, at least ones that involve redevelopment. Such suspicion is manifest, for example, in recent proposals to stimulate commercial and industrial development in the city in the areas south of the CBD. The density of the development in these areas tends to be low, which makes them relatively attractive for redevelopment, but the neighborhoods are also home to a substantial number of minority residents of the city.

There is still, then, a set of elected officials in Dallas that can be relied upon to favor policies that will facilitate the economic expansion of the city, whether by fostering a general political environment favorable to investment or by helping to rearrange land use. At a minimum, a majority of the city council members will be drawn to such policies. The new electoral system, the demise of the CCA, and the other changes have not meant disaster from the viewpoint of business interests committed to a vibrant business climate in the city. There have, nevertheless, been changes from the pure entrepreneurial political economy. While elected officials are drawn to or are acquiescent in growth strategies, they are in fact somewhat freer to offer their own interpretation of what this entails. They are more nearly coalition partners than they are members of the community of interest that characterized the alliance under the pure entrepreneurial variant; as such, they are more often inclined to take the lead.

The city manager's outlook is also more complicated under the present political economy. Again, however, he is drawn to progrowth strategies. In part, this simply stems from the factors already noted: the division of labor between state and market, his professional responsibility for the revenue base of the city, and his long-time horizon. He, even more than elected officials, must take investment in the city seriously in order to do his job and secure his professional reputation.

As important, although the manager is drawn to neighborhood, racial, and ethnic groups for reasons suggested above, he is not faced with elected spokesmen for these interests who are strongly pushing him to resist pro-growth strategies. The manager is essentially as free under the complex as under the pure entrepreneurial variant to pursue his own predilections, but more so than under the pure variant, he will tend to have independent interpretations of what pursuing such strategies will entail. This is because even when he is not under strong pressures from council members and spokesmen for various citizen interests to resist growth strategies, he does find it useful to accommodate their concerns as the strategies get worked out. Indeed, the present manager was hired, among other things, to be accommodating in this fashion. Once neighborhood, racial, and ethnic interests are politically expressed, it is, if nothing else, prudent not to ignore them.

An important part of the burden of arranging the necessary compromises falls then, and will continue to fall, on the manager. In contrast to the city business leaders, he has the necessary time, inclination, and skills to make the compromises. The consequences of this fact are important: whereas under the pure entrepreneurial political economy, business leaders could play an active role in making many city decisions, this is becoming increasingly less true. In the earlier political economy, when necessary, leading businessmen could sit around a table with the manager, the mayor, and the city council. What was needed was the capacity to choose, to be decisive, to rank projects, and the like. This was something that those who headed banks and business firms could do, or at least one might suppose that their special talent was the ability to make decisions. Under the complex entrepreneurial political economy, however, the required skills are those of arranging compromises and bargains, of negotiating and trading—areas in which those who run hierarchical organizations are less likely to excel.

The result is simply that the city manager inevitably will have a different appreciation of what is entailed in implementing the growth strategies. As much to the point, he will be able to say to business leaders that if they wish to achieve their goals, then they must take account of the political realities, and he knows what these are. Thus, as with elected officials, it is again more a case of a coalition with the business elite than a community of interest. The city manager is, in fact, becoming more like the mayor of a sizeable city and less like a staff person for leading businessmen.

The conjunction of gentrification, neighborhood organization, the costs of rearranging land use, city councillors who are elected from single-member districts, and a city manager who is not adverse to paying at least some attention to neighborhood organizations might be expected to complicate development politics. No doubt this has occurred. But more indicative of what is happening are two recent decisions to significantly alter land-use patterns. Both suggest that an alliance around growth is still vital and can engineer significant changes in land use.

Bryan Place was developed under what is essentially a local urban-renewal program, which did not entail public hearings and other restrictive regulations characteristic of the federal program. The local ordinance that made it possible was passed in 1975, the Area Redevelopment Plan, in which the city agreed to buy back from developers land that they subsequently had not been able to develop. The ordinance was later amended to reimburse developers for the interest costs that they had borne, as well as the original cost of purchase. Only land within a 2-mile radius of the center of the downtown was eligible for the program, and the advertised aim was to encourage housing near the central business district. The original funding for the program came from federal revenue sharing, so that the city did not need to commit any of its own funds. All that the city committed was its guarantee, which developers could then employ when trying to raise funds from banks. The attractions of the program are obvious. Local public authority was being used, but without public scrutiny. The city manager commented that "this is a private venture and doesn't become a public venture until the city is asked to acquire the property."[24]

As completed, Bryan Place is a development of some sixty acres at the edge of the downtown, in which a typical house or condominium costs on the order of $100,000 and up. In addition to contributing the guarantee of repurchase, the city also made a variety of changes in fire codes and minimum street lengths and closed some streets altogether. The result is a very attractive development that has already attracted the middle and upper managers who work in the central business district.

A further illustration that the alliance between the local business elite and public officials can still engineer significant changes in the face of the city can be found in the recent commitment made by the city and DART, Dallas Area Rapid Transit agency, to widen the major north-south expressway and to build sixty-nine miles of light rail above and below ground. In its first phase, the rail system is to have three stations downtown and forty-two stations outside the CBD. The initial commitment is for $1 billion; the targeted completion date is 1995. Dallas voters have already approved the plan, which is to be paid for in part by an increase in the local sales tax, by bonds, and by an additional mode of financing that is suggestive of how local business interests will be able to shape the development of the city even as its politics are growing more complex.

Local business corporations are to be solicited to pay for the cost of some of the stations. In return for their contribution, the stations will be located where the businesses find them most convenient.[25] Under the guise of public-private partnership, local corporations will be in a position to ensure that the route of the rail system will at least in part follow their preferences. With a little bit of exaggeration, we might say that they can simply buy at least the station locations that they prefer, rather than going through the arduous process of translating their money and organization into political influence. Purchasing what they wish is much easier.

The impression of an active alliance around rearranging land use is given added substance by the host of major projects around and near the central business district. Some of these are in the form of public-private partnerships in which, through a variety of land swaps, coordinated investment efforts, and related endeavors, major undertakings have been brought to fruition.[26] These projects have, with concomitant large-scale private investment, had a noticeable impact on the downtown. There is, simply put, a commercial boom, which extends to districts outside the downtown area. Perhaps most noticeable in all this is a downtown arts district, which contains a new art museum, performance facilities, and various commercial buildings. It covers several square blocks at the edge of the downtown, and it involved major land clearance. This is not the project of a city in which leading businessmen, developers, and public officials find it difficult to act with force and dispatch. No less can be said of the office and commercial boom.

CONCLUSION

With all these changes in the politics and economics of Dallas, the largest businessmen in the city, including major land interests, still can expect to find public officials who are sympathetic to facilitating the economic growth of the city. Public officials are more independent, and the links are more complex, but Dallas is still an entrepreneurial city. One need only note that the system of financing capital investment, which gives leading businessmen a privileged position, is still largely intact. More voices are now being heard in the city, but up to this point, at least, they have not made extensive links between public officials and business leaders very difficult to maintain, nor has the increased emphasis on rearranging land use prevented the relationship from continuing.

Development politics in Dallas occurs in the context of a city-manager system that does little to facilitate the development of political followings by elected officials. Not the least important point is simply that the City Charter is designed to dissuade council members from involving themselves in administrative matters. Although the temptation is difficult to resist and no doubt is sometimes given into, the manager and his staff, as well as those who are devoted to protecting the city-manager system, make it difficult for any councillor to do this as a matter of course. One of the principal sources of benefactions that an ambitious local politician can use and probably needs to use in order to build a political career is access to the local bureaucracy. Here can potentially be found favorable decisions for supporters and material benefits, including jobs. If it is difficult to do favors for valued political supporters, then it is difficult to have very many such supporters. All of this being so, elected officials are much less likely than are their counterparts in many other cities to have the skills to seek out discontent and to build coalitions that might draw them into stances that are critical of progrowth strategies.

NOTES

This essay appears in somewhat different form in Stephen Elkin, *City and Regime in the American Republic,* © The University of Chicago, 1987.

1. Unless otherwise stated, the analysis presented here draws on some fifty hours of interviews with a wide variety of local officials and political activists. Most of the interviews were conducted in the spring of 1982, though some were completed earlier.
2. See Stephen L. Elkin, "Cities without Power: The Transformation of American Urban Regimes," in *National Resources and Urban Policy,* ed. Douglas Ashford (New York: Methuen, 1980), and "Twentieth Century Urban Regimes," *Journal of Urban Affairs* 7 (Spring 1985): 11–28.
3. The best source on this early period is Harold Stone, Don K. Price, and Kathryn Stone, *City Manager Government in Nine Cities* (Chicago: Public Administration Service, 1940).
4. See the testimony of Dan Weiser, a local elections analyst, *Albert Lipscomb et al.* vs. *Wes Wise,* U.S. District Court for Northern District of Texas, Dallas Division, July 1974, vol. 4, pp. 56ff.
5. From 1931 until 1968 the city council was elected entirely at large; it contained nine members, six of whom had to reside in a designated district. In 1968 the number of city councillors was increased to eleven, and again a residence provision was employed.
6. See the testimony of George Allen, given in the case of *Lipscomb* vs. *Wise,* vol. 3, pp. 89ff.
7. See the testimony of Dan Weiser, *Lipscomb* vs. *Wise,* vol. 4, p. 56.
8. These data on campaign expenditures are from documents on file in the City Attorney's Office, City of Dallas.
9. *Lipscomb* vs. *Wise,* vol. 7, p. 57.
10. In addition to interview sources, the material on the CCA comes from Carolyn Jencks Barta, "The *Dallas News* and Council-manager Government" (Master's thesis, University of Texas, Austin, 1970). See also the testimony of Tom Unis, head of CCA during the mid 1960s, in *Lipscomb* vs. *Wise,* vol. 7.
11. The only exception was Wes Wise, who held office in the early 1970s. Wise was a popular local broadcaster and thus was one of the few sorts of people who had a sufficiently large independent reputation to contest a seat on equal terms with CCA-backed candidates.
12. Dallas is, in fact, the largest city in the United States with a city-manager form of government.

13. The material on the founding of the DCC is from Carol Estes Thometz, *The Decision-Makers: The Power Structure of Dallas.* See also "The Dynamic Men of Dallas," *Fortune,* Feb. 1946.

14. The solution of the water problem was the first big triumph for the entrepreneurial political economy. Indeed, the story is still regularly told in Dallas when outsiders need to be convinced of the civic-mindedness of local businessmen and of why a strong, well-organized business community is good for the city. The story is one of the civic totems of Dallas, and no doubt it is also passed on to new members of the business elite to explain why a politically active business community is a valuable thing.

15. In addition to the DCC, leading businessmen would also form special-purpose organizations to undertake particular projects.

16. See Mancur Olson, *The Logic of Collective Action* (New York: Schocken, 1971). For a parallel argument in another context see Stephen L. Elkin, "Political Structure, Political Organization and Race," *Politics and Society* 8(2) (1978): 225–51.

17. Dallas more than doubled in size from 1945 to 1957, and this expansion continued until recently, when it became increasingly difficult to annex because the surrounding areas were largely incorporated.

18. See Richard D. Brown, "Collective Bargaining and Public Employee Strikes," *Texas Business Review* 52 (Sept. 1978).

19. See the testimony of Dan Weiser in *Lipscomb* vs. *Wise,* vol. 4, p. 90.

20. John Rees, "Manufacturing Headquarters in a Post-Industrial Urban Context," *Economic Geography* 54 (Oct. 1978): 337–54.

21. A recent change in the Texas banking laws, which allows banks to do business all over the state, will probably further direct the attention of Dallas bankers away from city affairs.

22. See the account in the *New York Times,* 8 and 10 Apr. 1985.

23. See the account in John Fullinwider, "Dallas: The City with No Limits?" *In These Times,* Dec. 1980, pp. 17–23.

24. *Dallas Times Herald,* 24 July 1976.

25. See the account in the *New York Times,* 8 Sept. 1985.

26. See William A. Clagget, "Dallas: The Dynamics of Public-Private Cooperation," in *Public Private Partnership in American Cities,* ed. R. Scott Fosler and Renee A. Berger (Lexington, Mass.: D. C. Heath, 1982).

3

Fiscal Crises and Regime Change: A Contextual Approach

Robert F. Pecorella

In this chapter, Robert Pecorella enables us to see that regimes are not static. Drawing on the New York City experience, Pecorella shows how a city can have a cyclical pattern of regime change. "Prevailing coalitions" rise and fall, sometimes in response to forces that converge to restrict local policy discretion. Pecorella directs attention in particular to the capacity of financial interests to ally with state officials and then to intervene in city politics during times of fiscal crisis. This chapter forms an especially useful counterpoint to Stephen Elkin's chapter on Dallas. Whereas Elkin emphasizes continuities that grow from the relationship between privately held capital and popular control, Pecorella draws our attention to the potential for instability in this relationship.

In describing his approach as contextual, Pecorella also makes us mindful of the connection between local conditions and the national economy and even the international economy. While the question of fiscal condition comes from a complicated interplay between the local situation and the larger political economy, Pecorella shows that the city's fiscal condition forms a context within which the city's political relationships are worked out. Moreover, because a variety of groups outside the city's business and financial elite are involved in building coalitions, the New York experience serves also as an apt reminder that federal funds may play a key part in the ability of coalition builders to achieve the support of nonbusiness groups. The contrast with Dallas is again instructive. In that city, elite decision makers have, in some instances, foregone federal money in order to keep the governing coalition more narrowly based. In New York, the shrinkage of federal funds played a part in destabilizing the governing coalition of the 1970s.

New York and Dallas are alike in that both are financial centers. Thus, financial interests, which are important in all cities, play an especially significant role in New York, as they do in Dallas. That role, Pecorella points out, depends partly on a capacity to act collectively—that is, on having financial interests make their presence felt as a unified group.

The nature of business influence on local governance remains an unresolved yet critical issue in the literature on urban politics. Although the debate continues between those who view business as just another interest and those who view it as the elite interest in local politics, the gap that separates the two positions has narrowed in recent years. Proponents of the view that business interests are but one of many groups now wrestle with the notion of a "privileged position for business" vis-à-vis other groups. At the same time, advocates of the elite model must grapple with how receptive governmental officials are to distinctly nonbusiness interests.

Recent qualifications notwithstanding, the two positions offer only partially satisfactory analyses in that neither is empirically satisfying across time. What is required is an approach that recognizes the contextual nature of local politics. By suggesting that at any time, local group-power relationships are functions of larger socioeconomic and political forces, this chapter offers such an analysis. With New York City as the focus of analysis, I employ this contextual approach to illustrate how fiscal crises in the history of that city transform existing alignments of interest groups to the distinct advantage of business, specifically financial, interests. In immediate terms, this transformation results in public-sector retrenchment as coalitions of financiers and state politicos exercise directive influence—that is, control of policy options—over local officials. In the long term, the interest-group realignments that accompany fiscal crises result in regime changes in New York's mode of governance..

Fiscal crises, defined as the closure of short-term credit markets to city debt offerings, are central to the analysis. Such crises during the 1870s, the 1930s, and the 1970s are considered to have been fulcrum points in New York's political evolution that fundamentally altered existing political arrangements.[1] The first crisis, in the 1870s, ushered in the beginnings of institutionalized machine rule; the second crisis, in the 1930s, resulted in the ascendance of reform politics and the welfare city; and the crisis in the 1970s introduced a corporatist era in city governance. From the contextual perspective, these crises serve the same analytical purpose as do the bifurcating issues that set the stage for "critical elections" at the national level: they result in fundamental realignments of political power.

Before proceeding, however, I review three familiar approaches to urban politics—the pluralist, the statist, and the stratificationist—which incorporate distinct analyses of urban governance in general and of the most recent New York City fiscal crisis in particular. Although insightful analyses of the substantive and methodological issues that separate these schools of thought are available elsewhere, a brief discussion here serves as a useful frame of reference for presenting the contextual approach.

APPROACHES TO URBAN POLITICS

Pluralist theory suggests that local politics evolves incrementally through a process of accommodation between and among a diverse and wide-ranging assortment of interest groups.[2] From this perspective, the multitude of groups in the system as a whole, the extent of crosscutting cleavages within and overlapping memberships among the various groups, and the social consensus on democratic norms ensure the fluidity of group competition within an open political system. Even interests that attain preeminence in a particular policy area are constrained by the actual or potential mobilization of countervailing forces.

In recent years, however, a number of noted pluralist scholars who responded to obvious paradigmatic anomalies in their model have amended group theory to include notions of a distinctive role for business interests in the American polyarchy. Indeed, John Manley contends that such qualifications give rise to a neopluralist paradigm, although the shape of this revised model remains unclear.[3] What is clear, however, is a growing disquiet among pluralist scholars concerning the self-regulating nature of social equilibrium.

Recent qualifications notwithstanding, pluralists continue to emphasize group competition in analyzing the politics of urban fiscal crisis and retrenchment. Charles Levine, Irene Rubin, and George Wolohojian argue that New York's fiscal crisis resulted from economic decline after the effects of a temporary imbalance in the configurations of local group power.[4] This imbalance, generated by the windfall growth of urban social programs during the 1960s, reformulated the relationship between interest groups and city officials, thus permitting a coalition of social spenders to increase the government's fiscal obligations. The combination of slower economic growth and federal retrenchment during the 1970s generated pressures on the city's budget, which the existing governing coalition, committed as it was to extending public services, could not deal with. Consequently, a more conservative coalition of business interests, state government, and fiscally conservative local officials assumed power in order to manage the retrenchment. The crisis atmosphere aside, the twin concepts of social equilibrium and incrementalism are very much in evidence in those authors' conclusions: "Power has shifted somewhat from the city's municipal unions to business groups. These shifts have been gradual and do not represent a total reversal of prior political relationships on city politics."[5]

Pluralist theory has engendered two distinct sets of critics: one statist, the other stratificationist in perspective. First, a number of observers who subscribe to the group basis of politics argue that the traditional pluralist model ignores the importance of formal public authority. These critics argue that the lack of a statist perspective in modern pluralist societies results in a disaggregated social order in which issues of process supersede issues of substance in regard to formal procedure.[6] From this perspective, pluralism has degenerated into a pattern of group retrenchment in specific policy areas that do not have a central authority with the legitimacy to evaluate or coordinate claims.

From the statist perspective, urban fiscal crises are the predictable consequence of governments' inability to choose among competing claims on public resources. Such crises are not necessarily the result of economic decline or of imbalances in group competition; they are the consequences of "weak governance and lack of public control." Martin Shefter presents a picture of fiscal irresponsibility that results from the inability of New York City officials to assert the role of public authority.[7] By acceding to the demands of municipal unions for higher wages and of minority groups for increased social services, city officials have incorporated new and expensive claims on the public treasury. By refusing to risk alienating homeowners with further increases in taxes, officials have maintained artificially low revenue bases. By combining the two processes, governmental weakness has produced fiscal crisis.

While statists question pluralist assumptions concerning the self-regulating nature of group competition, stratification theorists challenge the basic principles of group theory. From the latter's perspective, local politics is essentially the domain of local business and financial elites whose influence on policy overrides that of any other group in the city.[8] Urbanization itself is a consequence of actions taken by economic elites, and urban policy making continues to reflect the primacy of these elites in modern cities. Stratification theorists argue that by concentrating on open decision-making processes as their units of analysis, pluralists miss the critical systemic role that economic elites play in local politics.

To stratification theorists, New York City's fiscal crisis in the 1970s reflects the costs of servicing the business and financial sectors of the local economy as well as the public burdens that have been produced by the self-serving activities of economic elites. Jack Newfield and Paul DuBrul, for example, locate the roots of the fiscal crisis in the capital construction projects and in the tax expenditure programs that were designed to socialize corporate production costs and to secure high rates of return for financial investors.[9] These ever-increasing costs, together with the decision by large banks to "dump" city bonds in favor of more profitable investments in 1974, precipitated the fiscal crisis in New York City.

In recent years, each of these perspectives has had a claim on empirical validity. During the 1950s, pluralism appeared to have modeled quite astutely the dynamics of American politics. At the national level, political conflicts were moderated by the distributive capacities of economic growth as the welfare state, created by Democrats, was institutionalized in a Republican administration. In American cities, the social crisis awaited discovery. Cleavages between haves and have nots and between native and immigrant cultures were considered to be "treatable" through continued economic growth and ethnic assimilation. Wallace Sayre and Herbert Kaufman's summary of their quintessential pluralist analysis of New York City politics exemplifies the conventional view of the period. While acknowledging the existence of "defects . . . accompanying virtues," they conclude:

> The most lasting impression created by a systematic analysis of New York City's political and governmental system as a whole are its democratic virtues: its qualities of openness, its commitments to bargaining and accommodation among participants, its receptivity to new participants, its opportunities for the exercise of leadership by an unmatched variety and number of the city's residents new and old.[10]

As political conflicts during the 1960s and the early 1970s intensified, however, statists emerged to confront anomalies in the pluralist model. As group competition degenerated into open, frequently violent group conflict, politics in American cities took on a distinctly nonpluralist tone. In the social upheavals of the period and in the fiscal instability of a later period, statists saw evidence of the predictable breakdown of pluralist equilibrium.

If pluralist theory seemed to be a reasonable guide to politics during the 1950s and if its statist critics appeared to offer plausible explanations for the increasingly uncontrolled conflict and fiscal crises of a later period, neither had a great deal to offer concerning retrenchment politics in the 1970s. The emergence of centralized authority in the form of quasi-public agencies, such as the Municipal Assistance Corporation and the Emergency Financial Control Board in New York, the Financial and Policy Service Board in Cleveland, and Economic Development Agencies in Detroit, fitted into a pattern of business control of local governments. To argue that this process of extragovernmental centralization was necessary in order to cope with crisis is reasonable though not incontestable; to argue that this process reflected self-regulating group equilibrium, temporary imbalances in group competition, or the absence of coherent public authority is utterly unconvincing.

It is clear that the three approaches differ as to the causes and effects of fiscal crisis. To pluralists, fiscal crises are anomalous events that balance the effects of equally anomalous periods of windfall growth; to statists, these crises are the predictable results of the absence of public authority in pluralist societies; and to stratificationists, these crises result from the greed and power of local economic elites.

In dealing with retrenchment, group theorists are faced with paradigmatic dilemmas. If urban politics is either self-regulating group competition or an example of the absence of coherent authority, whence did the authority to manage retrenchment arise? If it arose from emergency powers—that is, from outside of paradigmatic relationships—why were the agencies that were managing retrenchment dominated by large financial interests? And if emergency circumstances require that financiers intervene into local decision making, what does this say about the influence of these interests generally? These questions are particularly salient given the recurring pattern of crisis and financier intervention in American urban history.

Stratificationists were understandably anxious to address these questions. Because of the systemic power that economic elites wield, the directive role that financial interests play during retrenchment is not unexpected in a stratificationist analysis. However, although stratification theorists offer paradigmatically consistent explanations for the form that retrenchment politics takes, their analyses of noncrisis politics are frequently circular and unconvincing.

The contextual approach addresses the limitations in previous models by analyzing the details of retrenchment politics within their larger socioeconomic and political contexts. Employing this approach, I examine both retrenchment politics and regime change in New York during the 1870s, the 1930s, and the 1970s. I contend that differences in the three periods notwithstanding, there exist patterns of political behavior during and in the aftermath of fiscal crises which can best be explained contextually.

THE CONTEXTUAL APPROACH

Periods of fiscal crisis and retrenchment reflect the contrasting pressures that emanate from the socioeconomic and political environments of local governance. The socioeconomic context of American governance—private ownership and control of productive capacity—has evolved from the early competitive stages of the Industrial Revolution, through the latter periods of corporate consolidation, and into the most recent era of the postindustrial service economy. The liberal political context has been characterized by the increasing enfranchisement of social groups and the consequent democratization of representative modes of government. Inherent tension exists between the socioeconomic priorities of capital production, efficiency, and centralization, on the one hand, and the political demands for resource allocation, accountability, and decentralization, on the other.[11]

Although this tension is ubiquitous in American politics, it is particularly intense at the local level, where government "closest to the people" coexists with highly mobile private capital. Because local governments are required to balance their budgets, they confront the socioeconomic pressures for fiscal responsibility and the political demands for resource distribution without the option of deficit spending, which is available to federal officials. The immediacy and the relative rigidity of constraints at the local level are reflected in the fact that fiscal crises represent a breakdown in socioeconomic constraints and that retrenchment indicates a failure of political constraints.

Two broadly defined sets of constituencies embody the dual constraints on local politics: large-scale business interests and attentive nonelites. The nature of political interactions between these sets of interests, indeed the bifurcation between them at any historical moment, is a function of the larger socioeconomic and political forces that they represent.

Because the production of wealth in the United States occurs exclusively in the private sector and because government depends on producers of wealth for the resources that it is charged with allocating, interests that are involved in large-scale capital accumulation are critical to the local political economy. There are two types of such interests in American cities: large industrial concerns and financial institutions. Several observers have noted the influence of industrial concerns in cities where only a few industries support the local economy.[12] However, New York's diversified export base has largely insulated its government from the often-decisive political pressures that industrial concerns wield in more dependent cities.[13]

Financial institutions, on the other hand, have been tied inextricably to New York's political economy.[14] As the source of capital for entrepreneurs, financial institutions promote economic growth; as the source of capital for housing, they help to maintain neighborhood stability; and as purchasers of city debt, they provide resources to ease short-term cash-flow problems and to generate long-term capital projects. These traditional components of financier influence are writ even larger in the nation's, indeed in the world's, financial center. Although it overstates the case to argue that in all areas, New York's elected officials must produce policies that are acceptable to financial interests, it is certainly true that officials must anticipate the reactions of these interests in policy areas that are relevant to these interests.

Attentive nonelites, on the other hand, are active participants in city politics who exert influence to the extent that their participation translates into votes or into potential instability in the system. Obviously, under the rubric of attentive nonelites, a wide diversity of interests exists, ranging from middle-class homeowners, who desire minimal property-tax assessments and basic public services, to lower-income claimants, who require extensive public services. Diversity of interest aside, the distinctive characteristic of attentive nonelite influence is that it exists outside of the socioeconomic context defining the interactions of financial institutions and city government and that it is therefore dependent on overt political action.

The influence that financier and attentive nonelites have on city government affects and is affected by the fiscal situation—that is, the degree of balance between local revenues and expenditures. Indeed, the contextual approach suggests that the range of issues that are relevant to financial interests is dependent on the fiscal situation within which the issues emerge. The fiscal situation is reflected in three possible budgetary outcomes. *Fiscal stability,* or relative budgetary balance, indicates economic growth sufficient to address both incremental increases in existing demands and new claims on resources. *Fiscal stress* refers to temporary imbalance in the revenue/expenditure base, which is produced by an economic downturn, and/or to an increase in group demands. *Fiscal crisis,* as discussed above, is a closure of short-term credit markets to city-debt issues brought on by continued budgetary imbalance.

Each period of fiscal crisis in New York's history has witnessed changes in the prevailing interest-group alignment, which is reflected in the emergence of an active and unified coalition of financial interests that are seeking to restore fiscal stability and in the further segmentation of attentive nonelite groups, each of which is seeking to protect past political gains. These changes, coupled with the intervention of state government, have severely limited the autonomy of city officials and have resulted in public-policy changes in New York. In the immediate crisis situation, these changes are evident as retrenchment politics; in the long term, they help to explain the regime changes that follow crises.

FROM MACHINE TO REFORM TO POSTREFORM

In 1871, reacting to the increasingly obvious fiscal improprieties of the Tweed Ring, reformers secured a court injunction to prohibit city officials from collecting new revenues and from incurring additional debt.[15] The injunction transformed a period of investor skepticism and fiscal stress into one of credit-market closure and fiscal crisis.[16] The 1871 crisis, therefore, was part of an overall strategy to depose Boss Tweed, to reform city government, and—most important—to reestablish "fiscal responsibility" in New York City.

The precrisis period, which Shefter has characterized as the era of "rapacious individualism," had been marked by the rule of competing political gangs.[17] The Tweed Ring, the most successful of these gangs, maintained its political base by providing a "piece of the action" to a wide variety of interests, financing its largesse through the sale of public debt. Between 1867 and 1871, the level of municipal debt rose threefold, to over $90 million.[18] The city's debt level increased with the acquiescence of financiers who purchased and underwrote bonds. However, questions concerning the city's ability to manage the funds, which culminated in exposés of official corruption in the *New York Times* during the summer of 1871, shook investor confidence in city offerings.[19] After the disclosures, Mayor A. Oakey Hall's and Comptroller Richard Connolly's denials of fiscal problems were as ineffectual as they were predictable.

The reform coalition that employed fiscal pressure to topple the Ring included prominent state politicos and representatives of virtually all of the large financial institutions in New York City. Indeed, the success of the "bankers strike" was dependent on unity of purpose among financiers and their allies. The Committee of Seventy, the most prominent of the reform organizations that opposed the existing regime, "included at least eighteen bankers and brokers whose names appeared over and over again during the decade as advisors to city officials."[20] The committee, which was chaired by banker Henry Stebbins, conducted its often-secret strategy sessions at the Chamber of Commerce's offices on Henry Street.

State politicos and financiers, bolstered by daily press accounts of the crisis, sought indictments of city officials, secured the appointment of Andrew Green as special deputy comptroller to manage the city's fiscal affairs, and prevailed upon Governor John Hoffman to appoint Judge Charles O'Conor a special state attorney general to investigate city affairs. The power of the Tweed Ring was effectively broken as the reformers, with William Havemeyer at the head of the ticket, swept the 1872 elections. More importantly, the era of gang rule in New York was ended, because fiscal decision making was centered in individuals who were beholden to state government and to financial interests and because Tammany Hall was restructured.

After the immediate period of crisis, governance in New York was restructured. The coalition of financiers and state politicos installed "Honest John" Kelly as the leader of Tammany Hall. Throughout his tenure as county leader and later as city comptroller, Kelly maintained an essentially conservative fiscal posture, thereby addressing the demands of both financiers and the "swallowtail," or upper income, faction of Tammany Hall for stability.[21] In fact, such fiscal conservatism, reinforced by the panic of 1863, has been credited with helping city government avoid a fiscal crisis during the panic of 1893.[22]

Kelly's machine, however, was more than a conduit for upper-stratum interests. Under Kelly's leadership, the machine addressed the concerns of attentive nonelite groups by institutionalizing the Democratic party's presence in ethnic neighborhoods through the establishment of a hierarchically coordinated ward-based political organization.[23] Kelly formalized the financing of elections and the dispersal of patronage, two key elements of machine power. District leaders became less individual political entrepreneurs and more representatives of the larger machine organization. In short, Kelly's Tammany Hall—born in fiscal crisis, shaped by the overt power of financiers and state politicos, and attentive to newly arrived immigrant groups—initiated sixty years of functionally centralized but geographically decentralized machine government in New York City.

Although the Tammany machine, under Kelly's successors Richard Croker and Charles Murphy, evolved into the preeminent political force in New York City, it was never free from reform challenge. By the late nineteenth century, progressives, who were interested in governmental activism as a means of dealing with the more damaging social consequences of industrialization, and large business interests, which viewed government intervention as a means of decreasing competitive uncertainties, were united in their opposition to the machine. This coalition of progressives and business interests, with their emphases on cosmopolitan issues and supracommunity support groups, represented a fundamental challenge to comparatively parochial machine rule. Although the increasingly sophisticated reform movement managed to win control of the mayoralty several times during the height of machine power, reformers were unable to institutionalize their victories and to replace the machine regime in the early years of the twentieth century. Once again, as in the 1870s, the catalyst for regime change in New York City was fiscal crisis.

The world-wide depression of the 1930s produced substantial shortfalls in expected revenues, and it increased demands on city resources. Despite tax increases, revenues fell in 1931 and 1932 by nearly $50 million, expenditures increased by over $100 million, and debt service soared to nearly one-third of expense-budget outlays.[24] Twice in 1932, city officials implemented retrenchment measures in return for further credit from the city's major financial institutions.[25] In 1933, city officials, facing imminent fiscal crisis, were forced to "negotiate" a Bankers Agreement with financiers who had refused to roll over any more short-term debt.[26]

The Bankers Agreement was the culmination of three years of political activism by the city's major financiers. Throughout the period, a coalition of financiers, using their access to credit markets as a negotiating tool, had pressured the Jimmy Walker/John O'Brien administration to cut back on city programs and on employee salary levels. By the summer of 1933, it was evident that in the absence of further dramatic retrenchment, the financial community would close credit markets to city debt. In a series of meetings, the financiers, assisted by the intervention of Governor Herbert Lehman and the state-run Municipal Economy Commission (MEC), forced city officials to virtually relinquish control of the city's fiscal policy. On 1 November 1933, in the manner of heads of state, representatives of the major financial institutions and city officials formally signed the Bankers Agreement, which had been drafted earlier.

The Bankers Agreement averted immediate bankruptcy. However, the machine, severely constrained in its ability to deliver services by the concessions to financiers, entered the 1933 elections divided and weakened. Machine preeminence in city politics, a preeminence that started as part of the structural changes resulting from the fiscal crisis of 1871, ended in the wake of the 1930s fiscal crisis, with the ascendence of Fiorello LaGuardia's reform administration.

LaGuardia's fusion administration addressed the financiers' concerns by reaffirming the Bankers Agreement and by implementing the economy bill of 1934. This bill instituted payless furloughs for most city employees, which resulted in an average salary reduction of 4 percent across the board; required county officials to reduce their budgets by 10 percent, forcing layoffs and pay cuts at the borough level; and—reflecting the reformers' desire to rationalize governmental structures—gave to the mayor the power to consolidate and reorganize many city agencies.

In addressing the demands of attentive nonelites, the administration initiated the modern welfare city in New York by bringing New Deal programs and money to bear on social problems.[27] Faced with unprecedented demands for economic assistance, reformers were operating under the severe fiscal constraints of retrenchment. Using federal funds, city officials provided assistance to victims of the economic downturn. As a consequence, political interactions moved from the ward level of machine politics to the city-wide level of reform, and political power left the machine bosses and gravitated to the city bureaucracies.

In the 1870s, John Kelly addressed the concerns of activated financiers by restructuring the Tammany machine. Six decades later, reformers centralized governmental structures in order to address the financiers' demands for retrenchment and used federal funds to address the claims of attentive nonelites for services. In each period, the centralization of fiscal authority, coupled with policies designed to incorporate attentive nonelite groups into the political structure, resulted in regime change in city governance.

By the 1970s, the welfare city that LaGuardia's reformers had created had been institutionalized by succeeding administrations. Indeed, the scope of the local public sector increased dramatically during the years after World War II as the influx of an essentially service-demanding population from the rural South, the increasing demands of municipal unions, and the local share of federal social programs put upward pressure on fiscal outlays.[28] In fact, relative budgetary balance was maintained during the 1950s and early 1960s by the overall economic growth and by the infusion of federal money into city coffers. However, over time, fiscal stability gave way to fiscal stress as national and regional recessions, local depression, and a leveling of federal aid caused revenues to decrease and expenditures to increase, while fiscal gimmickery sharply extended New York's short-term debt.[29] By 1974, after several years of fiscal stress, it had become increasingly obvious that New York was facing fiscal crisis.

Financial interests, which had profited for years by purchasing and underwriting city debt, became increasingly concerned with and vocal about the city's fiscal situation in the early 1970s. As the city's deteriorating fiscal condition became a threat to the financial community's immediate interests, their common problems overrode normal competitive constraints on behavior. Because the welfare city encompassed so many claimants and such a great degree of decentralized policy making, control of the fiscal situation demanded more extensive and concerted action during the 1970s than during past crises. Accordingly, from 1974 on, we witnessed a pervasive intrusion of financial interests into the city's affairs, beginning with overt pressure upon city officials to retrench government and culminating with a state-imposed solution to incorporate direct financier intervention. By September 1974, New York City was, for all intents and purposes, being governed by its creditors.[30]

The 1970s fiscal crisis and the mode of retrenchment that it engendered reformulated relationships in the welfare city. While fiscal authority was virtually removed from the city's elected officials and was centralized in state politicos and financiers, control of local land-use and service-delivery functions were spread more widely among the city's community districts. The welfare city was weakened on two fronts—one by adaptations to deal with the fiscal crisis; the other by charter reforms to cope with legitimacy problems.[31] Although separate phenomena, these two aspects of politics in New York during the 1970s combined to produce regime change as the welfare city was replaced by the corporatist city. This new regime, personified in the neoconservative administration of Mayor Edward Koch, was fiscally centralized under watchdog agencies and highly conservative budgetary techniques (such as Generally Accepted Accounting Principles, or GAAP) and was politically decentralized through a system of institutionalized community boards. The new regime is attentive to the interests of upper-income wealth producers, on the one hand, and the white middle and working classes on the other.

THE POLITICS OF RETRENCHMENT: GROUP BIFURCATION

During periods of fiscal stability or fiscal stress, local politics is characterized by relative openness to group demands, shifting coalitions among various interests, and incremental adjustments in fiscal policy. However, during periods of fiscal crisis, a clear division develops between financial interests that are concerned with economic and political stability, on the one hand, and, on the other hand, attentive nonelites who are seeking to protect past political gains that would be threatened by retrenchment. As the allocation of resources becomes a zero-sum game and as issues are perceived increasingly as redistributive, the control of municipal finances becomes the paramount concern, and the accommodation between socioeconomic and political constraints that are embodied in the existing regime breaks down.

Fiscal crises unify and activate financial interests at the same time that they segment and weaken the attentive nonelite groups. During crises, financial interests broaden their involvement and increase their influence in local politics for three reasons. First, in order to protect their investments, these interests become concerned with a wide gamut of issues, such as union contracts and service allocation, which formerly were dealt with in the political sphere through the distributive policies characteristic of fiscal stability. Second, because of their expertise in economic matters and their professional standing with creditors, financiers can effect fiscal relief through their access to credit markets. And third, their prestige in the community as a whole—a prestige that is nurtured by media coverage, which understates the financiers' involvement in helping to generate injuriously high levels of debt while it emphasizes their "civic concern" during crisis—enables representatives of these interests to assume directive responsibilities in local government for which there are no discernible procedural rationales.

On the other hand, there are a number of reasons why the influence of attentive nonelites is minimized during periods of crisis. First, these groups operate exclusively in the political sphere, where their activities and demands are subject to intensive media scrutiny and public attention. Consequently, during periods of crisis, the attentive nonelites' access to officials appears more as part of the problem than as the solution to it. Second, these groups depend on elected officials' receptivity to their claims. As noted, however, the onset of fiscal crisis dramatically diminishes the influence that elected officials have on the local scene. Third, attentive nonelite groups, which are diverse during periods of fiscal stability, are further segmented during periods of crisis, as each group struggles to protect its own specific interests from retrenchment.

This transformed group alignment—unified and active financial interests, on the one hand, and segmented and weakened attentive nonelite groups, on the other—has ensured that fiscal crises in New York City have been dealt with in a manner consistent with socioeconomic exigencies while it minimizes political constraints. Ironically, then, the political sphere, which integrates the demands of attentive nonelites during periods of fiscal stability, is what has stifled such input during periods of crisis.

THE POLITICS OF RETRENCHMENT: THE LOSS OF LOCAL AUTONOMY

Among the immediate consequences of group realignment during crisis is the restructuring of formal political power in the city. To understand this process of change it is important to remember that although fiscal stress always precedes fiscal crisis, fiscal stress rarely leads to fiscal crisis. In most cases of fiscal stress, local officials have no way of knowing whether budget imbalances are temporary or have longer-term implications. These officials, however, have powerful incentives to view budget problems as temporary, since the officials are understandably anxious to avoid the political costs that service cutbacks or widespread increases in revenue would incur among their attentive nonelite support groups. Accordingly, local officials tend to employ short-term strategies—such as selective tax increases, which are often aimed at business interests, and augmented debt offerings—to address the immediate imbalance in local budgets. If fiscal recovery follows close on the heels of fiscal stress, these strategies are but footnotes to the balanced-budget requirements of city government. If, however, budgetary imbalances deepen, these same strategies sharply exacerbate an already deteriorating situation and become the focus of public attention. Thus, the indeterminate evolution of fiscal stress, coupled with the incentives that local officials have to conduct politics as usual under conditions of stress, explains why when a crisis develops, it is viewed by many as essentially a management problem, divorced from its larger socioeconomic and political roots.

Unquestionably, politics as usual is not the case during periods of crisis. During the initial stage of crisis, state governmental officials, who are concerned with the effects of local problems on their own fiscal situation, become increasingly involved with local issues. In union with representatives of financial interests, whose access to credit markets affords them de facto power during crises, state officials, who have de jure authority, assume a more active role in local fiscal policy. As the range of issues relevant to state officials and financiers expands and as their involvement in local politics becomes increasingly unidimensional and overt, the range of options available to local officials contracts. In their need to reopen credit markets, local officials are faced with a Hobson's choice. If they accede to the financiers' demands for immediate and dramatic retrenchment, the officials alienate the attentive nonelite support groups that constitute their political base; if the officials resist such pressure in order to maintain their base of support, they risk municipal bankruptcy. Regardless of which strategy the local officials choose—and there is intense and immediate pressure to choose the former—they soon become weakened actors on the local political scene.

The assumption of fiscal responsibility by two sets of actors who are relatively insulated from local political pressures allows the service cutbacks, employee reductions, and tax increases—the effects of which are felt most directly by attentive nonelites—to be implemented at the local level. In short, the legal authority of state government, the economic power of financial interests, and the weakened political position of local officials assure that local policy is no longer a local matter and that accountability is no longer a countervailing force to the efficiency of management during crisis periods.

THE POLITICS OF RETRENCHMENT: DEVELOPMENT POLICY

The bifurcation of group interests, the loss of local autonomy, and the appropriation of fiscal power by state politicos and financiers have dramatic impacts on local public policy. As Peterson has observed, local policy can be considered either developmental, redistributive, or allocational in emphasis.[32] Development policies are designed to produce social benefits by encouraging private investment and by promoting urban growth. These policies, which serve the immediate demands of business interests in the hope of generating "trickle down" collective benefits, are the clearest indication of socioeconomic constraints on local government. Redistributive policies address the social problems that result from the unequal distribution of resources among city residents. These policies, which are directed at the demands of lower-income attentive-nonelite groups, may have negative impacts on the local economy bcause they entail an essentially unproductive use of public funds. Allocational policies also involve the distribution of city services. Although such services are allocated to all residents, they are particularly salient to lower- and middle-income sectors of the population, which have relatively few alternatives to governmental services. In that context, allocational policies primarily address the demands of attentive nonelites.

During periods of fiscal stability, local public policy is a function of the prevailing balance of group power as well as the political priorities of elected officials. During such periods of growth, the allocation of services increases incrementally city-wide, with neighborhood winners and losers reflecting either "unpatterned inequalities" or differential political influence among communities;[33] redistributive policies are determined by local political culture and by the level of organization among lower-income groups and their allies; and the extent of development policies reflects whether private investment and locational decisions are occurring in a buyer's or in a seller's market. During periods of fiscal stress, local officials, who are constrained by the immediate political need to address the demands of their attentive nonelite support base by means of allocational and/or redistributive programs, balance municipal budgets with temporary, distinctly nondevelopmental policies, such as increases in business taxes. Finally, during periods of fiscal crisis, local policy is almost exclusively a function of financiers' and state politicos' demands for cutbacks in allocational and redistributive programs and for a reemphasis on development policies.[34]

FISCAL CRISES, RETRENCHMENT POLICIES, AND REGIME CHANGE

If New York City's fiscal crises had done nothing more than unleash the socioeconomic forces of retrenchment, they would remain notable historical phenomena. However, the most recent fiscal crisis has been characterized as "a pivotal event . . . redefining the very nature of our cities"[35] and as a "major transformation . . . in the governmental system of New York City."[36] One observer contends that the 1975 fiscal crisis produced "a legacy of new politics qualitatively different from that before the crisis."[37] Indeed, the contextual analysis that I have presented above suggests that each of New York's three fiscal crises since the 1870s has resulted in fundamental and long-term changes in city governance.

To understand these dynamics, we must address periods of fiscal crisis and retrenchment as part of large cycles of regime stability and change. Retrenchment is controlled by interests and is constrained by socioeconomic exigencies, which require that the expenditure cutbacks and revenue increases that are necessary in order to bring local budgets into balance be implemented at the expense of attentive nonelite groups. Therefore, reformulating the precrisis methods of addressing attentive nonelite interests is the central and immediate priority of retrenchment managers during fiscal crises. However, once the immediate crisis has been resolved or appears to be on the way to resolution, political constraints on local government once again become operative. State-government and financier control of local decision making, possible because of group alignments and local-government failure during crisis situations, must be brought into line with the political constraints that promote representative institutions as the normal arrangements at the local level of government. In effect, the socioeconomic priorities of capital production, efficiency, and centralization, which are undervalued before and are preeminent during periods of crisis, confront the political priorities of resource distribution, accountability, and decentralization after a crisis. The institutional balance between these twin constraints defines the state of the current regime.

In more operational terms, political regimes reflect the legal constraints on local government as well as the tension between center-city and community-based influence on policy. After the immediate adaptations to crisis, these issues are confronted anew in a political environment that necessitates the dismantling of a prior set of arrangements and its replacement by another. This environment includes the active involvement by financiers in local decision making; the diminished and disaggregated influence of attentive nonelites; and a weakened formal political structure. The regime changes that are produced by the confrontation over basic issues within a fluid political environment reveal themselves in patterned ways. First, the existing ruling coalition (regime) is replaced by a new coalition, supported by financiers and some attentive nonelite groups. Second, local government's role is redefined by the new leadership in ways acceptable to the new ruling coalition. And third, the new regime institutionalizes its presence through structural changes in city governance, which directly affect the balance between center-city and community-based influence on policy making.

Such regime changes are evident in the three periods of crisis discussed above. As a consequence of adaptations to fiscal crisis during the 1870s, New York's era of "gang rule" was superseded by an extended period of machine rule, in which functionally centralized authority (the boss system) coordinated business involvement in urbanization, while geographically decentralized legitimation mechanisms (ward-based representation) addressed the claims of immigrant groups. The machine era in New York reached its apex of power at the turn of the century, under the leadership of Charles F. Murphy, and lost its political dominance during the fiscal crisis of the 1930s at the hands of LaGuardia's reformers. Reform, which is institutionalized in New York as the welfare city, geographically centralized authority in center-city government while it functionally decentralized power among a host of administrative agencies.[38] Business and attentive-nonelite interests were both served by center-city governmental agencies, although distinctly different types of agencies handled the demands of business and of attentive nonelites.[39] The reform regime experienced its high point during Robert Wagner's years as mayor and began its collapse during the second Lindsay administration, a collapse that culminated in the fiscal crisis of 1975. Currently, the welfare city is being transformed by a regime that has functionally recentralized fiscal authority in quasi-public boards and has geographically decentralized land-use planning and service-monitoring authority in the system of community boards. The evolution of this corporatist regime remains an open question, although thus far it has tended to favor upper-stratum interests and, to a lesser extent, white middle-class communities.

It appears that the political regimes in the history of New York City have experienced a three-stage life cycle of initiation, consolidation, and fragmentation. Each of these periods evidences its own distinctive group balance of power, degree of local autonomy, and mix of public policy. As the life cycle evolves, a regime's stabilizing or centripetal components, which reflect socioeconomic constraints, are displaced by its adaptive or centrifugal tendencies, which reflect political demands.[40] Although each stage of a regime lends itself to an empirically satisfying analysis by the pluralist, the statist, or the stratificationist perspective, only the contextual analysis addresses the dynamics of urban politics and thus provides explanations for local politics across time.

According to the contextual approach, periods of regime initiation follow closely upon fiscal crises and are evident as basic changes in city politics. Group interests bifurcate to the distinct advantage of financiers, who, together with state politicos, assume directive power over local policy making. Consequently, local officials are weakened dramatically by the onset of crisis. These changes result in the establishment of crisis management, the delegitimization of the existing regime, and the beginning of new political arrangements. The virtual determinant influence of financial interests during these periods offers substantial empirical support for a stratificationist view of New York City politics.

Regime consolidation is a period in which the demands of the socioeconomic and political contexts of local politics attain relative balance. This period—the pinnacle of regime legitimacy—sees the coordinated integration of attentive nonelite groups into the regime's base of support, thus allowing both responsiveness and stability. The mix of public policy is, more than at any other time, a function of the balance of competing political forces. The responsive and stable nature of local politics, as reflected in the relative social-equilibrium characteristic during periods of regime consolidation, fits well into the pluralist paradigm of group politics.

The final period of regime fragmentation is characterized by continued group incorporation, without the centripetal force to hold coalitions together. The existing regime, which has now been in power for several decades, is unable or unwilling to attempt such coordination, and consequently the regime's socioeconomic and political balance is weighted against fiscal stability and in favor of group integration and political responsiveness. Public policy is no longer a function of coordinated competition; rather, it is a consequence of group entrenchment. This period in the regime's life cycle is modeled quite well by the statist critics of pluralism.

The contextual approach highlights the fact that fiscal crises and retrenchment politics are more than the results of either economic downturn or governmental weakness. These crises are, in fact, the consequences of those historical junctures when regime fragmentation coincides with economic weakness. Political and economic variables are each necessary but, considered alone, are insufficient explanations of fiscal crisis. As interdependent phenomena, however, these twin sets of variables explain the onset of crisis, the adaptations that are selected in order to cope with crisis, and the long-term effects of such events on local politics.

NOTES

1. See Martin Shefter, *Political Crisis/Fiscal Crisis* (New York: Basic Books, 1985).
2. See Robert Dahl, *Who Governs* (New Haven, Conn.: Yale University Press, 1961); and Nelson Polsby, *Community Power and Political Theory: A Further Look at Problems of Evidence and Inference,* 2d rev. ed. (New Haven, Conn.: Yale University Press, 1980).
3. See John Manley, "Neo Pluralism: A Class Analysis of Pluralism I and Pluralism II," *American Political Science Review* 77 (June 1983): 368–89.
4. Charles Levine, Irene Rubin and George Wolohojian, *The Politics of Retrenchment* (Beverly Hills, Calif.: Sage Publications, 1981).
5. Levine, Rubin and Wolohojian, *Politics of Retrenchment,* p. 28.
6. For examples of this perspective see Theodore Lowi, *The End of Liberalism,* 2d ed. (New York: W. W. Norton, 1979); and Douglas Yates, *The Ungovernable City* (Cambridge, Mass.: MIT Press, 1977).
7. Martin Shefter, "New York City's Fiscal Crisis: The Politics of Inflation and Retrenchment," *Public Interest* 48 (Summer 1977).
8. The classic analysis from this perspective is Floyd Hunter's *Community Power Structure* (Chapel Hill: University of North Carolina, 1953). See also G. William Domhoff, *Who Really Rules* (Santa Monica, Calif.: Goodyear, 1978); and Clarence Stone, "Systemic Power in Community Decision Making: A Restatement of Stratification Theory," *American Political Science Review* 74 (Dec. 1980): 978–90.
9. See Jack Newfield and Paul DuBrul, *The Permanent Government* (New York: Pilgrim Press, 1981), chap. 2.
10. Wallace Sayre and Herbert Kaufman, *Governing New York City* (New York: Russell Sage, 1965), p. 738.
11. Madison recognized the tension between political accountability and economic inequality. See his analysis of factions in Clinton Rossiter, *The Federalist Papers* (New York: New American Library, 1961), pp. 79–80.
12. See Robert Goodman, *The Last Entrepreneurs* (Boston, Mass.: South End, 1979); and Matthew Crenson, *The Unpolitics of Air Pollution* (Baltimore, Md.: Johns Hopkins, 1971).
13. Matthew Drennan and Georgia Nanopoulas-Stergiou, "The Local Economy and Local Revenues," in *Setting Municipal Priorities 1981,* ed. Charles Brecher and Raymond Horton (Montclair, N.J.: Allanheld, Osmun, 1980).
14. The term "financial interests" encompasses bankers and brokers, insurance companies, and real-estate developers (the "FIRE" group).
15. *New York Times,* 8 Sept. 1871.
16. See Seymour Mandelbaum, *Boss Tweed's New York* (New York: Wiley, 1965), chap. 8.

17. Martin Shefter, "The Emergence of Political Machines: An Alternative View," in *Theoretical Perspectives in Urban Politics,* ed. Willis Hawley (Englewood Cliffs, N.J.: Prentice-Hall, 1976).

18. See Edward Durand, *The Finances of New York City* (New York: Macmillan, 1898) pp. 145–50.

19. See *New York Times,* 8, 22, and 29 July 1871.

20. Mandelbaum, *Boss Tweed's New York,* p. 81.

21. In the years after the fiscal crisis, tensions developed between fiscal conservatives and businessmen as the latter group sought public subsidies during the extended retrenchment imposed by fiscal conservatives.

22. Jon Teaford, *The Unheralded Triumph: City Government in America, 1870–1900* (Baltimore, Md.: Johns Hopkins Press, 1984), chap. 1.

23. See Alfred Connable and Edward Silberfarb, *Tigers of Tammany* (New York: Holt, Rinehart & Winston, 1967), chap. 6.

24. See William Whyte, *Financing New York City* (Philadelphia: American Academy of Political and Social Science, 1935), pp. 29–40.

25. Reports in the *New York Times* of the early 1930s highlight the Walker/O'Brien administrations' concessions to financiers' demands for cuts.

26. For a review of the Bankers Agreement see William Beyer, "Financial Dictators Replace Political Boss," *Municipal Review,* Apr. 1933, p. 164.

27. Much of the information on LaGuardia's social reforms is based on Charles Garrett's *The LaGuardia Years* (New Brunswick, N.J.: Rutgers University Press, 1961); and William Paul Brown, "The Political and Administrative Leadership of Fiorello H. LaGuardia As Mayor of New York, 1934–1941" (Ph.D. diss., New York University, 1960).

28. See Emanuel Tobier, "Economic Development Strategy for the City," in *Agenda for a City,* ed. Lyle Fitch and Annmarie Hauck Walsh (Beverly Hills, Calif.: Sage Publications, 1970), pp. 27–85; Raymond Horton, *Municipal Labor Relations in New York City* (New York: Praeger, 1973); and Jesse Burkhead, "The Political Economy of Urban America: National Urban Policy Revisited," in *The Social Economy of Cities,* ed. Gary Gappert and Harold Rose (Beverly Hills, Calif.: Sage Publications, 1975), pp. 49–68.

29. See Charles Morris, *The Cost of Good Intentions* (New York: McGraw-Hill, 1980), pp. 131–36.

30. See Robert Bailey, *The Crisis Regime* (Albany: State University of New York Press, 1984).

31. For an analysis of the "trade-offs" in fiscal-crisis legislation and charter revisions of 1975 see Robert F. Pecorella, "Coping with Crises: The Politics of Urban Retrenchment," *Polity* 17 (Winter 1984): 298–316.

32. Paul E. Peterson, *City Limits* (Chicago: University of Chicago Press, 1981), chap. 3.

33. See Bryan Jones, *Governing Urban America: A Policy Focus* (Boston, Mass.: Little, Brown, 1983), pp. 350–65.

34. See Charles Brecher and Raymond Horton, "Retrenchment and Recovery: American Cities and the New York Experience," *Public Administration Review* 45 (Mar./Apr. 1985): 267–74.

35. William Schultze, *Urban Politics: A Political Economy Approach* (Englewood Cliffs, N.J.: Prentice-Hall, 1985), p. 16.

36. Donald Haider, "Sayre and Kaufman Revisited: New York City Government since 1965," *Urban Affairs Quarterly* 15 (Dec. 1979): 139–53.

37. Bailey, *Crisis Regime,* p. 179.

38. See Theodore Lowi, "Machine Politics—Old and New," *Public Interest,* Fall 1967, pp. 83–92.

39. See Roger Friedland, Francis Fox Piven, and Robert Alford, "Political Conflict, Urban Structure, and the Fiscal Crisis," in *Comparing Public Policies: New Concepts and Methods,* ed. Douglas Ashford (Beverly Hills, Calif.: Sage Publications, 1978), pp. 197–226.

40. The terminology is borrowed from Sayre and Kaufman, *Governing New York City,* pp. 720–21.

4

Coalition-Building by a Regional Agency: Austin Tobin and the Port of New York Authority

Jameson W. Doig

Cities are not the only local units of government that engage in development activities, and not all regimes are city centered. Jameson Doig's account of Austin Tobin's early career with the Port of New York Authority shows how an independent agency can engage in building a regime. Doig's chapter highlights the role that this bi-state agency has played in numerous facets of development in the Greater New York region.

One of the significant activities the Port Authority has controlled is the area's airports. How the agency gained that control is an intricate tale of coalition-building. It was part of a general effort in which the press, financial institutions, and other business organizations were among the allies that Tobin saw as useful in his effort to move the Port Authority from its cautious, averse-to-risk stance to an active and entrepreneurial one. That the Port Authority gained control of the region's airports, in the process overcoming jealousies among local jurisdictions and outmaneuvering bureaucratic rivals such as Robert Moses, is testimony to the importance that political leadership and skill play in the shaping of arrangements through which an area's development is carried out.

Doig's account of Tobin's leadership also traces the emergence of a national association—the Airport Operators Council. Before that association was formed, local airport operators were not organized, so that the major carriers could, as Doig points out, "pick them off one by one in demanding low charges for airport use." What was at stake was whether the airlines would place the major burden of air-

port improvements on local taxpayers or whether the airlines would be made to contribute substantially to those improvements through their user fees. Tobin's success in forming the Airport Operators Council placed much of that burden upon the carriers. This experience raises the question of whether cities could reduce the taxpayers' direct share of development costs. By improving their analytical capacities, exchanging information more extensively, and at times acting jointly, cities could perhaps shift costs onto the profit makers and, in general, become better bargainers with private investors.

As Doig's account makes clear, cooperation and collective action should not be taken for granted. Their achievement is itself a political feat, countering what is often a natural tendency toward apathy or even mutual antagonism. Relationships among and between public authorities and private businesses are significantly influenced by who is organized for collective action and who is not. Tobin saw the advantages of collective action, and he had the skill and resources to succeed in bringing it off.

During the three decades between the late 1930s and the late 1960s, a team of career officials at the Port of New York Authority used the resources and flexibility available at this bi-state agency to build political coalitions that would support their efforts to redirect their own agency and to reshape broader public policies. They led the fight against the FDR-Morgenthau plan to strip tax exemption from municipal bonds; they battled Robert Moses and elected officials in New York City and Newark, in order to gain control of the region's major airports and important marine terminals along the New Jersey shore; they cooperated with city officials to construct massive truck terminals in Newark and Manhattan and to build the world's largest bus terminal in mid-Manhattan—also over Moses's opposition. Working jointly with Moses and state highway officials, they added new bridges and major highways to the region's arterial system. During these years they also experimented with a major containerport, built the World Trade Center, and reluctantly took control of an important rail link that connects Newark, Jersey City, Hoboken, and Manhattan. And they led the successful effort to gather the airport operators across the country into a national alliance whose goal was to develop and operate air terminals without taxpayer subsidies.

The efforts of this band of career officials—Austin Tobin, Daniel Goldberg, Walter Hedden, Lee Jaffe, and their colleagues—illustrate the advantages that independent public authorities can have in shaping public policy, especially in the fields of physical development and construction. And they suggest some analytic and political strategies that can be used by public officials more generally.

Their leader in these three decades and more was Austin J. Tobin, who had joined the Port Authority in 1927, when Calvin Coolidge was in the White House and the Authority had no bridges or marine terminals or, indeed, any operating facilities at all. Rising through the ranks in the Law Department, Tobin was chosen in 1942 as the agency's executive director, and his days and nights thereafter were occupied almost entirely with the programs and the needs of the Port agency. He was, from this perspective, an exemplar of the career civil-service tradition.

However, if that tradition implies neutral competence in the service of goals and policies decided elsewhere (by elected leaders and by the electorate), then perhaps he was not the ideal civil servant. For Austin Tobin enjoyed the exercise of power too much, looked forward too eagerly to the challenge of battling vigorous opponents, and had too clear a vision of how his agency could shape the future of the New York metropolis to sit in careerist harness, awaiting orders. He was, in brief, too entrepreneurial to be neutral.

The press often treated Austin Tobin as though he were the Robert Moses of the Port Authority; the reality is much more complex. For unlike Moses and some other government entrepreneurs, Tobin was a team builder, not a solo acrobat. He attracted to the Port Authority men and women of high potential and often of quality already proven, and he encouraged them to stretch their own mental and entrepreneurial wings. They experimented with new techniques in engineering, planning, and other fields; they challenged legal constraints and often won; and a dozen or more became leaders in their own professional associations—in regional planning, public administration, engineering, law, marine development, aviation, and other fields. Moreover, Tobin recognized that he was uncomfortable in talking with the press and in the give-and-take of political bargaining, and he reached out for practitioners who could employ these black arts with skill and thus shore up his individual weaknesses, turning them into institutional strengths.

While Tobin was the clear leader during his decades at the Port Authority helm—far more than *primus inter pares*—to understand fully the evolution of the agency during these years would require that we explore the activities, successes, and failures of this large entrepreneurial team. It was an association of complex individuals, whose personal styles and values sometimes generated sparks of conflict and longer battles, resolved at times by reassigning responsibilities or quiet resignation. If Tobin was directing a team of stylish horses, it was on occasion a quite unruly team!

This essay, which is drawn from a longer study of Tobin and the Authority, first outlines the origins and early activities of the Port Authority, and then describes the strategies employed by Tobin and his colleagues to gather and use political influence in several policy arenas: the conflict in the late 1930s on the FDR-Morgenthau proposal to abolish tax exemption for municipal bonds; the development of airports and marine terminals in the New York region after World War II; and the creation of the national alliance of airport operators.

THE JOINING OF REGION AND OPPORTUNITY

Keen instruments, strung to a vast precision
Bind town to town and dream to ticking dream.
—Hart Crane, *The Bridge*

When Hart Crane began his epic poem on the Brooklyn Bridge, in the 1920s, the New York area had just taken its third major step in four decades to challenge localism in outlook and politics with the banner of "regionalism." Historically, the cities and towns clustered about Manhattan had been deeply divided—torn into parts first by wide rivers and bays and then by the state line, which separated the densely populated New York communities and their eastern suburbs from New Jersey's wary and often jealous cluster of smaller towns—Hoboken, Jersey City, Newark, and dozens more. The first of the three major steps to join what God and early politics had put asunder was the Brooklyn Bridge. Completed in 1883, it leaped over the wide East River and brought the growing population centers of Brooklyn and Long Island into easy congress with Manhattan's thriving employment districts.

The second step was a matter of political rather than engineering design. In the 1890s, a campaign to combine the independent city of Brooklyn with Manhattan and nearby territories was carried forward in earnest. And though many Brooklynites opposed the merger, and some Manhattan politicos were uncertain too, the state legislature finally adopted a new charter in 1897, which consolidated Brooklyn, Manhattan, the Bronx, and rural Queens and Staten Island into a "Greater" New York on the first day of January 1898.

The third step, also political but more tentative in the joining of regional forces, brings us to Austin Tobin and our story. In the early twentieth century, commercial activity in the bi-state New York region expanded rapidly, and each state sought to increase its share. For some political and business leaders in northern New Jersey, economic growth and vitality seemed much more likely if marine and rail traffic could be attracted from Manhattan and Brooklyn to their own shores, and both public criticism and legal action were directed toward that end. New York interests challenged the New Jersey effort and sought to maintain the competitive position of the eastern side of the harbor. But some of its spokesmen also emphasized the need for cooperative bi-state action to reduce acute congestion in the harbor and at major terminal points and to enhance the economic vitality of the entire region in meeting challenges from other East Coast ports.[1]

The intellectual leader in developing the case for bi-state cooperation was Julius Henry Cohen, an imaginative lawyer who was familiar with the Port of London Authority (created in 1908) and who urged that a bi-state port authority be created to undertake the necessary regional effort. This proposal, first put forward in 1918, generated extensive opposition, particularly from local politicians in New York City and Jersey City—who feared a loss of local sovereignty and who were unhappy that a new agency might be created which would not be easily controlled for patronage and partisan purposes. As a result of the opponents' efforts, the strong regulatory and planning powers envisioned by commissions that were studying the bi-state issue were omitted from the final proposal. However, with wide support from business and civic groups on both sides of the Hudson River, bills creating the Port of New York Authority as an interstate compact agency were passed in Trenton and Albany early in 1921, and the compact was then approved by Congress.

On 30 April 1921, the Port Authority came into being. It was governed by a Board of Commissioners—half appointed by the governor of each state for six-year terms—and its mandate was extremely broad: established by the two states as their joint agency to ensure "faithful cooperation in the future planning and development of the port of New York," the Authority was empowered to construct or purchase, and to operate, "any terminal or transportation facility" within the Port District, which extended—across 300 cities and towns—for 25 miles into each state. However, it was given no power to raise revenues by taxation or to pledge the credit of the two states; the Port Authority would have to rely on grants from other agencies and devise a program that otherwise would be financially self-supporting.[2]

For those who favored the creation of the Authority, a major hope was that the agency could devise and implement a plan to reduce the congestion and cost of freight handling by rail and water in the Port area. The Port Authority's staff devoted several years to this effort during the early 1920s, but the private railroad lines refused to cooperate, blocking any improvement in rail facilities. The Authority then turned to studies of vehicular bridges that might aid freight and passenger movement in the region, and by 1926 it had obtained approval from both states to construct three bridges between New Jersey and Staten Island, as well as a vast span across the Hudson River.

The Port Authority's potential and the opportunities for challenging work there attracted Austin Tobin to the bi-state agency. Born in Brooklyn in 1903, Tobin attended Holy Cross College, where he graduated near the top of his class. Returning to his hometown in 1925, he enrolled at Fordham Law School, taking classes in the evening while casting about for what he should do next.[3] In 1926, a friend of Tobin's was hired by the Port Authority's Law Department, and he urged Tobin to apply too. The Authority's general counsel was Julius Henry Cohen, who by now had a national reputation for his innovative approach to important legal and substantive problems.[4] The prospect of working with Cohen, together with the Authority's expanding general program, attracted Tobin, who applied and joined the agency as a law clerk in February 1927. A year later, law degree in hand, he was promoted to assistant attorney in Cohen's office.

Within a few years, however, the Port Authority and Austin Tobin appeared to be on divergent trajectories—the Authority slipping slowly downward; Tobin spreading his wings, moving up.

For the Port Authority, the decade of the 1930s opened with great achievement and much promise. By 1932, the agency had built an inland freight terminal in Manhattan, it had completed three bridges between New Jersey and Staten Island, and its great George Washington Bridge—the longest suspension bridge in the world—now spanned the Hudson River. Through adroit maneuvering, the Authority had also taken control of the Holland Tunnel and its lucrative toll revenues. With its own financial security strengthened and vehicular traffic expanding, the agency then obtained legislative approval to construct a new vehicular crossing—the Lincoln Tunnel—beneath the Hudson River.[5]

Under the impact of the depression, however, automotive traffic declined drastically, yielding barely enough revenue during the mid 1930s to pay debt service on the outstanding bonds. A mood of caution soon permeated the board and the senior staff. Led by Chairman Frank Ferguson, a conservative banker from Jersey City, the Authority sought no new duties and behaved as though its main goal was "to retire debt in all haste."[6]

In the Port Authority's Law Department, however, the atmosphere was not one of prudent investment and caution, but of lively challenge and legal inventiveness.[7] The intellectual leader was Julius Henry Cohen, and Tobin was one of Cohen's small band of assistants; in Tobin's efforts during these years we see many of the characteristic traits that shaped his later career and the Port Authority's direction for decades to follow.

In 1928 the agency identified a site in lower Manhattan for its inland freight terminal. Condemnation procedures were required in order to obtain portions of the site, and in 1930 Cohen turned that task over to Tobin, who was named to the new post of real-estate attorney. When the Authority announced that it was planning to erect an office building on top of the freight terminal in order to generate revenue on the terminal site, private interests sued. Tobin met with Cohen and suggested that "since this case is related to our real estate concerns, I assume you want me to take it."

Cohen agreed, Tobin took the lead in preparing the brief, and Cohen then argued the case, which the Port Authority won in the lower court in 1934.[8]

While this case was in the courts, the Internal Revenue Service initiated a series of actions, arguing that salaries paid to employees of the Port Authority (and similar agencies) were subject to federal income taxes. Since Tobin was already involved in (real-estate) tax litigation, he again approached Cohen with the suggestion that since this was "another tax case," he should take it on too. Again Cohen assented.

TOWARD A NATIONAL ALLIANCE

By 1935, Tobin was in charge of all tax litigation for the Port Authority and was anxious to shed the "back-water" image of a "real estate lawyer."[9] Cohen accepted his argument that a change of title was appropriate, and Tobin was promoted to assistant general counsel. In the same year, he recruited Daniel Goldberg, who was fresh out of Columbia Law School and at the age of twenty still too young to take the bar examination, to join the Port Authority's staff. Because the issue of tax exemption for salaries affected many municipal and state agencies, Tobin and Goldberg then contacted attorneys general in several states, as well as other public authorities, and obtained supporting briefs; indeed, Tobin and Goldberg drafted the briefs submitted by New York State and by the American Association of Port Authorities.

The Port Authority and its allies won the initial court round but finally lost the salary cases in the United States Supreme Court in 1938 and 1939.[10] Franklin D. Roosevelt and Henry Morgenthau, Jr., then took the next step, as expected: they challenged the tax-exempt status of bonds issued by state and local governments and their agencies. In 1938, the administration's allies in Congress created a special Senate committee to consider legislation that would strip tax exemption from these securities; a detailed Department of Justice study supporting the Morgenthau position was provided to the committee; and hearings were scheduled for early 1939. FDR and his advisers were known to be strongly in favor of such legislation; they argued that tax exemption of income from the bonds gave undue benefits to investors, many of whom were wealthy individuals. A "short and simple statute," as Roosevelt put it, would solve the problem.[11]

Tobin then went to Cohen and to General Manager John Ramsey with the suggestion that the Port Authority, building on the alliance developed in the salary fight, take the lead in opposing the administration's proposal. That proposal, he argued, was particularly threatening to the Port Authority's ability to sell bonds and carry forward its program, and he urged that the Authority use its own greater flexibility in allocating staff and funds in order to underwrite and direct the campaign.[12]

Cohen, Ramsey, and the commissioners accepted Tobin's analysis, and Tobin and Goldberg then turned to the attorneys general of New Jersey and New York State, who agreed to send telegrams to the attorneys general across the country, calling for a meeting on the tax-exemption issue. At that meeting, Tobin and Goldberg spoke, pointing out that federal taxation of state and municipal bonds would increase financing costs by 25 percent or more and that this would require higher state and local taxes and might drive some cities into bankruptcy. The assembled officials agreed to join together in a Conference on State Defense in order to resist the "inevitable onslaught" from the federal government. Tobin was named secretary and was asked to develop a plan of action.

During the later half of 1938, Tobin and his aides devised a strategy and, with the endorsement of the conference's titular leaders, carried it out. They traveled across the country, visiting state capitals and city finance offices, urging that letters and telegrams opposing the Treasury's plan be sent to members of Congress. They located experts who were willing to testify against the administration's plan, and they helped prepare the needed testimony. They sent out frequent reports to their allies, discussing substantive issues and political developments. ("It was Tobin's idea and a great tool—to keep all the people around the country informed and to unify their efforts," recalled one member of the team.) Tobin was the editor, and "he made sure Cohen, Ramsey and the Commissioners saw copies," noted another person who was active in the campaign.

Tobin had tremendous energy, and his enthusiasm infected the staff in New York and their allies across the country. "We put in 100-hour weeks," an associate recalled. "He worked as hard as anyone, and he gave us opportunities to try out our own ideas; and he gave credit when one of us made a useful contribution," another remarked. "Austin inspired great loyalty. We loved to work for him."

Until this fight, Tobin had had almost no contact with people in the financial world. But now Tobin and his aides met with top bankers in New York and other leaders in finance; and they in turn got to know Austin Tobin and his remarkable organizing ability.

At the Special Senate Committee hearings in early 1939, Tobin orchestrated the opposition to the administration's plan, and he and his associates helped prepare the testimony presented by state and local officials, investment bankers, scholars, and civic associations. Then they turned to the House Committee, which was scheduled to hold hearings that summer. They believed that the ten Republicans on the House Committee were opposed to the proposal, but there were fifteen Democrats who if not "educated" might be expected to support FDR. So they identified the congressional districts of these fifteen, divided them into two groups, and Tobin and Goldberg took off on their own campaign swings. With them they carried information on the tax rate and debt of each city and town in each district; they met with the mayor and the city council ("or the city manager, or whoever would talk with us"), and they explained the impact that the administration's bill would have on the town's debt. And they got results: resolutions from cities and towns across the country landed on the doorsteps of the Democratic committee members. By the fall of 1939, neither the House nor the Senate had much appetite for the proposal, and though the Special Senate Committee voted for the bill by a bare majority, lobbying by the Conference on State Defense continued, and when the bill reached the Senate floor in 1940, it was defeated. This was a "bitter defeat for the Administration," one participant later recalled.

But Morgenthau and Treasury were only temporarily subdued; having lost in Congress, they soon turned to the courts. In March 1941, the Internal Revenue Service (IRS) targeted several individuals who held tax-exempt bonds issued by public authorities and began proceedings to collect income taxes on the interest from the bonds; one of the individuals was Alexander Shamberg, a long-time commissioner of the Port of New York Authority. So Tobin and his colleagues went back to work, devoting much of 1941 to preparing the briefs and organizing the effort to counter the IRS position in the courts.[13]

This was an exciting time in the Law Department, especially in Austin Tobin's division. Julius Henry Cohen was nearly seventy, suffering from health problems, and not very active, but he gave plenty of leeway to his colleagues. Tobin and his aides were fully engaged during these years, handling real-estate issues arising from the freight terminal and the Lincoln Tunnel project, while battling the Roosevelt administration on the tax issue. The main problem facing Tobin and his associates was that they were joined to a large organization that seemed to be going nowhere.[14]

AN ENTREPRENEURIAL TEAM
TAKES CONTROL

By early 1942, the Port Authority had been operating under tight financial constraints for ten years, and with World War Two now under way, gasoline rationing would soon be in force. Traffic would probably decline again, and more staff members of the Authority might have to be laid off. John Ramsey, the agency's top staff member, was reluctant to "tackle a whole new round of problems": he was eligible to retire, and he decided that it was time to leave.

But who should replace him? One group of commissioners, led by Chairman Frank Ferguson, favored Billings Wilson, then assistant general manager, who could be counted on to exert strong managerial control—

reducing expenses while maintaining the bridges and tunnels in good repair. Overall policy would be set by banker Ferguson and his colleagues, with excess revenues being used to pay off the bonds.

To another group of commissioners, Ramsey's departure offered an opportunity to break free from the cautious approach of the previous decade. What was needed was an executive team which would look ahead to the economic opportunities facing the New York region once the war was over, and which would identify projects that the Port Authority might undertake to aid the region's economic growth and then devise strategies to gain public support for the agency's plans. This faction was led by Howard Cullman, a wealthy New York commissioner who had worked closely with Alfred E. Smith when Smith was governor of the state; Cullman had welcomed appointment to the Port Authority Board in 1927 as a way to help keep the New York region a vital commercial center. Cullman was energetic and a risk taker, and he found the cautious approach of Ferguson and his allies uncongenial.[15] As Tobin took on the legal issues confronting the bi-state agency, Cullman got to know him, and he liked the young man's style, his enthusiasm, and his capacity to develop a dedicated staff, as well as Tobin's ability to carry out complex strategies in the political arena.

In a series of meetings during the spring of 1942, Tobin emerged as the choice of a majority of the commissioners, and on 1 July he took office as executive director of the Port Authority—a position he would occupy for nearly thirty years.

Tobin had already demonstrated—in his work on the tax-exempt bond issue—the talent and the inclination to identify new goals and to marshal support inside and beyond the Authority. Soon after becoming the executive director, he applied these qualities in new and complex directions—in identifying larger missions for the Port Authority, in developing and nourishing external constituencies in support of the new goals and programs, in creating internal constituencies for the new initiatives (while neutralizing opposition), and so in acting as an "entrepreneurial" leader.[16]

Although Austin Tobin appeared in these ways to reach beyond the tradition of a "neutral" career official, it would be incorrect to view Tobin and his Port Authority colleagues simply as freewheeling entrepreneurs, indifferent to the shackles of legislative control and the sentiments of the general public, going their own way much as did the railroad barons of the nineteenth century. No major program initiatives could be undertaken by the Port Authority without legislative support; indeed, the legislatures of two states—New Jersey and New York—had to vote their approval. And the influence of the two governors was potentially overwhelming: they could block any new program by failing to sign legislative bills; moreover, every month they received the minutes of actions taken by the Port Authority's commissioners, and each governor held the power to veto any and all items in those monthly minutes.[17]

Within the domain of the Port Authority, too, Tobin operated under substantial constraints, for the Authority's policies were formally determined not by the executive director but by the Board of Commissioners—twelve individuals appointed by the governors, six from each state—who relied upon Tobin and his staff for "day-to-day management of the organization."[18]

These factual characterizations do not, however, adequately capture the reality, which is more interesting and more complex. For years on end, the legislatures of both states and the two governors carefully delineated functions and policies for the Port Authority—but they did so, with few exceptions, in response to the Authority's own carefully developed proposals. During the 1940s and 1950s, Tobin and his staff devised impressive plans for improving transportation and terminal facilities in the New York region and took them to business leaders, local officials, and the press for discussion and—quite often—for applause. The Port Authority's own commissioners were also informed, at an early stage; a few of them made suggestions that modified the proposals in modest ways, and many of the commissioners used their own enthusiasm and persuasive energy to convince their colleagues in the business world to support these plans. Governors and other key officials in Trenton and Albany were consulted too.

And then these plans, crafted with imagination and skill, honed and modified in negotiations with influential leaders and groups, were laid upon the legislative desks—with a promise that the Port Authority would cover all costs. For once World War II had ended, the traffic across Austin Tobin's bridges and through his tunnels, later joined by the revenue from airports and marine terminals, generated enough income that the Port of New York Authority could pay out of its own pocket for every new project its officials proposed. Perhaps it was not surprising, then, that throughout these years state officials were generally willing to approve the Port Authority's plans, which arrived with wide public and press support, which would not cost a penny in state taxes, and which might, if approved and carried out, reflect credit on governors and legislators too. Even if some of these officials might prefer that these funds be employed in other ways—for other transportation programs or even for hospitals or education—those choices were not presented, and essentially were not available. And so the projects favored by Tobin and his aides went forward. Not all of them through thirty years of plans and proposals, but many, large and small.[19]

NEW GOALS AND WELL-CRAFTED CONSTRAINTS

There was also a cat in a willow basket, from the partly-opened lid of which
she gazed with half-closed eyes, and affectionately surveyed the small birds
around.

—Thomas Hardy, *Far from the Madding Crowd*

Until he was chosen to be executive director, in the spring of 1942, Tobin
had been absorbed in matters of law and politics. He had devoted little attention to the transportation and economic-development problems facing
the New York region or to the possible role of the Port Authority in meeting
those challenges. During the summer and fall of 1942, Tobin spent long hours
reading about these issues and opportunities, and he gathered around him
staff members who could help him devise strategies to meet the region's
needs. Walter Hedden, the agency's top planner, was especially crucial; now
promoted to head the new Department of Port Development, Hedden worked
closely with Tobin in developing plans for the postwar ear.

By June 1943, Tobin and Hedden had completed a preliminary study
of the Port's problems and had identified a number of activities that the
Port Authority might undertake to help maintain the region's position as
"the gateway for world commerce." Included on the list were several projects that had been proposed by Hedden and others in earlier staff reports—
truck terminals, produce centers, and a large bus terminal in Manhattan.
Tobin and Hedden also suggested other and larger tasks—the Port Authority
might take over the dilapidated piers in New York City and along the New
Jersey waterfront, reconstruct them, and operate a series of marine terminals; and perhaps it should take on a central role in the development
of air transport in the bi-state region.[20] Tobin appreciated the marine terminals and the airports for their potential; perhaps he even hungered a bit
for them; but like Thomas Hardy's cat, he would need to be patient, making plans while awaiting the right time to pounce.

Tobin then went to the board to obtain funds for detailed studies in each
project area. Chairman Ferguson and two of his conservative allies objected
to Tobin's plans, and a few other members of the twelve-person board supported Ferguson, though reluctantly, in deference to his long service (since
1934) as chairman of the Port Authority. The board majority stood with
Tobin, but during the next year the board's enthusiasm was at times only
lukewarm.

Then, at the end of 1944, one of Ferguson's strongest supporters on the
board died, and the term of another expired, and their successors turned
away from the chairman. At their February 1945 meeting, the commissioners
replaced Ferguson with Howard Cullman and named Joseph Byrne of New
Jersey as vice-chairman. Both were enthusiastic advocates of vigorous Port

Authority efforts to reach out in new directions, and both were strong sup-porters of Austin Tobin. At last the board was essentially unified behind Tobin's leadership and ready to support an aggressive Port Authority role in grappling with the region's problems. It was a state of harmony that would last for more than two decades, until the battles of Tobin's final years.

AIRPORTS AND MARINE TERMINALS: STRATEGIES FOR ACTION

Even before the board had ousted Ferguson from the chairmanship, Tobin and his aides had begun the analytical and public-relations efforts that would permit them to take control of the region's major airports and a large chunk of its marine facilities as well. These strategies, begun in 1943 and extend-ing into the 1950s, were pursued with the following guidelines as central.

1. *The "self-supporting" criterion.* The Port Authority would undertake construction projects, rehabilitation programs, and other activities only if the new facilities would, in the long run, generate enough income to meet their total costs. Having no direct access to tax revenues—and very limited access to federal and state grants—the Authority's leaders were unwilling to commit their funds and energies to any project that seemed likely to become a permanent drain on the agency's revenues. Therefore, careful studies of consumer demand and other market factors, and of construction methods and costs, were essential. The possibility of federal aid or other outside funding that could reduce the total to be funded through the Author-ity's bridge-and-tunnel revenues should also be actively explored.

2. *The need for "regional balance."* The creation of the Port Authority in 1921 had been possible because business and political leaders had ten-tatively agreed to replace conflict with cooperation in seeking economic growth for the New York region; but suspicion between officials of the two states had not been abolished by waving the Port Authority wand. Tobin and his associates realized that proposals to aid commercial vitality in New York must be balanced with projects to aid the cities of New Jersey, whose elected officials were always ready to denounce the agency for charging their citizens fifty cents per car to journey to Manhattan.

3. *The passive stance of the Port Authority.* The agency's leaders believed that its political and public-relations position would be weakened if they took the initiative by announcing a range of programs the agency was ready to undertake; for that initiative would encourage the fears of those who viewed the Port Authority as a sort of octopus, reaching out to claim new domains and to squeeze the life from municipal government. Therefore, Tobin and his aides preferred to have suggestions for Authority action emanate from others—from business associations, civic and planning groups, mayors and governors—permitting the Authority to respond to such requests. If a project involved action to take over an existing municipal activity, it was es-

pecially crucial to have the initiative come from other groups in the region. The Port Authority would then gather the best experts, study the proposal, and report the experts' conclusions. Whether any action should then be taken to require the Port agency to go forward with a project would be the responsibility of the elected officials at the two state capitals.

4. *The need to deflect political pressure for reducing bridge-and-tunnel tolls.* Before the war, there had been recurrent efforts to require the Port Authority to reduce the fifty-cent charge on its bridges and tunnels.[21] With the probable increase in postwar traffic, the Authority's toll revenue would rise, and pressure to reduce the fifty-cent rate might become intolerable. However, such action would siphon off the surplus funds needed if the Port agency was to reach into new fields. Therefore it was important to develop a portfolio of useful projects and to ensure that influential business and civic groups were ready and willing to press for action to carry out such projects. Then any campaign for toll reduction could be challenged, and perhaps defeated, because of the trade-offs involved: If the tolls were reduced, less money would be available to carry out projects that were "urgently needed" to enhance the economic vitality of the region.

These four guidelines represented a complex mix of real constraints and public-relations strategies. They tended to be ingrained in all Authority staff members whose activities in the 1930s involved both analytical studies and political negotiation; thus the previous experience of Tobin and some of his assistants was invaluable. But many of the Authority's projects in the postwar world would require learning how to operate in new terrain—where technological uncertainty was greater and where a tradition of municipal control made Port Authority initiatives more difficult politically.

Using the confidential 1943 report as a basic inventory of possible Port Authority activities, Tobin marshaled and deployed the agency's resources for action. A complex array of analytical studies, behind-the-scenes negotiations, and public battles then followed, as the Port Authority moved to build two massive truck terminals and a gigantic bus terminal; to take over the marine terminals at Newark and Hoboken, with a solid try for New York City's piers—an effort that failed; and to wrest the most glamorous transportation projects of the postwar era—the airports—from Newark's political legions, from New York City's mayors, and from Moses's own competing agency. The effort to extend the Port Authority's reach in these several directions occupied the first ten years of Tobin's thirty-year reign in office. To illustrate these entrepreneurial patterns, we focus below on the Tobin initiatives that involved the most complex strategies—those which brought the Newark and New York City airports and Newark's seaport into the Port Authority's fond embrace.[22]

During the fall and winter of 1943/44, Hedden and Tobin created a small staff to analyze the prospects for growth in air transport in the postwar era, the costs of developing major airport facilities across the bi-state region, and the income that could be expected from airline leases and terminal concessions to offset these costs. They also met with federal officials to urge that federal aid be provided for airport development. Similar studies and negotiations were carried out by Tobin's staff in the seaport area. By early 1945 it seemed clear that if given the opportunity, the Authority would be able to modernize and operate major airports and selected marine terminals in the New York region on a break-even basis.

Here, however, a major challenge faced Tobin and his associates: the attitude of the regional press, local governmental officials, and the general public. For years, the Port Authority had faced hostile editorials from the suburban New Jersey press and criticism from citizens and politicians on both sides of the Hudson. A major complaint was the Authority's "exorbitant" bridge-and-tunnel tolls; and some people were suspicious of its wealth, unhappy about neighborhood disruption caused by its construction efforts, and fearful that its leaders were mainly interested in helping Manhattan maintain its economic dominance over the hinterland. Any plans to expand the agency's activities would generate unease, and proposals to add marine terminals and airports might encounter vitriolic opposition—particularly if the Port Authority reached out toward Newark's and New York City's airports and seaports, which generated municipal pride and a modicum of patronage jobs for the party faithful.

Tobin recognized that a skillful public-relations strategy would be needed to gain public support and to blunt municipal opposition, and he obtained the board's approval to hire a specialist to lead that operation. The goal would be to develop close ties with reporters, editorial writers, and civic and business leaders across the bi-state region—so that the region's opinion leaders would come to understand the importance of airport and seaport development to the region's economy and the advantages that the Port Authority could bring if it were invited to take on these challenging tasks.

To help gather allies to the Port Authority's cause, Tobin hired Lee K. Jaffe, who was named director of public relations in 1944. Tobin and Jaffe "hit it off immediately," as a close observer recalled, and she was soon included in policy meetings with Tobin, Hedden, chief engineer John Evans, and the agency's airport planner, James Buckley. Building on a decade of experience as a reporter and governmental press officer in Washington and New York, Jaffe established close working relationships with editorial writers and reporters on all of the region's daily newspapers, kept them constantly informed of new studies and human-interest stories in the Port Authority's domain, and suggested ways of making a story newsworthy.[23] By late 1944 and 1945, stories and editorials on the Authority's concerns about air and marine transport were appearing with increasing frequency, laying the groundwork for editorial and public support for the Authority to take a central role in postwar air and seaport operations.

In addition to a careful economic analysis and a skillful public-relations program, Tobin's strategy involved a crucial third element—developing close relationships with experts engaged in surveys of the airport and seaport issues and in studies of broader development needs in the New York area. By 1944/45, Hedden and his aides were working with the Regional Plan Association and with the United States Department of Commerce and other federal agencies in developing a plan for airports in the region. Most important, with the assistance of Joseph Byrne, his board's vice-chairman and a leading citizen of Newark, Tobin had made contact with planner Harland Bartholomew, who had been engaged in 1943 by Newark's business leaders to study that aging city's development needs. Early in their studies, Bartholomew and his associates concluded that the expansion of Newark's airport and the revitalization of its decaying marine terminal would be vital steps in aiding the city's postwar economy, but that the city government lacked the managerial talent and the political capacity needed in order to convert these two havens of patronage into engines of economic growth. Confidential meetings between these planners and Authority staff members led to an informal understanding—that the Port Authority stood ready to study a possible takeover of the Newark airport and seaport *if* Bartholomew were to take the lead in recommending Port Authority operation as desirable.

And so he did. In October 1945, the Bartholomew report was made public, and its conclusions were spread prominently across page one of the region's newspapers: in view of the Port Authority's large staff with "long experience in all forms of transportation" and its tradition of using "good business practices," the Authority should be asked to lease and operate Newark's airport and marine terminal. In addition, Bartholomew set forth an argument which would frame the airport issue in a way consistent with Tobin's long-range goals: seaport and marine-terminal development throughout the New York region should be part of an "integrated" system, the report concluded, and the "greatest usefulness" of Newark and other air and sea terminals would only be attained when they were all combined in a coordinated regional system.[24]

The Newark planning board, composed of civic and business leaders in the city, soon endorsed the Bartholomew proposal and urged the Port Authority to meet with Newark's elected officials to explore the possible takeover of the airport and marine facilities. Tobin moved cautiously, however, for he knew that interstate rivalry was ingrained in the hearts and minds of some Newark officials.[25] The Port Authority could properly allocate the staff time and funds needed for a definitive survey only in response to an official request from the city, Tobin said; then it would be "our statutory duty" to comply. The city fathers then reluctantly asked and the Port agency quickly agreed to go forward with a study.

Now the Port Authority could turn to larger game—New York City's two airports and those who guarded their gates, New York's mayor and its other major-domo, Robert Moses.[26] During his twelve years as mayor, Fiorello H. LaGuardia had fought successfully to displace Newark as the region's primary air-traffic center, and in 1944 and 1945 he had pressed for large city appropriations to improve LaGuardia Airport and to develop Idlewild— now Kennedy Airport—as the Northeast's greatest air terminal. In January 1946, however, the "Little Flower"was succeeded by William O'Dwyer. The new mayor preferred to husband New York's capital funds for schools, streets, and other urgent needs, and he endorsed an alternative suggested by Moses—the creation of a new City Airport Authority to develop and run the two air terminals. And when a citizens' group proposed Port Authority operation as better, O'Dwyer attacked that view. The mayor said he was "astonished" by the proposal, for it would involve "an abject surrender of the city's planning powers" to an agency subject to control by the two governors— thus giving New Jersey's governor the ability to "determine whether Newark instead of Idlewild" would be the region's international air center.[27]

In order to counter the Moses-O'Dwyer plan, the issue would have to be redefined for the business and political leaders of the region. Prompted by the Authority's leaders, the major daily newspapers began to carry stories which framed the issue of air transport in a larger perspective—as a long-term investment program, requiring millions of dollars before the air terminals could be self-supporting; as a complex package of engineering and administrative challenges, which could best be carried out by an organization with a highly qualified technical staff and a proven track record; and as a regional problem, which could best be resolved through coordinated planning and action, not through narrow competitive actions by individual cities. The Port Authority's commissioners took the lead in preaching the regional gospel, and their speeches against the "barriers of provincialism" were picked up and amplified by friendly reporters and editors.[28]

A BITE OUT OF ROBERT MOSES

These energetic efforts did not halt Robert Moses, who, with O'Dwyer's support in hand, strode to Albany to urge that state legislation creating his City Airport Authority be enacted forthwith. By early April 1946 both houses of the legislature had voted for his bill, Governor Dewey had signed it, and three commissioners selected by Moses and the mayor were sworn in and stood poised to take control of LaGuardia and Idlewild airports.

To block Moses' strategy, Tobin would now need to devise alliances with several crucial groups—the airline executives; the investment-banking community, whose members would have to purchase the new authority's bonds before the Moses enterprise could sign contracts and move ahead with expansion plans; and influential business and political leaders, whose support for Port Authority operation might permit the bi-state agency to gain control of the two New York fields before the City Authority could develop its own plans.

The airlines were readily brought into the Port Authority camp. Their leaders were already wary of the City Airport Authority, for they knew that agency could turn LaGuardia and Idlewild into first-rank postwar airports only if it could tap a large pool of funds. O'Dwyer had already made it clear that city tax revenues could not be counted upon; and the other readily available source—so Moses had argued publicly—would be sharply increased fees, levied by the Airport Authority on the airlines themselves. In contrast, the Port Authority could draw on growing bridge-and-tunnel revenues to build the airfields and terminals the major airlines would need as traffic increased. The airline executives supported the Port Authority cause through informal contacts with business and governmental leaders, and by commenting publicly on that agency's abilities and vision. Invited to view the Authority's developing plans at Newark, for example, airline officials expressed "great surprise and gratification" at the Port Authority's ideas for that airport.[29]

Members of the investment community also had their doubts about the City Airport Authority's ability to repay any bonds it attempted to float. In the spring of 1946, Moses urged the City Authority's commissioners to issue $60 million in bonds to finance the development of Idlewild Airport, but financial experts who were friendly to the Port Authority informally contacted O'Dwyer, to warn him that the City Authority's solution to the airport problem would probably not work.

Meanwhile, Tobin and Hedden pressed ahead toward completion of the Newark studies. Stories soon reached the press which linked the Port Authority's plans to "25,000 new jobs" in the Newark area, and on 30 July, Tobin announced a $55-million program for Newark Airport which would "provide one of the greatest airports in the world."[30] In New York, sentiment began to turn away from the Moses-O'Dwyer Airport Authority; and among the city's business leaders, pressure for O'Dwyer to ask the Port Authority to study New York's air-terminal needs intensified.

Moses denounced the idea, but he was soon outmaneuvered. Cullman and Tobin had already begun to hold informal meetings with Harry F. Guggenheim, who chaired the City Airport Authority, and in late July he resigned, urging the mayor to "get the airports out of politics" and to turn them over to the Port Authority. Then a leading investment banker, Eugene

Black, who had worked closely with Tobin on the fight for tax-exempt bonds, called O'Dwyer and paved the way for a meeting at which the mayor, Tobin, and Cullman explored how the Port Authority might best proceed. On 2 August 1946, O'Dwyer abandoned Moses's plan and asked the Port Authority to study the takeover of the New York airports, in order to "relieve the city of a tremendous burden of future airport financing."[31]

Tobin and his aides quickly responded, and in December the Port Authority announced a $191-million proposal to rehabilitate and expand New York's two airports. Moses's creation, still alive though headless, said it could do the job for less than half that total. For the financial analysts and editorial writers in the region, the choice was easy: the Port Authority had outlined a far more ambitious program, which seemed more likely to meet the needs—or at least the hopes—of the city's business community; and the Port agency had great financial resources and staff expertise, especially compared with the untried, unfunded City Airport Authority. Moreover, the Port Authority's extensive efforts to persuade the region's opinion leaders to think in regional rather than narrower terms now paid dividends, as commentators noted that airports are "a regional business" and therefore desirable meat for the Port agency's bi-state jaws.[32]

Moses then abandoned his City Airport Authority, but he did not abandon all hope. In early March he persuaded O'Dwyer that the city government should keep the airports and run them with a "bare-bones" investment strategy. Again, the Port Authority's legions swung into action: Tobin and Jaffe explained the options in meetings with the editorial writers and commentators, who then attacked O'Dwyer for relying on a "makeshift, patch-and-ragtag program" and urged that the Port Authority do the job. A close friend of Tobin's in the banking community met with O'Dwyer to emphasize the dangers of adding the airport burden to the city's existing debt obligations. And Tobin offered to modify the original Port Authority proposal, providing the city with three-fourths of any net profits at the airports, rather than the 50-50 split that had been proposed initially. On 17 April 1947, the Port Authority and the city agreed that the bi-state agency would develop the city's airports under a fifty-year lease. What the mayor had denounced a year earlier as "abject surrender of the city's planning powers" was now an accomplished fact.[33]

TASTY MORSELS ACROSS THE BAY

In Newark, meanwhile, the Port Authority's July 1946 plan had met with enthusiastic support among local business leaders and New Jersey editorial writers, but the proposal was vigorously attacked by Newark's elected officials. After several months of negotiation, Tobin was doubtful that the city commissioners would soon agree to Port Authority operation of the local airport and marine terminal. In October, looking back over his agency's long experience, he reminded the Port Authority's commissioners that perseverance, not quick victory, was a hallmark of Port Authority tradition: "The history of every . . . project is one of protracted effort, of temporary set-backs, of opposition that at the time seemed immovable."[34]

Two months later, however, with the proposal for the New York airfields nearly completed, Tobin and his allies began to tighten the noose around the necks of the reluctant Newark city commissioners. The Newark Planning Board's chief consultant, Harland Bartholomew, returned to the city to urge that its air and marine terminals be transferred to the Port Authority in order to save Newark's taxpayers from the burden of $47 million in capital improvements needed at the two facilities. Tobin and his New Jersey commissioners met with Alfred Driscoll, who had been elected governor of the state in November 1946; and in January, Driscoll announced his support for Port Authority operation of the two terminals. Working in harmony, the *Newark News* and Port Authority leaders urged Newark's city fathers to act and warned them that the Port Authority's large plans for Idlewild and LaGuardia Airports would soon outstrip other air terminals, which would then be little more than "whistle stops on a suburban line."[35]

Still the city's elected officials hesitated, and early in the fall, Tobin and the New Jersey board members again asked Governor Driscoll to lend a helping hand. Driscoll then reminded the Newark commissioners that they would need his support for state programs to help Newark and other older cities; and in four days of intensive discussions with local leaders, he pressed them to accept the Port Authority's offer.[36]

The combined forces of local, regional, and state pressures overcame the attractions of municipal independence and patronage, and the city fathers finally succumbed. On 22 October 1947, Newark and the bi-state agency signed an agreement leasing the city's airport and marine facilities to the Port Authority for fifty years. Now air-transport services on both sides of the Hudson could be planned and developed on a "truly regional basis," Tobin commented to his board. Moreover, Tobin noted, in adding Port Newark, the Authority had also taken an important step toward the "unification of pier and waterfront activities" throughout the region.[37]

ACROSS THE COUNTRY ONCE AGAIN

As it turned out, the conflicts leading to Port Authority takeover of the region's major air terminals were only the first of several battles that would occupy Tobin and his aides in this new field; and the next conflict came directly on the heels of the 1947 victory. During the initial Port Authority studies in 1946/47, Tobin had been assured by his staff and outside experts that LaGuardia and Idlewild airports could in time become self-supporting operations, under the leases that the airlines had signed with Mayor LaGuardia. Tobin's assurance that those contracts need not be renegotiated was welcome news to the airline presidents, who knew that Robert Moses wanted to tear up the leases and squeeze more money out of their metallic hides. As a result, the airlines actively supported Tobin's campaign against the Moses stratagems and aided Tobin in the Newark battle as well.

By early 1948, Tobin realized that he had received bad advice. The New York air terminals could not become self-supporting unless the LaGuardia leases were sharply revised to produce more revenue. The airlines objected to any changes, and a long battle ensued, punctuated by Governor Thomas E. Dewey's active intervention to achieve a tentative agreement in 1949; final negotiations were not completed until 1953. Meanwhile, indignant at the intransigence of Juan Trippe, Eddie Rickenbacker, and the other airline executives, Tobin launched a campaign built on his experience in the bond fight of the 1930s; and this brings us to the final case in this chapter.[38]

Until 1948, municipal airports across the United States were operated much as some sports stadiums are today—as "loss leaders" whose operation was subsidized by tax dollars, with the tax burden justified because of the jobs generated at and near the airport, and because of the advantages of "municipal prestige" and business vitality which allegedly flowed from having an airport and providing local air service to other cities. Most city airports were operated by line departments (marine and aviation, or recreation, typically), whose leaders had little professional or continuing interest in the economics of airport service and who rarely exchanged information on airport costs, services, or possible innovations.

This system served the short-run interests of the major U.S. airlines quite well. The landing charges and other airport service costs (levied by the airports on the airlines) were kept low—about 10 percent of actual costs and about one-fifth of comparable charges at European airports. The major five or six U.S. carriers (Pan Am, Eastern, American, etc.) maintained informal contact with each other as they pressed municipal airports for long-term, low-cost leases; and if a city balked and asked that an airline pay higher rates, the airline would threaten to by-pass the city in setting its major route pattern, and that threat was usually enough to quiet the upstart. Moreover, the airport operators were not organized, so that the airlines could readily pick them off one by one in demanding low charges for airport use.

In the longer run, however, the fact that the airports were losing money meant that they could modernize and expand only when the city government was willing to allocate funds to that city department instead of to schools or roads. As air travel expanded after World War II, the airlines were faced—especially in busy air centers like New York, Chicago, and San Francisco—with small, outmoded quarters and with reluctant municipal owners. The ability of the airlines to achieve higher levels of service and profit was, in effect, being undermined by their traditional tendency to measure "success" in airport rates by how low the rates were—that is, by how much the airlines could shift their costs to the city exchequer and other tax sources. In time, certainly, the system would have to be changed; but through the 1940s and early 1950s, the airline policy makers focused on the short-term goal of minimizing charges, even though that undermined their own preferred long-term goals of airport expansion and efficient management of the air terminals.

Enter the Port of New York Authority. Having announced that the airports would be made self-supporting, Tobin and his aides bent every effort in 1946 and 1947 to find ways to ensure that, in a few years, the airports would at least break even financially. Creative efforts were used to add revenue via stores, restaurants, and other concessions. But by early 1948 it had become clear that the "LaGuardia leases" would provide far too little return in relation to costs and that higher charges would be needed if a "break-even" operation of the airports were to be achieved. When the airlines resisted renegotiating the leases, Tobin did two things: he fought them tooth and nail to break the local leases; and he sent his chief aviation aide, James Buckley, around the country to explain to the operators of the other large airports what the facts of airline charges and strategies were.

Tobin and Buckley then took the initiative (in 1948) in establishing an organization of airport executives—the Airport Operators Council (AOC)— which provided a way for the municipal operators to exchange information and bring counterpressure on the airlines. Within two or three years, devising strategy and exchanging information through the AOC, the municipal agencies had recruited skilled executives and negotiators and had achieved the upper hand in setting the charges that the airlines paid for airport use. Led by the Port Authority's newly hired real-estate expert, Robert Curtiss, the AOC also helped the airport officials to redesign airport facilities so that substantial income would flow in from concessions. The net result at the large airports has been to reverse the outflow of tax dollars to subsidize airports and, instead, at many airports, to generate a net income.

The long-term result is that this more "entrepreneurial" approach to airport management has permitted airports to modernize and expand more rapidly than would have been possible under the old "tax-drain" approach and that airlines have, in terms of their own profitability, benefited. In the context of this study of the Port of New York Authority, the argument is that one of the major ways in which Tobin and his aides have had an impact on the American economic system has been their leadership, through the AOC, in altering the attitudes and relationships that have shaped the development of airport services and the air transport system nationally.

LEADERSHIP, COALITIONS, AND THEIR IMPACT

[For] officials at every level . . . a keen appreciation of the real components of their organization is the beginning of wisdom. These components will be found to stretch far beyond the government payroll.[39]

Austin Tobin and his colleagues found it easy to think and to act in these expansive terms. Reaching far beyond their own agency, they gathered sympathetic attention and then support, developed alliances with private interests and other public officials, and waged battle—for programs that would strengthen their agency and their own capacity to function and that would, as they viewed it, strengthen the economy of the New York region and perhaps aid the vitality of American society more generally.

In *City Limits,* Paul Peterson argues that the transportation and other development-oriented programs of public authorities and city agencies are examples of "consensual politics," in which "conflict within the city tends to be minimal, decision-making processes tend to be closed . . . [and] local support is broad and continuous." Indeed, Peterson singles out the activities of Tobin's Port Authority and Robert Moses's agencies, especially as they operated before the 1960s, as exemplars of his theme—that there is "no place" in this policy arena for "contentious group conflict."[40]

As the early pages of this chapter indicate, consensual politics is what the Port of New York Authority often preferred and sometimes was able to obtain. But the charm of Tobin's rhetoric, which Peterson quotes in his text, seems to have diverted that careful observer from a conflict-filled reality.[41] In the airport and seaport cases in this chapter and in other initiatives during these postwar decades, Tobin and his associates were compelled to battle jealous local governmental officials, private corporations, and local residents who viewed the Authority's proposals as dangerous to their own political and economic advantages. So the agency found it essential to enter the political arena and to devise and nourish coalitions which could overwhelm these opponents. Sometimes, too, the opposing coalition was stronger still, and the Port Authority lost.[42]

As Clarence Stone argues in his opening chapter in this volume, these patterns are found in cities and regions across the country. Economic-development proposals and programs often generate sharp conflict, rather than widespread agreement on what policies will best benefit the entire city. Certainly the pattern of alliances in the airport and Newark seaport cases supports Stone's position. It is worth noting, however, that in some cases described in this chapter, each city (and there are dozens of cities and towns involved) *does* speak with a single voice. When faced with a strong external threat, a city—like a nation—is more likely to adopt a unified position; and in the cases of the fight for tax-exempt bonds and the problem of airline leases, the cities could use the perception of a common enemy to facilitate cooperation with others in the same plight.

Moreover, these alliances were built on long-term advantages, and the coalitions have survived. The Airport Operators Council continues to be a central clearing house for information on airport fees, terminal design, airport security, and other issues. The Conference on State Defense, which was active throughout the 1940s against Treasury Department efforts to reduce or eliminate tax exemption for municipal bonds, was revived in the 1950s; and subsequently, its members have pursued the same protective goals into the 1980s through joint action of several related organizations, in which Port Authority staff members have central roles.[43]

In contrast, the coalition that supported the Port Authority's takeover of the air and sea terminals was a temporary alliance of business leaders in Newark and New York, of newspaper editors and civic associations, together with the airline executives and a few elected officials, which dissolved in 1947, once the Port Authority's goals had been achieved. Or perhaps that misstates the central point: better phrased, one might say, "The alliance is ended; long live the alliance." The particular coalition that Tobin constructed to attack the bastions of Newark, New York City, and Emperor Moses ended once the airports and Newark's seaport had been won. But those victories did not suspend Norton Long's "iron law of alliance-building": no government agency will endure and thrive if it does not continually reach out for broader support in its relevant communities. As the Port Authority pressed forward with new plans and projects in subsequent years, it called again and again on these allies of the 1940s, adding and dropping particular groups as their interests coincided or were likely to collide. And during periods of quiescence, Tobin and his staff maintained continual, friendly contact with those whose active support would often be needed in future battles—business leaders in Newark and New York, the editorial boards of the *New York Times* and several other daily newspapers, the leaders of the Regional Plan Association and other influential civic groups, the two governors and their staffs, and key legislative leaders in Albany and Trenton. In time, even Robert Moses was neutralized and added to that friendly coterie.[44]

The Port Authority's successes were not, of course, an unmixed blessing. To gain control of New York City's airports and Newark's airport and marine facilities was to remove important areas of policy choice from the direct responsibility of local citizens and their elected officials. These outcomes may be defended on the grounds of increased efficiency and benefit to the local and regional economy, but the trade-off is a loss in terms of democratic politics.[45]

However, in the other two cases considered in this chapter—the fight over tax-exempt bonds and the creation of AOC—the ledger seems more clearly favorable. While there are certainly trade-offs that could be examined, the outcome in both might be claimed as a victory for local political vitality and economic strength, as well as providing clear benefits to the Port Authority.

If one asks, "Under what conditions are coalitions likely to be formed?" the cases discussed in this chapter suggest the wide variety of motivations and organizing efforts that would need to be described in order fully to answer this question. Looked at another way, however, these cases have important elements in common, suggesting a few generalizations that might hold across a wide range of situations.

To note the dissimilarities first: the Conference on State Defense arose as a *defensive* response to a threat from the national government—a court suit and a Congressional bill, in the late 1930s, that would have ended tax exemption for municipal bonds. The second case, involving an alliance that supported the transfer of the region's major airports and Newark's marine terminals to the Port Authority, was essentially an *offensive* coalition, bent on changing the traditional pattern of policy making for these important facilities of commerce and local pride. The third, focused on the creation of a national association of local airport operators, was motivated by *both dangers and opportunities*. The local operators were municipal agencies and authorities which met continuing operating deficits through grants and other subsidies paid for largely by the local taxpayer. That source was becoming restive, and city mayors resisted airport managers' pleas when schools, highways, and hospitals were competing for the same moneys. The opportunity was that these airfield managers could expand their airport enterprises and become municipal heroes, if they could pool their political power and use business strategies in order to exact larger fees from the airlines and to build rental income through the creation of thriving restaurants and other concessions in each terminal.

Those elements are dissimilar; but others are not. In all three cases, one individual and his close associates played a central role. The coalitions form *not* because of unplanned collisions and conjunctions of need, nor because several "similarly situated" people met to explore important issues confronting them and then concluded, through reasoned examination, that they would all benefit through allied action. Instead, the personal drive and needs and vision of one man were crucial; and his analysis and strategies for action described a sort of "Rational Model of Coalition-Building." Austin Tobin identified goals that were important to him personally and strategies to achieve those goals—to break free from the "backwater image" of a "real-estate lawyer" by challenging FDR's taxation scheme; to make the work of the Port Authority more interesting, and his own job more challenging, by wresting airports and marine terminals from the mayors of New York and Newark and from Robert Moses; to make the airports pay their own way and to give the Eddie Rickenbackers of the world a well-deserved punch in the snout, by challenging the airlines' monopoly strategy with countervailing political and economic power. Tobin then inventoried the obstacles to be overcome in order to achieve his preferred goals and identified the strategies needed to surmount those obstacles. Among those strategies were the creation of alliances with other groups and institutions which might benefit if the objectives of Tobin and the Port Authority were achieved. To Tobin and his aides, therefore, the "mobilization of resources" to achieve their goals entailed—in these three cases and in essentially all others during the Port Authority's history—not only the allocation of staff time and money and the preparation of technical plans to guide and support their efforts, but also, as a central element, the building of external coalitions of support.[46]

Tobin's ability to construct alliances and act successfully in these and other cases was not, certainly, entirely of his own making. Even exceptional leaders depend on opportunities provided to them by external factors and by the special strengths of their own organizations; and they are also constrained by traditions, economic trends, and technological forces which they can only marginally affect. Thus the capacity of Tobin and his Port Authority to behave as "rational actors" was greatly facilitated by certain advantages that his agency shared with other semi-independent public authorities, but with few other governments in the New York region. Most of the agency's income was gathered via tolls and rents at its own facilities, which meant that its officials could target funds for study, alliance-building, and other action without waiting for approval from legislative appropriations committees or executive budget officers. Policy making was lodged in a board of twelve commissioners, appointed for overlapping six-year terms, which provided some insulation from elected officials and some advantage, too, in attracting high-quality staff members interested in working on complex long-term projects, who could be confident that the Authority would be able to sustain a focus on a program through several years despite the vagaries of politics.

Moreover, several of the agency's early projects were visible, highly regarded structures: the George Washington Bridge, the longest single-span crossing in the world; the Bayonne Bridge, which won prizes for its design; and the less glamorous but crucially important Holland and Lincoln tunnels. So the Port Authority had, by the late 1930s, earned a reputation among business leaders and the general public as an agency that "got things done"; and that reputation provided a basis for access to decision makers in the region and for obtaining cooperation from others around the country who were helpful in the three cases described in this chapter and in others in later decades.[47]

Even with these advantages, Tobin and his aides probably could not have wrested the airports and the marine terminals from Newark and New York City if their city governments had not suffered from great weaknesses—a tradition of patronage and poor management at their seaports, and legal limitations on municipal debt which constrained their ability to float bonds for capital improvements.

Had these factors been otherwise, Tobin's successes during the 1930s and 1940s might have been modest indeed. However, once presented with interesting opportunities, as Herbert Kaufman comments, Tobin "seized every one of them with a sure hand."[48] And when he grasped these opportunities, Tobin carried the issue forward in ways that offer lessons for local public officials and for governmental executives generally. He and his aides identified potential sources of political support in the business community and in civic associations, at the state capital, and in other cities. They gathered detailed information on the specific advantages that would flow to their potential allies from adopting the Port Authority's preferred approach and on the drawbacks of other alternatives. They employed experts to analyze development options, markets, and revenue flows and to provide the valuable stamp of objective approval for their plans. They worked closely with local reporters and editors and, through newspaper articles and editorials, made a complex and confusing world of regional growth and political choices much clearer—and more favorable to their own designs.[49] And so they helped the New York region prosper, though at some cost to local control, and built broader networks which could help other cities. And the Port Authority prospered too—its leaders gathering political experience, and reputation, which in the 1950s and beyond would permit them to build further coalitions and add still other projects—new marine terminals, bus and rail programs, highway projects, and large office buildings—to the vast Port Authority diadem.

NOTES

This essay is drawn from a study of leadership strategies, innovation, and accountability at the Port of New York Authority during the years 1932 to 1972. Financial support has been provided by the Lavanburg, Sloan, and Daniel and Florence Guggenheim Foundations. The author acknowledges with thanks the assistance of the following individuals who were directly involved in some of the events or who were closely associated with the officials whose work is described in this essay: Harland Bartholomew, Charles Breitel, Joseph Byrne, Jr., Stacy Tobin Carmichael, Mortimer Edelstein, John Fitzgerald, Roger Gilman, Daniel Goldberg, Sidney Goldstein, Lee Jaffe, Doris Landre, Edward Olcott, Harvey Sherman, Austin Tobin, Jr., Rosaleen Skehan Tobin, Robert Tuttle, Robert Wagner, Sr., and John Wiley. Helpful comments on drafts of this paper were also provided by Erwin Bard, Fred Greenstein, Erwin Hargrove, Pendleton Herring, Herbert Kaufman, Duane Lockard, Alpheus Mason, Richard Stillman, Clarence Stone, and Martha Weinberg. In gathering and organizing the materials, the assistance of Bevin Carmichael and Julianne Bauer is gratefully acknowledged.

Some of the materials in this essay are taken from a longer manuscript to be published by the Johns Hopkins University Press in a volume titled *Leadership and Innovation: A Biographical Perspective on Entrepreneurs in Government,* edited by Jameson W. Doig and Erwin C. Hargrove.

1. The political and legal conflicts during these years are described in Erwin W. Bard, *The Port of New York Authority* (New York: Columbia University Press, 1942), chap. 1.

2. The quotations are from the interstate compact, reprinted on pp. 329–39, ibid.

3. For additional information on Tobin's early years and his developing social and political values see the chapter on Tobin in *Leadership and Innovation,* ed. Jameson W. Doig and Erwin C. Hargrove (Baltimore, Md.: Johns Hopkins University Press, forthcoming in 1987).

4. In addition to devising the interstate-compact strategy which led to the creation of the Port of New York Authority, Cohen had done path-breaking work on the arbitration of commercial disputes.

5. The Holland Tunnel connected Canal Street, in lower Manhattan, to Jersey City; and the George Washington Bridge ran from 178th Street to Fort Lee, New Jersey. When completed, the Lincoln Tunnel would join midtown Manhattan at Fortieth Street and Weehawken on the Jersey side. For additional discussion of these developments see Michael N. Danielson and Jameson W. Doig, *New York: The Politics of Urban and Regional Development* (Berkeley: University of California Press, 1982), chap. 6; and Bard, *Port of New York Authority,* chap. 7.

6. Bard, *Port of New York Authority,* p. 266.

7. The unusual character of the Port Authority as a governmental agency generated much controversy and required much legal nimbleness. The Authority was the first agency in the United States to be constructed as a semi-independent "authority" and also the "first instrumentality with continuing administrative functions to be created by an interstate compact, thus serving as the agent of more than one sovereign" (Joseph Lesser, "Great Legal Cases Which Have Shaped the Port Authority," *Port Authority Review* 7 (1969): 5; Bard, *Port of New York Authority,* p. 280). Consequently its staff was continually confronted with complex problems of legal drafting, and many of its actions generated court suits by those who argued that the agency was exceeding its appropriate, but not yet clearly defined, powers.

8. *Bush Terminal Co. v. City of New York and Port of New York Authority,* Sup. Ct., N.Y. Co., 1934. The suit alleged that a mixed terminal and office building exceeded the Authority's statutory powers and that any such facility should pay full real-estate taxes, rather than a lower amount, which the Authority would normally pay in lieu of taxes.

9. The discussion of Tobin's attitudes and actions during the 1930s is based on interviews with those who worked closely with him in the Law Department during these years.

10. *Helvering* v. *Gerhardt,* 304 U.S. 405, 1938; *Graves* v. *N.Y. ex. rel. O'Keefe,* 306 U.S. 466, 1939.

11. "President Seeks Tax Immunity End . . .," *New York Times,* 18 Jan. 1939. Discussion of the bond issue is based on the author's interviews no. 22, 42, 51, and

201; J. H. Cohen, *They Builded Better Than They Knew* (New York: Julian Messner, Inc., 1946), pp. 317–28, 357–58; Bard, *Port of New York Authority,* pp. 276–77.

12. Because of budgetary restrictions set by legislative committees and central budget offices, it was difficult for state agencies and local officials to shift funds and personnel in the middle of a budgetary year; the Port Authority could reallocate funds and shift duties readily, as long as the Board of Commissioners approved.

13. See Brief for Petitioner, in *Commissioner of Internal Revenue* v. *Shamberg's Estate,* 144 F. 2d 998, 2d Cir., 1944. The Treasury Department also tried again in 1941 and 1942 to obtain congressional action, but without success. See, e.g., "States Will Fight Federal Tax Plan," *New York Times,* 10 Jan. 1942.

14. As Erwin Bard concluded in his definitive study of the Authority's first two decades: "Its policy has become totally receptive rather than aggressive." The agency sat passively, Bard concluded, "on dead center" (*Port of New York Authority,* pp. 320, 327).

15. "Howard liked new things," an associate recalled, "and he loved to bring new things into being" (interview 68). See also the extended review of his activities in "Howard S. Cullman, 80, of Port Authority, Dies," *New York Times,* 30 June 1972.

16. As these comments suggest, "entrepreneurial leadership"—as the term is used in this essay—involves both the identification of new possibilities *and* sustained efforts to implement the new designs. This perspective is used in a comparative study of governmental leadership that is being conducted by a group of researchers with grants from the Alfred Sloan and the Lavanburg foundations; for further discussion of the concept see chapter one in Doig and Hargrove, *Leadership and Innovation.*

17. As Tobin commented some years later: "Very few authorities are so completely subject to review by the elected representatives of the people. This is a complete answer to the alleged autonomy of the Port Authority" (statement at the joint public hearing of New York State Assembly Committee and New Jersey Legislative Commission, 5 Mar. 1971, p. 36).

18. Austin Tobin, "Management Structure and Operating Policies in Public Authorities: The Port of New York Authority" (1963 speech), p. 3.

19. To use an analogy suggested by one close observer of the Port Authority's activities at the state capitals, the Port Authority chef would appear before an assembled throng of hungry legislators, one of whom calls out, "What is on the menu today?" "Excellent bluefish, sir!" responds chef Tobin. "OK, but I think I'd like beef," the legislator replies. "Ah, but the bluefish is excellent, and it's free. And there isn't anything else on the menu today," the chef explains. "We'll take bluefish!" the legislators cry in unison.

20. The quotation and other information in this paragraph are taken from the Tobin-Hedden report on the "port planning program," dated June 1943. I am indebted to Edward S. Olcott, who held Hedden's post in recent years, for locating the document.

21. These included the George Washington Bridge and the Lincoln and Holland tunnels between New Jersey and Manhattan, plus three bridges between New Jersey and Staten Island (Bayonne, Goethals, and Outerbridge).

22. Other activities of Tobin's years as executive director (1942–72) are described in the chapter on Tobin in Doig and Hargrove, *Leadership and Innovation,* and in a separate paper on the final decade, J. W. Doig, "In Treacherous Waters" (mimeographed, 1986).

23. "She always had the facts," recalled one of the region's best veteran reporters, "and if you needed more, she would get them and call you right back. . . . She was head and shoulders above anyone else in the public-relations field."

24. Quotations in the text are from Bartholomew's draft report, October 1945. The report also noted that the Port Authority, in contrast with the Newark city government, was in a financial position to underwrite large construction projects; this statement was based on the Authority's own projections of postwar traffic on the bridges and tunnels.

25. Tobin had received a forceful reminder of Newark's concerns only a few months earlier, when the possibility of Port Authority operation of its airport and seaport had been suggested publicly by Vice-Chairman Byrne. Newark Commissioner John A. Brady had attacked the proposal as "municipal suicide" which would cause Newark's destiny as a great air and marine terminal center to "vanish into the stratosphere." He also criticized the Authority's "powerful, arrogant administrative staff" for its tendency to treat Newark as a "service station for Manhattan" (see "Brady Attacks Port Proposal," *Newark News,* 30 Apr. 1945).

26. The discussion below draws upon Herbert Kaufman's detailed case study "Gotham in the Air Age," in *Public Administration and Policy Development,* ed. Harold Stein (New York: Harcourt, Brace, 1952), pp. 143–97; and Port Authority documents. Robert Caro's massive study of Moses includes only a few lines on this important Moses venture and defeat (*The Power Broker: Robert Moses and the Fall of New York* [New York: Knopf, 1974], pp. 763, 766–67).

27. Quoted in *New York Times,* 9 Feb. 1946.

28. See, e.g., "Regional Air Plan to Solve New York–Newark Issue?" *Christian Science Monitor,* 3 Jan. 1946; "Area Airport Authorities Seen Needed in U.S.," *New York Herald Tribune,* 13 Jan. 1946; "City Airports and State Lines," *New York Herald Tribune,* 13 May 1946.

29. See "Airlines Fear Moses Authority," *New York Post,* 6 Feb. 1946; "Air Lanes," *Newark News,* 18 Mar. 1946.

30. See, e.g., "25,000 in Port Jobs Predicted," *Newark News,* 27 July 1946; "Newark Airport Projected to Rival Idlewild," *New York Herald Tribune,* 25 July, 1946. Tobin announced at the same time an $11-million plan for Port Newark (see Port of New York Authority, *Development of Newark Airport and Seaport,* July 1946).

31. See "Airport Proposal Derided by Moses," *New York Times,* 25 July 1946; "O'Dwyer Invites Port Authority to Run City Airports," *New York Herald Tribune,* 3 Aug. 1946; Kaufman, "Gotham in the Air Age," pp. 171ff.

32. E.g., Leslie Gould, "Port Authority Offers Better Airport Deal," *New York Journal American,* 14 Feb. 1947.

33. The negotiations are summarized in Kaufman, "Gotham in the Air Age," p. 190. The "makeshift" quotation in the text is from Allan Keller, "City Air Leadership Periled," *New York World-Telegram,* 20 Mar. 1947.

34. Weekly Report to the Commissioners, 4 Oct. 1946. By 1946, only Chairman Cullman had served as long as Tobin (both having joined the agency in 1927), and eight of the twelve members had served less than five years each.

35. The comment is from a speech by Cullman, which is quoted in "Time for Decision," an editorial in the *Newark News,* 19 May 1947; see also editorials in the *Newark News,* 23 Jan. and 28 Mar. 1947.

36. See "The Wider View" (editorial), *Newark News,* 12 Oct. 1947; Driscoll's letter to the mayor of Newark, reprinted in the Weekly Report, 18 Oct. 1947; and Tobin's summary of the governor's efforts, in the Weekly Report, 25 Oct. 1947.

37. The quotations are taken from Tobin's Weekly Report to the Commissioners, 25 Oct. 1947.

38. The information in this section is drawn mainly from interviews with those active on "both sides" of the controversy in the 1940s and 1950s, together with

documents in Port Authority files. For useful published information see Joseph L. Nicholson, *Air Transportation Management* (New York: Wiley, 1951), chap. 6; Frederick L. Bird, *A Study of the Port of New York Authority* (New York: Dun & Bradstreet, 1949), chaps. 12–14; John R. Wiley, *Airport Administration* (Westport, Conn.: Eno Foundation, 1981), chaps. 7 and 8; *Airport System Development* (Washington, D.C.: U.S. Office of Technology Assessment, 1984), chaps. 6 and 7.

39. Norton Long, "Power and Administration," *Public Administration Review* 9 (Autumn 1949): 259.

40. Paul E. Peterson, *City Limits* (Chicago: University of Chicago Press, 1981), pp. 132–34.

41. "An authority is designed," explains Tobin, "to put revenue producing public facilities on their own feet . . . ; to free them from political interference," and to permit them to use "the administrative standards of a well-managed private corporation" in carrying out their duties (quoted in Peterson, *City Limits*, p. 134).

42. E.g., in the 1940s and 1950s the Port Authority's proposal to take over the Hoboken piers was blocked for several years, because of local opposition; its plan to rehabilitate and operate New York City's piers was defeated; its proposal for a Manhattan bus terminal was held up for several years because of opposition from Robert Moses and the Greyhound Bus Company; and its plan for a large jetport in New Jersey was permanently blocked through the efforts of local residents and others. One important source of resistance in these cases was the perception of the Port Authority as an "outside" agency, reaching for valuable local property; there were other important factors, too, which made it difficult for the Port Authority to employ the "consensual" political mode.

43. The Airport Operators Council is now the AOCI (International). The AOCI, the American Association of Port Authorities, and the Municipal Finance Officers Association (MFOA) are the main members of the alliance that has defended tax exemption during recent congressional deliberations; a Port Authority official chairs the relevant MFOA committee. Of course the ability of each city to speak with a single voice on these issues has been aided by the fact there are few citizens within any of the cities who perceive their financial or other interests as being harmed by the policies advocated by the Port Authority and the other members of these coalitions.

44. See the chapter on Tobin in Doig and Hargrove, *Leadership and Innovation,* for a summary of these patterns during the 1950s and 1960s.

45. For further discussion see Annmarie H. Walsh, *The Public's Business* (Cambridge, Mass.: MIT Press, 1978), esp. chap. 12, and Jameson W. Doig, "Answering the Grand Inquisitor." More generally, see Theodore J. Lowi, *The End of Liberalism,* 2d ed. (New York: Norton, 1979), pp. 177ff.; Clarence N. Stone, "Efficiency versus Social Learning," *Policy Studies Review* 4 (Feb. 1985): 484–96; Michael Walzer, *Radical Principles* (New York: Basic Books, 1980).

46. For further discussion of the conditions under which coalitions are likely to form see the analysis of business-government relationships in Dallas, in the chapter by Stephen L. Elkin in this volume, as well as James Q. Wilson, *Political Organizations* (New York: Basic Books, 1973), pp. 267–72, 275–77, 317ff.; and Barbara Hinckley, *Coalitions and Politics* (New York: Harcourt Brace Jovanovich, 1981), chap. 4.

47. On these general and specific advantages see J. W. Doig, " 'If I See a Murderous Fellow Sharpening a Knife Cleverly . . . ': The Wilsonian Dichotomy and the Public Authority Tradition," *Public Administration Review* 43 (1983): 292–304.

48. Letter from Kaufman to the author, 14 Sept. 1984.

49. In their discussions with newspaper editors, in their speeches, and in their public reports, the creation and nourishment of political symbols was a central

strategy. Like David Lilienthal's "grass roots democracy," the themes of "non-political administration" and projects created "without cost to the taxpayer" were a significant part of the armor and the lance used by Austin Tobin and his agency, as they fended off politicians seeking favors and critics seeking assistance for programs that would not be financially self-supporting.

5

More Autonomous
Policy Orientations:
An Analytic Framework

Susan E. Clarke

Jameson Doig's account of Austin Tobin's leadership at the Port of New York Authority is followed in this chapter by a further examination of the role of public officials in development policy. Drawing on her comparative study of development activities in American cities as well as on a review of current literature generally, Susan Clarke looks at the issue of state autonomy. She asks if there is evidence of governmental action independent of various societal pressures, and she indeed finds such evidence. Public officials in the local community display a variety of policy orientations, and these are not always congruent with the preferences of major business interests or other powerful groups in society.

While the mobility of investment capital constrains local officials, they nevertheless have numerous considerations to weigh in determining how to respond to that fact. Local elected and administrative officials may well have different stakes in local development strategies. And as Clarke points out, a variety of policy responses are possible. After all, some participants are oriented mainly toward short-term and particular distributional demands, while others may be concerned more with long-term institutional viability. The latter group may seek arrangements under which particular concessionary demands can be resisted and more autonomous decisions can be made. Coalition-building strategies pursued by elected and administrative leaders and resulting institutional arrangements thus mediate the way in which societal pressures are transmitted to public decision makers. In comparing four communities, Clarke thus shows that

*the character of a regime is more complex than the broad structural
constraints within which it is shaped.*

INTRODUCTION

Despite electoral imperatives and economic constraints, development-policy
choices that American communities make are more varied and less predictable than current theories anticipated. This suggests either that these
choices are truly idiosyncratic or that the logic and assumptions embedded
in analytic models of local development politics are inaccurate or incomplete.
The latter is especially likely, given the inadequacies of extant models in
explaining situations in which the direction of these choices cannot easily
be traced to public preferences or class interests. Such circumstances signal
the possibility of relatively autonomous policy choices—some decisional independence of the state from its structural basis.[1]

Such a proposition is at the heart of contemporary debates on the relative
autonomy of the democratic state. It challenges strict Marxist interpretations of state and society as well as liberal theories of representative
democracy.[2] It also raises important normative and theoretical questions not
generally considered in discussions of local development politics. As Eric
Nordlinger points out, the society-centered biases of both pluralist and Marxist models make it impossible to consider autonomous state actions in accounting for policy decisions.[3] The value of applying the relative-autonomy
perspective to local development politics lies in its analytic distinction between societal and state interests; rather than assuming the dominance
of economic imperatives or the irrelevance of local political choice, this
distinction allows for situations in which local development-policy choices
may be relatively independent of the preferences of dominant economic
interests.

Drawing on this theoretical argument, this essay establishes an analytic
framework for developing predictive statements about the content and direction of development-policy orientations in American communities. It
characterizes orientations as more or less independent from the preferences
of economic interests and specifies those societal and state interests that
have a stake in more autonomous orientations. Analyzing variations in
development-policy orientation in Los Angeles, Atlanta, Dayton, and Kansas City in terms of three alternative policy models underscores the importance of taking into account institutional interests as well as economic constraints in studies of local development politics.

ORIENTATIONS TO LOCAL
ECONOMIC-DEVELOPMENT POLICY

More autonomous policy orientations imply distinctive direction—that is, policies that diverge from the preferences of economic interests—as well as a distinctive content. The substantive content will vary by community but can be distinguished by prescriptions for the more equitable allocation and distribution of the risks and costs of investment, as well as more equitable distribution of its benefits; policy orientations also incorporate distinct notions of political authority: "Which interests should participate in and be deferred to in the course of framing public policy."[4] Orientations to local economic-development policy can be characterized, therefore, in terms of varying degrees of decisional independence: those which merely reflect business preferences for policies that minimize their costs, maximize their profits, and restrict political voice; those which resist these pressures; and those which resist business pressures and alter the economic and political terms of private investment in a community.[5] Certain features of the local setting provide grounds for anticipating both more and less local autonomy in development issues.

CONSTRAINTS ON LOCAL DECISIONAL INDEPENDENCE

The distribution of interests and resources in the American political system, as well as the constraints that are imposed on local policy makers by the constitutional and fiscal systems that link central and local governments, discourage autonomous local policy orientations. In effect, these factors constitute a null hypothesis regarding the likelihood that local officials will establish policy orientations independent of societal pressures. Gordon Clark argues that local autonomy is a function of institutional arrangements of power and authority between different tiers of the state.[6] In Clark's typology of ideal types, autonomous communities are ones that are free from the oversight of higher authority and that have the power to legislate and regulate the behavior of residents. According to these criteria, the autonomy of American communities is legally and politically circumscribed by constitutional provisions and judicial decisions that limit their initiative and subject them to the review of higher authorities. The rights and responsibilities of local governments are those which the individual state governments grant. Local powers of taxation, in particular, are severely restricted; in most states, local governments must rely on property taxes, sales taxes, and user fees for revenue to provide services. These taxes tend to be regressive and inelastic; these limits on fiscal initiative and the political difficulties involved in increasing the tax rates place additional resource constraints on the ability of local governments to set their own agendas.

As part of a weak federal system functioning in a capitalist economy, local governments in the United States are dependent on the locational decisions of private firms for their revenue base. Since the factors that affect locational decisions vary, both among firms and over time, local officials are always uncertain about the type and the amount of incentive that will be necessary in order to influence a firm's investment decision. This asymmetry—the "corporate surplus," as Bryan Jones and Lynn Bachelor characterize it—benefits the firm: it presents a further opportunity to reduce investment costs, even if the factors that state and local governments control are not actually major cost factors in the firm's operations.[7] This local fiscal dependency is now exacerbated by increasing rates of capital mobility among multiplant national and multinational firms seeking profitable investment opportunities. This economic context—that is, firms seeking to increase their rate of return through minimizing the costs of investment—biases the likelihood that local governments can make efficient use of public resources when they try to encourage firms to invest in their jurisdictions. Local governments will always overspend, or grant larger subsidies than necessary, to attract investment. The structure of American public finance further exacerbates this economic bias by encouraging interjurisdictional competition for households and firms whose tax contribution to the city appears to be greater than the costs of services demanded. Competition for such groups encourages firms to play one community against another and bids up the community's costs in attracting investment.

The limited expertise of the local public sector in development finance is a further constraint on greater decisional independence. Even with an improvement in technical expertise and information, however, the intelligence of local decision making is profoundly constrained by the lack of institutional coherence. The fragmentation of local political structures, the diffuse political power among elected and administrative officials, and the weakness of intermediary organizations in most cities hamper coherent bargaining and concerted public action. Viewing the local state as a decision maker, which makes choices "on the basis of some collective interest or intention,"[8] is especially problematic, although the degree of institutional coherence can be expected to vary by city and over time.

The logic of both economic and political processes, therefore, argues against expecting local officials to act in ways that are counter to firms' preferences. (1) Local officials have few legal powers that will allow them to take the initiative in bargaining with firms in regard to investment decisions. (2) There are specific limits on the officials' flexibility in finding new ways to raise revenues. (3) Many local actions are subject to review by state and federal governments, both of which are responsive to different constituencies and neither of which gains from increased local intervention in economic activities. (4) The officials have limited information about the factors that influence the firms' behavior. (5) Decision making by national and multinational firms is relatively indifferent to and removed from local initiatives. (6) Interjurisdictional competition encourages concessions to attract firms. (7) Fragmented local power structures mitigate against consensus on economic-development goals and strategies, as well as the ability to implement them if they could be agreed on.

OPPORTUNITIES FOR MORE AUTONOMOUS DEVELOPMENT POLICIES

Features that constrain local policy choices—namely, the "systemic power of business" and the need to facilitate private investment in the community—also create opportunities for more autonomous choices. In order to accommodate these structural imperatives, the local state has a collective interest in maintaining the legitimacy of its political authority and its capacity to address the diverse demands being made by capital and citizens. This requires decisional independence, rather than merely brokering group demands. In contrast to the exogenous factors that mobilize a bias against autonomous policy choices, this need to sustain legitimacy and capacity constitutes an endogenous pressure for decisional independence and the potential initiation of change from within the state.

The degree of autonomy will vary: resisting business preferences (e.g., Cleveland's refusal to grant tax abatements) offers deductive grounds for characterizing policy orientations as more autonomous, but the strongest arguments can be made for those policies that resist business preferences and alter the terms of investment. "Linkage development policies," which have been adopted in cities such as Chicago and San Francisco,[9] are examples of the latter; they impose nonmarket conditions on developers to satisfy public-sector preferences for values that the market could not or would not otherwise provide. Some of the factors contributing to these variations are discussed below; here, the focus is on the opportunities for some decisional independence stemming from the need of local policy makers to balance class interests, to build constituencies that will accommodate diverse group interests, and to enhance intrastate resources in order to enhance the authority and the capacity of the local state.

The need to balance class interests is a prominent feature of contemporary Marxist theories of the relative autonomy of the state.[10] The Marxist perspective emphasizes how the bourgeoisie's short-sighted view of its own interests can force the state to adopt a stance of relative autonomy—one that is free from identification with the interests of any one class—in order to effectively serve the long-term collective interests of capital. Em-

pirical analyses indicate that the mediation of conflicts among capital factions and top-down efforts to encourage the organization and coordination
of local economic interests occur with some regularity.[11]

The accommodation of diverse social consumption and capital needs by
public officials is necessary for maintaining the legitimacy of liberal democratic states; under certain conditions, this need to build political constituencies of diverse interests leads to more autonomously determined local
agendas. Both Marxist and rational-choice perspectives, for example,
hypothesized that greater fiscal austerity would force local officials to curb
public expenditures for social needs and to increase the public sector's support of investment activities in order to "facilitate capital accumulation"
and to sustain the polity's access to credit.[12] Empirical studies, however,
report divergent responses to these imperatives. Although local cuts in social
expenditures have been significant, they have not been as severe or as ubiquitous as predicted, nor do they reflect a patterned response. Changes in
local fiscal policies do not wholly reflect either responses to political exigencies or concessions to business interests; rather, they suggest strategic policy
choices on the part of local officials who are acting to preserve the state's
legitimacy and to protect long-term institutional interests in retaining
budgetary control and resources.[13]

In addition to these concerns about legitimacy, the local state's interests
in enhancing its authority and control may also encourage policies that promote decisional independence and political change. The institutional nature
of the state creates interests in maximizing power, control, and autonomy.
Specific agencies also have a stake in seeking both greater decisional independence and resources to improve their relative position. Nordlinger, for
example, defines state preferences as divergent individual preferences of
public officials, based on their "weighted intrastate resources" (not the individual resources of the officeholder).[14] These preferences presumably reflect
needs to garner or protect financial and political resources, to expand domains, to improve interorganizational position, and to maintain organizational coherency. Some of the institutional strategies for doing so are re-
counted in Jameson Doig's study of the Port of New York Authority, in which
he suggests that initially peripheral organizations must be especially astute
in building the client groups and the backing needed to support their
organizational ambitions.

A number of variable, community-specific conditions may complement
these ubiquitous interests: locational advantage, external fiscal resources,
the intervention of national or state authorities, and the degree of coherence
in local public and private sectors. For example, because the uneven nature
of economic development ensures that some communities are more attractive investment sites than others at different times, local officials in these
communities would have the latitude, if they choose, to exercise some deci-

sional independence.[15] "Linkage development policies" in San Francisco, California; Boston, Massachusetts; Santa Monica, California, lend credence to this argument; but other analyses indicate that these orientations are not confined to cities in high-growth areas. At different times, Hartford, Connecticut; Burlington, Vermont; and Cleveland, Ohio, have adopted development policies that were counter to local economic interests; and distressed cities such as Newark, New Jersey, and Toledo, Ohio, have done so for specific projects.[16] It appears that although locational advantage increases the opportunity for decisional independence, such choices are not determined by locational advantage or fiscal distress.

Greater mayoral discretion and greater bureaucratic autonomy in development issues also is linked to national and subnational fiscal aid; Ted Robert Gurr and Desmond King, for example, make this argument in their comparative study of central/local relations in the United States and in Great Britain.[17] The implication that local discretion declines with less external aid, however, overlooks the independent fiscal authority of many quasi-public development agencies. The more likely outcome is that these agencies will have greater influence relative to line agencies; their degree of decisional independence is more likely to be a function of ideological views and institutional interests than of social pressures. Other forms of external intervention are also important. Both in Martin Shefter's account of New York City's fiscal crisis and in Doig's study of the Port of New York Authority, intervention by state officials increased the local officials' latitude in making specific decisions. Similarly, the "broker" role of the staff of the United States Department of Housing and Urban Development in its Urban Development Action Grant program encouraged local officials in some communities to strike harder bargains with developers who were seeking subsidies.[18]

Varying degrees of coherence and coordination among business interests, community-based groups, and the public sector may also influence the possibilities for decisional independence. A fragmented business community is not sufficient grounds for anticipating greater policy discretion, however; Doig's account of the coordinative role of the Airport Operators Council underscores the need for some degree of institutional coherence in the public sector, while Sophie Body-Gendrot's study emphasizes the importance of community-based coalitions. Strong bases of political organization outside the business community may be a necessary but not sufficient condition for more decisional independence; their policy effects increase when allied with external third parties, as in Body-Gendrot's study, or when organizational resources include more than votes. But many groups who would appear to benefit from more autonomous orientations act as if they see their interests as congruent with those of business. This raises the question of who actually has a stake in more autonomous policy orientations.

PRIVATE INTERESTS AND PUBLIC AUTHORITY
IN LOCAL POLICY PROCESSES

A necessary precondition to legitimately asking why development policy orientations vary across communities, however, is to identify interests that have a stake in greater decisional independence from economic preferences, more equity-promoting policies, and broader representation of interests in policy processes. Looking for manifest expressions of such interests would yield sparse results; given the constitutional, economic, and fiscal constraints noted above, groups that actively pursue these goals are uncommon. A comprehensive analysis of the stakes in local development policies requires taking into account latent as well as manifest interests in different development-policy orientations. Identifying latent interests involves viewing groups as being embedded in larger sociopolitical structures and in spatial values; it also involves attributing interests to groups in terms of their social roles in these relationships.[19] This makes it possible to specify the policy orientations that such groups in all cities would be expected to adopt, to predict their actions in terms of these roles and the resources that are available to them, and to analyze the conditions under which these interests do or do not act as anticipated. I argue that the latent interests of three local groups—territorial groups, elected officials, and administrative officials— are served by more autonomous policy orientations but that a number of barriers limit the pursuit of these interests.

TERRITORIAL GROUPS

Groups that have territorial stakes in development activities include neighborhood groups that organize around land-use issues and minority groups that use their physical segregation as the basis for community identity as well as for political mobilization. Their latent interests in development policy center on promoting orientations that define the neighborhood in terms of the use values that are important to residents rather than its exchange value for developers.[20] Policy orientations that address these latent interests would include the use of public authority to increase the equitable spatial distribution of growth benefits. and to expand spatial representation in making development decisions.

Yet despite these stakes, neighborhood groups are most likely to articulate particularistic demands on the political system and are least likely to have access to political power. As Mancur Olson points out, such groups lack the resources to internalize the costs of making broad equity demands; they can only afford to make short-term distributional demands regarding their share of wealth and service.[21] Organizational factors, rather than resources, appear to be a major constraint. Greater coordination and cohesion among territorial groups would increase their capacity to internalize these costs. But in the United States, historical splits between the concerns of community and work place, the continuing political and ecological fragmentation of metropolitan areas, and racial hostilities among neighborhood groups hamper such efforts. Territorial interests are further diluted by biases in federal policies that encourage community groups to adopt corporate norms, structures, and procedures and that lead to the displacement of equity concerns by efficiency criteria. Thus, despite their stakes in more equity-oriented policies and greater political voice, a number of factors limit the articulation of these latent interests of territorial groups.

LOCAL ELECTED OFFICIALS

These officials have a latent interest in increasing the public's voice in the allocation of growth benefits and in minimizing the public's internalization of the costs and externalities of growth; policies that incorporate such principles would increase the resources available to local officials and would enhance their reputations, prestige, and career prospects. But electoral and economic imperatives constrain the manifest expression of these interests; with few exceptions, local elected officials are part of local prodevelopment coalitions, and they perceive a "mutual community of interest" with developers.[22] Local officials' economic and electoral calculations are complex. They seek to maximize the efficiency of their bids for investment—ensuring that the package is attractive enough to bring in investment—while minimizing regret by not bidding so high that the costs to the community in terms of new services, foregone tax revenues, and other indirect costs will outweigh the benefits. At the same time, these officials must accommodate the interests of their electoral constituencies in order to sustain the latter's support. Uncertainty about the preferences and needs of both businesses and voters confounds these calculations; they are further constrained by political norms about the relations between public authority and private interests. As a consequence, local elected officials are most likely to adopt development policies that reflect business preferences and that offer symbolic participation or representation to noneconomic interests. Such strategies appear to further the economic well-being of the community, to garner material and symbolic benefits for the politician, and to assuage electoral interests. Strong ideological beliefs and supportive constituencies are necessary conditions for expecting elected officials to do otherwise.

LOCAL ADMINISTRATIVE OFFICIALS

The latent interest that local administrative officials have in development-policy orientations reflects institutional needs for power and control, rather than societal pressures. This fact coincides with the attributes that are associated with more autonomous policy orientations—that is, a greater public voice in the distribution and allocation of the costs and benefits of development. Both line agencies and quasi-public development agencies potentially gain from policies that both bring in additional revenues and create new arenas for public organizational activity. Quasi-public agencies can ensure that these revenues, gained through their negotiations, are channeled to the agency for redistribution, rather than to general-revenue accounts. The ability to secure such agreements from the private sector affirms the specialized knowledge and expertise that the administrative agency controls. Both this affirmation and the independent resources that accrue to the unit contribute to the organizational maintenance needs of the unit itself, as well as to its influence relative to other state agencies. Satisfying these institutional needs can lead to relatively autonomous choices.

Whether local administrators act on these latent interests depends on the perceived congruence between these institutional interests, on the one hand, and individual career aspirations, professional norms, and ideological beliefs, on the other hand. Individual administrators, for example, are responsive to professional norms and to the career incentives that are embedded in policy subsystems of federal and state officials; but these may conflict. These professional and political norms support public participation in development decisions, for example, but also emphasize the need for efficient and rational routines and decision processes. Administrators will also be affected by organizational features, such as the agency's revenue dependency, its constituencies, and its operating rules and procedures. Line agencies that are dependent on budgetary allocations, for example, are at greater risk and have less to gain from promoting these strategies than do quasi-public organizations. The constituencies of line agencies are more likely to be grant-oriented clients, and their activities are constrained by civil-service and bureaucratic norms. The incentives to act differ significantly. Variations in organizational composition of the public sector, therefore, are likely to be associated with differences in policy orientations.

EXPLAINING VARIATIONS IN RELATIVELY AUTONOMOUS POLICY ORIENTATIONS

The three models of the policy-choice process that are discussed here offer different explanations of how policy makers arrive at strategic responses to these imperatives and interests.[23]

POLICY IN RESPONSE TO ELECTORAL NEEDS

This model explains policy choices as they reflect politicians' efforts to maximize their chances for reelection by making decisions that are congruent with the preferences of the majority. These efforts lead them to use resources, such as time, money, and influence, in ways that are apt to gain the greatest electoral advantage. According to this model, the policy outcomes that result from this exchange of resources reflect a series of compromises that balance competing societal interests and that best respond to what the public wants. The normative implication is that groups which control votes and other resources important to elected officials will be assured of political access. There are numerous critiques of both the normative and the empirical assumptions of this model, but a great deal of evidence suggests that politicians do act as if these considerations are significant.[24]

If coalitions and policy choices are determined by electoral interests, we would anticipate policy orientations that do not resist societal pressures and that include minimal, primarily symbolic citizen representation in development policy. Since there are strong electoral interests in preserving the existing political arrangements and coalitions, there is little to be gained by expanding interest representation and by risking a potential loss of support or opposition by those who are not included. The electoral model will be most effective in anticipating city policy choices when ideologies are indifferent or uncertain as to the nature of development issues, or when local administrative structures are uncertain as to their stakes in the issue. The model cannot account for cities that do more—or less—than would appear to be required by electoral calculations and the demands of social groups. In such circumstances, ideological and institutional factors must be taken into account.

POLICY IN RESPONSE TO IDEOLOGICAL CONCERNS

On many occasions, ideological and electoral interests will converge; but on some issues, ideological concerns may motivate officials to act in ways that are opposed to their electoral interests. The results will be policy orientations that will differ significantly from those anticipated by the electoral/organizational model. Local development ideologies that lead to different policy orientations vary in their emphases on constitutionalism, on rationalization, on pluralistic bargaining, and on norms of participation, as well as in their prescriptions for governmental intervention into economic activities.[25]

Local officials who share Community Conservationist beliefs, for example, value hierarchical rational planning over pluralist bargaining in reaching policy decisions. These officials also support broader public participation in development politics; Dale Rogers Marshall, Rufus Browning, and David Tabb, however, argue that the preference is for consultative participation, rather than substantive representation, given the concomitant value placed on rationalized procedures.[26] The distinctive ideological features are the emphasis on a public role in rationalizing development processes and on some extension of democratic participation in these processes.

In contrast, local officials who act from the Liberal Pragmatist position emphasize the importance of pluralist bargaining as a means of representing interests. This suggests opposition to the institutionalization of interest representation in development-policy processes or the vesting of new interests in established structures, because this would disrupt extant political relationships. Such officials defer to economic interests on development issues and allocate the benefits of publicly assisted development in terms of political influence rather than in terms of broader equity principles. The likely outcome is a pork-barrel approach to economic development.

Marshall, Browning, and Tabb's characterization of Progressive Conservative sentiments suggests that local officials who hold these views would see the public interest as being congruent with business and financial interests but would value an efficient and entrepreneurial public sector. As a result, Progressive Conservative policies would endorse active public-sector involvement in large-scale economic-development activities; those who are guided by these ideological concerns are relatively indifferent to participation norms but may resist participation that appears to distort "rational" development strategies.[27]

Ideological concerns are most likely to dominate when electoral interests are either unclear or stalemated, thus giving local officials a certain latitude to maneuver and mediate according to their particular beliefs and values. These concerns may also prevail when local administrative agencies are uncertain about their interests or when they share similar ideological perspectives with elected officials.

POLICY AS A RESPONSE TO INSTITUTIONAL INTERESTS

This model explains development-policy orientations as responses to organizational structures, norms, and routines. The unit of analysis is not the individual administrator but is the institution itself; the assumption is that these institutions "define and defend" role interests other than the aggregate interests of the individuals in the organization and that they are more than arenas for contending societal interests.[28] The institutional interests of local development agencies, therefore, may result in policy orientations that cannot be explained by electoral interests or by the ideological concerns of local officials. Instead, these orientations further agency needs to increase administrative resources, to advance individual career interests, to protect operating procedures, and to enhance institutional capacity. Institutional interests are most likely to influence policy outcomes when electoral interests are stalemated or when ideological coalitions cannot link specific policy alternatives with their ideological perspectives and thus remain quiescent. Under these circumstances, development-policy orientations may be "more liberal than those promoted by political processes" as a consequence of satisfying certain institutional interests and needs.[29]

FOUR CITIES

Development policies in four cities—Atlanta, Georgia; Dayton, Ohio; Kansas City, Missouri; and Los Angeles, California—reflect variations in equity orientations and policy representation that illustrate the effects of different policy interests. Kansas City's economic-development projects often include arrangements that will enhance the city's direct benefits as well as expand development participation by nonbusiness groups. The arrangements for their new hotel and convention-center facilities included allocating 20 percent of the construction contracts to minority contractors, setting aside jobs for workers eligible for CETA (Comprehensive Employment and Training Act), vesting minority-owned corporations that have equity shares in the project, and negotiating the city's participation in the net cash flow from the project. At least a third of the city's recent development projects included similar features. In contrast, Atlanta's development policies include few equity-promoting or representation-expanding features that might counter the interests of economically powerful groups. None of their Urban Development Action Grant (UDAG) projects have conditions similar to Kansas City's, and only a small proportion of loans made through federal programs have gone to minority firms.

Dayton's orientation, on the other hand, institutionalizes the representation of affected interests on the City-wide Development Corporation board that allocates public development funds. Substantive policies emphasize job retention and creation rather than the direct fiscal benefits negotiated by Kansas City. This orientation corresponds to community concerns about severe dislocations of the labor market as Dayton shifts from a blue-collar industrial economy to an office-based service economy. Los Angeles' policy orientation is splintered: it tends to include either direct public benefits, as in Kansas City, or greater participation, depending on the administrative agency involved. Los Angeles lacks any institutionalized representation of affected interests but often includes neighborhood/minority involvement in projects implemented through line agencies. There are few instances, however, in which the neighborhood organization gains direct benefits, as in Kansas City. This is consistent with previous policy settlements in Los

Angeles, which tend to deter the development of autonomous neighborhood political organization.[30]

Sorting out these orientations in terms of the three policy models that have been presented above illustrates the conditions under which economic interests prevail or under which more autonomously determined agendas emerge. The electoral model, for example, appears best in explaining Atlanta's policy orientations. Atlanta continues to be dominated by a coalition of city officials, corporate leaders, and middle-class black leaders who concur on the community-wide benefits of downtown revitalization. The current black mayor, Andrew Young, embraces the downtown-revitalization strategy more enthusiastically than did Maynard Jackson, whose modest efforts to support black community development were depicted as pork-barrel politics. The mayor's advocacy of business interests is not constrained by organized labor or territorial interests; labor is weakly organized, as in most southern cities, and is likely to become even more fragmented as service jobs replace industrial employment within the city. The concessions that have been made to the black community on development issues have been primarily symbolic. Although the city has an ordinance requiring minority participation in projects that involve the disbursement of city monies, enforcement of the ordinance has been uneven. Furthermore, projects that provide for resident representation are rare.

The electoral model is sufficient to explain Atlanta's economic-development orientations, given the congruence of ideological sentiments with business interests and given the lack of coherence among public development agencies. Officials in Atlanta, including Young, act as if they are guided by Progressive Conservative sentiments; but electoral interests appear to outweigh ideology. Atlanta's policies were not significantly different during Jackson's administration, despite his Liberal Pragmatist views. Furthermore, Atlanta's administrative structure for economic development is a relatively new structure and is still being beset by the fragmentation that characterizes Atlanta's public sector. The city-wide, quasi-independent Atlanta Economic Development Corporation, for example, shares policy responsibilities with numerous other city departments, including the Department of Aviation. In the absence of supportive electoral constituencies, alternative ideological views, or strong institutional claims, deference to business interests is likely to increase as competition with suburban communities intensifies and as the threats of firms to leave the city for alternative sites become more viable.

Electoral concerns shape policy orientations by default in Los Angeles. Although Mayor Thomas Bradley articulates Community Conservationist concerns, and there is an entrenched, professionalized administrative structure for development policy, these factors are diluted by the city's diffuse political structure. In Los Angeles' weak-mayor, strong-council nonpartisan government, development interests are articulated almost exclusively through electoral channels. Bradley has used economic-development policy as a tool to centralize power in his office, but members of the city council continue to exert considerable influence in shaping policies according to their electoral concerns. Racial and neighborhood groups have greatest access to programs and funds that are administered by line agencies whose budgets are controlled by the city council. With cuts in federal programs, however, these funds are declining, and the council's attention is turning towards the resources in agencies that the mayor controls.[31]

The effects that policies have on institutional interests such as those of the Community Redevelopment Agency (CRA) are weakened by the fragmentation of policy authority. Economic-development responsibilities are shared by the mayor's Economic Development Office (EDO), the CRA, and the Community Development Department (CDD). Development orientations differ by agency: the CRA enjoys powers of eminent domain and authority for tax-increment financing. The CRA's strategies emphasize a strong public planning role, but there is minimal public participation in CRA projects, and the CRA is frequently criticized for using public authority to benefit corporate interests at the expense of low-income groups. In contrast to the CRA, which is relatively autonomous, is exempt from civil service, and is self-financing, the CDD depends on council allocations and federal funds for resources, is bound by civil-service regulations and bureaucratic procedures, and is directly accountable to the city council. The CDD, its council patrons, and its neighborhood constituencies tend to be grants-oriented and to emphasize the inclusion of minority groups and enterprises in CDD projects. With the decline in federal funds, CDD administrators are shifting to a more entrepreneurial, competitive funding approach, but they are being hampered by the conflicting preferences of council members and community groups.

Institutional interests shape policy orientations in Dayton and Kansas City. Dayton has lost 25 percent of its blue-collar jobs during the period 1976 to 1986. The need for new investment is significant, but there is little evidence that elected officials favor more concessionary business policies. In part this may be due to the insulation that the commission form of government provides, but Dayton's policy orientations are distinctive even in comparison with other cities that have the same political structure. A more likely explanation is the way in which the city's political institutions are structured to encourage consensual policy making and the accommodation of a broad range of community interests. The City-wide Development Corporation is a quasi-public economic-development policy institution; it serves as a policy forum where representatives of business, community, and labor, along with public officials, make decisions on allocations of city development funds. Substantively, this exercise of public authority is used to balance neighborhood and downtown projects. Policies often feature innovative financing and job-creation strategies. The institutional coherency that is generated by this use of public authority has resulted in development policies that cater neither to electoral nor to economic interests.

Similarly, the Kansas City Council for Industrial Development (KCCID) is a private nonprofit agency that includes representation from small business, labor, and black business councils, in addition to representatives of the larger business community. This special authority was set up in the early 1980s in response to a study that criticized the extreme fragmentation of Kansas City's development administration. The KCCID coordinates the activities of a number of private and public development organizations and initiates its own projects as well. From 1979 to 1986 it has been responsible for nearly four hundred development projects in the metropolitan area. It is not part of the formal political structure. A line agency of local government, the Community Development Department, is often included in these projects, but as a lesser partner, contributing in-kind services and acting as liaison with the city council. Neither the mayor nor the city council takes a lead in development issues, but there is little demand for them to do so. The financial and business communities prefer minimal governmental involvement in development activities, and a growing number of minority organizations view their past involvement with governmental programs as a dead end. Many organizations, especially those with young leadership, prefer more entrepreneurial ventures, working with the private sector through nonprofit organizations. Labor organizations focus on job opportunities in the greater metropolitan area; they make few demands on the city government.

As a result, the field is wide open for KCCID to define policy alternatives and to meet institutional needs through these policies. The professional norms and ideological views of a number of KCCID administrators have injected concerns about equity into these policies through a series of trust arrangements that provide services, such as housing, that would not be available by relying on city or market resources. These programs rely on corporate contributions rather than on extracting corporate profits. After their initial capitalization, the programs are organized so as to be self-financing. In addition, KCCID's requirement that segregated minority communities be represented in its projects has granted de facto representation to these territorial interests in Kansas City's development policy making. As a consequence, Kansas City's policy orientation is frequently reflective of territorial and minority interests, which often gain direct economic benefits from participation in development activities and are ensured a political voice through institutionalized representation on the primary policy-formation body.

Some interesting features of policy orientations in these four cities cannot be fully accounted for in terms of electoral or administrative interests;

they suggest that ideological factors are also significant, even though none of these cities is characterized by a progressive coalition. Bradley's concerns for the economic and political enfranchisement of blacks in Los Angeles, for example, and for enhancing the rationality of the decentralized, fragmented governmental structure have resulted in policies, such as the Watts shopping center, that might otherwise have faltered. Interestingly enough, he is also credited with having initiated a cooperative mayor-council approach to city-wide issues such as redevelopment.[32] In Kansas City a "good government" ethos that dates back to the breakup of the Pendergast machine does not directly encourage public officials to act counter to electoral and economic interests in "the public interest," but it does emphasize efficiency in govermental activities and the inclusion of organized groups in development activities. It is probably best described in terms of the Community Conservationist ideology, but with a greater emphasis on efficiency in government operations than in Bradley's version.

CONCLUSIONS

These analyses suggest that electoral and ideological models do not provide sufficient explanations for variations in policy orientations. The importance of the institutional model derives from the institutional nature of the state. In order to maintain the local state's legitimacy, authority, and control, local officials can neither be instruments of capital nor administrators of the national state; rather, they must make strategic choices that may differ significantly from those demanded by social groups. This creates some potential for anticipating policies that reflect broader values and interests than those expressed through fragmented pluralist policy processes. This is due to the coincidence between such policies and institutional interests in obtaining greater power and control. Most likely these policies will continue to be defined and legitimated in terms of dominant social values and can only be pursued in agencies that have a language and a clientele that support these alternative orientations to local economic-development processes. The key distinction here is that the institutions shape this process, rather than merely reflect societal consensus or special constituencies. Neither Dayton nor Kansas City exemplifies a positive, goal-oriented local state; but the development institutions in each city have played a significant role in molding policy orientations and in legitimating these policies through the inclusion of affected interests. The argument is not that these institutional structures have resulted in better policies but that they have produced different policies from those that are preferred by dominant interests in the communities and from those that accommodate the complex goals and interests of diverse groups.

NOTES

1. See Roger Benjamin and Raymond Duvall, "The Capitalist State in Context," in *The Democratic State,* ed. Roger Benjamin and Stephen L. Elkin (Lawrence: University Press of Kansas, 1985).

2. See Stephen L. Elkin, "Pluralism in Its Place: State and Regime in Liberal Democracy," in *The Democratic State.*

3. Eric A. Nordlinger, *On the Autonomy of the Democratic State* (Cambridge, Mass.: Harvard University Press, 1981).

4. J. David Greenstone and Paul Peterson, *Race and Authority in Urban Politics* (Chicago: University of Chicago Press, 1976), p. xvi. Stone notes in the concluding chapter that progressive coalitions are likely to favor the use of public authority for equality-promoting initiatives and for increasing the representativeness of development policy processes.

5. This typology is based on Stephen D. Krasner's continuum of relational state autonomy, but it omits his fourth category—namely, orientations that resist societal pressures, change private behavior, and attempt to change economic and social structures (*Defending the National Interest: Raw Materials, Investments, and the U.S. Foreign Policy* [Princeton, N.J.: Princeton University Press, 1978], p. 22). Local policy choices are not apt to have a direct effect on these larger structures; however, Bryan Jones and Lynn Bachelor argue that the lagged effects of more limited choices theoretically could bring about some degree of change in these relations (Bryan D. Jones, Lynn Bachelor, with Carter Wilson, *The Sustaining Hand* (Lawrence: University Press of Kansas, 1986). Policy orientations that inject new principles and norms into policy processes may have interactive effects that, over time, alter the perceptions of affected interests; in this way, policy orientations could shape future development politics.

6. Gordon Clark, "A Theory of Local Autonomy," *Annals of the Association of American Geographers* 74 (1984): 195–208.

7. Jones and Bachelor, *Sustaining Hand.*

8. James G. March and Johan P. Olsen, "The New Institutionalism: Organizational Factors in Political Life," *American Political Science Review* 78 (1984): 739.

9. See examples in Pierre Clavel, *The Progressive City* (New Brunswick, N.J.: Rutgers University Press, 1986).

10. See Mark Kesselman's review of these theories, "From State Theory to Class Struggle and Compromise: Contemporary Marxist Political Studies," *Social Science Quarterly* 64 (Dec. 1983): 826–45.

11. See Martin Shefter, *Political Crisis/Fiscal Crisis: The Collapse and Revival of New York City* (New York: Basic Books, 1985). Also, Doig's chapter in this volume illustrates an unsolicited state initiative to reduce the suboptimal decisions that characterize the interactions of airline operators and municipal airport agencies.

12. This hypothesis is put forward most persuasively by Roger Friedland, Frances Fox Piven, and Robert Alford in "Political Conflict, Urban Structure, and the Fiscal Crisis," in *Comparing Public Policies,* ed. Douglas Ashford (Beverly Hills, Calif.: Sage Publications, 1978), pp. 197–225. It is also implicit in the theory of urban politics that Paul E. Peterson sets out in *City Limits* (Chicago: University of Chicago Press, 1981).

13. See Terry N. Clark and Lorna C. Ferguson, *City Money* (New York: Columbia University Press, 1983); see also, Irene Rubin and Herbert Rubin, "Structural Theories and Urban Fiscal Stress," in *Cities in Stress,* ed. M. Gottdiener (Beverly Hills, Calif.: Sage Publications, 1986).

14. Nordlinger, *On the Autonomy of the Democratic State.*

15. Harvey Molotch and John Logan discuss this view and its normative implications in "Urban Dependencies: New Forms of Use and Exchange in U.S. Cities," *Urban Affairs Quarterly* 21 (Dec. 1985).

16. See examples in Clavel, *Progressive City;* see also, Alexander Ganz, "Where Has the Urban Crisis Gone?" *Urban Affairs Quarterly* 20 (June 1985): 449–68. Susan E. Clarke describes project-specific examples in "The Local State and Alternative Economic Development Strategies: Gaining Public Benefits from Private Investment," an unpublished paper presented at the 1984 annual meeting of the Association of Collegiate Schools of Planning, in New York.

17. Ted Robert Gurr and Desmond King, *The State and the City* (Chicago: University of Chicago Press, forthcoming). Stephen Elkin includes similar propositions in his analysis of urban-land-use politics in "Pluralism in Its Place."

18. Shefter, *Political Crisis/Fiscal Crisis;* HUD's brokering role is described by Susan E. Clarke and Michael J. Rich in "Financial Federalism: Trends toward Intergovernmental Management of the Local Economy," an unpublished paper presented at the 1982 annual meeting of the American Political Science Association, in Denver, Colorado.

19. See Greenstone and Peterson, *Race and Authority,* for a discussion of latent-role analysis. Molotch and Logan, in "Urban Dependencies," describe urban conflicts in terms of spatial values; and Jeffrey Henig takes a similar approach in analyzing neighborhood mobilization over redevelopment plans in *Neighborhood Mobilization: Redevelopment and Response.* (New Brunswick, N.J.: Rutgers University Press, 1982).

20. See Molotch and Logan, "Urban Dependencies."

21. Mancur Olson, *The Rise and Decline of Nations* (New Haven, Conn.: Yale University Press, 1982).

22. Elkin, in "Pluralism in Its Place," delineates these mutual interests.

23. These models are derived from Greenstone and Peterson's analysis of factors that influence variations among cities in implementing the War on Poverty programs. They considered two alternative but complementary models that together could account for local variations: the electoral/organizational model and the ideological model. Although Greenstone and Peterson discuss how local bureaucratic structures modify the effects of both ideological and electoral factors, the administrative structure is treated as an intervening factor, rather than as an institution that is capable of making choices that reflect state needs or interests that are independent of social group pressures or sheer organizational maintenance needs. The institutional model included here allows for such possibilities.

24. See Clarence Stone's critique "Systemic Power in Community Decision Making," *American Political Science Review* 74 (Dec. 1980): 978–90.

25. These categories are based on Greenstone and Peterson's adaptation of Robert Agger, Daniel Goldrich, and Bert E. Swanson's typology of political ideologies that support particular governance arrangements and processes; see *The Rulers and the Ruled* (New York: Wiley, 1964).

26. Dale Rogers Marshall, Rufus Browning, and David Tabb, *Protest Is Not Enough* (Berkeley: University of California Press), p. 278.

27. E.g., see Siegrun F. Fox, "Who Opposes Public/Private Financial Partnerships for Urban Renewal?" *Journal of Urban Affairs* 7 (1985): 27–40.

28. March and Olsen, "New Institutionalism," p. 738.

29. Gordon L. Clark and Michael Dear, *State Apparatus: The Structure and Language of Legitimacy* (Winchester, Mass.: Allen & Unwin, 1984), p. 193.

30. As noted by Dale Rogers Marshall, *The Politics of Participation in Poverty* (Berkeley: University of California Press, 1971); also see Greenstone and Peterson, *Race and Authority.* Atlanta's development policies are described by Clarence Stone in *Economic Growth and Neighborhood Discontent* (Chapel Hill: University of North Carolina Press, 1976); also see the account in R. Scott Fosler and Renee A. Berger, *Public-Private Partnership in American Cities* (Lexington, Mass.: Lexington Books, 1982). Earlier projects in Atlanta and Dayton are described in Marshall Kaplan, Sheldon P. Gans, and Howard M. Kahn, *The Model Cities Program: The Planning Process in Atlanta, Seattle, and Dayton* (New York: Praeger, 1970). My characterizations of city development-policy orientations are based on analyses of activities in federal economic-development programs, which were conducted as part of a larger study of local economic-development strategies.

31. See Alan L. Saltzstein, Raphe Sonenshein, and Irving Ostrow, "Federal Grants and the City of Los Angeles: Toward a More Centralized Local Political System," a paper presented at the 1984 annual meeting of the American Political Science Association; also, Alan Saltzstein and Raphe Sonenshein, "The Council Ascendant: The Case of Los Angeles," a paper presented at the 1986 annual meeting of the Western Political Science Association.

32. Saltzstein and Sonenshein, "Council Ascendant."

6

Grass-roots Mobilization in the Thirteenth Arrondissement of Paris: A Cross-National View

Sophie N. Body-Gendrot

Efforts to shape urban regimes are not restricted to public officials and business elites. In this chapter, Sophie Body-Gendrot traces the efforts of neighborhood actors to form a coalition and to make strategic alliances that are compatible with a progressive agenda of urban development.

In her study, Body-Gendrot brings a cross-national perspective to bear on the study of development policy. She contrasts the French tradition of centralization and reliance on public authority with the American tradition of decentralization and the extensive use of private associations. However, grass-roots political activity is not missing from the French experience, and Body-Gendrot also traces the steps that a neighborhood movement took in mobilizing successfully to replace commercial development with a more diverse and socially concerned form of development. She cautions, however, that extraordinary circumstances enabled the neighborhood movement to succeed.

In turning to the grass-roots mobilization itself, Body-Gendrot stresses that the neighborhood movement was able to be effective because middle class groups played a central role in drawing the coalition together and in pressing government officials to take favorable actions. This middle-class element enhanced the resources of the neighborhood association and enabled it to be seen as acting largely within the bounds of established social relations, not in opposition to them.

In putting this single case of neighborhood mobilization into perspective, Body-Gendrot reminds us that there is a broader context in which profit-minded developers enjoy significant structural advantages. Among them, the institutional interests of the executive branch often favor large, privately controlled developments. This drive, the Paris experience suggests, is not dependent on economic competition among local governments, American style. So, while political mobilization can make a difference, it does not occur in a neutral arena. Still the relevant factors are complex. In the Thirteenth Arrondissement, administrative interest in a large privately developed project was countered by popular support that was more attuned to the communal values of the neighborhood. In the working out of these conflicting forces, the ideological predispositions of various actors proved to be significant.

In Western societies, while most investment initiatives come from the market, government nevertheless plays an important role in shaping development. The interaction of private and public decisions gives rise to and is sometimes influenced by social mobilizations and conflicts. This chapter, which is a case study of a grass-roots mobilization in one of the older areas of Paris, examines the claims and actions of citizens who opposed an announced plan of urban renewal and sought instead a plan that was more in line with the wants and needs of those living in the neighborhood. As a case of grass-roots mobilization, it offers a chance to consider why such movements succeed or fail in efforts to influence the development process. In the consideration of this question, special attention is given to the French setting and how it differs from the American setting.

STRONG-STATE SOCIETIES
VERSUS WEAK-STATE SOCIETIES

France is a society with a strong-state tradition. The state refers to differentiated forms of political power exercised by actors who claim to be acting in the name of the general will. This notion is critical. "If the general will is to be able to express itself, it is essential that there should be no partial society within the State and that each citizen should think only of his own thoughts," Rousseau wrote.[1] According to such a perspective, all intermediate bodies, organizations, and associations, as partial societies between individuals and the state, are condemned as perverters of the general will. French government and administration have been notably insensitive to outside citizen input. The development of associations in France has been smothered ever since the Middle Ages. It has been fought, among others, by the centralized Catholic Church, wishing to prevent lay members from carrying on religious activities. The Church and the monarchy have combined their efforts toward centralization. State power is not fragmented by other governmental structures such as provinces, counties, cities, or neighborhoods. The weak Parliament, the judicial system, and the media hardly check the state's extensive powers.

Another element of strength comes from the role played by the public bureaucracy—that is, large teams of administrators and technocrats who are the guardians of the public interest. They are supposedly insulated from politics, and they are meant to apply laws and regulations impartially. Whether this is true or not is unimportant as long as this view is widely shared by the public and is held as a desirable goal.

Ministerial cabinets head bureaucratic departments and constitute an effective decision-making body which is able to resist pressures from interest groups, even those within their own departments. Compared with fragmented centers of decision and authority in the United States, the cabinets can both define state policies and have them implemented coherently. For instance, in 1970, when President Georges Pompidou expressed the wish to associate his name with large-scale operations of urban renewal, all of the involved ministerial cabinets coordinated their efforts to pursue that goal.

To sum up this point, the bureaucratic corps shares a common view of the mission, the options, and the investment risks that belong to the state. The similar education and training grounds of top civil servants give them a judgment of where specific interests are compatible with the state's interests and of what type of conduct on the part of decision makers and the public are appropriate. The relationship between the state and French businesses is one of cooperation, but as a counterpart, the economic market is subordinated to the political system and sometimes to arbitrary decisions. Business representatives almost never penetrate the state apparatus.

In the United States the tradition has been strikingly different. The powers of the national state were limited from the start, while decentralized structures and organized forms of participation were legitimate and encouraged. Alexis de Tocqueville has emphasized how, in the United States, "associations are, as it seems, the only private bodies aiming at controlling the State," how "society is activated by itself and upon itself," for "there is power only within itself," and that wherever at the head of a new enterprise there is government in France and a lord in England, there is an association in the United States.[2] Changes in the United States are initiated by the grass roots, thanks to strong representative institutions, whereas in France the state is thought of as the main source of progress.

For several reasons, there seems to be no equivalent American approach to a general interest defined by unified state structures. First, American interest groups—the ones that Rousseau called the partial societies—compete to obtain policies favorable to their aims, and they mobilize all their energies in order to be heard and to be on the public agenda. The resulting pork-barrel policies are a function of the skills of the groups involved; some *may* structure projects in the public interest. The boundary between public and private is often blurred, and government often intervenes on behalf of and at the request of private interests.

Second, the American bureaucratic corps and official elites come from heterogeneous backgrounds, including business, and such fragmentation lessens the authority and the legitimacy that are necessary to define and defend a public interest that is superior to those of powerful self-oriented lobbies. Social corporatism can thus expand, because it is largely unopposed by a state that wishes to protect its own differentiated stratum of decision.

Third, in a decentralized, weak-state society, the local level is the locus of contradictions between demands for capital expansion, which enlarges economic resources, and demands for social expenditures, which may increase votes. Local governments in the United States have little autonomy. As in France, their initiatives are limited by constitutions, higher jurisdictions, and judicial decisions. Their tax powers are also constrained. What is the difference then with a centralized country such as France? The tax structure and the revenue base are different. Local governments in the United States compete intensely to attract private investments in order to increase their revenues. This progrowth orientation may subordinate the political process to economic forces.

In France the fiscal crises that American cities experienced are unknown. Despite the new decentralization laws of 1981–84, which give local governments more leverage in regard to their expenditures, local governments in France are spared the rigorous competition of their American counterparts. The progrowth orientation is at the national level. It is easier for French decision makers, acting in a closed, insulated environment, to plan which investments will be best for which city, then to negotiate from the top with private firms, and, next, to send the good or bad news to the local levels, which are not accountable to their voters for such decisions. However, even a strong state doesn't operate in a vacuum, and the context influences the decisions that are made. Accordingly, the state may have to modify previous policies when it is in its interest to listen to organized interests, as the following case study will demonstrate.

The French tradition of authority enables elites to guide policy. Certain groups are encouraged to carry on a dialogue with state representatives, but other groups are not. The French state has the leverage to act independently of interest groups, which are almost illegitimate and are limited to a reactive role. In the United States, it is more difficult to shut out organized interests.

How, then, are particular wills protected in France? Specific interests are not as well protected as in the United States. For instance, some state interventions and regulations may startle Americans who are used to free enterprise. At this writing, for example, a French entrepreneur cannot open a local funeral parlor (agreements were made at the turn of the century between municipalities and monopolistic firms), discount book prices by more than 5 percent (the state protects small bookstores), or lower the price of gasoline (which is fixed by the state).

Organized interests can, however, appeal to the Council of State, a consulting and judiciary body constituted of higher civil servants whose advice is not binding for the state. One function of the council is to rule on citizens' claims against the administration. As a redresser of wrongs, it may decide that administrative action was illegal—as will be shown in the case study—and grant damages to the plaintiffs. This function, however, is limited. As Hayward points out, a third of the council's decisions remain unenforced, the council's backlog of cases is estimated at three years, and seventeen thousand cases currently await judgment.[3] Moreover, enforcement of the council's judgments frequently depend on administrations that may be the object of the trial. Consequently, victories that are obtained by associations of private citizens either through the Council of the State or the judicial power are, as we will see, especially significant.

To sum up this general outlook, one should emphasize that a strong, centralized state has tactical advantages that a weaker state, fragmented and open to the influence of conflicting interests, lacks. Such broad features should obviously be reinterpreted on a case-by-case basis: their sole function here is to contribute to the understanding of the context of the case that will now be developed.

BACKGROUND: SETTING AND HISTORY

At the south of the Left Bank, the Thirteenth Arrondissement is one of the oldest working-class neighborhoods in Paris, interwoven with tight social networks of lifetime residents. It is said to have as many as two hundred neighborhood and civic organizations, a figure that represents a record in the city. The intense communal life dates back from the end of the nineteenth century, when the Thirteenth Arrondissement was still a village on the outskirts of the city and consisted of small houses surrounded by gardens and when open cafés were a focus of social interaction. In the subneighborhood of Maison Blanche, in the southern part of the Thirteenth Arrondissement, as in a painting by Renoir, townspeople would picnic on the green on Sundays, then dance to the music of the *guinguettes* (dance pavilions).

The names of the streets in the neighborhood are witnesses of the social life of that time: rue des berges, rue du pré aux curés, and so forth.

Numerous residents of the Maison Blanche neighborhood have not moved since World War II, and they constitute its social foundation. The war promoted tight solidarity amongst them, and after the war, life was still village style and based on exchanges, highly personalized relations between the shopkeepers of small retail stores and their customers. Its characteristics reveal a multiplicity of activities, residential stability, and the proximity of work places, including small manufacturing firms.

Today, the Maison Blanche neighborhood is mixed ecologically and socially. New residential projects coexist with a very significant number of public-housing towers; both are next to old-stock housing and cheap hotels. The new Chinese immigrants have taken over numerous stores, which they have converted into restaurants. Small industrial plants are scattered along a scarcely used circular railway. Bars and five-cents stores attract the large working-class population, while modern supermarkets and stores are also used by the middle-class families from the residential towers and middle-size buildings.

Urban Restructuring

Urban renewal started in the Maison Blanche area at the beginning of the 1970s. As a prime minister of General Charles de Gaulle's and then as president, Georges Pompidou wanted to leave his imprint on the Parisian territory, and vast projects under the auspices of the state were undertaken. The Thirteenth Arrondissement was to be renovated into a "Renaissance center" and completely modernized. To replace slums and blight, the new orientation in urban planning called for skyscrapers and intensive development. While beneficial to those who profited from it, this process worsened the position of low-income residents, particularly of renters who were going to be displaced.

Within a few years, towers of thirty-five floors popped up everywhere in the neighborhood. Among the tracts to be renovated in the Maison Blanche area, the B-10 lot was spared for a few years. Official plans revealed that it, like other areas in the neighborhood, would be renovated to provide better housing in place of old-stock dwellings. In May 1973 the land was bought by a profit-oriented developer named SOFIREX, a dummy organization composed of banks and insurance companies. A resident describes this purchase as "an irresistible temptation to raze old homes and to erect a forest of towers with a few necessary facilities on the location." A majority of renters and shopkeepers were promptly displaced; but there was virtually no overt opposition.

When a gas explosion providentially destroyed the two remaining buildings, land was cleared, and SOFIREX had a free hand to start building. However, the company was not interested in building housing that would accommodate neighborhood residents and yield little profit. The most profitable operation for the developer was to build two office buildings, of five and fifteen floors. This would be simple to do architecturally, and it would result in little nuisance but high rents. In the new project, green spaces, which once were supposed to occupy 30 percent of the land in that neighborhood of high density, disappeared. The construction plan called for 118,150 square feet of offices to be built on 37,650 square feet of land. The surrounding streets would be narrowed, and few parking spaces were planned. Nevertheless, at the end of 1974, SOFIREX received its construction permit from the state.

The proposed development was advantageous for the public authorities. In every country, selling land to developers represents huge incomes and taxes, street renovations, and other improvements. In the present case, economic development also meant the relocation of displaced residents. The urban-development law that was passed during the Pompidou era provided for the by-passing of urban regulations and for special treatment and concessions to owners of capital on a case-by-case basis.

THE CONTENDERS

The opposition, when it emerged, consisted of two groups: older residents and younger middle-class families. The older residents had not moved during the land-clearing period, because they thought that new and better housing would be built on the B-10 lot, and they began to react at this point for several reasons.

(1) For all of them, the sense of dispossession from their neighborhood by the construction of so many towers was overwhelming. "We were threatened to perish by suffocation. . . . We could no longer see the sky and breathe with these walls of towers surrounding us. . . . We were saturated, we couldn't bear one or two additional towers," people said. Saturation was the key word.

(2) People were shocked to discover that offices would be built in an area where most of the residents were tenants in uncomfortable homes. Even profitable housing could have been acceptable, whereas, in the words of a resident, "offices destroyed their roots." For some time, residents had been asking for gardens, schools, and better housing; and they discovered that the developer had more clout than they did in obtaining favorable decisions from the administration.

(3) In a material way, the construction works were a nuisance. Not only did excavations threaten the foundations and walls of small homes in the

surrounding streets, but the new office towers would block the view of tenants in nearby buildings, and the towers would look directly into the apartments of tenants.

A second social group of residents was concerned as well by those issues. They were younger, more politicized middle-class intellectuals who rented apartments in the new residential buildings on the adjacent streets. Contrary to the American situation and the governmental efforts to encourage ownership through financial incentives, most of the Parisian residents are renters. The renovation of the center of the city progressively displaced new middle-class families to the periphery of the city, while their incomes allowed them to avoid being pushed with the working-class to the suburbs. This intellectual middle class often takes pride in living in a traditional neighborhood, side by side with the elderly who own or rent their small houses; and there are very few signs of social segregation between the two groups, which are linked by the same attachment to the neighborhood. The group of younger residents also opposed the high-rise project, contesting it as a matter of principle, since they did not approve of having banks make a profit from urban-renewal activities. Profit is not a hallowed word in many intellectual and administrative circles in France.

FROM COMMUNITY DEFENSE...

Individual actions were undertaken to check the SOFIREX development, first by asking if the company had been authorized to build offices instead of the housing that was officially planned. This approach met with little success. The administration defended its decision; allegedly, it had "lost" the first plans; the models of the renovated area had been destroyed by fire; the law authorized alterations in permits; and no further decision was possible. Residents should not worry: their homes were not being threatened.

In the meanwhile, excavation was proceeding full speed, digging deeper than was originally intended on the B-10 site. A few residents decided to turn to their elected officials. In January 1976, with the support of the Left, a demonstration took place on the site, and a defense association was created, bringing together concerned tenants and owners.

In March, cracks began to appear on the outside walls of homes adjacent to the excavation. The newborn organization then took several steps. It contacted all the local officials, whatever their political label, to get their support. It wrote a letter to the Paris prefect, the state's representative, asking for a revision of the construction permit. At the same time, the organization started a very important campaign of information and mobilization: meetings, panels, door-to-door canvassing, and so forth. With 120 members, in two months, the organization had gathered 900 signatures of residents supporting the claims that housing, not offices, should be built on B-10. The rule of the organization was that each member should contact neighbors to elicit their support and their membership in the organization. Leadership built a sense of trust between older and younger members, and all recognized that important stakes were at issue. Because of their dedication and sophistication, the organization's leaders were respected by the administrators.

The protest organization produced an imposing file for lobbying with their elected officials to the Prefect's Office. They also orchestrated a media campaign, and articles about their mobilization were published in the national morning papers. One reason for this lobby's being taken seriously was that the renewal of B-10 was treated as an issue that was broader than the concerns of eleven hundred families. The cause was a good one: Why new offices, while others in the same area remained empty? Why offices, while so many public services were lacking in this densely populated neighborhood?

Although the local authorities were not averse to the people's claims, bureaucratic inertia nevertheless impeded their efforts. It was difficult to have access to the administrative staff; the people's right of expression was not recognized; and the administration shared the view that the public interest is better served if the public keeps out of it. In Europe, as in America, officials defend their expertise. In France, government is seen as the locus of expertise, and civic activity is seen as a threat to rational judgment. Hence, there is a tendency to keep governmental decisions secret, to move quickly to implementation, and to rule out participatory forms.

However, as the residents' common will grew more determined, the protest organization increased its resistance. It linked its action to those of other organizations in the neighborhood which had mobilized against the residents' displacement in urban-renewal operations. Community opinion was aroused. Huge meetings had taken place in the Thirteenth Arrondissement against the Renaissance restructuring (Etats Généraux), and these meetings had enabled organizations to discuss openly the problems of the neighborhood and to move toward an alliance. The press gave wide coverage to these events.

In June 1976, a sit-in took place on the B-10 site: symbolically, the residents stopped the bulldozers and the cranes. All the local councillors were present. At this point, the organization came to the conclusion that SOFIREX should be taken to court. It was not going to be easy to take a legal action to have the permit canceled: five levels had already been dug underground. Yet for its first anniversary in January 1977, the organization obtained its first victory: the administrative court ordered a suspension of the construction works. It was an important step for the residents: they became conscious that collectively they could oppose projects that had been imposed upon them. It now seemed unlikely that office towers would be built on the site. "The position of the developer had become precarious," a commentator recalls, "he would need a new construction permit adjusted to the urban development regulations which had been recently published and as those regulations were very restrictive, the profitability of a real estate operation was dubious." With the support of their local councillors, the residents then decided to try to exert control on the future of the B-10 site.

. . . TO NEW CONSTRUCTIVE PROPOSALS

In contrast to hierarchical administrative processes, the organization decided to set up a vast democratic consultation of the Maison Blanche residents. For three months, contacts were made through the existing networks, meetings took place in the projects, and militants distributed pamphlets at the open market on Sundays and explained the goal of their action. This very unusual process in a French neighborhood (people are not used to being consulted and asked to express their wishes) was successful, and a common will emerged from all these encounters. Since the residents were all too poor to buy the site themselves, the best solution would be to have the city buy the lot and act as a packager to accomplish the community's wishes. We face here a distinct cultural pattern of the French, who are accustomed to appeal to the prince for their needs, rather than to form a neighborhood development corporation that they themselves would control.[4] Among the requests that the residents put forward were those for a day-care center, housing for the elderly, low-income housing, and walks for pedestrians. People also wanted gardens, a swimming pool, and a recreation-and-crafts center. These grass-roots demands attracted a lot of support, and a local architect offered to draw the plans without charge.

In the fall, the plans were ready. An open-door meeting provided all the neighborhood residents with an opportunity to come and comment; and on that occasion, fifteen hundred letters of petition were sent to the city, with the support of the local branches of all the political parties. Numerous organizations (parents' associations, the greens, defense organizations, etc.) also came by, and an umbrella organization, Liaison 13, was then created.

A NEW SHOWDOWN

At the end of 1977, a second victory was achieved by the organization: the developer had lost his court appeal before the Conseil d'Etat, the supreme jurisdiction (like the Supreme Court in the United States). Work was definitely suspended on the B-10 site. However, the permit was still valid as long as the administrative court had not canceled it. The judgment took place in July 1978, and it was a third victory for the organization and its lawyer. The administrative court canceled the permit on the grounds that too many derogations revealed an abuse of power.

The organization had now to exert its pressure on the city. In 1977, Paris acquired a new status. Before the change, most of the city expenditures were financed by national sources via annually calculated grants or a fixed share. Local demands were conveyed by the prefect, acting as an intermediate agent between the local government and the state; then the choice of urban designs and public services was made centrally by the Ministry of Equipment (the equivalent of the Department of Housing and Urban Development of the United States government) and other concerned ministries to establish priorities among various local projects.

In 1977, President Valéry Giscard D'Estaing gave back to the city of Paris the status it had lost at the end of the nineteenth century after the Commune episode. Not only did the city gain an elected mayor, but it also received forms of autonomy in urban matters, with appropriate sources of funding. The mayor and the city council were free to choose which public services the city would provide and where, and to tax the neighborhoods accordingly.

In 1978, Jacques Chirac was elected as the new mayor, and the neighborhood organizations had to deal with new administrative "interlocutors." Would they be ready to listen to people's needs and to implement their wishes? To increase pressures, a press conference was set up, and thirteen national and local newspapers with varied political orientations gave favorable coverage to the initiatives of the two-hundred-member organization.

However, the first reaction of the new administration was to side with the developer. In that respect, the French situation was not different from the typical experience in American cities.[5] The developer had produced a new proposal: office towers would be replaced by residential towers, which could still make a decent profit; and the company had appealed to the Conseil d'Etat to obtain a revised construction permit.

The organization had to act rapidly and decisively. Mobilization efforts were increased, and 1,620 people signed a petition expressing their demands. A campaign of information was undertaken for the administration as well as for the residents: models built by student architects representing what the B-10 site could be like in a grass-roots approach were exhibited for the first time. They depicted an island of communal life, with gardens and patios surrounded by medium-rise housing. A services center would help the elderly, while a day-care center would welcome young children. A recreation-and-sports center would be a locus of social interaction in the neighborhood. For two years (1979 and 1980) continuous pressures were exerted on the mayor's office, the city council, the state's representatives, the press, and the Conseil d'Etat. Again, fifteen hundred post cards were sent to the mayor. Yet the city's strategy was to gain time and to delay making its decision. Officially, the answer was that the demands couldn't be received as long as the Conseil d'Etat had not made a judgment.

The fourth victory came in May 1981, as the Left came back to power: the cancellation of the developer's permit was definitive. It had taken the residents five years of continuous legal battles—the suspension of the construction in 1976, followed by a victory against the appeal of the developer in 1977, the cancellation of the construction permit by the administrative court in 1978, and the defense action against the second appeal—to win in the legal arena. The weakness of the developer's defense, the changes in the political climate, and a new urban philosophy had contributed to this success. No elected official had sided openly with the developer. However, the organization had now to prove itself further.

In the fall, pressures were exerted on the city administration to have it use its power of eminent domain and to buy the still privately held site via the Office Public des Habitations à loyer modéré (OPHLM)—that is, the public-sector agency responsible for the construction of subsidized housing. From that moment on, the OPHLM became the prime "interlocutor" of the organization. However, the residents would not be satisfied with medium-rise public housing. They were determined to obtain the facilities that had been specified in the consultation with the neighborhood. Yet the OPHLM could only finance the public housing: the state administration would have to provide further funding for services of benefit to both the city and the residents. As the mayor and his administration didn't have the same political orientation as the government and the ministerial cabinets, the neighborhood faced no easy victory.

Eventually, in April 1982, the B-10 site was purchased by the OPHLM. The plans provided for ninety-four housing units, a sports center, stores, a recreation center, a public garden, and patios. The swimming pool, which would have necessitated a municipal staff, had evaporated. What about the day-care center? The organization took advantage of the new decentralization law, which had created neighborhood councils to hear such demands. Skillfully, the leaders defended the needs of all the young working mothers, and the project was unanimously approved by the representatives of all parties and then by the mayor. The sixth victory took place in December 1982, when the construction permit granted for B-10 was modified and a day-care center was included in the administrative plans.

However, it would take three more years of efforts and determination to obtain the adequate funding. Finally, in April 1985, after a nine-year struggle, construction started on the site: the residents had won, and celebrations could take place.

GRASS-ROOTS MOBILIZATIONS
IN COMPARATIVE PERSPECTIVE

Our interpretation of the B-10 struggle goes beyond the limits of this Parisian neighborhood: it aims at pointing out the similarities of processes going on in the working-class neighborhoods at the center of large cities, whether they are in the United States or in Europe.

Large cities in which land is costly do not usually seek to help lower-income groups or listen to their needs, unless they are constrained to do so. Conflicts are thus apparent between the economic policies that are pursued and the neighborhood needs for facilities and services. The local level of government constitutes the locus in which these conflicts are the most salient. Twofold policies are usually pursued: (1) Those that give economic interests and the more affluent segments of the population incentives for investments in order to enhance the revenue base. Edward Koch, the mayor of New York City, states explicitly: "The main job of government is to create a climate in which private business can expand in the city to provide jobs and profit. It's not the function of government to create jobs on the public payroll."[6] In Paris the economic domination over the political system has been less overt than in large American cities, in which the direct subsidizing of business is a widely accepted practice. However, during the Pompidou era, French *étatisme* coincided with market domination. The "better city" appeared as a more middle-class and affluent city. (2) Those policies that allow the displacement of low-income strata who are less profitable taxpayers. "In general, the state aims to make available to private firms, developers, and elite institutions land with aesthetic and transportation advantages once 'undesirable' populations are removed."[7] In Paris, important fragments of the working-class were thus—willingly or not—moved to the suburbs,[8] while gentrification was encouraged. The rationale for such policies was that communities should be grateful to receive modernization and the elimination of blight, and individual hardships should be accepted. This explains why there was little opposition in 1970, when speculation spread in the Thirteenth Arrondissement (urban struggles started after two years of economic development, around 1972, and were usually led by political radicals, not by the traditional leftist parties). Thus, despite a weak tradition of grass-roots participation, opposition did develop.

In various cities, social forces have mobilized to attempt to change the balance of power and to resist unwanted development plans. However, across national boundaries, grass-roots mobilizations face the same obstacles: (1) lengthy bureaucratic or legal processes, and (2) fragmented decision centers among various administrative agencies.[9] In our case the organization's leaders had to lobby the prefect's cabinet, the various agencies within the

Ministry of Equipment, the mayor's office, and other local agencies dealing specifically with associations and construction. Then, when the proposals were ready, they had to exert pressures on the OPHLM, on the Ministry of Health and Social Affairs (for the day-care center), on the Ministry of Cultural Affairs (for services for the elderly), on the Ministry of Youth and Sports (for the sports center), and overall on their elected officials. The segmentation of the decision centers, the character of the governing coalitions, and the isolation of neighborhood residents' actions from the main allocation decisions contribute to the limitations on effective access of neighborhood representatives to the complex matrix that surrounds development. (3) Not only is it difficult to find administrative aides who will admit their responsibilities in a controversy, but also such aides frequently move from one function to another because of bureaucratic restructuring; thus, months of efforts to establish contacts are lost.

Opposition organizations also face internal problems. The composition of their membership may lack coherence. In the United States, owners rarely side with renters, blacks with whites, or low-income strata with middle-class ones; and fragmentation is increased by bureaucratic devices.[10] In our case, tenants who lived directly in slums were probably too alienated to react, and many younger renters in public housing didn't feel rooted enough in the neighborhood to be concerned: for them, the Thirteenth Arrondissement was only a temporary location on their way to ownership in the suburbs. However, part of the success that the organization experienced came from the unusual coherence among its members. The rich network of personal interactions and social institutions in the neighborhood proved to be a valuable resource in community political mobilization.[11]

WHY DO SOCIAL MOVEMENTS SUCCEED?
WHY DO THEY FAIL?

Successful protest organizations must be able to highlight weaknesses or contradictions in the plans they oppose. In the present case, the residents first fought against high-rise office buildings: not only did such buildings cause a nuisance; they were also unnecessary, as office buildings were already underused in the area. Then the residents refused high-rise residential housing for ecological and ideological reasons. One observer suggested that if the developer had, at one point, reduced the project to a medium-rise construction, he would probably have won. The neighborhood aim was to impress on decision makers the population's right to express its needs and to find ways to have them taken into account.

Unlike the segmentation that often pits one group against another in American low-income neigborhoods, a real osmosis cemented older inhabitants and middle-class intellectuals, owners and renters, experts and rank-and-file citizens. The older inhabitants had the ability to disseminate information rapidly through preconstituted social networks. They knew instinctively where the "natural leaders," the "little Joes," were to be found; which stores would be useful to spread information; and so forth. They were motivated by a common will: they liked their neighborhood; they were not antigrowth, but they wanted to exert some control on the intrusion of modernity on their territory.

The middle-class representatives possessed savoir-faire. One of them had a leftist past and had already participated in struggles against urban renewal and displacement in the Thirteenth Arrondissement in 1972. As has been the case with other political activists who have been disappointed by the evolution of extrainstitutional actions, he had involved himself in neighborhood activities that contained a prospect of constructive planning. Other leaders had previously been involved in civic and church activities in the neighborhood. All the leaders were either renters or owners of apartments in residential projects of two hundred or three hundred units, and their charismatic personalities enabled them to act as key connections to different networks: residential, political, religious, civic, and so forth.

The leaders' professional occupations also provided additional resources. Two of the active members were connected to public and private urban fields, a third one worked at the office of the attorney who dealt with the B-10 restructuring, and a fourth directed a youth community center which provided facilities to the organization. Among the members of the neighborhood organization, an architect and a lawyer had spontaneously sided with the cause and had offered their expertise and skills to the residents.

The middle-class factor is an important element which partly explains the success of the mobilization and the capacity to negotiate with various administrators and local councillors. The same language, the same codes, and the same references, with the ability to adjust the argumentation to the function of each interlocutor, enable neighborhood leaders to communicate effectively. In contrast, another mobilization in an adjacent street, Moulin de la Pointe has failed because (1) there were conflicts among the residents: some found an interest in keeping the neighborhood as it was, whereas others accepted renovation as a desirable operation; and (2) the language of class struggle that the militants used had antagonized the older inhabitants and the administration from which they were seeking to extract concessions.

In the B-10 case, horizontal as well as vertical linkages brought useful resources to the organization, which received the help of other neighborhood organizations. The leaders avoided cooptation and kept a respectable distance from the political parties, without refusing their help. Again, we find an important difference with the American situation of low-income neighborhoods which often lack adequate political representation. In France the role of local elected officials was essential in amplifying the organization's efforts. Why should the leaders seek the help of parties? Cultural patterns explain this attitude. The notion of local involvement against state policies usually has little resonance among the traditional segments of the population, because centuries of centralization have accustomed people not to concern themselves with the problems of their neighborhood but to exert pressures on their representatives to have them find solutions. This phenomenon helps explain the high levels of voting turnouts at local elections (75–80 percent). Moreover, the French process of accumulating offices (*cumul*), which allows a local elected official to accomplish functions at higher levels and to become a representative in Parliament or a minister, is a counterweight to centralization and reinforces the weight of representative democracy. This belief can be a deterrent to direct participation. In our case, both approaches were combined: grass-roots involvement and the use of political channels of action. The latter proved very useful when the leftist parliamentary representative of the Thirteenth Arrondissement became, after 1982, the minister of Equipment and Housing. However, the leaders of the organization knew that if they wanted to keep the largest possible base, they would have to resist the attempts that all the political parties were constantly making to coopt them and to claim victories for actions that had been led independently of their support. After each election, the leaders of the organization had to make public comments emphasizing their political independence and denying to political representatives the right to exploit the benefits of their actions.

Due to the leadership's sophistication and charisma, not only were political antagonisms avoided, but social coherence was emphasized as well. Progressively, the older residents also acquired the knowledge of how to "play" the rules of the game and to behave in the same way that middle-class entrepreneurs did in wealthier neighborhoods. Conversely, the public-housing proposals did not provoke disapproval by middle-class families for two reasons. Public housing in Paris is not stigmatized, as it is in American cities. In the same buildings, along with apartments for low-income families, decent lodgings are provided at low cost to middle-class civil servants and to politically protected families. Consequently, in Paris, multifamily public-housing units are not a concentration of all the underclass. In the present case, 20 percent of the ninety-four units are set aside for city administrators.

Cross-class cohesion was also encouraged by the fact that the middle-class families living in the Thirteenth Arrondissement, when they made the choice to move into the neighborhood, recognized its traditional working-class character. Social heterogeneity can be politically advantageous.[12] Moreover, objections to additional public housing were reduced by the prospect of gaining facilities and better environmental conditions (a day-care center, a sports-and-recreation center, a public garden, etc.). The weight of the general consensus and the grass-roots character of the neighborhood planning also muted objections.

Finally, governmental policies and economic conditions are not to be neglected in the analysis. They are sources of urban effects, no less so than the actions of the neighborhood movement. It seems unlikely that the neighborhood would have been successful without favorable changes in the policy priorities of governmental officials. Outside pressures were all the more accepted because governmental priorities in urban matters were changing.

The Renaissance operations in the Thirteenth Arrondissement were planned in 1966, when the economy was favorable, and they started in 1971. Yet, in 1973, the first oil shock provoked changes in the orientation of urban development. High-rise buildings, which consume a lot of energy, no longer proved to be very profitable. When Valéry Giscard d'Estaing was elected president in 1974 by only 50 percent of the electorate, the state withdrew from these large-scale construction projects. The ecologists' movement influenced the climate of opinion, and a new urban philosophy emerged in the production of space: it was now desirable to abandon crass urban architecture and to undertake smaller, more ad hoc, and piecemeal projects in a green environment. Housing officials were pressured by higher strata of command to please the other half of the electorate and to maintain a diversity of people in the neighborhoods of large cities. It was acknowledged that excessive concentration of working-class families in the suburbs caused numerous problems.

Jacques Chirac himself, the new mayor of Paris, agreed with this view. Although, like an American mayor, he needed the support of the business community and of the affluent taxpayers, he knew that his electorate was also composed of the petite bourgeoisie and of lower-income traditional strata that he didn't want to antagonize. As a consequence, he never opposed the construction of public housing in working-class areas; and as long as the OPHLM was taking the financial risk, he knew he could gain advantage from the operation and use of B-10 as a showcase.

Most administrative middle-rank officers were also convinced that B-10 was a good cause that would serve their image. When the funding was approved by the top administrative management—that is, the Ministry of Economy and Finance and the Ministry of Equipment—the project met with no real opposition as it moved down the hierarchy for implementation.

The coming to power of the Left was also a favorable element. The two years preceding the elections had been years of austerity after the second oil shock. They had aggravated the housing crisis in Paris: people couldn't afford to buy apartments because of high interest rates, and there were few vacancies in rental properties. When the Socialists arrived in power, housing policy had to catch up with popular demand. Many promises had been made during the electoral campaign, and low-income families became the prime beneficiaries of governmental endeavors. The first two years of social democracy were marked by huge public expenditures to support policies of redistribution: construction started again in the city as a means to fight unemployment, and public housing and public facilities were approved as measures that would keep the population as diverse as possible in the city—a desirable goal for elected officials of all political labels—and as a demonstration of the changes introduced by the new Socialist elites.

Our study indicates that a new direction in urban development and a change in the balance of political power were obtained by a conjunction of opposition by a neighborhood movement, of specific public policies, and of new economic circumstances. Such outcomes, however, are not necessarily long-term victories in terms of popular demands. At some moments, the balance of forces may be such that the citizens are able to obtain development concessions that are consistent with social-welfare concerns; yet the general orientation of economic urban development in Western post-industrial countries does not differ greatly in the long run from one society to another, and it is unlikely that even progressive elites can consistently pursue redistributive policies to answer the needs of their constituents. Successful mobilization, even when it reaches across class lines, as it did in the Thirteenth Arrondissement, is still reactive to development policies based largely in partnerships between public officials and private investors. This is the case in France and the United States alike.

NOTES

1. H. W. Ehrmann, *Politics in France,* 4th ed. (Boston: Little, Brown, 1983), p. 183.

2. Alexis de Tocqueville, *De la démocratie en Amerique,* 2 vols. (Paris: Gallimard, 1961), 2: 125 and 1: 56, 63.

3. J. Hayward, *The One and Indivisible French Republic* (New York: Norton, 1973), p. 127.

4. Sophie Body-Gendrot, "Public Policy, Community Action: A Review of the American Model," a paper presented at the Tocqueville Conference, Paris, 5–7 May 1985.

5. Susan S. Fainstein et al., *Restructuring the City* (New York: Longman, 1983).

6. Quoted in Ira Katznelson, *City Trenches* (New York: Pantheon, 1981), p. 4.

7. Fainstein, *Restructuring the City,* p. 251.

8. Manuel Castells, "Theoretical Propositions for an Experimental Study of Urban Social Movements," in *Urban Sociology: Critical Essays,* ed. C. Pickvance (New York: St. Martin's Press, 1976).

9. Robert Friedland, Frances Fox Piven, and Robert Alford, "Political Conflict, Urban Structure, and the Fiscal Crisis," in *Comparing Public Policies: New Concepts and Methods,* ed. Douglas Ashford (Beverly Hills, Calif.: Sage Publications, 1978).

10. S. Body-Gendrot and J. Turner, "Ethnicity and Class: Politics in Manhattan's Lower East Side," *Ethnic Affairs* (Fall 1983).

11. See Jeffrey R. Henig, *Neighborhood Mobilization* (New Brunswick, N.J.: Rutgers University Press, 1982).

12. Ibid., p. 163.

7

The Arts Coalition in Strategies of Urban Development

J. Allen Whitt

Up to this point, the chapters have focused on the development experience in particular cities. A range of situations has been described. Allen Whitt's chapter marks a change of scope, directing attention to forces at work that may affect the composition of governing coalitions across a wide range of communities.

In this chapter on the arts coalition in urban development, Allen Whitt shows that strategies for growth are undergoing change as cities themselves are being transformed into administrative and service centers of a postindustrial society. Just as the encouragement of tourism emerged as a growth strategy, so has the promotion of arts and culture districts. Whitt's chapter shows how fluid the lines of conflict and cooperation are in city development politics. While there is some natural tension between profit seeking and a refined quality of life, the emergence of arts coalitions indicates that there are overlapping interests as well.

Downtown centers of art and culture are useful to central-business-district interests in their competition with suburbs. In addition, such centers can unite historic preservationists and developers, and mixed-use projects can serve to lessen popular resistance and to provide means whereby city officials can use development to add to the public amenities that a community enjoys.

By focusing on a national trend, Whitt also brings into focus a role that can be played by national advocacy groups and alliances in encouraging local coalitions.

In recent decades, a political coalition of new dimensions has formed within the United States. It is a coalition whose main thrust is not to elect politi-

cians to office, nor is it one whose aim is to institutionalize a liberal or conservative philosophy. Rather, the glue that binds this diverse coalition
together is the desire to use cultural institutions to foster urban development and to bring mutual benefits to the members of the coalition. In particular, the coalition believes that the performing arts (ballet, orchestra,
theater, opera, stage shows, etc.) can play useful roles in the redevelopment
of central cities and in boosting the economic life of the metropolitan area—
two venerable and potent inducements to political coalition building.[1] A national trend has developed in which numerous cities are attempting to use
an arts strategy to help renew their downtowns, to make themselves attractive to potential investors and footloose corporations, and to lure the corporate, professional, and administrative personnel who will populate the
urban service-oriented economies of the future.

The presence of the arts in cities is of course not a new phenomenon:
cities have always been centers for artistic production, and the arts frequently have had an influence in shaping the character and economies of
cities. Nor are political ties between public officials, commercial interests,
and arts advocates restricted to this decade. In such cities as New York the
arts have long been of great importance, and arts supporters often have been
wealthy and politically powerful. Art has been important in other cities too,
as, for example, in Louisville, Kentucky.[2]

Rather, my argument is that because of recent changes in the arts, in
the ways they are financed, and in cities themselves, the arts have come
to be seen as of increasing importance in urban development across a range
of cities in the United States. The arts/development coalition is now of
broader constituency, more focused, and seemingly more influential than
ever before. In numerous cities, art now is being used to fuel what Harvey
Molotch has called "urban growth machines."[3]

THE GROWTH OF PUBLIC AND
PRIVATE SUBSIDIES FOR THE ARTS

Since the late 1950s, both public and private funding for the arts has increased greatly. Major milestones in this growth were the Ford Foundation's
establishment in 1957 of its first program on arts and humanities;[4] the
publication in the early 1960s of a report, "Problems and Prospects of the
Performing Arts," by the Rockefeller Brothers Fund; and the rising concern
for the arts within the powerful big-business organization known at the time
as the National Industrial Conference Board (now called the Conference
Board).[5] In 1967, Ford and Rockefeller money established an influential arts-
advocacy organization within the world of the top corporations, the Business
Committee for the Arts (BCA).[6] The BCA has reported that private-business

support for the arts has risen from \$22 million in 1969 to \$506 million in 1982.[7] Within the public sphere, the most significant event was the establishment of the National Endowment for the Arts and the National Endowment for the Humanities in 1965. Funding for the National Endowment for the Arts had increased from \$2.5 million in 1966 to \$149 million by 1978.[8]

Increased funding caused what some have called an "explosion" in the growth of performing-arts organizations and programs around the country. For example, an official of the National Endowment for the Arts reported that the number of dance companies has multiplied ten times, and the number of theater companies has multiplied twenty times in just over two decades.[9] The burgeoning of arts groups and programs in the cities produced a great demand for new arts facilities and performance spaces; this has led to a situation that has been described as a "housing crisis" in the arts.[10] Physical development became part of the arts agenda, development that has often been targeted for central cities in order to maximize attendance. Public and private subsidies, the pressure for the development of physical structures in inner cities, and the transformation of cities into service economies—all made possible the coming together of a new coalition, a coalition focused on an arts strategy for urban development.

THE SPECIAL APPEAL
OF THE ARTS AS A STRATEGY

Members of the arts coalition advance a number of interrelated arguments in favor of the arts as a strategy for urban development: it has been said that the arts are now a "major new industry";[11] that they pump money directly into the urban economy (through wages to artists, demands for artistic supplies and services, spending on restaurants and shops and taxicabs by attendees, etc.);[12] that they encourage physical development and historic preservation (e.g., newly constructed cultural centers or the conversion of old schools and theaters into modern arts facilities); that they promote related development in a "synergistic" way (as in the growth of nearby shops, office buildings, restaurants, hotels, convention centers, etc.);[13] that they add vitality and "animation" to city streets by bringing people downtown after normal working hours;[14] that by bringing in people from outside the city—in a process akin to traditional "tourism"[15]—to spend money downtown, they help central cities to compete more effectively with other cities and with their own suburbs;[16] that the arts are a "clean" industry that contributes to the local quality of life; that the arts support the move toward in-town living and gentrification; and that they are especially attractive to corporate and other high-level personnel who work in the service, administrative, and professional portions of today's city economy.

THE NEW ARTS-CENTERED
DEVELOPMENT COALITION

The major actors in the alliance are large corporations, developers, banks, arts groups, and officials of the federal government. At the local level, these groups are joined by local and state governments, city planners, local arts organizations and arts advocates, and, often, historic preservationists.

Developers, especially, are a powerful part of urban-development schemes in that they not only are deeply involved in the growth politics of individual cities but also are increasingly national in their operations and interests. As Joe Feagin points out, construction is the largest industry in the United States and much of that construction is urban. The process is becoming more centralized as development corporations become larger and build projects all over the country (and sometimes overseas as well): "A few hundred developers and financial institutions now construct and finance most major and many smaller urban development projects." As will be discussed below, the "multiple-use development," or MXD, is a favored form of development.[17]

The link between corporations and the arts has been made tighter in the 1980s by President Ronald Reagan's policies of federal cutbacks in funding for governmental programs and the concomitant encouragement of reliance on private sources of funding. These policies are reflected in the Private Partnership Office, which was created by the National Endowment for the Arts, and by the establishment of the President's Committee on the Arts and Humanities. The Arts and City Planning Conference, which met in San Antonio in 1979,[18] and the Arts' Edge Conference, which was held in Pittsburgh in 1981,[19] were made up of the groups listed above. A Harvard Business School study of arts-based revitalization in six cities notes that all were founded on close ties among "the major social, political, business, and important special-interest groups."[20] The report reaches the overall conclusion that "of all factors contributing to success, perhaps the most important components are the combination of energetic personalities with ties to the power structure of the community, core corporate leadership, and a broad base of public support." The head of the Cultural Alliance of Greater Washington (D.C.) spoke of the mixed-use development efforts in that city as a "model partnership between private business and the arts," one that "provided a direct response to the Reagan administration's challenge to increase private-sector support of the arts."[21]

THE INCENTIVES FOR THE PARTNERS

CULTURAL MXDs

The Urban Land Institute defines three categories of arts-related development projects: "mixed-use buildings," or structures that combine arts and commercial activities in one building (such as the Museum of Modern Art in New York City, with its attached residential tower); "mixed-use developments" or MXDs, complexes of structures physically connected to each other, as in a cluster of buildings that houses a professional theater, a concert hall, a hotel, shops, and restaurants; and "arts districts," analogous to historic districts, in which a whole and relatively large area of a city is designated and zoned as a mixed cultural and commercial district.[22] Work has started in Dallas, Texas, on a prominent example of an arts district, a sixty-acre publicly and privately developed area across the north end of downtown, which will contain a fine-arts museum, a symphony hall, galleries, artists' studios, hotels, office buildings, and other establishments. It is said that real-estate "developers across the country have expressed interest in the Dallas Arts District."[23] Redevelopment that uses cultural MXDs and related projects can be found in a variety of cities, and the trend appears to be increasing across the country.

MXDs are central to the partnership and the political coalition. In order to get all of the mutual benefits for the parties in the coalition, it is often stressed that cultural MXDs must be "well-planned" and integrated into the surrounding social and commercial landscape,[24] putting the arts, as one arts planning consultant puts it, "right smack in the middle of the action" by avoiding "the cultural Ziggurt principle,"[25] which some see as characterizing certain earlier-vintage, relatively isolated "cultural palaces," such as Lincoln Center in New York City.

A report by the Urban Land Institute summarizes some of the inducements presented to developers, local governments, and arts organizations by MXDs that include arts components.

> Private developers, seeking ways to create a strong and distinctive market image, include arts and amenities to draw the desired consumers to these complexes and to extend the activity cycle to evenings and weekends.
>
> Public agencies, whose goals are to strengthen downtown areas with development programs that attract residents, workers, and visitors, are willing to share the financial risks of including amenities and cultural uses in mixed-use projects.
>
> For arts organizations, faced with operating costs rising higher than traditional funding sources can support, the use of real estate development rights or the opportunity to participate in major urban development projects can provide a way to gain new facilities and to supplement their funds.[26]

SPECIAL LEGAL, TAX, AND FINANCIAL ARRANGEMENTS

MXDs that incorporate the arts are attractive to the partners because they provide a form of development that is in part publicly and privately subsidized, through federal grants (e.g., National Endowment for the Arts grants, which are usually given on a matching basis), through tax breaks and local government support, and through corporate and foundation giving. For example, a combination of business money, foundation money, contributions from individuals, funds from the National Endowment for the Arts, the Indiana Arts Commission, and part of an urban-development action grant received by the city of Indianapolis was used to renovate a 1927-vintage movie theater (located downtown near a new Hyatt Regency office-building complex) and to convert it into the home of the Indiana Repertory Theater.[27]

There are many ways in which financial arrangements can be made in order to provide incentives to the partners. One article by a financing specialist,[28] for example, outlines fourteen different financing strategies, including revenue bonds, special assessment districts, tax-increment financing, the creation of special taxes, urban enterprise zones, special leasing arrangements, and density trade-off zoning.

One interesting variation of the latter strategy is known as "air rights transfers": "What is involved is the amount of space above a building short of what applicable zoning permits. If the air rights above building X can be transferred to building Y (to permit Y to exceed its zoning-permitted height), then building X's air rights have significant value."[29]

In New York City, there have been two major cases in which air rights were sold. In the South Street Seaport project, an area of historic buildings, the air rights over those buildings were bought by banks (headed by David Rockefeller's Chase Manhattan) and were sold to developers in Lower Manhattan, which resulted in such developments as the Continental Insurance skyscraper four blocks from the Seaport.[30] The Museum of Modern Art (MOMA) sold a quarter-acre of its air rights (over property it owned next to the museum) to developers who built an expensive residential tower nearby. The partnership was cemented by the fact that the developers got the tower they wanted, MOMA received $17 million for the air rights and from continuing income from the Museum Tower condominiums,[31] and the city acquired extra tax revenues. People outside the partnership have not necessarily been pleased, as the fifty-two-story tower project is said to have brought "dismay" to others in the city,[32] who have protested both the changed character of the area and the height and space taken up.[33]

In some cases the city strikes explicit deals with developers in order to get arts facilities built. During the tenure of Mayor John Lindsay, developers wanted to build large office buildings in New York City's theater district.

A former city official explains: "We simply told developers who came to us for various kinds of technical variances that unless they built theaters in the office buildings, they were not going to get their variances." There is not likely to have been much if any coercion, however, because, as the same official notes: "Developers have learned that arts activities increase their property values."[34] Other observers have put it thus: "For developers, providing arts facilities is also a way of getting a leg up on the competition in an increasingly tight commercial real estate market." In San Diego, developer Ernest Hahn is reportedly contributing $1 million toward the building of two legitimate theaters to be located in his shopping mall. Similarly, in the massive Bunker Hill redevelopment project in Los Angeles, the plan is for a developer to provide operating subsidies for new performing-arts spaces in order to "gain the zoning bonuses needed to build an office, housing, and retail development."[35]

Other more conventional financing means are also used. One, described as a "standard real-estate transaction in private development," brings local government, developers, and arts organizations into a direct partnership. In order to provide incentives for developers, the city acquires a piece of historic property, such as a theater, and sells it to a developer. The developer in turn syndicates it to investors looking for tax breaks on their other income. The city leases the property back from the developer and sets up a nonprofit corporation to run the theater in which arts groups will perform.[36] These and other complex legal and financial arrangements are common in the cultural-development business.

In addition to the inducements offered to developers for the renovation of historical buildings (i.e., a 25 percent tax credit, plus accelerated depreciation allowances),[37] the nonprofit-corporation form has advantages for development. Arts organizations have long used the nonprofit form in order to be able to receive public and private funding.[38] Likewise, nonprofit corporations are often used to spearhead arts-related development efforts because they, too, are allowed to receive foundation money.[39] Also, for philanthropic contributions that are given directly to arts and other organizations, corporations get a tax deduction of up to 10 percent of their taxable income.[40]

The Arts and Commercial Interests

The evolving role of the arts in commercial and urban development has not only tended to bring arts organizations more and more into the urban-growth coalition, however indirectly; it has also raised issues among arts advocates concerning the proper relationship between art and the drive for profit and growth. Some, such as arts consultant Richard Weinstein, see the fusion of art and commercialism as good. He argues that the traditional separation between art and commercial interests is unhealthy because it frees the commercial sector from moral and ethical constraints and allows the arts to retain their "purity" and elitist nature. "If I were building a cultural facility," he says, "I'd build it in a mall."[41]

It is not difficult to understand the attractiveness of commercial involvement to many arts organizations. They have long had to depend on support coming from sources beyond their immediate audiences, such as rich patrons, government grants, and money from foundations and corporations. Many arts groups see partnership with local government and developers in MXDs and similar arts-based development schemes as a way of generating additional needed funds, possibly obtaining facilities contributed by developers, and maybe reaching wider audiences. Citing the example of the New York Museum of Modern Art's tower project, arts consultant Richard Weinstein urges more commercially oriented values and practices upon arts organizations: "If you absorb as a cultural institution a defined portion of the risk [of a commercial development venture] that the private sector ordinarily accepts, the rewards can be tremendous."[42] The former head of the Cultural Alliance of Greater Washington asserts that for the arts "to survive and thrive in an urban environment, within the constraints of the economics of these times, such a partnership [between art and business] is vital."[43]

In spite of the obvious incentives, however, it is not clear how arts organizations will feel about the new relationship in the longer run. The new forms of development that are taking place, for instance, sometimes pose problems for arts organizations. In addition to philosophical debates about commercial involvement and some resistance among arts groups, the nonprofit legal status of arts organizations places some tax-related and other constraints upon commercial ties.[44] There also have been public controversies over such things as the Museum of Modern Art's role in developing a fifty-two story residential tower. A rather common feature of arts development has been the creation of a single performing-arts structure, as in the case of the recently completed $33.5-million Kentucky Center for the Arts in Louisville, which is designed to serve theater groups, opera companies, symphonies, ballets, road shows from out of town, and other performing companies. Problems often arise in such facilities because resident groups commonly feel that they must put up with physical conditions that are less than ideal for their own needs (e.g., poor acoustics for the orchestra in a theater that is fine for stage plays), that centralized administration (the operation and maintenance of the hall, the printing of programs, etc.) is sometimes inflexible and inefficient, that they have reduced autonomy, and that they are placed in greater competition with the other arts groups for funds and audiences.[45]

THE SYMBOLIC AND POLITICAL ATTRACTIVENESS OF THE ARTS

In addition to the reasons already advanced, the arts have a great deal of symbolic and political appeal to the development coalition. Even more than research and development or "hi-tech"—and certainly far more than traditional industries—the arts are seen as "clean," and thus productive of a "good" kind of urban development and a higher "quality of life." Arts development is, at least for the time being, largely noncontroversial. While some opposition might surface against having new industries move into town, who can be against the arts? The head of the Design Arts Program of the National Endowment for the Arts has phrased it thus:

> Urban development projects are so complex that, inevitably it seems, constituencies organize against them for various reasons. . . . The arts, however, are like Mom and apple pie; they're consensus-makers, common ground. People can easily focus on the arts activities in a new project, instead of dwelling on the complicated costs and benefits public support for private development activity usually entails.[46]

In addition to anticipated market synergy between culture and commercialism, part of the appeal that the inclusion of an arts facility in an MXD has for a developer is, no doubt, that it helps to make public subsidies for development, as well as the fact of development itself, more palatable to potential opponents. Thus, an arts strategy might, in certain cases, be tried as a kind of Trojan horse for local "rentiers" and developers in a bid to overcome resistance,[47] particularly in large and controversial displacement projects such as Yerba Buena in San Francisco.[48]

Another aspect of the arts that is often stressed is that the arts supposedly help to promote social unity. Sharon Zukin sees the political significance of what she calls the recent rise of the "Artistic Mode of Production" to lie in its stress upon social harmony, inner meaning, anti-materialism, and limited expectations.[49] The street fairs and other animation projects that the city of Baltimore sponsored are said by organizers to be "things that will bring people together and not pull them apart."[50] The former festival director of New York City believes that such events allow people "to claim the open spaces of their cities" and to learn to trust each other; they also help "to heal the paranoia of urban life."[51] Ralph Davidson, who is chairman of Time, Incorporated, and is a member of the Committee for Economic Development, asserts that the arts "bring us together, united in our appreciation and awe."[52]

It is an open question as to how much the arts really do create social cohesion within a commmunity. To the extent that development interests feel that they have such an effect, however, the arts can become another component (such as professional sports teams) that may be used in local efforts to generate "boosterism" and the "we feeling" of community.[53]

CONCLUSION

I have argued that the arts are becoming a part of what Harvey Molotch has identified as the urban growth machine.[54] This has been possible—and perhaps necessary—because of the changing relationships between business, the arts, and government and because of the political and economic obstacles that have arisen to block older, industrially based strategies for urban growth.

Because the movement toward the significant inclusion of the arts in downtown development is relatively new, it is too soon to say just what the actual fate of such strategies will turn out to be in the longer run. As in the case of tourism,[55] systematic studies and data are lacking. The arts can probably never, by themselves, provide the economic strength or infusion of outside money that was possible under the heyday of industrialism.

The arts, however, are indicative of, and contributory to, the conversion of central cities into corporate administrative and service centers, a process that, in the broad historical perspective, has been under way since the advent of what David Gordon calls the "corporate city."[56] To the extent that the arts strategy proves successful in transforming the central city by helping to generate the conditions for redevelopment and the growth of capital investment, the strategy may also be thought of as part of the process of what Norman and Susan Fainstein have called the Europeanization of American cities, featuring offices, tourism, historical preservation, and "the redirected social gradient which places the upper classes back in the middle of town."[57]

Central-city growth does not benefit everyone equally; it gives most to the middle and upper classes. The development of a larger arts presence in central cities is even less likely to benefit everyone equally; the greatest direct benefits will be to upper-income groups, who are the most frequent attenders at arts performances. According to the work of Paul DiMaggio and Michael Useem, for example, professionals, who constitute only about 15 percent of the work force, account for about 56 percent of arts audiences; blue-collar workers, who make up 34 percent of the work force, account for only about 4 percent of arts audiences; blacks are similarly underrepresented.[58]

The older style of urban renewal that dominated cities during the 1950s and 1960s generated political controversy over the issues of displacement of poorer residents of the central city. Even though the use of the arts as

a tool for urban transformation and redevelopment is currently almost
without controversy, the strategy may eventually inspire protests and
political conflicts too, because, as Dennis Judd and Margaret Collins have
observed, the most recent form of urban renewal, which stresses such things
as tourism, and conventions, "is usually directed exclusively toward the
affluent."[59]

The arts/development connection and the rise of the arts coalition have
as yet been largely undiscovered and unanalyzed by social scientists.
Analyses instead have focused on the rise in downtowns of services or
tourism or the convention business, but almost never on the role of the arts
per se, and even more rarely on the arts as a growth *strategy*.

I have tried to show that the arts strategy has some unique characteristics that make it somewhat distinct from these other categories and
therefore worthy of analysis in its own right. The arts/development connection has been firmly established in actual practice, and the strategy has
been and will continue to be an important shaper and mirror of fundamental processes affecting our cities.

NOTES

1. See, e.g., Clarence N. Stone, *Economic Growth and Neighborhood Discontent*
(Chapel Hill: University of North Carolina Press, 1976); J. Allen Whitt, *Urban Elites
and Mass Transportation: The Dialectics of Power* (Princeton, N.J.: Princeton University Press, 1982).

2. Allen Share, *Cities in the Commonwealth* (Lexington: University of Kentucky
Press, 1982), pp. 109–22.

3. Harvey Molotch, "The City as a Growth Machine," *American Journal of
Sociology* 82 (Sept. 1976).

4. Sharon Zukin, *Loft Living: Culture and Capital in Urban Change* (Baltimore,
Md.: Johns Hopkins University Press, 1982), p. 101.

5. From a pamphlet published by Business Committee for the Arts (BCA)
"Culture and the Corporation," undated.

6. BCA pamphlet, "Business Committee for the Arts," undated.

7. BCA pamphlet, "Why Business Supports the Arts," undated.

8. Paul DiMaggio and Michael Useem, "Cultural Democracy in a Period of
Cultural Expansion: The Social Composition of Arts Audiences in the United States,"
Social Problems 26 (Dec. 1978): 180.

9. Michael Pittas, "Foreword," in *The City as a Stage: Strategies for the Arts in
Urban Economics,* ed. Kevin Green (Washington, D.C.: Partners for Livable Places,
1983), p. 6.

10. Phyllis Lehmann, "Where Will All the Dancers Dance?" in *The City as a
Stage,* p. 16.

11. Pittas, "Foreword," p. 6.

12. Luisa Kreisberg, "Economic Insurance," in *The City as a Stage,* pp. 24–25.

13. Harold Snedcof, *Cultural Facilities in Mixed-Use Development* (Washington,
D.C.: Urban Land Institute, 1985), p. 14.

14. Sandra Hillman, "Leveraging Prosperity in Baltimore," in *The City as a Stage*, pp. 98–99.

15. Dennis Judd and Margaret Collins, "The Case of Tourism: Political Coalitions and Redevelopment in the Central Cities," in *The Changing Structure of the City: What Happened to the Urban Crisis?* ed. Gary Tobin (Beverly Hills, Calif.: Sage Publications, 1979), pp. 177–99.

16. American Council for the Arts, *The Arts in the Economic Life of the City* (New York: American Council for the Arts, 1979), p. 67.

17. Joe Feagin, *The Urban Real Estate Game* (Englewood Cliffs, N.J.: Prentice-Hall, 1983), pp. 39, 8, 64–84.

18. American Council for the Arts, *The Arts and City Planning* (New York: American Council for the Arts, 1980).

19. Green, *The City as a Stage*.

20. Harvard Business School, "Cultural Revitalization in Six Cities," in *The City as a Stage*, pp. 26–28.

21. Peter Jablow, "The Arts and Commercial Development," in *The City as a Stage*, p. 50.

22. Snedcof, *Cultural Facilities*, p. 23.

23. Robert Goetsch and Mary Haderlein, "Art for Downtown's Sake," *Planning*, July/Aug. 1983, pp. 11–13.

24. Frank Spink, Jr., "Foreword," in *Cultural Facilities*, p. 5.

25. George Clack, "Footlight Districts," in *The City as a Stage*, p. 13.

26. Snedcof, *Cultural Facilities*, p. 10.

27. Benjamin Mordecai, "A Movie Palace Goes Legitimate," in *The City as a Stage*, p. 52.

28. Samuel Stone, "Fourteen Points," in *The City as a Stage*.

29. Ibid., p. 56.

30. Richard Weinstein, "Creative Financing," in *The City as a Stage*, p. 43.

31. Snedcof, *Cultural Facilities*, pp. 50–51.

32. Weinstein, "Creative Financing," p. 45.

33. Robert Peck, "Living over the Museum," in *The City as a Stage*, p. 47; Snedcof, *Cultural Facilities*, p. 50.

34. Weinstein, "Creative Financing," p. 42.

35. Goetsch and Haderlein, "Art for Downtown's Sake," pp. 10, 12–13.

36. Clack, "Footlight Districts," p. 15.

37. Zukin, *Loft Living*, pp. 165–66.

38. Paul DiMaggio, "Nonprofit Organizations in the Production and Distribution of Culture," in *Handbook of Research on Nonprofit Organizations*, ed. Walter W. Powell (New Haven, Conn.: Yale University Press, forthcoming), p. 36.

39. Harvard Business School, "Cultural Revitalization," p. 26.

40. Cultural Assistance Center, "Business Partners for the Arts," in *The City as a Stage*, p. 63.

41. The developer was quoted in *The City as a Stage*, p. 32. As noted earlier, developer Ernest Hahn has in fact put up money for the construction of two arts facilities in his San Diego shopping mall (Goetsch and Haderlein, "Art for Downtown's Sake," pp. 12–13).

42. Weinstein, "Creative Financing," p. 45.

43. Jablow, "The Arts and Commercial Development," p. 51.

44. American Council for the Arts, *The Arts in the Economic Life of the City*, p. 109; Peck, "Living over the Museum."

45. Marc Freedman, "The Elusive Promise of Management Cooperation in the Performing Arts," in *Nonprofit Organizations in the Arts*, ed. Paul DiMaggio (New York: Oxford University Press, forthcoming).

46. Quoted in Clack, "Footlight Districts," p. 13.

47. Harvey Molotch, "Capital and Neighborhood in the United States," *Urban Affairs Quarterly* 14 (Mar. 1979).

48. Harvey Molotch and John Logan, "Tensions in the Growth Machine," *Social Problems* 31 (June 1984).

49. Zukin, *Loft Living,* p. 105.

50. Hillman, "Leveraging Prosperity," p. 98.

51. Karin Bacon, "The Rhythm of City Life," in *The City as a Stage,* p. 105.

52. BCA pamphlet, "Improving the Business Climate: Business and the Arts," undated.

53. Molotch, "City as a Growth Machine," pp. 314–15.

54. Ibid.

55. Judd and Collins, "Case of Tourism."

56. David Gordon, "Class Struggle and the Stages of American Urban Development," in *The Rise of the Sunbelt Cities,* ed. David Perry and Alfred Watkins (Beverly Hills, Calif.: Sage Publications, 1977).

57. Norman I. Fainstein and Susan S. Fainstein, "Restructuring the American City: A Comparative Perspective," in *Urban Policy under Capitalism,* ed. Norman Fainstein and Susan Fainstein (Beverly Hills, Calif.: Sage Publications, 1982), p. 170.

58. DiMaggio and Useem, "Cultural Democracy," pp. 187–91.

59. Judd and Collins, "Case of Tourism," p. 197.

PART 2

CONFLICT AND CONFLICT MANAGEMENT

8

Reexamining a Classic Case of Development Politics: New Haven, Connecticut

Clarence N. Stone and Heywood T. Sanders

Part 2 of this book gives particular attention to conflict within urban communities. While cities may have a unitary interest in economic advancement, that fact, as the following chapter by Clarence Stone and Heywood Sanders contends, does not preclude conflict over development. The pervasiveness of conflict underlies coalition-building and conflict-management strategies that are so central in city politics.

To be sure, public officeholders work at building consensus or at least majority approval for their policies, and they act in a context in which nearly everyone endorses the general notion of economic growth. In this chapter, however, which reexamines the New Haven experience, and in the following chapters, which focus on other cities, political leaders display an overriding concern for coping with conflict. As the chapters in Part 2 indicate, conflict-management strategies and the coalition-building efforts that accompany them are varied.

Chapter 8 proceeds in two stages. The first is a critique of Paul Peterson's City Limits; *the second is a reexamination of the redevelopment experience in New Haven, Connecticut, during Richard Lee's mayoralty. New Haven holds special interest for students of urban politics. It is perhaps the nation's longest-running drama in the study of development politics, and the fabled mayoralty of New Haven's Richard Lee continues to be a subject of fascination and dispute. It is not surprising, then, that Paul Peterson drew on Robert Dahl's account of redevelopment there to illustrate the argument in* City Limits. *It is perhaps also predictable that Stone and Sanders would find this*

interpretation of the mayoralty of Lee—one that plays down conflict—to
be oversimplified and incomplete. These are well-drawn lines in the
New Haven debate. Stone and Sanders push beyond the general lines
of that debate, however, to argue that the full Lee mayoralty was quite
different from what it seemed to be in its early years. Put another way,
the actual carrying out of a development policy has a much-different
character from that of the promotional stage. Consensus is easier to
maintain during promotion than during execution.

After the publication of Theodore Lowi's review essay setting forth a typology
of policy arenas,[1] many political scientists have been attracted to a policy-
determines-politics formulation. In the field of urban studies a particularly
influential version of this formulation is one that Paul Peterson put forward
in his award-winning book *City Limits*.[2] That there is a sense in which policy
shapes politics is indisputable. Of course, people react politically in accordance with what they perceive to be at stake. But does that statement capture the basic dynamic of politics? We think not, especially in the field of
urban politics. We propose, then, to take the step of showing that Peterson's
conceptualization of the link between developmental policy and politics is
inadequate. We suggest an alternative view, one in which politics is a major shaper of developmental policy. New Haven provides an illustration.

PETERSON'S ARGUMENT IN BRIEF

City Limits is an enormously ambitious book. It makes very large claims,
and these claims must be understood in order to grasp the full import of
Peterson's argument about development politics. *City Limits* attempts to
reinterpret and synthesize the findings of pluralists and elitists and to accommodate the phenomenon of nondecision making as well. It does so
through the policy-structures-politics formulation. According to Peterson,
there are three categories of policy, each of which is identified with a distinct
set of political relationships. Development policy is an arena of decision making that is dominated by public and private elites operating consensually.
Allocative policies are characterized by conflict and bargaining, in line with
the pluralist view of urban politics. And redistributive policies, through
which benefits would be shifted from haves to have-nots, are largely excluded
from the local political agenda; in other words, they give rise to nondecision making.

In providing an overarching explanation of city politics, Peterson operates
deductively, not inductively. He starts with the economic situation of local
governments. Cities promote development, avoid redistribution, and allow

conflict and bargaining over allocative policies because the logic of their competitive situation dictates that they act in this manner. His full formulation is that a particular economic situation gives rise to policies, and policies structure political relationships. It is a powerful argument, and as Peterson says, it is consistent with the line of reasoning that both neoclassical economists and structural Marxists employ. Yet, for all of his claims about synthesizing, when Peterson moves from deductive argument to the actual world of urban politics, the result is a pluralist view. Can it be, after all these years, that Robert Dahl's *Who Governs?* remains the definitive word on the politics of cities?[3] We contend that the answer is no, and we believe that the slippage in Peterson's case for pluralism occurs in the translation of a deductive argument to the sphere of operational political realities.

Because the use of the word *pluralism* is certain to sound all kinds of alarm bells, let us explain why *City Limits* can be labeled "pluralist". This explanation should also indicate why Peterson's argument about development policy and politics is a key element in his overall depiction of city politics. In Peterson's policy-determines-politics formulation, there are two arenas of consensus and one of conflict. Development policy is an arena of consensus because it is in the interest of the whole community to enhance the city's economic position.[4] Redistributive policy is simply the other side of the same coin—redistribution is, in the main, avoided because it is harmful to a city's economic position. Allocative policies are neutral in their effect on economic position; therefore they are fair game for group competition. In *City Limits,* as in the classic pluralist studies, policy makers operate within the bounds of popular consensus on the large questions, and conflict is largely confined to narrower issues of allocation.[5]

Peterson, of course, is not simply reiterating pluralist arguments. His terms of analysis are quite different. Whereas pluralists talk about group interests, Peterson focuses on the city as a territorial unit. He sees it as a unit that is analogous to the business firm. Like the business firm, the city is driven by the logic of its place as a unit (hence, unitary interest) engaged in economic competition with other units. Peterson states: "Cities, like private firms, compete with one another so as to maximize their economic position. To achieve this objective, the city must use the resources its land area provides by attracting as much capital and as high a quality labor force as is possible" (p. 29; see also pp. 18–21).

Here, however, Peterson confronts a difficult problem in translation. The analogy of the business firm is quite limited. Citizens of a city differ in important ways from shareholders in a business firm. All shareholders benefit if the profit margin and the worth of a business firm go up. If a risk is taken, all either benefit or suffer. The consequences of business actions are external to the daily lives and the immediate social opportunities of shareholders. Moreover, shareholders, as shareholders, are related to one another in only a limited and formal way. The consequences of business action neither advantage one shareholder over another nor affect the quality of the attachments and relationships among shareholders.

The fruits of economic growth (good and bad) are not like business profits; they are not purely external to the relationships between citizens. Economic-enhancement efforts affect citizens differentially. Growth is not an unmixed blessing, and the losers are not necessarily compensated. Peterson confronts the issue indirectly, but he then proceeds to link the interest of each citizen with the economic advancement of the city as a corporate entity. He notes that within the urban community there are numerous and even conflicting social roles. But, he adds:

> All are structured by the fact that they take place in a specific spatial location that falls within the jurisdiction of some local government. All members of the city thus come to share an interest in policies that affect the well-being of that territory. Policies which enhance the desirability or attractiveness of the territory are in the city's interest, because they benefit all residents—in their role as residents of the community. (p. 21)

Thus, for Peterson, the city as a territorial unit has an interest that is conceptually separate from, but in reality related to, the interest of the people who are citizens of the city. Peterson observes that city residents "often have discordant interests." But he discounts that fact, and states: "By a city's interest, I do not mean the sum total of the interests of those individuals living in the city" (p.17). The city is, therefore, not its people, but a social structure with territoriality. Peterson contends, however, that because all citizens have a stake in the city as a territorial unit, there is an affinity of interest between these territorial units and the citizens who reside within them. While Peterson does not closely examine this affinity of interest, it is a basic assumption for his entire argument about development policy and politics. His characterization of development politics requires that he skim over the question of "discordant interests" and that he emphasize shared interest in the territorial unit. We think this is a fatal flaw. Had he focused more on the issue of the uneven and differential impact of development policy, it would have been less easy to talk about a unitary interest and, therefore, more difficult to treat the city as a utility-maximizing entity.

By-passing these complications, Peterson makes a seemingly plausible assertion that the economic well-being for the city is a prerequisite to other benefits. Hence it is rational for decision makers to pursue economic-enhancement policies, and it is rational for citizens to support such policies. Therefore development policy leads to a consensual set of relationships in which public and private elites cooperate, and their cooperation rests on a foundation of public support. This line of reasoning seems to assume Pareto optimality. Development policy, in Peterson's eyes, leaves almost no one worse off and leaves most people better off. At one point, for example, he talks about the benefits of development "for all members of the city" (p. 147). Thus, conflict has been defined away.

DEVELOPMENT POLICY
IN A PARADIGM OF RATIONALITY

If, as Peterson argues, development policy were characterized mainly by a unitary interest of the whole community in economic well-being, then there would be little basis for conflict. Consensus would be expected. According to Peterson, that is the specific way in which development policy shapes political relationships. Because it is not, in Peterson's analysis, a contest between winners and losers, but a matter in which all can win, development politics has a consensual quality. Group conflict is minimal, and support for development policy "is broad and continuous" (p. 132). Therefore, it is not appropriate to talk about one element's having power over another. Power is best thought of as "the capacity of the community as a whole to realize its objectives"; leadership is not the ability to impose one's will, but is that of being able to "persuade others to contribute to a common cause" (p. 148). Thus, Peterson maintains, local politics is low-key; it is "generally a quiet arena of decision making where political leaders can give reasoned attention to the longer range interests of the city, taken as a whole" (p. 109).

Peterson's view of development policy and politics is embedded in a paradigm of rationality. In his earlier work on school politics, Peterson, citing Graham Allison, states: "much of the finest work in [international relations] has been guided either implicitly or explicitly, by the assumption that nation-states are, or at least could be—purposive, efficient value-maximizing entities that rationally pursue certain strategic objectives."[6] It is likely, as the use of the idea of unitary interest indicates, that the treatment of development policy in *City Limits* is guided by a similar assumption of rational action. In the latter book, Peterson asserts that "generalizations about policy-making are more likely to be correct if they assume a degree of intelligence, reasonableness, and rationality on the part of those entrusted with local authority" (p. 133). He adds: "Most political leaders are reasonably able men and women with fairly well developed systems of information" (p. 133). On this point, Peterson puts forward a guarded claim: "Although information is imperfect and local governments cannot be expected to select the one best alternative on every occasion, policy choices over time will be limited to those few which can be plausibly shown to be conducive to the community's economic prosperity" (p. 30). Yet, while Peterson doesn't treat development policy as an exact science, he sees it as an arena in which there are shared goals and common terms of discourse. Despite discordant interests, city residents have a mutual concern about prosperity. Thus, Peterson argues, the citizens "know the kind of evidence that must be advanced and the kinds of reasons that must be adduced in order to build a persuasive case that a policy is in the interest of cities" (p. 22).

What Peterson describes is a policy arena in which there is a consensual goal. Priorities are not at issue, and the terms on which the goal is to be pursued are agreed upon. Therefore, policy making is a matter of choosing, within the available information and alternatives, what appears to be the best choice. Imperfect information can, on occasion, lead to mistakes, but better information brings about corrections.

Peterson therefore looks at heavy business participation in development policy as "apolitical," as an opportunity to garner a "halo effect" (p. 142). Since it is, in Peterson's eyes, a question of choosing a suitable means to pursue an agreed-upon goal, extensive business participation can be explained as a matter of involving people who are "well acquainted with the problem of fostering economic growth" (p. 148). Similarly, the secrecy surrounding planning efforts for development projects is explained as a matter of not raising false hopes until feasibility can be determined or of not tipping the city's hand to competing localities (p. 142). In short, Peterson argues that development policy gives rise to nonpolitical relationships. There is no need for bargaining over value trade-offs; no need for mutual adjustment between differentially affected interests. The specialized information known to experienced actors, not representation of a diverse constituency, is the guiding concern; and according to Peterson, it is appropriate that much of the decision making occur in isolation from the mass public. Unitary interests, rational choice, and decision making based on specialized knowledge are closely interwoven in Peterson's schema of development policy making. The irony of drawing inspiration from the work of Graham Allison is that Peterson did not follow Allison's lead in seeing the shortcomings of the rational-actor paradigm.[7]

WHAT HAPPENED TO POLITICS?

According to Peterson, developmental policies are usually electorally popular. Political leaders pursue economic development because it is good practice and widely recognized as such:

> By pursuing policies which contribute to the economic prosperity of the local community, the local politician selects policies that redound to his own political advantage. Local politicians, eager for relief from cross-pressures of local politics, assiduously promote goals that have widespread benefits.

And few policies are more popular than economic growth and prosperity.
(P. 29; see also pp. 24, 132, 145)

Astute politicians grasp that the collective benefits of economic growth
are politically popular,[8] and they do not hesitate to make alliances with
business. Lee in New Haven and Daley in Chicago, for example, understood
quickly "that what is good for business is good for the community" (p. 143).
But, Peterson maintains: "The city's interest in attracting capital does not
mean utter subservience to any particular corporation, but a sensitivity to
the need for establishing an overall favorable climate" (p. 28).

At the same time, Peterson argues that development policies don't just
happen. Inertia must be overcome. For many projects, disparate activities have
to be brought together in support of a common venture, and securing support for development proposals may require considerable political ingenuity.
Business executives and other actors do not want to invest time and resources
in plans that won't reach fruition. Peterson says of New Haven's redevelopment program under Mayor Lee: "Especially in the first year or two of local
planning, when rewards were distant and uncertain, it was difficult to get
much support" (p. 144). In this view, however, political benefit came to Lee,
because he could foresee the gain from redevelopment and because he was
skillful enough in the art of persuasion to unify a community effort behind
his vision. The political effort that was involved, Peterson argues, was not
one of how one faction prevailed over another. "In the developmental arena,"
he contends, "power is not best understood as a 'zero-sum' game, where one
person or group wins, at the expense of another. Instead, power is better
understood in systemic terms; it is the capacity of the community as a whole
to realize its objectives" (p. 148). Hence, when all of his cards are put on the
table, Peterson is very much a pluralist, largely reiterating the argument
of Robert Dahl in *Who Governs?* Heavy business involvement in development
policy is not a matter of dominance, not a matter of prevailing over other
interests; it is a matter of contributing to the capacity of the community to
realize its general well-being. Politicians lead, but they do so by persuasion.

Peterson acknowledges that the "consensual quality of development
policies does not hold in each and every case." There are exceptions. But,
he says, these exceptions "are unlikely to characterize the politics of large
and medium-sized cities" (p. 149).

THE FIT BETWEEN DEDUCTIVE TERMS
AND OPERATIONAL REALITIES

Our basic contention is that Peterson's use of the paradigm of rationality
prevents him from examining closely what needs to be analyzed. The deduc-

tive terms that are used to describe the city as a utility-maximizing entity serve poorly to guide our understanding of what shapes development policy. As the previous section indicates, Peterson puts forward a fairly simplistic view of development politics: business involvement is non-political, mayors practice the art of persuasion, and support for projects grows as they near fruition and as the benefits become more apparent. To be sure, Peterson also describes a politics of allocation in which there is conflict, bargaining, and identifiable winners and losers. Allocational policies are those that have neutral effects or no known effects on a city's economic position. These policies confer highly divisible benefits and are typified by housekeeping services and by rules of public employment.

In contrast, development policies are defined as "those that contribute to the economic well-being of the city" (p. 131). Peterson says that such policies are typified by projects "to attract industry to a community, to extend its transportation system, or to renew depressed areas within the city" (p. 132). In a footnote, he indicates that locational decisions are sometimes controversial (p. 240), and he acknowledges in passing that any particular project "may have elements within it that are developmental, others that are redistributive, and others that are purely allocational" (p. 133). Yet, he never takes advantage of these occasional qualifying statements to extend or elaborate his argument. He uses highway expenditures as his operational measure of development policy when analyzing data, and he generally sees development politics and allocational politics as fairly distinct arenas. However, the overall argument is underspecified in some crucial respects. Particularly important, but unexamined, is the fit, on the one side, between "development policy" as defined formally for deductive purposes and, on the other side, what in substantive terms or in ordinary understanding is "development policy."

Peterson writes as if the prevailing pattern is one in which substantively development projects (e.g., redevelopment, transportation, and business subsidies) have a known and positive effect on a city's economic position (his formal definition of development policy entails this positive effect). These are projects in which particular impacts (divisible benefits and costs) are less important than is their collective impact. Note, however, what happens if either of two assumptions that underlie this scenario is modified. Suppose that the net economic effect of what in substantive terms are development projects is uncertain to a significant degree. Then, what is substantively development policy becomes, in formal definitional terms, allocational policy. Yet, this mental conversion is obscure enough to cause problems of analysis. Or, relax the second assumption: suppose that actors on the urban scene are not primarily motivated by a concern with the impact of projects on the long-run economic position of the city as a corporate entity but that, instead, they are concerned primarily with the direct and fairly immediate impacts on their particular interests. If concerns about the allocation of particular costs and benefits prevail, the policy is not only allocational; it also matters greatly who is represented in decision making. Business predominance takes on a different light.

Why does Peterson not examine these eventualities? Apparently the paradigm of rationality stands in the way. Rationalist assumptions about policy making are ill-suited to dealing either with uncertainty or with preference orderings that are not unified.[9]

Peterson's policy-determines-politics formulation leads him to separate analytically what in empirical reality may be closely joined. Much case-study material suggests that conflict, not consensus, is characteristic of redevelopment and expressway issues.[10] Moreover, the efficacy of business-subsidy programs can be questioned. It seems likely, then, that many development-type projects actually have, in Peterson's terms, an allocational character, but without the openness and fluidity associated with pluralist politics.

Even when projects are promoted in the *name* of the interest of the whole community, political leadership has to confront a complex task of coalition-building. Peterson's analogy between the city and the business firm—aside from the inappropriateness of the citizen/stockholder parallel—fails to save his argument from the need to confront the issue of coalition-building and conflict management. The discipline of the market notwithstanding, business firms themselves are faced by this very same need.[11] Actors don't of necessity act on the basis of a desire to maximize utility for the corporate entity, or if they do, they operate—in accordance with their positions in the scheme of things—with widely divergent understandings of what utility maximization calls for. (This is the point of Allison's Models II and III.)[12]

By treating the city as a utility-maximizing unit, one ignores the possibility that a development project might offer uncertain *general* benefits but generate very definite costs and benefits that are *particular* in nature. Even where general gains are to be made, there is no guarantee that they will be pursued. Richard Nelson argues: "With many players in the game, and many subgames being played, it is not . . . clear that all gains that can be made will be made."[13] Coalition-building is thus necessary, and organizational policy reflects these efforts at coalition-building. Moreover, in the case of urban redevelopment and transportation, the typical project is hardly a Paretian move. Change brings forth fairly certain costs and high risks; hence opposition is likely. Coalition-building aims to bring together actors who will benefit enough with high-enough probability and low-enough risks to withstand opposition that the policies of the coalition may engender.

The political task, then, is not one of persuading members of a unit to support or acquiesce in a policy that will benefit all eventually. Instead, the task is one of putting together a coalition of needed and dependable supporters and of managing conflict by compensating or, in some way, isolating losers. Under these conditions, secrecy and selectively reporting information (not to mention "cooking" the data)[14] are not politically neutral acts.

With a complex political task to be done, no single approach is likely to appeal to all actors. Coalition-building and conflict management are done in a variety of ways. Variety is especially evident when, as is often the case, the projects at issue have a mixture of short-term and long-term effects, differentially incurred costs and benefits, direct and indirect costs as well as benefits, and varying degrees of risk incurred among the affected population.

Once the utility-maximizing notion is put aside in the face of such complications, analyzing the political task becomes centrally important. And the political task is not necessarily external to the policies that are being pursued. Governing officials *may shape policies to facilitate the political task*—that is, they may adopt policies that contribute to both building and maintaining coalitions and to managing conflict. To the extent that this is the case, the pertinent formulation is one in which politics shapes policy. Organizational analysis yields parallel situations. Dennis Palumbo and David Nachmias, for example, observe that organizational decision makers usually do not look for the most efficient way of solving a problem. Instead, they search for solutions that will serve the interests of the members of the policy-making coalitions.[15]

In short, our critique of Peterson is that by employing a paradigm of the city as a utility-maximizing unit, he makes inappropriate assumptions. We offer the following as an alternative set of assumptions.

1. Uncertainty surrounds the net long-range effects of many development projects, and in any event, many participants are more concerned about short-term effects than about long-term ones.

2. Similarly, many participants act on the basis of particular, rather than general, impacts. Even those who represent institutional interests concern themselves mainly with the particular interests of institutions to which their careers are attached.

3. Significant conflict surrounds development policy.

4. The city acts less as a utility-maximizing unit than as an aggregation of particular interests that must be held together by a combination of shared and overlapping purposes and strategic "side-payments." Political efforts in the form of coalition-building and conflict management are thus essential.

5. Because political efforts are more a matter of habit, ongoing adjustments, and judgment than of technical calculation, prevailing political arrangements vary from place to place and from time to time.

6. Concerned about protecting and using these political arrangements, key actors make substantive policy decisions in line with the interests of coalition members and with the maintenance needs of the coalition itself.

7. Policy responses to the economic position of the city are thus mediated through the politics of the city.

Paradigmatic debate is not a simple matter of hypothesis testing. Paradigms differ in the questions they pose and in the facts they point to. As a consequence, they offer contrasting pictures of the world. In the next section, we turn to the redevelopment experience in New Haven under Mayor Lee and look particularly at Peterson's characterization of Lee as an "able servant"—the archetype of leader as utility maximizer. We suggest an alternative view, based in a political paradigm.

THE POLITICS OF REDEVELOPMENT IN NEW HAVEN

Introduction

In the tradition of Robert Dahl's analysis in *Who Governs?* Peterson characterizes development politics in New Haven as politics in the service of the collective good of the community. Under the leadership of Mayor Richard Lee, New Haven's executive-centered regime was, in Peterson's eyes, the "able servant" of the community's business and nonbusiness interests alike. Peterson offers Oakland, California, as the contrary example. A council-manager city, without strong executive leadership, Oakland was widely presumed to be especially responsive to business interests. Yet its redevelopment effort appeared to be far less vigorous than the one made in New Haven. Peterson suggests that business and nonbusiness interests alike suffered, and he labels the Oakland government as an "inefficient slave." The irony that Peterson is playing upon is that in the one community, strong political leadership served economic interests well, whereas in the other community, weak political leadership, presumed to be especially responsive to business interests, by some accounts served economic interests poorly.

Behind Peterson's view of the two cities is the assumption that *the* political problem is one of overcoming inertia. It is, he believes, a problem of how to mobilize people on behalf of their shared interests in a more productive economy. Drawing on the New Haven case, Peterson suggests that this can best be done by a strong executive who has a flair for public relations—in other words, Richard Lee, New Haven's action-oriented mayor for eight consecutive two-year terms. Inherent in Peterson's comparison of New Haven and Oakland is a spectrum that runs from a point of greatest efficiency in mobilizing a development effort to a point of least efficiency in mobilizing such an effort. The implied standard is the amount of activity: greater activity not only requires more efficiency, but greater activity is also better for the community. Less activity is a sign of less efficiency and of less good accomplished.

Peterson's analysis has the appeal of simplicity. For him, cities are all alike in that they pursue economic productivity; they differ in that some pursue this goal with greater efficiency than do others. Elsewhere we have tried to show that several facts don't fit Peterson's analysis very well.[16] New Haven was, in reality, much less successful in carrying out redevelopment than has widely been thought. Oakland was a more active participant than has generally been acknowledged. Furthermore, redevelopment is not simply a matter of more or less. The mobilization of effort involves a set of arrangements in which some considerations come to weigh heavily, while others do not. We won't go so far as to say that "the medium is the message," that arrangements are the policy. We do contend that the medium through which development is pursued can shape policy in profound ways. As we reexamine the New Haven case for the appropriateness of the label of "able servant," we should gain some understanding of how politics shapes policy.

THE NEW HAVEN PROGRAM

In Richard Lee's New Haven, redevelopment politics centered on the use of the federal urban-renewal program. Lee invested heavily in the pursuit of federal aid for renewal, and he captured an impressive quantity of project grants. For the decade of the 1960s and into the early 1970s, New Haven's renewal allocation was unmatched in per capita terms. The city had more dollars per capita reserved for renewal projects than had any other city in the nation. Even in terms of total federal renewal aid, New Haven was among the top few communities in the country. In physical impact, that renewal effort was also impressive. Redevelopment programs affected the construction of a freeway connection and the routing of interstate highways; supported the development of a coliseum and a number of parking facilities; aided a new downtown shopping mall, office, and hotel complex; and renewed inner-city neighborhoods with new housing, schools, and community facilities. Those policies also appear to have provided real political returns as well. Richard Lee succeeded in gaining reelection at two-year intervals from 1955 through 1967. Yet the triumph of urban renewal in New Haven was not purely a triumph of Richard Lee, of his development administrator, Edward Logue, or of a host of capable bureaucrats.

Richard Lee came to the mayor's office after the federal approval of New Haven's first redevelopment project, Oak Street. He did succeed in moving that federal commitment toward the point of actual implementation, with the result that he could announce a final grant arrangement with the federal government in 1955. The movement of an early project from the planning to the execution stage was no doubt an accomplishment. Still, it was one that was repeated in hundreds of cities. Both Hartford and Stamford, Connecticut, began the planning work for their first renewal projects at about the same time as New Haven's Oak Street effort, and brought them to the final approval and execution stage at about the same time as New Haven. The implementation of a single renewal project would be a slim justification for a reputation of "able servant." The Oak Street project was by no means unusual in its size or accomplishments. It did provide some expansion room for the Yale Medical School, a great deal of expensive new housing, and a site for offices of the Southern New England Telephone Company. The project also cleared some 750 housing units and displaced a reported 544 families, most of whom were black. Oak Street was neither very substantial nor very unique in its size or its emphasis on "Negro removal." It did represent the first step in what was to be a series of federal commitments and a barrage of public announcements from the mayor's office.

Lee's real record of success at grantsmanship began in the wake of the first actual work in Oak Street. Throughout 1956 and 1957, New Haven received an unusually high level of federal commitments. Two projects in addition to Oak Street were approved by the Board of Aldermen in July 1955, and two more had been approved by September 1956. With relatively rapid federal approval in 1956 and 1957, New Haven's total of renewal aid came to more than $21 million in project reservations.

The quick accumulation of federal commitments represented a very narrow and particular achievement. New Haven's success at grantsmanship came at a time when there were no specific restrictions on the dollar commitments to individual cities. A state-level restriction affected only New York City, which had garnered about $113 million in reservations by late 1957. And the achievement of a large volume of reservations simply meant a large volume of fiscal promises by federal administrators. The actual business of renewal for an individual project could extend over ten, fifteen, or twenty years. The translation of federal commitments and accounting-book entries to local action was far more important and far more difficult. For example, the city's first project, which was begun in 1955, was not finally completed, with all the cleared land sold, until mid 1975. The major downtown project, Church Street, begun in 1957, was not finished until seventeen years later. And the final published report on New Haven at the end of 1975 still showed eight unfinished renewal projects.

Not only did the process of renewal take a long time in New Haven, the movement from planning to execution could be equally delayed. The State Street project, the fourth in New Haven's early efforts, which was approved in 1957, remained just a commitment and a financial promise until 1968. The city began serious work only after substantial federal prodding, and renewal and rehabilitation efforts continue there at this writing (1987).

The image of development success in New Haven, as indexed by federal dollars reserved, was thus very much a "paper" accomplishment during most of the 1950s and well into the 1960s. Richard Lee had succeeded in acquiring federal commitments for future funds and future activity. Implementation, with its difficulties, conflict, and escalating costs, was a very different (and unmeasured) matter.

THE FEDERAL ROLE

The volume of federal commitments to New Haven under Lee might still be considered a measure of something. Clearly, if federal renewal administrators, beseeched by claims from competing cities, expressed a preference for New Haven over some other deserving or energetic community, then we might well ask what was there about New Haven that had succeeded in impressing the federal government. To the extent that Lee's success was a product of Washington procedures, rather than of the quality of planning and leadership in New Haven, we can question the extent to which the mayor's office was extraordinarily able in serving the city.

The approval of New Haven's four major renewal plans came in a brief period, covering only two federal fiscal years. These projects and this period are what constitute the program's accomplishments, which have been variously celebrated by Dahl, by Wolfinger, and by Peterson.[17] During fiscal 1956 and fiscal 1957, the circumstances of the federal urban-renewal program were substantially different from that of earlier years, and perhaps unique over the program's history. The authorizations for the renewal program enjoyed a sharp increase, from $100 million annually between 1950 and 1955 to $200 million a year for 1956 and 1957. With the level of local requests for federal aid remaining roughly constant, an excess of funds was available in Washington. Rather than producing a year-end surplus of uncommitted monies, renewal officials were supporting local efforts and pushing funds out the door. These two fiscal years were thus unusually opportune ones for local officials. The approvals during fiscal 1956 included many of the largest project commitments ever made under the renewal program, with many individual projects being larger than New Haven's. New Haven received $12.6 million in project reservations during this period, but New Haven was certainly dwarfed by Washington, D.C., which acquired some $40 million in reservations.

The distribution of renewal funds came as a result of local applications. Washington could not and did not "tap" particular cities in the absence of formal applications; but it did respond to the pipeline of local requests in a first come, first served manner. Local applications were therefore not evaluated competitively. Whoever met the basic requirements for programs and projects got money. The task for federal administrators was therefore not to judge who was good and who was better. Their job was to commit funds quickly, with the volume of reservations granted rising from $27 million in 1954 and $68 million in 1955 to $212 million in 1956 and almost $240 million in 1957.

The ultimate test of New Haven's quality and of federal generosity is the rate at which the federal government approved local requests for renewal during this period. And the answer is that New Haven won at a contest that contained little competition. During fiscal 1956 the Urban Renewal Administration approved 99.49 percent of all dollar requests from cities. In the following year, still with a substantial surplus of federal funds but with an increasing level of local demand, the approval rate stood at 90.71 percent.

New Haven's success was the result of being on line at the right time and under the right federal fiscal conditions. Had it applied later, as local applications increased markedly in volume, its fiscal accomplishment undoubtedly would have been much less. The approval rate for new applications fell to 63.7 percent in 1958, and then to 36.4 percent in 1959. Federal renewal administrators imposed a moratorium on applications during part of fiscal 1958 and then, in September 1958, finally imposed a scheme tying the level of grant commitments to the size of a city's population.

New Haven did move quickly and at the right time to secure a windfall of federal grant funds. But it did so at a very early stage in the development and planning of renewal projects, with only the most cursory review by the Board of Aldermen. One measure of how tentative and uncertain the city's early plans were is provided by the evolution of its grant estimates. Applications for urban renewal typically provide an estimate of grant needs well before detailed planning is undertaken. This estimate is the amount that is reserved initially, subject to changes in the size, shape, and content of the project as it is planned. New Haven invariably altered its early estimates. The downtown Church Street project grew from $7.9 million to $13.3 million over a twenty-month period, and the Dixwell project added almost $6 million to its original estimate. New Haven effectively altered the scope and direction of its early renewal efforts after the commitment of federal funds. The city thus had effective leverage over federal officials, who were committed to financing projects that spread over more and more years, with an ever-growing financial tab. The original estimate of Church Street's grant requirement, $7.9 million, reached more than $32 million by the time the project was completed. New Haven's success at grantsmanship, as measured by the sums of renewal dollars that it received, was thus a partial result of the delays, changes in plans, and continual escalation in cost of some very tentative and ill-defined plans.

That New Haven managed an impressive accumulation of grant commitments in the 1950s, which expanded over the years, cannot be doubted. But this outcome was largely the product of federal bureaucrats interested in pushing their programs and in gaining their own success stories. As was noted in an analysis of the national renewal program that was made by staff members of the federal Bureau of the Budget in 1960, the grant-reservation system enabled "federal administrators to achieve maximum results by committing a grossly improportionate amount of Federal funds in the more aggressive cities."[18] And as H. Douglas Price argued in his review of *Who Governs?* "The more emphasis one puts on the important and unusual base of federal funds, the less weight need one attach to the Mayor's particular talents."[19]

Getting the grants was easy. The city's ability to move from paper commitments to new buildings and concrete results is the more relevant question. Peterson argues that development projects are hard to get under way, because they have distant benefits and uncertain rewards. The role of the able political leader is to overcome inertia, because once development is under way, the common benefits become evident. Yet for New Haven and for almost every other American city, this scenario inverts the political and administrative realities of renewal undertakings. General plans are easy to promote and endorse. The problems arise in choosing who is to be moved and what will replace them. The interests and requirements of the private real-estate and development market become paramount. And as forces over which local officials have no direct control begin to determine the results of renewal efforts, the promising electoral appeal sometimes turns into unfulfilled promises and disappointing results. Let us now turn to the questions of development implementation and the results in New Haven.

FROM PLANS TO REALITY

The opening years of Lee's mayoralty, from 1953 to 1957, were a time of initiating and "selling' urban renewal. The next stage, the execution stage, was to prove particularly long and difficult. The first real new development came in Oak Street in May 1957. Completion of this project, with all of its land sold off, did not come until 1975. Moreover, the execution phase of renewal was not only lengthy; it was also unpredictable. Even though the Oak Street project was a relatively modest effort, in which much of its land area was devoted to a broad expanse of expressway that came to an abrupt end just south of downtown, Lee's redevelopment team still faced serious problems as they attempted to sell developers on New Haven and to sell the cleared land. The difficulties of renewal in Oak Street were but a foretaste of the problems with Church Street, the downtown-core-area project. Although Church Street was largely cleared of buildings during the late 1950s, redevelopment took ten years.[20]

This slow progress of redevelopment was something of a public-relations problem for the city. Rebuilding always took longer than was planned, thus incurring the loss of tax revenues from vacant and undeveloped land. For some eleven years after federal approval of the State Street project, it remained largely a plan, with some broad outlines for acquisition and redevelopment. The city, which was beset by implementation problems on other projects, simply deferred any serious activity. As a result, on more than one occasion the federal government threatened to terminate the grant in the absence of local progress. The city succeeded in keeping the grant commitment and the federal dollars; but the intent of the plan and the promise of larger downtown renewal remained unmet. An elaborate scheme for new parking garages and companion retail development was stopped by neighborhood protests and the failure of projected highway improvements. At this writing (1987), the city is attempting to revive the State Street area with yet-another plan for renewal, this time emphasizing rehabilitation and the creation of new downtown housing, which again would be largely dependent upon additional federal aid.

By the late 1960s, the character of redevelopment politics was quite different from the executive-centered coalition and the aggressive renewal bureaucracy of the earlier era. Renewal efforts were distinguished by vocal conflict and debate that coincided with an increased level of racial tension and political disarray. The problems that New Haven eventually faced were little different from those of many other cities across the country. Renewal projects that were planned and announced with great fanfare and public enthusiasm often failed to deliver on the promise, as vacant land awaited a private market that placed small value on inner-city land.

ELECTORAL SUCCESS

In arguing the popularity of redevelopment in New Haven, Peterson states: "Mayor Lee was elected time and again at two year intervals for more than two decades after he began his renewal drive."[21] That Lee enjoyed a long period of electoral success, which culminated in an eventual voluntary retirement from the mayor's office, is indisputable. Nevertheless, the relationship between that record and the politics of redevelopment is open to interpretation. Raymond Wolfinger has suggested that Lee's short-term political strategy was based on "executing numerous intrinsically desirable minor projects which were presented as parts of the administration's comprehensive plans for civic betterment."[22] Wolfinger notes: "In September 1957 Lee's earlier accomplishments were still in the forefront of the public consciousness: the most frequently mentioned admirable features of this regime were, in order, new playgrounds, slum clearance, schools (especially the new high schools), and street paving."[23] New Haven's electorate was impressed by a combination of distributable goods, in the form of new streets and playgrounds, and by the start on Oak Street.[24]

The political rewards of Lee's early efforts can be read in the mayoral election returns. Lee entered office after a victory in 1953 with 52.4 percent of the vote. His 1955 percentage jumped to 65.6. By late 1957, with the public still seeing a combination of playgrounds, street paving, and slum clearance, his vote reached 69.4 percent, but at this point, little actual redevelopment was under way. The 1959 vote saw Lee's share drop to 61.8 percent, and in 1961, Lee's percentage of the mayoral vote declined even more, to 53.5. In the 1963 election, Lee's vote rose to 60.3 percent, and he maintained comfortable majorities for his remaining two elections, although he never undertook his much-speculated-about bid for higher office. His political career closed with his not being invited to his successor's inauguration.

Lee's problems with urban renewal did not prevent his regular and continued reelection. He was backed by a substantial party organization, the advantages of incumbency, his reputation as an activist, and significant patronage. Still, the fluctuations in voter support for him were symptomatic of the problems that many mayors faced. Progress proved difficult in New York and San Francisco, as well as New Haven. The short-term results of promised rebuilding were often less than purported, while the costs of local activity mounted and conflict often grew. The promise of vast federal grants was not easy to repeat at regular intervals, and even the appearance of declining electoral fortunes could be enough to dim the luster of an activist mayor. For example, in the wake of Lee's reduced margin of victory in 1961, the *New York Times* noted that his slim margin would hinder any bid to win his party's nomination for the United States Senate the following year.[25] Just as the image of success at renewal had aided him in previous races, the image of diminished voter appeal hurt him in 1961. In New Haven, development politics worked best at the announcement stage.

The apparently costless development programs did in fact have a financial cost to New Haven. Despite the fact that the city was unusually imaginative in meeting the matching requirements for federal renewal grants, the city experienced a tax increase in late 1960, which undoubtedly had some impact on the mayor and on the city. Lee was also assisted by the fact that Connecticut law allowed the city to issue bonds without a vote of the people. But the renewal effort did have a cost to the city, both in terms of the obligations on local taxpayers and of the alternatives foregone. We can properly ask if the development strategy that Lee chose brought the long-term results of economic growth and enhanced productivity that Peterson contends.

The downtown-renewal strategy chosen by Mayor Lee provided New Haven with some boost in its property values and with a new enclosed mall, office buildings, coliseum, and parking garages. But the emphasis on the downtown's role in retail sales was not borne out by subsequent public preferences or by the market. The Chapel Square Mall gradually deteriorated during the 1970s, eventually housing a vast number of vacant shops and a good part of the city's teenagers. The mall eventually required a major rescue effort by the Rouse Company, with a price tag to the city of about $5 million and with loan funds from banks, insurance companies, and Yale University. The city was also ultimately obliged to try to auction off the former Malley's Department Store, which closed in 1982 and which owed more than $1 million in back taxes. Overall, retail sales in the downtown core had plummeted over the years to less than 20 percent of the metropolitan area's retail activity.

The development of a downtown coliseum, which had a price tag of $23 million, was intended to provide a supplement to the retail strategy by drawing evening crowds to central New Haven. One release by the city argued that the city was going to be "the sports capital of southern New England."[26] The coliseum was promoted as being effectively self-supporting, with its 2,400-space garage generating revenues to supplement income from sports events and shows. Indeed, the structure was financed with revenue bonds issued by an independent Coliseum Authority. The reality of the center's operations has fallen far short of these promises. It has operated at a deficit for most of its history, including two of the last four years (1982–86). And that operating deficit excludes the principal and interest payments on the original bonds. The city has been obliged to support the coliseum debt with payments of about $1.5 million per year, passing the failures of the coliseum on to all of New Haven's taxpayers. Today the coliseum is in a state of physical decay: it is literally falling apart, and only a fraction of its 2,400 parking spaces are available for use, and therefore revenue. City officials are currently discussing whether to invest close to $20 million to repair it, or to simply tear it down and begin another renewal strategy.

Despite years of renewal effort aimed at both neighborhoods and downtown, there has been a regular loss of city population, which is down some 20 percent from its 1960 level. And while retail sales in current dollars have increased from $247 million in 1958 to $357 million in 1977, city sales in constant dollars have dropped precipitously. At the same time, the number of retail establishments in the city decreased from 2,300 in 1958 to 1,166 in 1977, and manufacturing jobs fell from 26,000 at the end of the 1950s to 13,800 in 1977.

The ultimate costs of New Haven's renewal efforts by the public sector have fallen on the city's residents and taxpayers. The property-tax rate more than doubled from 1958 to 1970, and the city has seen a massive increase in general-obligation debt, which had risen to more than $104 million by 1984. New Haven's per capita debt figure of $834.28 stands at roughly 2.5 times greater than the average for cities in its population range.

Development politics in New Haven proved to be difficult, time-consuming, expensive, and of mixed results. Former Mayor Lee, describing the city's overall effort in 1981, noted: "We thought we were doing everything right then, but now we realize a lot of it came out wrong."[27] Still, in 1983, one of Lee's successors, Biagio DiLieto, could describe the effort to renovate and salvage the Chapel Square Mall as "without a doubt the most important step we've taken in economic development" in more than twenty years.[28]

THE POLITICS OF ANNOUNCEMENT

It is certainly true that redevelopment, economic promotion, and grantsmanship policies can provide genuine political rewards for astute politicians. However, these rewards are quite fragile; they are subject to the vagaries of external events and to the need to produce concrete results.

Grant commitments and project planning provided Richard Lee with a unique opportunity during the mid 1950s. He was able to take advantage of the announcement of a federal grant in 1955 and of massive additional commitments in 1956 and 1957. Thus, if the "great prize" was federal grant money, Lee had won overwhelmingly. But what he had won at was the politics of *announcement,* rather than the politics of redevelopment. The process of actual redevelopment proved time-consuming, difficult, and politically treacherous. What was most appealing politically was the prospect of a revitalized city, paid for by the federal government. It provided the mayor with an image of accomplishment and forward motion, and this image is what generates popular support. Significantly, before becoming mayor, Lee's occupation was in public relations.

Image, however, is not the entire redevelopment story. Moreover, success at the federal-grants game did not ensure enhanced economic productivity. The Chapel Square Mall was an expensive project, and in recent years it has suffered from a substantial vacancy rate while perhaps sapping strength from the balance of New Haven's retail sector. The department-store situation is little better: one is now closed. Despite the Oak Street Connector, New Haven continues to face serious competition from suburban shopping malls, which are more convenient to motorists. If the redeveloped New Haven achieved economic advancement, it did so in a halting and uncertain manner.

As for Richard Lee, the "able servant" personified, he initiated large projects and played the announcement game with great skill. But as promise gave way to reality, conflict and allocational issues rose. Furthermore, a redeveloping New Haven displaced 20 percent of its population and contributed to social disruption, perhaps to civil disorder, and only uncertainly to economic well-being.[29] Mayor Lee's executive-centered coalition gave New Haven a highly active program of redevelopment. Whether that left New

Haven better off than it would have been under a more modest program is not so clear.

CONCLUSION

Holding office for sixteen years is no little accomplishment. Mayor Lee made himself the center of an entrepreneurial-style, executive-centered coalition. He cultivated the image of an activist, and as a former public-relations officer, he did it with skill. The New Haven urban-renewal program mirrored the political arrangements that Lee put together; it was long on the politics of announcement and image projection, but was short or at least uncertain on concrete accomplishments. The move from planning to execution was not a move characterized by gathering momentum; rather, it was one of increasing conflict and disputed priorities.

Inertia, it turns out, is not the only enemy of an effective policy of development. There are also conflicts among particular interests, and the move into implementation does not dissolve these conflicts in a sea of collective economic well-being. Instead, execution seems to heighten controversy and to compound problems. This is especially the case in cities, such as New Haven, that embarked on large-scale programs of clearance and renewal. The New Haven experience suggests that a high level of redevelopment activity was less a sign of efficient promotion of the collective good and more an invitation to conflict. Whereas Peterson indicates that development is a process in which initial resistance gives way to increasing support as the general benefits of development become apparent, the New Haven experience suggests that resistance grows as plans give way to concrete actions. Furthermore, reality proved to be more complex than the advance publicity had indicated. As a result, it became less certain that the collective good would be served. Particular concerns are always ready to occupy the center of the playing board in the development game. New Haven was no exception.

Not all of Mayor Lee's redevelopment efforts, it should be noted, went into downtown. That Mayor Lee also promoted neighborhood and housing improvements was significant. These efforts were not the product of a community consensus about what was economically beneficial; rather, they were the result of an ongoing effort to generate benefits to offset the costs being borne by various segments of New Haven's "renewing" community. Had New Haven been the beneficiary of an economic boom, Mayor Lee might have been more successful in offsetting losses with such programs. Instead, he appears to have been a mayor whose strongest points were good early timing and plentiful skill in promoting his image as a dynamic executive. While he retired from office undefeated, he did so without having been able to launch a candidacy for state or congressional office. His politics of image and announcement enabled him to build a broad coalition, and with the support of federal dollars, it carried New Haven into an ambitious program of redevelopment. That was politics shaping policy. However, because Lee's policy, in execution, imposed widespread costs that were not fully compensated for by community gains, he was unable to institutionalize his entrepreneurial style of executive-centered politics. That was policy shaping politics, but not in the fashion suggested by Peterson.

NOTES

Portions of this chapter are adapted from an article that we coauthored: "Developmental Politics Reconsidered," *Urban Affairs Quarterly* 22 (June 1987).

1. Theodore J. Lowi, "American Business, Public Policy, Case Studies, and Political Theory," *World Politics* 16 (July 1964): 677–715.
2. Paul E. Peterson, *City Limits* (Chicago: University of Chicago Press, 1981). Subsequent references to this book are noted in parentheses in the text.
3. Robert A. Dahl, *Who Governs?* (New Haven, Conn.: Yale University Press, 1961).
4. Cf. ibid., p. 61.
5. Cf. ibid., pp. 91–92, 310, 318.
6. Paul E. Peterson, *School Politics Chicago Style* (Chicago: University of Chicago Press, 1976), p. 112.
7. Graham T. Allison, *Essence of Decision* (Boston, Mass.: Little, Brown, 1971).
8. Cf. Dahl, *Who Governs?* p. 61.
9. Richard R. Nelson, *The Moon and the Ghetto* (New York: W. W. Norton, 1977), pp. 33–36.
10. In addition to the present volume see, especially, Susan S. Fainstein et al., *Restructuring the City* (New York: Longman, 1983).
11. Richard M. Cyert and James G. March, *A Behavioral Theory of the Firm* (Englewood Cliffs, N.J.: Prentice-Hall, 1963).
12. Allison, *Essence of Decision.*
13. Nelson, *The Moon and the Ghetto,* p. 147.
14. See Robert A. Caro, *The Power Broker* (New York: Alfred A. Knopf, 1974), pp. 962–64.
15. Dennis J. Palumbo and David Nachmias, "The Preconditions for Successful Evaluations," *Policy Sciences* 16 (Sept. 1983): 67–79.
16. Heywood Sanders and Clarence N. Stone, "Developmental Politics Reconsidered," *Urban Affairs Quarterly* 22 (June 1987).
17. Dahl, *Who Governs?*; Raymond E. Wolfinger, *The Politics of Progress* (Englewood Cliffs, N.J.: Prentice-Hall, 1974); and Peterson, *City Limits,* esp. pp. 144–45.
18. U.S., Bureau of the Budget, "Comprehensive Annual Grants for Urban Development," National Archives, record group 51.13, box 1, Dec. 1960, p. 3.
19. H. Douglas Price, review of *Who Governs?* in *Yale Law Journal* 71 (July 1962): 1593.
20. For details of the negotiations and delay see Wolfinger, *Politics of Progress,* pp. 298–356.

21. Peterson, *City Limits,* p. 145. Lee, it should be noted, served a total of sixteen years—not "more than two decades."

22. Wolfinger, *Politics of Progress,* p. 174.

23. Ibid., p. 183.

24. Ibid., p. 202.

25. *New York Times,* 8 Nov. 1961, p. 29.

26. Public Information Office, New Haven Redevelopment Agency, "A History of Urban Renewal in New Haven" (New Haven, Conn., 1968), p. 6.

27. *New York Times,* 11 Jan. 1981, sec. 23, p. 1.

28. Ibid., 9 Feb. 1983.

29. Fainstein et al., *Restructuring the City,* p. 49.

9

The Politics of Development in Middle-sized Cities: Getting from New Haven to Kalamazoo

Heywood T. Sanders

Although conflict is a central theme in this chapter by Heywood Sanders, his account of Kalamazoo, Michigan, could also be placed in Part 1 as an example of regime character in a smaller city. However, this examination of development policy in Kalamazoo is also an appropriate follow-through on the account of the New Haven experience. Some may assume that entrepreneurial-style leadership in the Richard Lee manner is universally admired. Activism is certainly regarded highly. Yet, as Heywood Sanders shows in the case of Kalamazoo, the active promotion of development projects is not always electorally popular. Community sentiment, as registered at the ballot box, may offer disapproval and enforce electorally a caretaker regime.

Homeowners and managers of small businesses are often cautious about public expenditures and the use of public authority to reallocate land use. Their view of what is in the community interest may result in opposition to efforts to intensify downtown development by means of large and expensive projects. It is perhaps significant that Kalamazoo has a much higher percentage of home ownership than does New Haven. But whether the political climate of Kalamazoo is shaped by the proportion of home owners, the absence of a Yale-centered form of "cosmopolitanism," or some combination of factors, it differs from that of New Haven. Kalamazoo's electorate, unlike New Haven's, was not willing to support executive-centered activism. Kalamazoo thus pursued a much more modest and cautious policy, and the city government steered away from any large-scale public involvement in allocating the costs and benefits of redevelopment. The New

Haven/Kalamazoo comparison suggests that development policy indeed reflects a community's politics.

From the early studies of power structure to today's analyses of urban
political economy and the role of the state, the position of business interests
and demands has long fascinated students of the city. The relevance of
business interests and issues was heightened in the 1960s with the combination of public concern about the "urban crisis" and the decline of the
center city and with the development and expansion of a host of federal-aid
programs aimed at physically reshaping the city and altering the character
of the urban economy. Academic analyses of urban development and redevelopment have long been dominated by the singular image of New
Haven, its reputed renewal successes, and the role of a powerful urban mayor.
New Haven has become not only a metaphor for urban pluralism but also
a symbol of the benefits to the larger community from a combination of
massive federal aid and vigorous local political leadership. Some observers
have also seen it repeated in other locales: "New Haven's version of the new
urban coalition sprang up in cities all over the country."[1]

It is thus not surprising that Paul Peterson chose New Haven as the centerpiece of his examination of the politics of development, with its consensus
politics and its benefits for downtown business, laborers, home owners, the
unemployed, and even politicians.[2] Yet just as Peterson's view of the benefits
and consensual politics of development is misleading, so too is his generalization from New Haven. The Connecticut city was a singular case, in everything
from the volume of promised federal aid to the strength of the mayor and the
party organization. The more common stories of local development initiatives
are tales of abortive plans, failed projects, and unimplemented programs.
Cities are obliged to compete with one another. But the terms and content of
that competition vary sharply from place to place. Cities are limited in their
policies, not simply by threat to mobile capital but also by a more substantial
and immediate set of fiscal imperatives. The mass public of voters and property owners has considerable potential to shape the size and quality of governmental activity. And for most middle-sized cities, any governmental
program or initiative that threatens to increase the local property-tax rate or
to benefit one group or geographic area at the expense of another will almost
certainly become an object of public debate and conflict.

THE LESSONS OF KALAMAZOO

The name of Kalamazoo, Michigan, is unlikely to generate nods of recognition among political scientists. Compared with a well-studied locale such

as New Haven, Kalamazoo has had virtually no place in the analysis and understanding of urban politics. But mention Kalamazoo to a group of urban planners, and the recognition is likely to be immediate. Kalamazoo's claim to fame among planners lies in its initiation of the first downtown pedestrian mall in the United States. The car-free mall has become so common today as to be a cliché among the list of solutions to the decline of business in the city center. Yet by planning and implementing the mall in 1959, Kalamazoo stands out as a development innovator on the order of Richard Lee's New Haven. Kalamazoo thus provides a reasonable site for an investigation of the politics and policies of downtown renewal in a medium-sized city, one that is clearly distinguished by a notable development initiative and collaboration between business and government.

With a 1960 population of just over 82,000, Kalamazoo stood at just over half the size of New Haven (at 152,000). Kalamazoo lacked the dominant presence of a major national university, but it was and is the home of Western Michigan University and Kalamazoo College. The city has also possessed, much like New Haven, an economy that blends both major manufacturing enterprises (paper production, Fisher Body, Checker Motors) and the headquarters of a major corporation, Upjohn, with manufacturing, office employment, and a major research center. The result is that Kalamazoo's population was slightly better educated and better paid than New Haven's. Yet other population characteristics show more marked differences, and hold more relevance for an understanding of the role and performance of local government and business.

New Haven, in 1960, was a largely ethnic city with a declining population. Kalamazoo had less than half New Haven's foreign-stock population (19.8 percent, compared to 42.2 percent) and was enjoying vigorous growth in the 1950s. New Haven, in 1960, was overwhelmingly a city of renters. About a third of the city's homes were owner occupied, in contrast to almost two-thirds in Kalamazoo.

These differences in ethnicity, growth, and housing character are central to an understanding of the two cities. With only a modest proportion of home owners, New Haven politics were probably not much affected by the resistance of property-tax payers to city spending and debt. The city's ethnic heritage merged with the existence of partisan local elections to create strong allegiances of party, ties to party organizations, and loyalty to party leadership.

Kalamazoo, like most medium-sized cities, was governed by a small city council, elected at large on a nonpartisan ballot, with much of the detail of city government being left to a city manager. The result was, and is, a very different sort of politics in the two cities, although the one in Kalamazoo might be structurally better suited to the representation of business interests and desires. These structural differences were accentuated by state requirements regarding debt. Connecticut communities were relatively free in their ability to incur debt. Kalamazoo's system required a referendum on general-obligation-bond issues, supported by a tradition of seeking direct popular approval for governmental undertakings. New Haven's Richard Lee faced the need for regular reelection but no requirement that each of his development initiatives and their financing be subject to a direct public vote. Kalamazoo's governmental arrangements assured that the city's population of taxpayers would have a substantial role on particular issues and that politics would regularly revolve around issues of the *cost* of local government.

The dominant position of fiscal concerns in Kalamazoo during the 1960s and 1970s was not a new or unexpected phenomenon. In the face of the social dislocations of the Great Depression, the city reduced public spending rather than embracing welfare or development programs. A taxpayer's ticket that demanded a reduction in city spending was elected in 1931, and the city gradually reduced its property-tax rate. By 1937, Kalamazoo could boast of being a "debt free" city—the only city of 50,000 or more in the nation with no local government debt.[3] The city's frugal policies of the 1930s suggest both the importance of debt and finances in local political debate and the persistent nature of public desires. While the city did issue bonds during the late 1940s and early 1950s, it did so only after referenda and for purposes such as sewage disposal, which involved broad and widespread community benefit.

"MALL CITY USA"

Kalamazoo began to grapple with the same kinds of urban problems as other communities in the 1950s. Public involvement with federally aided urban renewal began in 1956 with the initiation of planning or the Lincoln urban-renewal project. The effort was originally designed to deal with slum problems in an older neighborhood and to provide expansion room for local industry. There was a great deal of opposition to the project, however, despite the promise of increased tax revenues. Local residents objected to being forced from their homes. Others objected to the plan on the grounds of its cost to the city and the threat of public-housing construction. As a result, the city council scaled the project down in size, and the federal grant was reduced from $1.6 million to about $325,000. The protests effectively eliminated all clearance and displacement. The 418 residences in the area were affected only by a modest effort at rehabilitation.[4]

Kalamazoo's first experience with urban renewal was tentative and limited. The city avoided both the major public costs and the political repercussions of substantial clearance and relocation. And the Lincoln project, modest as it was, was to be the city's only successful effort at federally aided renewal. In comparison with New Haven's commitment of more than $790 per person in federal renewal aid by 1966 and a national average of $53.51, Kalamazoo's per capita renewal funding came to only $3.66.

At about the time that Kalamazoo was developing and implementing its sole urban-renewal project, it was beginning to plan for the future of the downtown core. The city's role developed from an effort by downtown businessmen to deal with the conventional problems of traffic circulation and parking. A small group of business leaders—the president of the city's largest bank, the president of a major savings-and-loan company, and the owner of the largest downtown department store—formed a downtown planning committee. The mayor urged the group to hire a different planning consultant, with a broader mandate for study, in an effort to recapture the economic fortunes and image of the central business district.[5]

Kalamazoo acquired the services of Victor Gruen, a Vienna-born architect and planner who had already acquired a substantial reputation as a designer of shopping malls, including the first enclosed mall in the United States. Gruen's proposal, produced in 1958, was both bold and expensive. It called for three phases of public action. The first efforts were to include a loop street system, encircling the downtown core; a series of pedestrian malls on existing city streets; and a number of new parking lots and garages. The second phase was to provide for the expansion of the perimeter roadway and an extension of the mall system, followed by a final program of new civic building and the renovation of existing stores and offices. The price tag for this ambitious plan was estimated at between $10 and $12 million for all three phases, involving a combination of assessments on downtown property, federal grants, and direct city expenditures. Despite a substantial reliance on the support and financial involvement of downtown owners, the full plan required major public action by the city and the use of federal urban-renewal aid.

The rhetoric of the Gruen plan neatly defined this investment in a small area of the city as a requisite for community betterment. The plan itself noted that it was "built on a philosophy and approach that will bring not only long range, but immediate benefits to the entire region . . . [and] establishes a concept which will fuse community interest into a force to assure and guide the healthy future growth of Kalamazoo." The appendix of the plan spelled out its implications in more specific fiscal terms: "In effect, public funds will help to create the environment and induce the climate in which private investment will thrive and grow, discovering increased opportunities for new and profitable enterprises. . . . Through this chain reaction, vigorous competition and higher property values will lead to an increased tax base which can be used to support vital public improvements."[6] The plan was thus presented in the broadest possible terms, as being vital to the central business district, the city, and the region and as being an economically reasonable if not profitable proposition for the city's tax base. This rhetoric not only presaged more contemporary calls for economic development; it also carried the refrain of community-wide need and betterment that had supported previous bond referenda for public projects. Yet despite the call for public action for community good, the notion of a costly governmental action was to prove a major stumbling block.

The reception of the Gruen plan by the business community was neither immediate nor unanimous. The mayor pressed for the plan as the only workable alternative to downtown deterioration, despite the reluctance of many smaller owners and firms. According to one account, "The formal leaders [the mayor and at least one councilman] were actual leaders supplying key actions in introducing, coordinating, and promoting the development plan."[7] Perhaps more important to public acceptance of the plan was the acquiescence of a single family, one that controlled about 70 percent of all downtown property. Although the combination of mayoral salesmanship and economic dominance ensured public action, they did not ensure the full implementation of Gruen's plan.

Kalamazoo eventually constructed a two-block pedestrian mall along Burdick Street in 1959 at a total cost of $58,315. Most of the money went to widening and improving sidewalks and to adding new lights and landscaping. The majority of the cost was assumed by property owners, although the city contributed about $28,000, and the construction was directed by the Parks and Recreation Department. By early 1959, Kalamazoo had pioneered a new form of downtown improvement. It had done so at minimal public cost, with almost no disruption to downtown business or to access, and with no displacement or relocation at all. The contrast to New Haven is obvious. Where Richard Lee secured vast sums of federal assistance for downtown renewal and then implemented a plan requiring substantial displacement and dislocation in the core area, Kalamazoo managed its version of revival on a fiscal shoestring, with no deleterious impact on downtown firms.

Kalamazoo's new image as "Mall City USA" involved only the most limited and least expensive form of the Gruen plan. Observing that the mall scheme was the final element of the larger plan, Gruen himself noted: "The citizens of Kalamazoo felt that this most dramatic feature should come first, and proceeded accordingly."[8] The pedestrian mall was implemented as the easiest and most all-benefiting element of a complex and expensive plan. The other elements, from a new set of streets to a complex of public parking lots, were deferred to the indefinite future. One relatively speedy addition was in the spirit and form of its predecessor. Another block of mall improvements, extending the pedestrian zone, was added in 1960 at a cost of $24,000.

The accomplishment of the three-block Burdick Mall was the first step in the larger downtown program. The full set of proposals, including the loop road (now called Central Parkway) and an urban-renewal project, was studied further by the city and its planning commission in the early 1960s. A federally financed urban-renewal feasibility study, undertaken during 1962 and 1963, indicated the merit of the original Gruen plan, and the city commission developed a broad Community Improvement Program in the summer of 1963 for public review. Carrying a local price tag of about $6 million, the improvement program was designed to join a range of local street improvements with the plan for a downtown loop road. It appeared that the commission members were intent on selling downtown improvements to the voting public as part of a larger, community-wide public-investment plan. Such a broadly distributive plan was probably a political necessity, because the commission came under fire both for the total cost of the plan and for the displacement that was likely to result from urban renewal. Rather than pressing ahead, the commission chose to allow a public advisory referendum on the bond issue required for the improvement program. In the words of the *Kalamazoo Gazette,*

> Tuesday's election will be of an advisory nature. The outcome will tell the City Commission whether it has public support of a program that includes a central parkway and urban renewal projects in the central business district, and major street construction throughout the city. The City Commission has promised to abide by the results of the election Tuesday. . . . The cost of the program to the owner of the average home has been estimated at $5.40 per year, or 45 cents a month.[9]

The referendum on the improvement issue was a necessary element in achieving the plan; it was also the first opportunity for a direct public say in renewal and downtown-investment policy. The achievement of the mall had been arranged at minimal public cost and without a public vote, through the support of the mayor and something of a consensus among major downtown business interests. The $6-million Community Improvement Program was a very different sort of product. The improvement plan was endorsed by a broad collection of local organizations from the Downtown Kalamazoo Association to the local chapter of the NAACP and the Kalamazoo Board of Realtors. There was also opposition, much of which was based on the issues of increased city taxes and excessive involvement of the public sector. One letter writer complained of the "creeping paralysis of socialism."[10] These public opponents were joined by one member of the seven-member city commission, who vocally dissented and railed against debt and higher taxes.

Popular concern over the tax and "socialism" issues proved decisive. The referendum went down to defeat by a vote of roughly 59 percent to 41 percent; it carried only thirteen of the city's forty-three precincts. The city commission had pledged to abide by the public's decision, and thus the ring-road and urban-renewal plans were effectively killed. Without public support for a bond issue, Kalamazoo had no means of financing either the street improvements that were called for under the original plan or a bold urban-renewal effort. The public's reaction is particularly relevant, because it came in the face of substantial formal agreement on the plan and a near-unanimity on the part of elected officials. The informal slate-making organization that had long dominated Kalamazoo's electoral politics should have been able to ensure the votes, as it had on previous capital-improvement issues. Yet a commitment on the part of commissioners and elites proved insufficient to command the support of the city's electorate on an issue that involved both a public threat and a direct cost.

The failure of the Community Improvement Program did not mark the end of formal efforts at downtown revitalization. Kalamazoo continued to seek federal urban-renewal aid, and it received approval for a $3.7-million grant in October 1964.

The new renewal effort contained the central elements of the 1958 downtown plan—a ring road around the downtown core; the clearance of land for apartments, light industry, and a local hospital; an extension of the three-block pedestrian mall; and expansion of the arts-and-cultural center bordering the business district. The new renewal plan was formally presented to the city commission in early 1967, after considerable work had been done by consultants and city staff. The commission quickly approved it by a formal vote of 6 to 0 on 7 February 1967. Despite the failure of the 1963 referendum and some ten years after the early planning for Kalamazoo's new downtown, a renewal effort and full implementation of the plan appeared to be at hand. It was not to be, however. One member of the city commission, who was absent when the vote was taken in February, mounted an attempt to force another referendum, first through a petition drive and then with a court suit. The result was that urban renewal in Kalamazoo was placed on hold again, as the courts attempted to sort out the need for a public vote and the responsibilities of the commission itself.

The first court decision, rendered in April 1967, declared that the commission's vote of the previous February was void and upheld the right to petition for a public referendum. The city appealed the decision to a higher court, but the fate of Kalamazoo's renewal program continued to depend on the local electorate. The November 1967 commission elections were based almost solely on the urban-renewal issue. And the prorenewal commission was roundly defeated. The commission member who had led the court fight and the petition drive received the largest number of votes, which automatically made him the mayor, while only two prorenewal incumbents remained on the seven-member commission. An editorial in the *Kalamazoo Gazette* noted: "It is doubtful that any further action in the field of urban renewal will be proposed by the new commission without considerable deliberation."[11]

The attempt to implement the Central Parkway South urban-renewal project in Kalamazoo ended with the 1967 election. The project was formally terminated in July 1968, and its federal grant was canceled. The twenty-year history of renewal and redevelopment planning in Kalamazoo was thus represented by the modest Lincoln rehabilitation project and by a collection of failed attempts at more substantial rebuilding in the downtown area.

The failure of urban renewal in Kalamazoo did not imply a failure of further attempts to aid the core area through public and private action. A major addition to the mall plan came in the mid 1970s with the construction of a multiple-use center on a full block bordering the pedestrian mall. The Kalamazoo Center project was a $16-million effort that combined a new hotel, retail facilities, restaurants, and a city-owned convention center. This project, like those that preceded it, was financed largely by the private sector with private funds. The city's contribution of public funds was limited to $600,000 from federal revenue sharing and another $3 million in contributions by private business.[12]

The Kalamazoo Center project was intended to attract major conventions to downtown Kalamazoo and to aid in altering the economic function of the core. The core area had been steadily losing retail establishments and employment to outlying shopping malls, and older hotels were gradually disappearing. Developed by the initiative of a new executive of the Chamber of Commerce, the Kalamazoo Center project was seen as a new source of downtown vitality and activity. Coupled with a one-block extension of the pedestrian mall in 1973, the center was one part of a continuing reaction to downtown decay.

Construction of Kalamazoo Center did not signal an end to downtown renewal efforts. City-planning professionals and business leaders continued to work on measures intended to support the core's retail position and its role as an office and governmental center. By the late 1970s the city had developed an elaborate plan for railroad consolidation, which was intended to alter the pattern of rail traffic, to provide both additional crossings of the railroad and river barriers at the edge of the downtown area, and to free up new land for business development and expansion. The rail-consolidation plan neatly tied broad popular concern with traffic delays and safety to larger objectives of downtown access and economic development. Despite the record of mixed public reaction to multi-million-dollar capital investments, the electorate approved the $7.5-million proposal at the polls in 1979. Yet rail consolidation, like other downtown efforts before it, was to face an uncertain future. The city sought additional federal, state, and private funds for the project as it continued detailed planning into the 1980s. But public concern began to develop over both the eventual costs of the project and the delays in implementing it. A group of antitax organizations had an amendment to the city charter placed on the ballot in November 1984, requiring that voter-approved bonds be sold within five years after approval. The charter revision was clearly aimed at stopping the rail-consolidation project and at restricting the city's ability to implement future capital projects. And it succeeded. The city was forced to place the rail-consolidation plan before the voters again, on 23 April 1985. And it was defeated.

THE LESSONS OF KALAMAZOO

Kalamazoo is at once typical and unusual as a middle-sized American city. Its 1960 population of 82,000 made it somewhat smaller than New Haven, Atlanta, and some of the other major sites of community-power studies. But it was not atypical of a range of communities that were neither national economic centers nor monopolized factory towns. How can we summarize Kalamazoo's experiences in the areas of urban renewal, redevelopment, and the politics of development from the early 1950s to the early 1970s?

First, Kalamazoo attempted to grapple with the economic situation of its downtown area with a modest effort to implement a system of one-way streets. That effort proved conflictual but was eventually successful. An early effort at slum clearance and redevelopment became embroiled in conflict and opposition from those faced with displacement. The plan was reduced in size and scope until all that remained was a limited effort at neighborhood rehabilitation, which had modest results and a tiny price tag. A bold effort at downtown revitalization and improvement, coupled with substantial public investment, was embodied in a plan prepared by architect/planner Victor Gruen. The Gruen plan did result in the nation's first downtown pedestrian mall. Yet that mall was only a very small piece of the elaborate plan, most of which was either deferred or ignored. An attempt to fulfill the larger objectives of the Gruen plan and downtown renewal by using federal urban-renewal aid began in the early 1960s. That effort also proved abortive: the plan was eventually blocked by negative votes on renewal and public spending. Kalamazoo retained its mall and finally capped it with the construction of Kalamazoo Center—a downtown civic center, hotel, and commercial complex that was largely funded and built by the private sector in 1975.

Kalamazoo succeeded admirably and, indeed, was a national innovator in one area of downtown revitalization. Yet it also failed at a broader downtown renewal effort tied to federal aid and substantial local public investment. Its successes were largely private ones—privately initiated and privately financed. Its failures were largely public ones, involving a larger role for city government or the application of federal programs to local conditions.

The coincidence of private success and public failure is precisely what makes the case of Kalamazoo so relevant to an analysis of the politics of economic development and redevelopment in American cities. The privatization of the city and the dominance of local business interests in its affairs tend together to create a situation that can stymie public action in the face of some private resistance or cost. It is important to note that only parts of Victor Gruen's ambitious plan for Kalamazoo were implemented. Those parts possessed the least apparent cost, the greatest immediate benefit, and the smallest role for the city government. Kalamazoo's business community and its downtown merchants had favored and supported plans for new arterial routes centered on the downtown and plans for transportation improvements that would have opened the city up for its outlying market area. But when it came to the imposition of a one-way-street system that would create differential costs and benefits, there was substantial opposition. So it was with the Gruen proposals. The simple pedestrian mall, with its highly specific costs and benefits, was acceptable because it imposed no burdens on the larger community of business firms. Any more elaborate or costly plan would have benefited some at the expense of others. And the total business community of Kalamazoo could not move forward in the face of such an internal split.

Public action, particularly in the renewal area, was repeatedly stymied by the threat and reality of public review. The need for a referendum in 1963, as well as the threat of one in 1967, effectively limited the ability of elected officials to develop and implement development plans. The local electorate's direct involvement in decisions about renewal was a serious impediment to public action. The circumstances of a referendum that was strictly limited to development plans presented a particular difficulty. Unlike general city elections, which involve broad issues of incumbent performance and a range of personalities and issues, the referendum reflected popular feeling only about the specific issue—namely, urban renewal. And that issue involved questions about the role of the federal government in local affairs, increased taxation and city debt, and the possible effects of displacement and relocation. Each of these issues played a part in the failure of public urban renewal and development in Kalamazoo, although local observers place the blame primarily on the threat of federal intervention and "creeping socialism." Kalamazoo had voted, both in 1961 and in 1963, not to create a city housing commission with the power to construct public housing. The city's persistently conservative electorate apparently had little patience for or interest in a vigorous local government and federal aid. And the possibility of placing these issues directly before the city's electorate proved crucial in quashing public action.

The issue of federal intervention was joined by the issue of taxation and debt. The urban-renewal program required a substantial local financial contribution either in cash or in supporting public works and capital improvements. Either alternative required city funds and *some* increase in taxes. Some cities, such as New Haven, were able to side-step a public vote on bond issues or taxes because of generous state laws or by means of self-financing improvements such as parking lots. But for most other cities, urban renewal was far from free. The issue of increased taxes was always a potent one, particularly where it was linked to benefits that would accrue largely to the downtown business community or major property owners. All of these issues were raised in Kalamazoo during the 1960s, and they served to make urban renewal, not some consensual program of community improvement, but a costly and threatening effort to aid downtown at the expense of the city's home owners.

Kalamazoo's business community wanted a local government that could provide some modest assistance to local growth and development, particularly in the form of infrastructure provision and enhancement. What it did *not* want was a city government that was large in size and scope and costly to local property owners and taxpayers. In Kalamazoo, as in many other cities, the principal items on the political agenda of local business were low taxes and limited government, even in the face of widespread need and community distress. While some downtown interests were vigorous supporters of the mall and its successor projects, downtown was but one very specialized part of a community that had broader interests and demands.

Kalamazoo presents a classic case of a city with an open political system and a great deal of "slack" in political resources. A dissident member of the city commission was able to organize petition campaigns that forced the holding of referenda on the city housing commission and on urban renewal; the antitax group forced through a charter revision in 1984. Despite the backing of the manager, the mayor, the majority of the city commission, and the business community, it was impossible to deliver on the promises of Kalamazoo's pioneering downtown plan. Leadership on the part of elected officials was not lacking, nor was the ability to plan and initiate public programs. Kalamazoo simply had a system that was open and responsive to broad public preferences and demands.

While Kalamazoo failed in its larger development efforts, it did succeed in the narrow business of mall building. And the differences between the success of the mall effort and the failure of urban renewal are instructive. The Burdick Mall provided a direct benefit to the largest and most important downtown merchants. It ran past the front doors of both the new J. C. Penney's department store, which was built in 1955, and the locally owned Gilmore Brothers department store. It included the three prime blocks of downtown retail activity. The mall promised great things for little money, but perhaps more importantly, it promised no bad or unpleasant things for the downtown area. In part because substantial property ownership rested in the hands of one extended family group, a limited downtown project that entailed limited public cost could be implemented. The mall project represented a form of public-private action in which the private was clearly dominant. That very private dominance required a project that all segments of the business community could endorse and ultimately live with. The prospect of urban renewal, with its obvious costs and control by the public sector, was a source of overt conflict.

Kalamazoo's pioneering effort at mall building became something of a national model. One study of downtown pedestrian improvements counted some sixty-seven cities that had mall projects as of 1977. Other communities emulated Kalamazoo's efforts, but not because the pedestrian mall was a sure solution for downtown ills. Indeed, many of the downtown pedestrian ways appeared to spur retail abandonment, and activity declined in some core areas. The mall model succeeded so widely because it offered to both the business community and the local electorate the promise of something—improved visibility and greater retail sales—for nearly nothing. The virtue of mall building was not that it could do much but that it could be developed and implemented at little public cost with only the most marginal political conflict. While some communities coupled mall development with large-scale renewal and rebuilding of the core area, most often the two- or three-block-long pedestrian mall, with an occasional planter or kiosk, stood as a lone monument to public concern for the economic place of the downtown center. Malls in such places as Decatur and Champaign, Illinois; Riverside, California; and Louisville, Kentucky, were not undertaken as rational responses to the need to compete with other communities or as efforts to advantage the city as a whole. They were built because they could be built in environments where downtown problems had little major claim on public resources, where business interests were often divided among themselves on issues of public responsibility and the costs of government, and where majority support for limited government could be readily enforced through the ballot box. Their purposes were as much symbolic as substantive, the downtown business' equivalent of the elected officials' politics of announcement.[13]

There are other more contemporary solutions to central-city economic ills that, like Kalamazoo's mall, appear repeatedly, endlessly in city after city. Domed stadiums, civic arenas, and convention centers appear regularly as public solutions to development needs at modest cost. With the aid of special purpose authorities, revenue financing, or taxes that can be shifted to conventioneers and out-of-town tourists, they appear to offer the virtues of enhanced economic activity without disturbing the local property-tax rate or fiscal balance. The expansion of Chicago's massive McCormick Place can be paid for with state taxes on hotels and horse racing and can be managed by an independent public authority. A new stadium in Indianapolis is paid for with foundation funds and private contributions. Each of these solutions depends upon either private financing or some public arrangement outside the realm of normal city politics. They testify to the fact that business interests are often able to dominate local development agendas. But they also suggest that in sustaining business-oriented development policies, *money* may be a more important element than political control or power. Businesses in Kalamazoo and elsewhere can define the possible in downtown revival or facility building because they foot most of the bill.

CONCLUDING FROM KALAMAZOO

Kalamazoo is but one locality in a much-larger universe of American cities. It achieved national recognition for an early and innovative approach to central-business-district revival. Yet it has also seen a host of public-development failures. Its abortive urban-renewal efforts appear in sharp contrast to New Haven's record of grantsmanship successes. Still, Kalamazoo is by no means alone. From 1950 to 1970 more than 520 planned urban-renewal projects were terminated by local governments, often because of a lack of public support or a failure of city financing. And a long stream of private projects and public initiatives for downtown, from new hotel complexes to people movers and cultural centers, exist only in the memories of the politics of announcement and the unfulfilled promise of action.

For Kalamazoo the politics of fiscal concern dominated the politics of development. Citizen opposition to debt and tax increases aborted a host of public actions. More recently, the city commission has been embroiled in an ongoing conflict over the granting of tax exemptions, made possible under state law. Commissioners debate the merits of job creation and expansion against the inequity of favored treatment and the larger taxes on the community, and they argue the need to compete with other governments versus "transferring the burden to the residents."[14] The 1985 city elections featured advertisements by Edward Annen, Jr., the successful mayoral candidate, who noted: "The last time your tax rate *DROPPED* was in 1981, Mayor Annen's last year on the City Commission!"[15]

The primacy of fiscal concerns is not a new element in urban politics, nor is it unique to the Michigan community. Describing the politics and finances of Houston, Texas, in 1960, Kenneth Gray noted the reluctance of the city to tax its residents. He quotes one top official as having said, "This city doesn't want to pay more taxes, period!" and concludes: "The general citizenry of Houston is no less vigorous than businessmen and big property owners in resisting taxes."[16] These totems of fiscal concern and restraint have regularly characterized urban regimes at various periods. A cycle of public fiscal expansion and retreat has been repeated at regular intervals in New

York City, and a number of other cities, including New Haven, have seen frugal, low-taxation regimes dominate for substantial periods of time. The difference that is particularly salient for Kalamazoo is the persistence of minimalist, or "caretaker," regimes over time. The structural and historical constraints on city spending and debt have not been effectively overturned or replaced by more-aggressive spending-oriented coalitions. The character of the city's home-owning population and the ethos of broad, community-wide interest have limited the ability of elected officials to alter the content of city functions and the size of the public fisc, even when they proposed new programs. And the reliance on nonpartisan elections and referendum review no doubt help to render elected officials guardians of civic virtue, rather than politically ambitious policy innovators.

The constraints on Kalamazoo come from within rather than from without. The city has long enjoyed an excellent credit rating and the fiscal ability to issue a large volume of debt. Indeed, as of mid 1985, Kalamazoo's debt limit stood at more than nine times its outstanding general-obligation debt. Kalamazoo could thus afford to issue new debt, and it could afford to tax itself more heavily. The city has resolutely avoided adopting a local income tax, for example, despite the fact that state law allows it to do so and that many comparable communities do tax local income. The private-capital markets were not a problem for Kalamazoo, and a few major firms did not act to quash all efforts at increased taxation and spending. The city was regularly pressed to do more, and its array of economic-development plans testifies to a host of available initiatives. Kalamazoo's citizens consistently *chose* not to expand development activities and policies, and they enforced that choice through the polls.

Kalamazoo's development history is one neither of total success nor of unmitigated failure. The city developed and implemented some public/private partnerships of both early and recent vintage, with the private sector assuming the bulk of the financial burden. Today, its overall economy is in reasonable condition. Yet its history is one of the repeated failure of governmental initiatives and of limits on business and economic leadership. Unlike the classic "elitist" community in which the business and economic elite easily manages its desires, Kalamazoo's economic powers have gotten far less than their full menu of development projects and public support. They have done so despite a substantial commonality of economic and political leadership. Indeed, the city's mayor in 1960 and 1961 was a member of the local family that owned the major downtown department store; he himself was the owner of a number of downtown properties. The coincidence of economic and civic leadership did not suffice to fulfill Kalamazoo's downtown development plans. Unlike the tales of mayoral leadership in pluralist New Haven, the reality in Kalamazoo has been a history of initiatives blocked, failed policy entrepreneurship, and a public reaction against the cost of specific public policies. Those failures came despite the attempt to link downtown revival and capital improvements to the symbols of community economic growth and job gain, as well as to a persistent rhetoric of city-wide necessity and advantage. The case of Kalamazoo simply fails to fit many of our models of development activity, from Paul Peterson's conflict-free requisite for economic competition to John Mollenkopf's notions of growth politics and policy entrepreneurship, as well as alternative images of the dominance of local growth coalitions.[17]

Renewal and development policies regularly led to overt political conflict in Kalamazoo because of the role of fiscal concerns and the central place of taxation questions. The mass of voters has been able to define the content both of fiscal policy and of political coalitions in the city. The results are a local politics that consistently revolves around issues of taxation and government cost and a government that is restricted in both revenues and functions. Kalamazoo's city regimes can properly be labeled "caretaker," not because development initiatives never arise, but because they lack a base of popular support. City government necessarily pursues traditional urban services and those few additional functions that are costless or nearly so. Even so common a governmental activity as a local bus system was crippled in Kalamazoo in 1985 with the referendum defeat of a tax increase, yet another vivid demonstration of public control and the preeminent position of fiscal concerns.

NOTES

1. Dennis R. Judd, *The Politics of American Cities: Private Power and Public Policy,* 2d ed. (Boston, Mass.: Little, Brown, 1984), p. 273.

2. Paul E. Peterson, *City Limits* (Chicago: University of Chicago Press, 1981), p. 147.

3. Willis F. Dunbar, *Kalamazoo and How It Grew* (Kalamazoo: Western Michigan University, 1959), pp. 187–88.

4. Ibid., p. 214.

5. For the history of the mall plan see Dunbar, *Kalamazoo;* Roberto Brambilla and Gianni Longo, *Banning the Car Downtown* (Washington, D.C.: U.S. Department of Housing and Urban Development, 1976); and Oliver P. Williams and Charles R. Adrian, *Four Cities* (Philadelphia: University of Pennsylvania Press, 1963).

6. Victor Gruen Associates, *Kalamazoo 1980* (Detroit: n.p., 1958), p. 35 and app.

7. Williams and Adrian, *Four Cities,* pp. 131–32.

8. Victor Gruen, *The Heart of Our Cities* (New York: Simon & Schuster, 1964), p. 331.

9. "CIP Goes before Voters Tuesday," *Kalamazoo Gazette,* 11 Aug. 1963.

10. "Debate Flares over Improvement Program," *Kalamazoo Gazette,* 30 July 1963.

11. Editorial "Charter Amendment Fails," *Kalamazoo Gazette,* 8 Nov. 1967.

12. On the development of Kalamazoo Center see Larry B. Massie and Peter J. Schmitt, *Kalamazoo: The Place behind the Products* (Woodland Hills, Calif.: Windsor Publications, 1981), pp. 202–4; and Louis G. Redstone, *The New Downtowns* (New York: McGraw-Hill, 1976), pp. 6–11.

13. Roberto Brambilla, Gianni Longo, and Virginia Dzurinko, *American Urban Malls* (Washington, D.C.: U.S. Department of Housing and Urban Development, 1976).

14. "Tax Breaks in City Slated for Case-by-Case Handling," *Kalamazoo Gazette*, 26 Nov. 1985.

15. Advertisement, *Kalamazoo Gazette*, 4 Nov. 1985.

16. Kenneth E. Gray, "A Report on the Politics of Houston" (Cambridge, Mass.: Joint Center for Urban Studies of MIT and Harvard University, 1960), pp. vi–30, 36.

17. John H. Mollenkopf, *The Contested City* (Princeton, N.J.: Princeton University Press, 1983).

10

A Critique of Neo-Progressivism in Theorizing about Local Development Policy: A Case from Atlanta

Adolph Reed, Jr.

In this chapter, Adolph Reed looks at the challenge of coalition-building that Atlanta's first black mayor, Maynard Jackson, encountered. In a black-majority city, Jackson needed to assume a policy stance that was responsive to this core constituency. Economic reality—in particular private control of investment—dictated, however, that Jackson also reach an accommodation with Atlanta's white business elite. Thus the election of a black mayor dramatizes the tension inherent in the political economy of American cities. Atlanta was no exception. Reed traces the working out of an accommodation—Jackson's embracing of the symbolically potent but substantively empty position of a south-side location for a new airport, the devising of a program to require that minority enterprises receive a share of the city's contracts, and the reluctant and modified acceptance of this program by white business interests. As an accommodation was worked out, Reed argues, the notion of a unitary interest proved itself to be more a matter of rhetoric than of reality.

Significantly, conflict over Atlanta's airport exposes the weakness of classifying policies as developmental, allocational, and redistributive. Not only did the building of the new Atlanta airport involve elements of all three, but much of the controversy surrounding this project centered on whether the consequences of various actions would fall into one category or another. The participants did not agree on whether a second airport was a development need, nor did they agree on whether minority-business requirements were allocational or redistributive. Overall, the experience of Maynard Jackson shows how complex the relationship is between political power based on electoral strength and economic power based on the private control of investment activity.

Local development policy typically is "promulgated through highly centralized decision-making processes involving prestigious businessmen and professionals," as Paul Peterson observes. "Conflict within the city," he notes further, "tends to be minimal, decision-making processes tend to be closed until the project is about to be consummated, local support is broad and continuous, and, if any group objects, that group is unlikely to gain much support."[1] That those processes are "closed" and "highly centralized" is not particularly inconsistent with democratic interests, in Peterson's view, because development—that is, any activity that enhances the municipality's revenue potential—is an interest of the city as a whole. In fact, it is fortunate that "local politics weakens the capacity for mass pressures, because by "keeping mass involvement at the local level to a minimum, serious pressures for policies contrary to the economic interests of cities are avoided."[2] Once popular intervention is circumvented, policy can be made through "informal channels" in which "the political resources that count are technical expertise, the power of persuasion, and the capacity to reason soundly."[3] Nor should we fret that this informalization and centralization of development policy either fuels inequitable concentrations of privilege or rationalizes the self-interested agendas of local power structures; for Peterson cautions:

> When developmental policies are considered, attempts to ascertain the power of one or another individual or group are probably pointless, if not misleading. In this policy arena the city as a whole has an interest that needs to be protected and enhanced. Policies of benefit to the city contribute to the prosperity of all residents. Downtown business benefits, but so do laborers desiring higher wages, homeowners hoping house values will rise, the unemployed seeking new jobs, and politicians aiming for reelection. Those who seem to have "power" over developmental policies are those who do the most to secure these benefits for all members of the city.[4]

Therefore, the closed character of development-policy processes, even though its most proximate underpinnings are the structural and systemic factors that screen out avenues for popular participation, is an expression, he suggests, of the consensual basis on which development policy rests.[5] Indeed, "the frequency with which responsibility for developmental policy is granted to groups and entities outside the main-stream of local politics" itself illustrates the existence of a "consensual politics of development";[6] because development is a collective interest, its actualization via policy and program need not be subjected to public scrutiny and debate and is a matter for technical concern only.

Yet, despite the fact that all the pieces fit neatly together, the picture rings somehow incomplete if not plainly false. To those students and citizens who have repeatedly seen development policy impose suffering and hardship on certain groups in the polity, notions of a consensual or collective city interest seem to be abstractions to a vantage point from which those very real victims blend into the background. Most often when he trumpets the unitary interest in development, Peterson himself seems not to notice them, although his tendency to choose the agentless passive voice at critical junctures in his account—for example, adverse popular pressures "are *avoided*"; responsibility "*is granted* to groups and entities outside the mainstream of local politics'—raises suspicions. However, in citing the virtues of minimizing popular involvement, he does acknowledge, almost in passing, that "it is the interests of the disadvantaged which consistently come into conflict with economically productive policies."[7] By denying the disadvantaged the opportunity to intervene, the local political system permits the articulation of development policy that realizes the interest of the city "as a whole."

When viewed through the lens of the historian of ideologies, Peterson's attempt to define a "city interest" exhibits a quaint quality. It harks back to an earlier period when Progressivist political science affirmed, perhaps more ingenuously than now, the prosperous burgher's self-congratulation by equating preservation and the expansion of his prosperity and cultural preferences with the public interest; so also does Peterson's view that endorses systematically induced limitations on popular participation because they provide space for disinterested, public-regarding elites to make rational development policy in the interest of the whole. That view rings with echoes of the various "democratic distemper" theories and similar hoary rationalizations of entrenched privilege. Other students of urban politics have disputed Peterson's contention that development policy is free—even in principle—from the self-interested, conflictual processes that he would consign to the "allocational" realm. His analytical distinction of developmental and allocational policy processes, that is, collapses as it slouches toward the empirical world.[8]

A market-rationality model of local development activity breaks down in part because even in the most objectivistic view imaginable, it is unlikely that there will always be only one clear direction through which to realize the "city interest." When more than one course contends, choices must be made, and the basis for choice inevitably includes not only calculations of abstract market rationality but also estimations of political feasibility. The latter of course entails, *inter alia,* accounting for which interests in the city can be mobilized on behalf of a given policy direction or given project and

which must be isolated or neutralized. To that extent an allocational element is woven into the texture of development activity very early in the
game; and that allocational element both undermines the premise that
development policy is fashioned above the fray of political conflict and implies that development is indeed a coalitional activity. Therefore, what Peterson sees as a consensus might just as likely reflect only the hegemonic position of a durable coalition.[9] In that light, the "city interest" that exhausts
itself in facilitating and realizing development might be simply an "interest"
imposed by a dominant politicoeconomic elite and may no more express in-
trinsic rationality than the divine right of kings truly expressed natural law.

This problem with Peterson's account grows in prominence with any increase in the proportion of the habitually "disadvantaged" among the city's
population, because by his own admission their interests are what conflict
most sharply with "economically productive" policy. The larger their cohort
in the polity, the greater the strain on the premise that either a transcen-
dent ideal or a de facto consensus legitimizes the pursuit of development
as paramount for the city's policy agenda. Only an "Orwellian logic" can support an argument that a policy decision that imposes substantial net costs
(ranging from physical displacement to the diversion of scarce budgetary
resources) on a large segment of a city's population and that is made without
its participation somehow expresses the municipal interest. (This reminds
us of the Brazilian general in the late 1960s who observed—proudly and
with no sense of irony—after several years of his junta's draconian economic
policy, "The economy is doing fine; of course, the people aren't.") Yet, precisely
such a logic currently grounds most public discussion of urban development,
and often it is applied, apparently as in Peterson's case, with the very best
intentions.

Not only is that logic normatively unsatisfactory, but it cannot give an
adequate response to a question that has most important implications for
democracy and for politicoeconomic equity in cities: How can local development policy proceed in a way that systematically disadvantages certain
groups in the municipality but that at the same time produces little political
challenge or conflict? To respond that discrete disadvantage melts away into
collective advantage is a mystification; to respond that there is no conflict
because there is consensus offers only the empty truism of tautology.

A path to more fruitful answers to that question, I believe, entails the
illumination of the ways in which actual development coalitions legitimize
policies, as well as policy courses, that have a broadly adverse popular impact. Because it is close to nature, as it were, that path avoids broad abstractions, such as the notion of a unitary city interest. Furthermore, this path
takes the existence of consensus as a starting point for the investigation
of the political dynamics surrounding development policy, rather than as
a post hoc defense for the premise of unitary interest or as a justification

for the lack of popular accountability in development politics. The examination of the mechanisms through which coalitions are formed and consensus is created on behalf of a development agenda restores a sense of the political to the discussion of local development activity, a consequence that must by definition be salutary to political scientists. Moreover, that restoration speaks to the intellectual usefulness of one of the several approaches that presently vie for proprietorship of the rubric "political economy." Most of all, however, restoring the political reminds us that even within sharp constraint in the urban polity, a span for choice does exist and that how those choices are made and by whom says much about the character of democracy in our society.

In what follows, I shall examine an instance of coalition and consensus formation in a policy context characterized by a clear pattern that concentrates the benefit on certain groups and the costs on certain others—namely, Atlanta during the Maynard Jackson regime during the 1970s. The centerpiece of this examination is the question, How did Mayor Jackson galvanize enough support and quiescence among the black electorate to cement blacks into the prodevelopment coalition despite the fact that the black community did not figure into the list of real beneficiaries? Answering that question, of course, requires attending to structural and ideological characteristics of the local political culture, as well as its prevailing concatenation of political forces and interests, as they impinge on development policy. This focus can yield an account of the anomaly of systematic disadvantagement that does not produce challenge or conflict. In addition, the Jackson administration is an excellent case for purposes of illustration in at least two respects: it was a black administration, and it reigned in Atlanta.

In few settings are the disparities between developmental and popular interests likely to be sharper than in a municipality governed by a black administration. For at least three reasons those disparities are thrown into greatest relief when a black regime governs. First, black administrations—by which I mean regimes that are led by blacks and that conform to Peter Eisinger's definition of "ethnoracial political transition"[10]—are more likely than not to come to power in cities characterized by general economic decline and comparatively high rates of economic privation among the citizenry.[11] Second, historically the social costs associated with development activity have been more likely to fall on blacks and on other nonwhites than on other groups in the polity.[12] Third, because of the nature of its core electoral constituency, the black administration is more likely than others to associate itself with an aggressively egalitarian rhetoric; moreover, representatives of black regimes often have their roots in activist, protest politics and therefore embody an imagery of antagonism toward entrenched elites, even beyond the assertiveness that is typical of other displacing elites.[13]

While the black administration highlights the tension between electoral and development constituencies, Atlanta is perhaps the archetype of the hegemony of development elites in local politics. There is no need to rehearse the central place that Atlanta has held during three decades of debate among urbanists and power-structure theorists. In addition to being a much-studied city, it is also one whose political culture has long been characterized by a pandemic civic boosterism that champions unfettered development as the engine and emblem of progress.[14] The path of that engine, moreover, has been such—throughout the period of the "Atlanta miracle"—as to concentrate the costs of "progress" repeatedly onto the city's quiescent black citizenry.[15] Empowerment of the Jackson regime in that context, as the symbol of a newly powerful black political voice, raised the clear specter of very sharp potential conflict over development policy.

Maynard Jackson's two terms (1974–81) as Atlanta's mayor were shaped to a considerable degree by a stormy relationship with the city's "business community"—principally the leadership of the Metro Atlanta Chamber of Commerce and Central Atlanta Progress—that was at the same time predictable and anomalous. Jackson's administration was dogged throughout his tenure with charges of being either overtly antibusiness or at least suspiciously inattentive to the business community's needs and interests. At the same time, however, no major development initiative that was taken during those eight years failed to elicit his enthusiastic support. Despite the absence of any concrete evidence of antagonism, however, the charges persisted, recycled regularly through the editorial pages of the *Atlanta Constitution* (and the *Atlanta Journal,* its afternoon version), which can be described with little rhetorical excess as the Chamber's chief ideological organ. In fact, Jackson's alleged hostility to business became a stigma from which his designated successor, Andrew Young, has striven mightily to absolve himself.[16]

In part, the perception that Jackson was not sufficiently responsive to business interests is simply an artifact of the process of "ethno-racial transition" and displacement. Business elites in Atlanta had governed the city directly for at least a generation, and both scholarship and local lore agree that City Hall and official governmental institutions were often less important as linkages in the public-policy process than were such private, voluntary associations as the Capital City Club, the Commerce Club, the Piedmont Driving Club, and of course the Chamber of Commerce itself.[17] It was not so much that political elites acquiesced to the desires of business elites or even that they shared the latter's interests and outlook. Rather, they were the same; the city's political leadership was designated by the business elite from within its own ranks, as the memoirs of Ivan Allen—the mayor who is most identified with the incorporation of racial progressivism into the city's sparkling New South image—attest.[18] The election of any black mayor, therefore, would have increased the degree of inconvenience suffered by business elites, if only by forcing them to venture into City Hall to conduct their affairs that involved the public sector. Having to accommodate those inconveniences combined with an overreaction to Jackson's early efforts "to do for blacks" to create an impression, however unfairly, that Jackson was hostile to business interests. Eisinger has observed that this reaction is a typical "response of a new minority uncertain of its position in the new order."[19]

Jackson's problems with those who spoke for the business community also were fueled by the latter's distaste for elements of Jackson's personality and political style. Ironically, the personal characteristics that members of the business elite found distasteful were closely related to those that had made Jackson more attractive to the voters than his more experienced black opponent, state Senator Leroy Johnson, in 1973. Jackson's initial mayoral candidacy was supported by an impressive list of business-community notables, including the chairmen of the boards of the Coca-Cola Company and two of the largest banks and John Portman, the Atlanta-based architect-developer, as well as the men who later would become the first two black presidents of the Chamber of Commerce.[20] Among those members of the business elite who accepted the inevitability of the transition to black political prominence, however, acceptance was by no means unanimous.[21] Jackson was the preferred candidate partly because of his youthful, energetic demeanor, his articulateness, and his social polish.

As Mack Jones has observed, racial transition in Atlanta "coincided with the plans of the business and commercial elite [to build] a series of modern luxury hotels, a modern sports complex, a sprawling convention center, a new airport and/or expand the existing one, and a billion dollar rapid transit system."[22] Those capital projects were pieces of a development strategy that was aimed at exploiting the city's "natural" advantage as a regional transportation center by enhancing the city's attractiveness to paper-work industry and by competing more aggressively for the convention and trade-show market. This strategy entailed selling Atlanta as "the next great international city."[23] In that context the coming of black political power could be turned into a benefit, especially if its inevitability were acknowledged anyway, by incorporating it into the marketing image of the progressive "New York of the South," "cultural center of the Southeast," New South "international" city.[24] Jackson's smooth, urbane style certainly was better suited to such a campaign than was Johnson's; the state senator was more "down home" in both idiom and demeanor and therefore was more likely to evoke an image of an earlier New South, no longer in vogue—namely, the one that was associated with unpleasantnesses such as Jim Crow, Ku Kluxism, and subterranean instability.

The problem, however, was that the very qualities of urbanity, articulateness, and polish that made Jackson an attractive choice to be the city's first black mayor also, as has been the case ever since W. E. B. Du Bois, led him to succumb to the disagreeable habit of mind that in the earlier day had been known as the assumption of "social equality." Therefore, Jackson was inclined to insist that his office of mayoralty be accorded the respect and deference to which it was formally entitled. This in turn meant that he was inclined to insist that his suitors come to City Hall to meet in his office and to ask for his support, rather than simply to inform him of their needs and assume his compliance. This posture was a shocking contrast to the longstanding norms of public/private interaction in Atlanta, and the added racial dimension to the shock led to charges that Jackson was "arrogant."[25] Similarly, his propensity to make his own patronage appointments and his attempts to give previously marginal groups representation in his administration fueled charges, which are commonly made against black (or populist) mayors, that he was a "poor administrator," that his regime suffered from "bad management" and "inept" appointments.[26]

Despite the rhetorical tempest, Jackson's record gives no reason to suspect that he ever would have considered breaking the longstanding public/private marriage that defined Atlanta's development policy. He unhesitatingly supported the implementation of the major development initiatives that his administration inherited—such as the construction of the MARTA (Metro Atlanta Rapid Transit Authority) rapid-transit system, the Bedford-Pine Urban-Redevelopment Project (a slum-clearance/redevelopment project in the urban-renewal mold), and airport expansion—and he was an avid proponent of the general framework for downtown development and revitalization. Indeed, even when Jackson sought, during his second term, to concentrate his energies on the problems of poverty and unemployment in Atlanta, his disposition was to define those problems in ways that conformed to the agendas of development interests. When, beginning in 1978 and continuing through the rest of his tenure, the annual Comprehensive Development Plan adopted unemployment as the city's principal concern, the administration's strategic thrust derived from the familiar premise that a rising tide lifts all boats. Thus, City Hall's intervention on behalf of the poor and the unemployed was centered in the economic-development unit of the Department of Budget and Planning, the Mayor's Office of Economic Development, the Economic Development unit in the Bureau of Housing and Physical Development (BHPD, in the Department of Community and Human Development), and the newly formed public/private Atlanta Economic Development Corporation. Each of those agencies, except for the BHPD unit, had been formed specifically to anticipate and respond to the needs of large private developers. Not surprisingly, therefore, the Community Economic Development Strategy that they formulated to address the needs of the dispossessed recommended that greater proportions of Community Development Block Grant funds be shifted from the direct provision of social services to infrastructural and fiscal support for private development, both within and outside the Community Development Impact Area.[27]

There lies the means through which the Jackson administration reconciled the interests of the black citizenry with the business elite's development agenda—that is, by defining the latter as the essential context for fulfilment of the former. On no issue was Jackson's reliance on this approach more pronounced than on the controversy over airport expansion and construction.

Momentum for somehow expanding Atlanta's airport facilities preceded Jackson's mayoralty. In one form or another, the discussion of expansion dates from as early as 1968.[28] By 1973 a consensus had formed among the significant interests—the airlines, led by Delta whose home base is Atlanta; the Federal Aviation Administration (FAA); city officials; local developers; and of course the Chamber of Commerce—that some measures needed to be taken soon to enlarge the airport's capacity. When Maynard Jackson was inaugurated in January 1974, the issue that confronted him was not whether some airport-development project should be undertaken but whether that project should be an expansion of capacity at the current airport site in Clayton County or the construction of a second airport.[29]

The airlines, which would have to approve any proposed expansion, for the most part were cautious about endorsing either of the options; they generally maintained a low profile in the debate, although Delta and Eastern dropped early hints that they might lean toward the construction of a second airport north of the city.[30] Developers, though, were not so much given to temporizing, and Tom Cousins—the developer of the Omni complex and the World Congress Center in the old railroad gulch in the southwest central business district (CBD)—took the initiative by putting together a partnership to acquire a 48,000-acre tract approximately thirty-five miles northwest of the city in Paulding and Polk counties, with the understanding that part of the tract would be available as a possible airport site.[31] Less than two months later, in September 1973, the FAA gave encouragement to the proponents of a second airport by exhorting the city to begin the project within five years. However, the Paulding-Polk site was not the only contender; Sam Massell's administration had paid over $5 million two years earlier for a 10,030-acre site in Dawson County to Atlanta's north; and a location in Henry County, to the city's south, was a third, albeit less favored, possibility.[32] The FAA and the Atlanta Regional Commission (ARC), the A-95 clearing house for the region, therefore undertook a study to determine the best location for a new airport, though this study itself was to become, as we shall see, a source of considerable controversy.

By the time that Jackson assumed office, the environment of municipal governance included a consensus among significant elites that a major commitment of new public resources to Atlanta's airport capacity was a pressing item on the city's agenda, and the weight of opinion tilted toward the construction of a second airport to the north. Shortly before his inauguration the lame-duck Board of Aldermen took a two-phase option—a token $1 for the first three months and roughly $250,000 to secure the parcel for the next seven months—on 30,000 acres of Cousins's Paulding-Polk site. The new mayor was in the position, therefore, of having either to carve out his own position from within a very tightly constrained policy context or to break altogether from a nearly unanimous consensus of significant elites, among them many of his own supporters.

While the concentration of elite support on behalf of airport construction would exert pressure on the mayor to "go with the flow," he was at the same time under pressure to deliver signs of good faith to his predominantly black electoral constituency. This pressure stemmed from at least two sources. First, Jackson, like other black candidates in electoral contests auguring racial transition, was packaged for black voters as a symbol of racial aspirations, a legatee of the civil-rights movement. This symbolic aspect of his candidacy had become increasingly prominent as his opponent in the runoff, incumbent Sam Massell, opted for a scarcely veiled racist appeal to white voters to "save" the city from black rule.[33] A second source of pressure was more concrete. Police brutality had become so flagrant in the black community that Jackson had had to pledge that he would fire the incumbent chief of police, John Inman, to assure the heavy black turnout that Jackson needed in order to win. For reasons that need not be given in detail here,[34] however, Jackson found removing Chief Inman more difficult than he had anticipated; as a result, very early in his first term, some of his less patient black constituents began publicly to question Jackson's commitment to the black electorate. In that environment the mayor needed to find some "black" position to take in regard to the airport issue, particularly as the controversy over alternative locations intensified.

Jackson found his "black" position in a strong endorsement of the principle of a second airport, coupled with an increasingly firm and vocal preference for the Henry County site on the southeastern fringe of the SMSA (standard metropolitan statistical area). This posture was shared by John Portman, who, like the mayor, argued that a northwestern location would exacerbate an already-extant tendency toward an uneven concentration of development on the city's north side. This tendency, they observed, threatened to drain Atlanta's downtown toward the northern suburbs. For Portman this position became enmeshed with his running rivalry with Tom Cousins, and it created considerable tension as their version of Maoists' "two-line struggle" spilled over into the politburo of Central Atlanta Progress.[35] For Jackson, advocacy of the Henry County location was also attractive because Atlanta's population distribution is such that blacks live primarily, if not overwhelmingly, in the city's southern quadrants. Even black suburbanization, which increased considerably during the 1970s and the early 1980s, has largely reproduced black enclaves in the southern half of Dekalb County and in nearby suburbs south of the city in Fulton County. On that basis, Mayor Jackson sought to tie black interests to the Henry County site by virtue of his claim that the construction of a second airport there would stimulate development on the city's south side and would thereby yield material benefits for Atlanta's black community.[36]

In fact, there was little reason to believe that a Henry County airport, which would have been nearly as far away from the city as the proposed north-side location, would have had any direct development impact on the communities in which black Atlantans lived. Nor would it have opened opportunities for black entrepreneurs that would not have been equally available at other sites. Indeed, ancillary development impact on black communities would have been most, but still not very, likely from the third option—namely, the expansion of capacity at the existing Clayton County location. However, when an unexpected turn of events returned that option to the agenda, the mayor vigorously opposed it.

To everyone's surprise, the preliminary report of the ARC's staff, which was completed in the spring of 1975 as the two lines on the second airport sharpened, indicated that there was no need for an additional airport after all. Instead, the draft recommended that the existing facilities be expanded and upgraded. Delta, which had long-since become vocal as an advocate of the Paulding-Polk site, attacked the report and, invoking support from the other airlines and from the Chamber of Commerce, urged discarding the recommendation and proceeding with construction plans. The city's finance commissioner, who was virtually autonomous under the new charter and was the Chamber's principal representative in the municipal executive department, followed suit.[37] Shortly thereafter, the ARC overturned the staff report and recommended that a second airport be constructed northwest of the city. The decision to overturn the staff report apparently was influenced by lobbying from Mayor Jackson and his chief black ally on the city council.[38] Although the mayor expressed his continuing preference for a southeastern site, it seemed that he was committed first of all to the idea of a second airport. Then, two months later, shortly after City Hall had announced its intention to purchase the Paulding-Polk site for $9.5 million, the ARC reversed itself again and canceled its earlier recommendation of that site. The mayor decried this last reversal as a "setback for Atlanta" and reiterated his commitment to a second airport, even in the northwestern location.[39] Nevertheless, fed in part by antiairport protest from Paulding citizens' groups, the ARC's decision that recommendations concerning the second airport lay outside the commission's seven-county mandate effectively killed off the second-airport option by blocking access to federal funds. The airlines, as well, apparently got tired of the bickering and contented themselves with the construction of a huge new terminal close to the existing Clayton County location.

For his part, Mayor Jackson succeeded in defining the issues at stake in the airport-construction controversy in a way that identified his black electoral constituency's interests with one pole of a debate over options within a development-policy agenda that actually had little bearing on that constituency. To that extent he succeeded in neutralizing potential black opposition that might have been transferred from the parallel conflict over the reorganization of the city's public-safety department, a conflict that pitted the Chamber-centered elite directly against the black community.[40] At the same time, he succeeded in assuring that elite that, despite his combativeness over the right to control his own administrative public-safety appointments, he could be counted on as a team player with respect to the Chamber-endorsed development agenda and furthermore could help to cement black support. Finally, he succeeded even in the failure of the second-airport plan, because the decision to build a new terminal next to the existing one in the near-southern SMSA enabled him to claim a partial victory for his south-side preference. Those successes, though, were soon to be lost in the acrimony that resulted when the mayor sought to intervene in the development agenda by officially factoring a black-claimant status into the allocational component of the airport-construction project.[41]

In concert with the city's new and widely noted Finley Ordinance (named for its author, Councilman Morris Finley), which laid out extensive guidelines to enforce minority participation in municipal contracts, Mayor Jackson announced that he would aggressively seek to involve minority-owned firms in all contractual phases of the airport-construction project. This plan quickly came to be known by one of its components—the "joint venture" provision that called for nonminority contractors to form limited joint-venture partnerships with minority-owned firms in order to receive special consideration in the competitive-bidding process. That proposal generated almost unanimous opposition from the business elite. For months the *Constitution* railed editorially and otherwise against the administration's affirmative-action and contract-compliance efforts, particularly as they intersected the airport-construction project. Awards and near-awards of a few dubious contracts to old cronies fueled the fires of opposition. The generally articulated oppositional line was that the construction of the new terminal was too important to be subjected to a "social experiment," no matter how noble. Somewhat more shrill voices charged "reverse racism" and unnatural governmental interference in the activities of firms.

As the lines of confrontation tightened, the mayor opted, first, to stand his ground by emphatically reiterating his rhetorical commitment to the joint-venture strategy and to the principle of favoring firms that had substantial minority representation. Consequently, he found himself, upon entering the last year of his first term, under increasing attack from significant elements of the development coalition. Predictably, that attack led blacks to rally around both the mayor and the joint-venture idea, but the black support turned out to be a double-edged sword.

By early 1976 a combination of the airlines' indirect threats to withhold financial support for construction and the business community's threats to back a strong candidate against Jackson in 1977 led the mayor to tilt toward compromise on his commitment to the joint-venture program. Specifically, the compromise entailed (1) the softening of City Hall's official position on minority involvement; (2) the appointment of the business community's designee to supervise the entire airport-construction project; and (3) the removal of the recalcitrant commissioner of administrative services, an aggressive black woman who had incurred the enmity of practically the entire business elite in her capacity as administrator of the joint-venture/contract-compliance program. In exchange, Mayor Jackson was assured the acceptance of the more modest version of his minority-contracting agenda and unanimous support in his bid for reelection.[42] Jackson's black supporters, however, displayed mixed emotions over his willingness to accept the compromise, especially because it required the dismissal of a black commissioner who was well known in the black community. Charges circulated on the margins of the black political elite that Jackson had sold out to the "downtown power structure," and Emma Darnell, the displaced commissioner (technically she was not fired but was reorganized out of her job because her department was abolished), ran against Jackson in 1977. She received no significant support, though, and the mayor was reelected with 77 percent of the vote.

What can the Maynard Jackson experience tell us about the politics of local-development policy? First of all, although in both instances of controversy over airport construction Jackson accepted the business elite's development agenda, his attempts to meld blacks into the coalition met with drastically different responses. In the first instance his efforts were favorably received by the coalition because he simply chose sides in what essentially was a debate over what Peterson would call "allocational" issues. None of the three (or four, counting Dawson County) potential options was clearly preferable in technical terms. Therefore, the decision could be derived only through the tug of war between very particularistic interests. Certainly, the ARC's waffling back and forth on its "expert" recommendations does not give much comfort to those who would argue that such development-policy decisions are made on the basis of an impersonal, extrapolitical rationality. As mayor, Jackson had to take some position on the issue, and he chose one that was already a legitimate item in elite policy debate and that enabled him to express a claim, albeit only a symbolic one, on behalf of his black electoral constituency.

Jackson's effort to reinvent the south-side option as a black interest reflects a variant of Peterson's view of the translation of potentially redistributive demands into allocational or symbolic ones.[43] Jackson's success at reinvention suggests one of the mechanisms through which the black administration can mediate the tension between electoral and governing constituencies. By virtue of his representation of his position as the "black" position, he added an epicycle of racial self-defense to blacks' consideration of policy options; to that extent, Jackson shifted the basis for black response to policy debate away from substantive concern with the potential outcomes and toward protection of the racial image and status, as embodied in the idiosyncratic agenda of the black official. In this way it becomes possible for black officials to maintain support from both their black constituents and the development elites that systematically disadvantage them.

In the second instance, Jackson sought to reformulate the allocational element of the development agenda to include a niche for blacks. One point that stands out about this controversy is that it is sometimes very difficult to distinguish between redistributive and allocational dimensions of public policy. In fact, the controversy centered precisely on whether the proposed minority-contracting program was redistributive or allocational. Jackson argued that it would have no impact on production timetables or on cost effectiveness and that it was only a matter of assuring that minorities received "parity" in budget allocations. His opponents contended that the program would produce delays, weaken investor and bidder confidence, and drive up costs and therefore that it was an inappropriate "social experiment"—that is, a redistributive program. To the extent that his proposal challenged an entrenched pattern of privilege with respect to allocation, it did in fact contain a redistributive component, at least insofar as the program implied a marginal redistribution of privileged access to public resources via the contract-award process. Nevertheless, if one abstracts from the self-interestedness of the discrete actors involved, the program's focus was on modifying the allocational dimension of a development-policy objective.

Another noteworthy characteristic of the second controversy is that Jackson's program incurred such uniform hostility in part because it represented an attempt to assert a version of black influence over the determination of the allocational rules of the game in the development-policy process. In Atlanta's political culture, such an assertion constituted a radical departure from business as usual and was therefore unacceptable to the business elites, even though the version of black interests that were asserted accepted the developmentalist premises and agenda around which the business elite cohered. The problem was not that the black administration or the prospective black subcontractors or joint-venture contractors were unreliable with respect to the agenda. The problem was simply that they were supposed to be cue takers exclusively, even though their claimed representation of the aspirations of a popular black constituency no doubt raised some questions about their reliability. Eventually, however, even in Atlanta, the business elites recognized the virtues of the black administration's capacity to displace potential conflict by reinventing development agendas that had potentially disadvantageous outcomes for black constituents as campaigns for the defense of racial self-respect embodied in black officials. But that is the story of the Andrew Young regime.

What does all this say about the critique of Peterson with which this paper began? Most important is that consensus around development policy derives from political processes that some interests are not allowed to have a voice in and that are largely defined and dominated by significant economic interests. Moreover, neat analytical distinctions between different posited policy types are difficult to sustain in places where matters rather approximate William James's "bloomin', buzzin' confusion." These two points, of course, do not speak well for a notion of unitary interest in development, which in practice is often little more than a cudgel with which to enforce an entrenched pattern of privilege.

NOTES

1. Paul E. Peterson, *City Limits* (Chicago: University of Chicago Press, 1981), p. 132.

2. Ibid., p. 129.

3. Ibid.

4. Ibid., p. 147.

5. Ibid., pp. 121–28.

6. Ibid., p. 133.

7. Ibid., p. 129.

8. Todd Swanstrom, *The Crisis of Growth Politics: Cleveland, Kucinich, and the Challenge of Urban Populism* (Philadelphia: Temple University Press, 1985), pp. 15–17.

9. See the article by Stone and Sanders in this volume.

10. Peter K. Eisinger, *The Politics of Displacement: Racial and Ethnic Transition in Three American Cities* (Orlando, Fla.: Academic Press, 1980), p. 5.

11. See, e.g., Richard P. Nathan and Charles Adams, "Understanding Central City Hardship," *Political Science Quarterly* 1 (Spring 1976): 47–62; and Katherine L. Bradbury, Anthony Downs, and Kenneth A. Small, *Urban Decline and the Future of American Cities* (Washington, D.C.: Brookings Institution, 1982), esp. pp. 6–7.

12. See, e.g., Clarence Stone's study of urban renewal in Atlanta, *Economic Growth and Neighborhood Discontent* (Chapel Hill: University of North Carolina Press, 1976); and John H. Mollenkopf, *The Contested City* (Princeton, N.J.: Princeton University Press, 1983).

13. Albert K. Karnig and Susan Welch, *Black Representation and Urban Policy* (Chicago: University of Chicago Press, 1980), pp. 12–13, 23.

14. See M. Dale Henson and James King, "The Atlanta Public-Private Romance," in *Public-Private Partnership in American Cities: Seven Case Studies,* ed. R. Scott

Fosler and Renee A. Berger (Lexington, Mass.: Lexington Books, 1982), pp. 293–337.
Cf. Bradley R. Rice, "Atlanta: If Dixie Were Atlanta," in *Sunbelt Cities: Politics and
Growth since World War II,* ed. Richard M. Bernard and Bradley R. Rice (Austin:
University of Texas Press, 1983), pp. 31–57; and Ivan Allen, Jr., with Paul Hemphill,
Mayor: Notes on the Sixties (New York: Simon & Schuster, 1971), passim.

15. Stone, *Economic Growth;* also see Mack H. Jones, "Black Political Empowerment in Atlanta: Myth and Reality," *Annals,* Sept. 1978, pp. 90–117.

16. A flavor of Young's insistence on cultivating a rapport with the business community can be gleaned from Art Harris, "The Capitalistic Gospel According to Rev.
Young," *Atlanta Constitution,* 22 Sept. 1985.

17. Allen, *Mayor,* remains the most illuminating source on this motif in Atlanta's political culture; see also Floyd Hunter, *Community Power Succession: Atlanta's Policy Makers Revisited* (Chapel Hill: University of North Carolina Press, 1980).

18. Allen's story of his own recruitment and grooming for political office is il-
lustrative; see *Mayor,* pp. 9–16.

19. Eisinger, *Politics of Displacement,* p. 81.

20. Henson and King, "Atlanta Public-Private Romance," p. 306.

21. For an examination of the representative of the element that refused to accept the idea of black rule see Russ Rymes, "The Tide Turns Again for Dillard Mun-
ford," *Atlanta Journal/Constitution Magazine,* 23 Nov. 1980, pp. 14ff.

22. Jones, "Black Political Empowerment," p. 109.

23. Ibid.

24. Thus Birmingham, Alabama; New Orleans, Louisiana; and Charlotte, North
Carolina, also have elected black mayors with considerable support from the business
elite.

25. Rice, "Atlanta," pp. 51–52; Eisinger, *Politics of Displacement,* p. 81.

26. Henson and King, "Atlanta Public-Private Romance," pp. 306–7; Eisinger,
Politics of Displacement, p. 83.

27. This programmatic orientation is articulated in Mayor Jackson's "State of
the City, 1980" (21 Jan. 1980) address and in the "Action Plan to Combat Poverty
in Atlanta," prepared for the Mayor's Poverty Task Force by his Department of Budget
and Planning, 21 May 1981.

28. Raleigh Bryans, "Airlines Hint OK of Move of Terminal," *Atlanta Constitution,* 22 July 1973.

29. Sam Hopkins, "FAA Gives Push to 2nd Airport Here," *Atlanta Constitution,*
8 Sept. 1973; Gene Tharpe, "Possible Airport Site Acquired Near Dallas," ibid., 28
July 1973; Jim Gray, "Airport Study Urged," ibid., 10 Oct. 1973; and idem, "Airport
Welcome," ibid., 20 Jan. 1974.

30. As the debate unfolded, the airlines—especially Delta—became increasingly
candid and adamant in stating their preference, which was for the Paulding-Polk
option (see Jim Merriner, "Mayor Raps Airport Site Option Cost," *Atlanta Constitution,* 13 May 1974; Tharpe, "Possible Airport Site Acquired").

31. Tharpe, "Possible Airport Site Acquired."

32. Ibid.

33. See Jones, "Black Political Empowerment," p. 107.

34. Ibid., pp. 109–11.

35. Margaret Shannon examines the Portman-Cousins rivalry in "The Battle
of Downtown Atlanta," *Atlanta Journal and Constitution Magazine,* 22 July 1979,
pp. 10ff.

36. Jones, "Black Political Empowerment," p. 10; also see Frederick Allen,
"Airlines Fear 2nd Airport Never Will Be," *Atlanta Constitution,* 26 Jan. 1975.

37. Raleigh Bryans, "Delta Chides ARC Report on Airport," *Atlanta Constitution,* 2 Mar. 1975.

38. Jim Merriner, "City Still Seeks Southside Airfield Site," *Atlanta Constitution,* 3 Apr. 1975.

39. Jim Merriner, "City Not Bound by ARC Vote," *Atlanta Constitution,* 2 July 1975.

40. See Jones, "Black Political Empowerment."

41. The following discussion draws freely from almost daily coverage of the joint-venture controversy in the Atlanta press, as well as from Jones, "Black Political Empowerment."

42. Jim Gray, "Compromise Okayed on Joint Ventures," *Atlanta Constitution,* 10 Feb. 1976.

43. Peterson, *City Limits,* pp. 178–82.

11

New Orleans: Mayoral Politics and Economic-Development Policies in the Postwar Years, 1945–86

Robert K. Whelan

Robert Whelan's account of New Orleans, Louisiana, shows that neither its politics nor its development policy has been static. Famous for the dominance of patronage politics, New Orleans and the state of Louisiana were slow to enter the era of executive-centered development politics. A city political leadership that was held in low regard, a strong tradition of historic preservation, and a business elite that was never unified for action in the manner of its southeastern neighbor, Atlanta, Georgia, or its southwestern neighbor, Dallas, Texas, added up to a context in which the aggressive pursuit of development was slow in coming. Even when it came, entrepreneurial activism may have owed more to the presence of a newly mobilized black constituency than to extraordinary business effort and power.

The uneven course of development policy and politics in New Orleans invites speculation about the connection between regime character and development efforts. The old regime in New Orleans may well have been especially sensitive to the concerns of small-property holders and for that reason may have been reluctant to push hard for an aggressive program of redevelopment. Fears about costs and disruption, we saw earlier in the case of Kalamazoo, can engender opposition by home owners and small businesses. In the case of New Orleans, a more activist public effort came only after the city's electorate was diversified, but also in combination with an extensive use of state and federal money. Whelan's account of New Orleans thus suggests that intergovernmental funds are themselves important in managing conflict around development. In New Orleans, with federal

216

money diminishing and the state of Louisiana in a fiscal crunch, City Hall, under a new mayor, has recently backed away from its highly activist stance and faces a struggle even to fund basic services. Development efforts in New Orleans thus seem to be particularly dependent on state and federal funding.

Conflict remains ever near the surface. Whelan indicates that the struggle between preservationists and the proponents of maximum development is ongoing and that interwoven with the shifting political alignments in New Orleans, there is a set of unresolved issues about development. Just as there is no stable governing coalition, there is no consensus on what the best development strategy is, who should pay for development efforts—that is, why intergovernmental money is so important—and what risks should be taken.

As the political-economy approach to urban politics has developed in recent years, scholars have become more aware of the links between the economies of cities and the economies of nation states. New Orleans, as a port near the mouth of the Mississippi River, has been especially affected by economic cycles. Throughout its history, New Orleans has been known as a city that has had its "ups and downs," that has experienced periods of "boom and bust."

What is the relationship, if any, between economic cycles and political events in cities? In a provocative and groundbreaking study, Martin Shefter has suggested that cycles of reform in urban politics are fundamentally intertwined with the fiscal crises of cities.[1] Stephen Elkin, in a brilliant, broad-ranging paper, introduces the concept of an "urban regime,"[2] which ties together continuities in urban economic development and patterns of politics.

In Elkin's analysis, urban regimes have three main components: an alliance between land interests and city politicians, which makes major decisions about land use; a stable electoral coalition; and the relationship of functional bureaucracies to the land-use alliance on issues related to the economic position of the city (e.g., police services).[3] Elkin identifies three regimes in recent American politics: the privatist regime, the pluralist regime, and the federalist regime. For the purposes of this paper, we will use Elkin's typology.

THE PRIVATIST REGIME, 1945–70

At the end of World War II, in 1945, the mayor of New Orleans was Robert S. Maestri, an Italian-American who had become mayor of New Orleans in 1936, with the support of the Old Regular organization (New Orleans' version of the traditional urban Democratic machine) and Huey Long's organization in Baton Rouge, the state capital. During his early years in office, Maestri compiled a record of civic achievement. The mayor reduced the municipal debt and improved the delivery of city services. Maestri pursued a busy program of public construction, aided by funds from the Federal Works Progress Administration. After Maestri's reelection in 1942, the administration stagnated. Changing times and attitudes made the machine's deficiencies more visible. During the war years, New Orleans was a wide-open town, in which prostitution and gambling flourished. The spoils system dominated New Orleans politics, and each ward leader and assessor had his own small political organization. Vice, corruption, and favoritism dominated the later Maestri years, in a climate that was ripe for reform.[4] Blacks held only the most menial jobs in city government; and major bureaucracies, such as the police force, were still segregated. Police mistreatment of blacks was a common occurrence.

In summarizing the state of the urban regime at the start of the postwar era, the following can be said: (1) The land-use alliance was happy with the fiscal policies and economies of Maestri's first term in office. At the end of the war, the Chamber of Commerce and other business interests wanted the construction of a union passenger station and other infrastructure projects. (2) The machine provided a steady base of votes. In return for "favors" such as jobs, preferential treatment in service delivery, and so forth, the machine received middle-class and working-class votes. These white voters were small-property owners, who supported a "caretaker" government that provided minimal services. Some blacks always voted in New Orleans as Republicans, but large numbers of blacks didn't vote until after the United States Supreme Court outlawed the white primary in 1944. (3) Functional bureaucracies were not highly professionalized, because the civil-service system was not introduced until this era. The maintenance of city streets and garbage-collection services both declined during Maestri's later years in office.

With the support of many of the city's civic and business leaders, DeLesseps ("Chep") Morrison, a young state representative and a veteran of World War II, was elected mayor in 1946. Morrison's victory over the incumbent, Maestri, was seemingly a victory for reform forces over the Democratic machine. During his early years in office, Morrison fulfilled some of the promises of reform. He created the New Orleans Recreation Department (NORD), which gained national recognition for its programs. He was also very active in the national urban lobby. The adoption of a new strong-mayor charter in 1952 was a major achievement of the Morrison years. Reform, however, is not to be confused with regime change. As Elkin points out, "Many reformers were as much interested as machine politicians in facilitating private development of the city."[5]

The earliest major postwar redevelopment efforts centered around the clearance of a slum area in downtown New Orleans, which housed many black families. A new railroad station and a civic-center complex were built, with financing from the city, the state, and the railroads. The project included the construction of a union passenger terminal and the building of an expressway linking the downtown area with residential neighorhoods near Lake Pontchartrain and with suburban areas. The civic-center complex included the new City Hall, the main public library, a municipal court building, a state office building, and a state-court building. This was the major physical development effort of the Morrison years. While it provided badly needed public facilities, the new railroad terminal arrived at a time when railroad travel was declining significantly. Furthermore, the Housing Authority of New Orleans (HANO) failed to provide new dwellings for the black citizens who were displaced.[6] First proposed in 1947, the new terminal opened in 1954, and the new City Hall in 1957. The lack of state enabling legislation for urban renewal and the lack of state support from a government that was dominated by rural segregationists who had little interest in the problems of urban New Orleans and its substantial black population were significant constraints on any other major urban-development efforts by the Morrison administration.

In short, the privatistic regime, as it existed in the Morrison era had several characteristics. (1) There was a land-use alliance, which was hampered by the lack of state enabling legislation for urban renewal, but which still achieved significant development of physical facilities for the city. Municipal bonds financed such projects as the civic center and the union terminal. The land-use alliance also strongly supported international-trade activities, such as the building of the International Trade Mart, an exhibition hall and office building, which opened in 1948.

(2) Morrison's Crescent City Democratic Association replaced the old machine. Despite the advent of civil service and the development of a classified personnel system, there were still many opportunities for patronage politics. Although there were some class differences in Morrison's base of support (there was more upper- and middle-class support but less working-class support), the privatistic regime depended on the support of white home owners.

Blacks began to vote in substantial numbers after World War II, and black voters generally supported Morrison. Morrison was known as a "moderate" segregationist. There were material benefits for the black community during the Morrison years; the integration of the police force, improved city services, and the construction of public housing. Nonetheless, need always was far greater than the city's response, and racial discrimination prevailed. In particular, Morrison and the New Orleans business community failed to provide leadership during the school-integration crisis of

1960. Segregationist extremists dominated public events, and the racial strife of that era left a bitter residue that permeates black-white relations in the metropolitan area even today. Although our main concern here is urban development, the relationship of the school system to urban development and a comparison with cities where school integration was more amicable (e.g., Atlanta) are instructive.[7]

(3) The city's functional bureaucracies were reorganized, particularly in areas important to the land-use alliance. A new city-planning-commission structure was created in 1946. Its professional staff was involved in the design and planning of major public improvements, such as the modernization of drainage, streets, and fire equipment, in addition to the terminal and the civic center. Police scandals were frequent, but police brutality and corruption were not a major focus for the land-use alliance.

Morrison was succeeded as mayor by Victor Schiro, a stalwart of the Democratic machine. On land-use issues, Schiro was instrumental in the widening of Poydras Street, a key downtown artery, from two to six lanes. He also strongly supported the building of the Superdome.

Perhaps these years—the 1960s—are better known for an unsuccessful initiative, the proposed Riverfront Expressway. Others have told this tale in great detail, but in brief, the expressway proposal would have placed an elevated highway along the French Quarter's river front.[8] New York planner Robert Moses first suggested the expressway in the 1940s. The plan had the support of downtown financial and business interests organized into an umbrella coalition known as the Central Area Committee, the Chamber of Commerce, and some local and national politicians. Against the plan were historic preservationists, affected neighborhood groups, and some civic elites. The project was finally defeated by a decision of the United States secretary of transportation in 1969. What is important for our purposes here is that in this instance, a unified business community's strategy to promote economic well-being by building an expressway conflicted with another strategy—preserving the city's most historic area, particularly the waterfront. Some observers see this as an instance of "productive non-action." Historian Arnold Hirsch argues that "the attraction of a French Quarter unspoiled by Moses' elevated highway was critical to the 1970's revival of the Central Business District."[9]

THE PLURALIST REGIME, 1970–78

New Orleans has often been called a backwater. The city is set off geographically from other American metropolitan areas, and it is frequently said to be behind the times. While cultural and geographic factors were important, political considerations were certainly vital, too. New Orleans lagged behind in urban redevelopment for several reasons. (1) State enabling legislation for urban renewal did not exist until 1968. (2) Political leadership was lacking: Morrison was distracted by races for governor and by personal problems in his later mayoral years, and Schiro was not a dynamic mayor. (3) Business-community leadership was not cohesive. In contrast to other cities such as Dallas,[10] which are known for a cohesive, unified business elite that has an integrative vision of the community, the New Orleans land-use alliance is characterized by its fragmentation. Some observers of New Orleans attribute this fragmentation and the lack of leadership to the time and attention given to Mardi Gras, the city's annual celebration. More charitable observers note that much civic energy during the 1960s was expended on an abortive effort to resite the port.

This situation was what Maurice ("Moon") Landrieu inherited when he was elected mayor in 1970. Landrieu was a transitional figure in New Orleans' political history. As a member of Mayor Morrison's Crescent City Democratic Association, Landrieu had strong ties with the city's traditional civic elites and political organizations. As a state legislator during the early 1960s, Landrieu had stood alone in support of the integration of New Orleans' public schools. His courageous actions were remembered by black voters, who strongly supported Landrieu in his two mayoral campaigns. Landrieu was elected by a coalition consisting of the overwhelming majority of blacks and a minority of whites. In addition, Landrieu's administration signaled the end of political dominance by an urban political machine with traditional values.

The story of New Orleans' redevelopment during the 1970s has been told by several other observers.[11] Suffice it to say here that the city of New Orleans has pursued an economic-development strategy that emphasizes the revitalization of the central business district and the promotion of tourism. Central to that effort was the construction of the Superdome, a downtown sports arena and convention center. The Superdome and other downtown-development projects brought an infusion of external finance capital.

There are problems with the choice of tourism as a major strategy for economic development. As one classic analysis of the New Orleans economy has noted, the tourism orientation of economic development is almost totally unrelated to the problem of the low-income population.[12] Tourism jobs are largely low-paying, low-skill, dead-end service jobs. Moreover, tourism is controlled by external interests. For example, only two of the many major downtown hotels are owned by citizens of New Orleans. There were some benefits from the tourism strategy for the low-income black partners in the Landrieu political coalition. Sherman Copelin, a black political activist allied with Mayor Landrieu, was awarded a major service contract for the Superdome. Supporters of Copelin's political organization, SOUL, and other blacks received service jobs at the domed stadium.[13]

Assessments of the Superdome vary. City officials say that the Superdome has been an economic catalyst that has aided in generating more than
$2.5 billion in construction and renovation and has sparked the rejuvena-
tion of a deteriorating central business district. A study that was commis-
sioned by the Louisiana Stadium and Exposition District concluded that
the Superdome has been a very good investment for the city and the state,
because of the beneficial economic impacts. On the negative side, the Superdome never achieved its goal of becoming a multipurpose facility. It does
have many conventions and trade shows, but it is not ideal for that purpose,
as evidenced by the construction of a new convention center for the city,
which opened in 1984. The Superdome is too large for most concerts, but it is
ideal as a professional sports facility. However, because New Orleans does not
have a major-league baseball team, the Superdome is used on only ten days a
year for pro sports, by the New Orleans Saints football team.[14] In the face
of a severe state fiscal crisis, state legislators have proposed that the Superdome be sold, so as to avoid the annual operating losses. The threatened
move of the Saints and the sale of the team in 1985 created a situation in
which the state government provides heavy subsidies to the Saints. Because
of the crisis that was caused by falling oil prices, the state has problems
in meeting its financial obligations to the Saints. It is clear from this discussion that the costs and benefits of large-scale urban development are complex. Moreover, it seems that any detailed analysis of costs and benefits in
the Superdome or related situations would point up deficiencies in Peterson's "unitary model" of urban economic development.[15]

The role of the state government in these development initiatives must
be noted. State monies were crucial in the widening of Poydras Street and
in the construction of the Superdome. Moreover, the passage of state urban-
renewal enabling legislation in 1968 made the city eligible for federal urban-
renewal programs. State-government support of all these ventures can be
attributed to the state's traditional penchant for construction projects, which
benefit the usual network of contractors, builders, and so forth, and to the
national political aspirations and moderate images of Governors John
McKeithen and Edwin W. Edwards, who succeeded the segregationist governors of earlier years.

During the mayoralty of Landrieu, the city became heavily involved with
federal economic-development programs. Two major projects that were undertaken by the Landrieu administration with federal monies from the
Economic Development Administration (EDA) were Armstrong Park and the
Piazza d'Italia. Armstrong Park is a thirty-two-acre park and entertainment
complex at the periphery of the French Quarter; it is built around the
Municipal Auditorium. The Piazza d'Italia occupies a city block and consists of a plaza, a fountain, and historic buildings, which are to be restored

for hotel and commercial uses. These were the earliest economic-development efforts by the city government, and neither has achieved its potential. The city found both projects costly to operate and difficult to lease under city ownership. Again, any reasonable assessment would find a mixed picture of costs and benefits to the city.

In examining the pluralist regime during the Landrieu administration, I found, first, that the land-use alliance made major advances as the central business district (CBD) boomed. Landrieu's efforts were not limited to the CBD. Major efforts and money went into projects in the French Quarter. Several streets became pedestrian walkways. Jackson Square was closed to traffic, and Jackson Square and the French Market were restored. Moon Walk, named after Landrieu, is a pedestrian walkway that provides a magnificent view of the Mississippi River from the French Quarter.

Second, I found that there were continuities in New Orleans politics. "Machine-style" politics continued, and the white-home-owners constituency was placated in numerous ways (e.g., by the reconstruction of city finances, improved city services, etc.). The involvement of blacks in city government was a significant achievement. Bob Tucker, a black businessman, was one of Landrieu's top mayoral aides, and blacks held such key positions as chief administrative officer and finance director. Landrieu was responsible for the appointment of the first black city councilman. Blacks also obtained jobs at the middle and lower levels of city halls. By the end of the Landrieu administration, blacks held 40 percent of the jobs in city government. The public sector has been a continued channel of access for blacks and a place in which the mayor has the opportunity to provide distributive benefits for his supportive constituency.[16]

Third, I found that the city's functional bureaucracies worked in ways that were amenable to the land-use alliance. The Downtown Development District, a special district funded by taxes from downtown businesses, was established in order to make physical improvements in the downtown area. City finances were revamped, with taxes and fees being raised. Landrieu's access to state and federal governments assured a steady flow of funds from the higher levels. The amount of park space in the city doubled, because of the use of federal funds.

THE FEDERALISM REGIME, 1978–86

Ernest ("Dutch") Morial, who was first elected mayor in 1977, was the city's first black mayor. As such, Morial is a truly historic figure. He got his start in the civil-rights movement and the legal battles of the 1960s. In both of his runoff elections—in 1977, against Joseph DiRosa, and in 1982, against

Ron Faucheux—Morial defeated white candidates by obtaining virtually all of the black vote while earning an appreciable minority of the white vote—20 percent in 1977, but only 13 percent in 1982.

Morial's administrations emphasized economic development, which utilized federal monies until federal funds were cut back during the later part of his second term. Federal money brought planning requirements with it, and the city undertook detailed economic-development planning for the first time at the beginning of Morial's administration in 1978. EDA monies provided a planning staff, which was required to write an Overall Economic Development Plan and a Comprehensive Economic Development Strategy, in order for the city to remain eligible for economic-development dollars. Both of these were collapsed into a single document, the Economic Development Strategy. The 1979 document *New Orleans Economic Development Strategy* is the best statement of the Morial administration's economic policies. The overview includes a discussion of the quality of life and the perceived business climate, the labor force and its socioeconomic characteristics, and recent trends in the port, tourism, and the CBD. The plan then discusses significant economic problems, such as the failure to attract new industry, the loss of existing firms, the shortage of suitable industrial-park sites, and the decline and disinvestment in older-neighborhood commercial shopping areas. The report then presents the goals and program elements of the city's economic-development strategy, including financial assistance to small businesses, the long-range industrial-land-use plan for the Almonaster-Michoud Industrial Corridor, and the growth potential of the CBD and other areas.

New Orleans has been extremely active in the Urban Development Action Grant (UDAG) program, a federal program that was instituted in 1977. Two major activities of the UDAG program funds are providing infrastructure and gap financing for project development. Three concepts that are central to the UDAG program are targeting, leveraging, and public-private partnerships.[17] The UDAG program targets its funds to distressed cities, using a variety of measures of hardship. Because New Orleans has older housing and a high-poverty-level population, it is invariably high on any list of distressed cities. Leveraging involves using public funds to stimulate additional private investment. The idea behind the UDAG program is that federal grants will leverage private-sector investments, which will help to revitalize economically distressed communities. The final important concept is partnerships. Cities will enter public-private partnerships with developers as a result of negotiations in the UDAG, but the program also assumed that there would be partnerships involving all levels of government, as funding sources, and neighborhood residents.

The city's first UDAG was the construction of a new wharf and a new dry dock on the West Bank in the Algiers district of the city. The project was undertaken with the Dock Board and Todd Shipyards for a cost of $1.75 million. The city's largest UDAG is for the Exhibition Hall (New Orleans Convention Center) and Sheraton Hotel project. The city received $14 million, which represented 16 percent of the cost of a new convention facility, not including the land. The Exhibition Hall, which served as the Louisiana Pavilion for the 1984 World's Fair, is now open as a convention center. Most recently, the city has employed a UDAG for the construction of single-family homes for low- and moderate-income groups in east New Orleans.

The most controversial UDAG in which the city has participated is Canal Place, a downtown mixed-use project that straddles the boundary of the historic French Quarter. Canal Place has pitted preservationists, who fear that the scale and height of the project will damage the coherence of the historic district, against developers and city officials, who see the project as helping to provide the jobs and taxes that the city needs in order to sustain itself.[18] To allay the fears of the preservationists, the city has adopted a "managed growth" strategy, by which development is focused in areas where high-intensity land uses already exist. This strategy has worked reasonably well, but as the pressures for downtown development mount, the preservationists may find themselves losing ground. To illustrate, the height limitations in the French Quarter were waived for the extension of the Jackson Brewery development along the river front in 1985, despite the opposition of preservationists. Such controversies again point up conflicting objectives in economic development, as development along the river front frequently clashes with the desire to preserve the city's historic waterfront district. Economic development along the river front may well benefit a city that has a depressed economy, especially in the short run. At the same time, river-front development may well spoil one of the city's major assets: a remarkable supply of historic and architecturally interesting buildings, especially in the French Quarter.

A review of the Morial years shows at least three things. (1) Major downtown development projects that were favored by the land-use alliance were vigorously pursued during Morial's administration. Most of these projects were funded with federal government monies, through such programs as Community Development Block Grants and UDAG's. One major thrust away from downtown was seen in Morial's effort to develop the Almonaster-Michoud Industrial District. While this effort was (and still is) an admirable attempt at diversification, this large industrial area needs substantial infrastructure development at a time when federal and local funds are dwindling. The ultimate fate of this effort is uncertain.

(2) Morial's constituency base was very different from that of his predecessors. Many black supporters of Morial were rewarded with city-hall positions and city contracts. Morial also remembered his constituency base in economic-development programs, which were aimed at the neighborhoods.

Such programs as Neighborhood Commercial Revitalization and small-business loans were aimed primarily, though not exclusively, at the black community. Morial's white supporters were largely from the middle and upper-middle classes. Many of them were rewarded with appointments in areas of interest to them, such as seats on the Audubon Park Commission.

(3) The city's functional bureaucracies were professionalized, as the city's economic-development activities increased. Mayor Morial established the Office of Economic Development to plan, establish, and manage the city's economic-development efforts in the creation and retention of jobs and taxes. One of the mayor's top four aides—the mayor's executive assistant for planning and development—oversees the city's development strategy. Another mayoral office, the Office of Economic and Fiscal Analysis, is in charge of forecasting revenues and economic and land-use information. The city's traditional line bureaucracies, including the City Planning Commission, supported economic-development efforts and increased their professionalization during the Morial years.

POSTSCRIPT: THE POSTFEDERALIST REGIME, 1986–

In 1986, New Orleans voters elected Councilman Sidney Barthelemy as their mayor. In a runoff election against state Senator William Jefferson, voters were faced with a choice between two black Democratic candidates, who both seemed liberal in terms of their stated policy preferences. Barthelemy was elected by a rather unusual coalition; he received the overwhelming majority of white votes and a substantial minority of black votes. This election reversed a traditional political process. In many instances, blacks chose the white candidate who was least inflammatory to them. In this election, white voters selected the least objectionable black, presumably on grounds of personality and style.

On economic-development issues, the Barthelemy administration has a somewhat different tone from that of its predecessor. The mayor's main assistant is called the executive assistant for development. The word planning was omitted, rather conspicuously. Officials of Barthelemy's administration have been quoted as saying that economic development "is the responsibility of the Chamber of Commerce." This attitude is an unfortunate one, because in fragmented New Orleans the Chamber does not only serve New Orleans. It represents six other parishes in the River Region, and its actions might not always serve the best overall economic interests of the city. The Chamber has a small-business base, and again, its policies don't always reflect the broader interests of the community. Moreover, the Barthelemy administration seems to be wedded to a continuing emphasis on tourism. In a public forum on the city's economy in the fall of 1986, the executive assistant for development said that "there was nothing wrong with tourism as a strategy."

Mayor Barthelemy quickly discovered that there was a significant difference between electoral coalitions and governing coalitions. In a September 1986 referendum, the mayor's proposal for a $195 services fee to maintain basic city services was rejected by an angry electorate. In the same election, New Orleans voters turned down a millage increase for more public-school funding, a proposal that was opposed by much of the business community. The white voters, who overwhelmingly supported the mayor's election, overwhelmingly opposed his service-fee proposal. Black turnout was low. With federal funds diminished and with few local options, the city turned again to an unpopular earnings-tax proposal. The point here is that Barthelemy became mayor at a time when the era of federal largesse had ended. At the local level, imaginative initiatives and thoughtful strategies were necessary in order to cope with the fiscal crisis.

CONCLUSIONS

While any conclusions must be speculative and tentative, it is my judgment that the New Orleans downtown business community does not seem to be the dominant force that the downtown business community is in many other American cities. Admittedly, the role of business in policymaking—including agenda setting and the implementation of policy—should never be underestimated.

Indeed, when we look at New Orleans, we find the Chamber of Commerce and City Hall working very closely on economic-development and other issues. The "land-use alliance" was evident throughout the postwar era. The Morial administration had especially close working relationships with major local and national developers, who developed hotels, retail businesses, and office space downtown. Many projects provide examples of thriving "public-private partnerships."

The question, however, is, *Why* has this land-use alliance not dominated New Orleans politics? One major reason is the fragmentation of policy makers, both public and private. This fragmentation takes a number of forms. First, there is a fragmentation of effort. Numerous city and state agencies are involved in the economic-development fields, and there is little coordination among them. The Chamber of Commerce is involved in its own economic-development efforts, which don't necessarily coincide with the city's efforts. Indeed, the Chamber was somewhat resentful when the city "invaded its turf" with its entry into the economic-development field during the 1970s. Second, there is a fragmentation of jurisdiction. The city government is only one government in a metropolitan region. Relations between

New Orleans and other area governments, especially Jefferson Parish, have been highly conflictual. There is little sense of any regional cooperative effort. In an earlier period, the 1940s, Mayor Morrison was proud of his efforts to bring a major Kaiser Aluminum plant to Chalmette, Louisiana, in suburban St. Bernard Parish. Third, there is a fragmentation of time and attention on other civic projects and on recreational activities, especially Mardi Gras. Finally, there is competition and controversy over many issues that simply would not exist, or would not be tolerated, in other cities. To cite a few examples, recent years in New Orleans have seen fissures in the power structure on such issues as who would develop a choice piece of riverfront property, what sort of image campaign, if any, the city should undertake, and the legalization of a statewide lottery and casino gambling for New Orleans.

A second major reason for the lesser business dominance is the structure of interest groups in the city. First, there is no one "peak" downtown business organization, which dominates policy making and agenda setting in the fashion of Central Atlanta Progress, in Atlanta, or the Greater Baltimore Committee, in Baltimore.[19] Second, other groups, such as preservationists and black grass-roots political groups, seem to be more of a countervailing force to urban-development interests than they are in many other communities. The fact that blacks are a significant part of the city's dominant political coalition keeps concerns about unemployment before the politicians. Moreover, displacement has never been employed as vigorously as in other cities, possibly because of the combined political strength of grass-roots black politicians and the preservationist movement.

NOTES

1. Martin Shefter, *Political Crisis/Fiscal Crisis: The Collapse and Revival of New York City* (New York: Basic Books, 1985).

2. Stephen L. Elkin, "Twentieth Century Urban Regimes," *Journal of Urban Affairs* 7 (Spring 1985): 11–28.

3. Ibid., p. 13.

4. Edward F. Haas, *DeLesseps S. Morrison and the Image of Reform: New Orleans Politics, 1946–1961* (Baton Rouge: Louisiana State University Press, 1974), pp. 7–25.

5. Elkin, "Twentieth Century Urban Regimes," p. 19.

6. Haas, *DeLesseps S. Morrison*, pp. 57–62, 72–73.

7. On the integration of the New Orleans public schools see Robert L. Crain, *The Politics of School Desegregation: Comparative Case Studies of Community Structure and Policy Making* (Garden City, N.Y.: Anchor Books, 1969), pp. 250–322.

8. See the excellent case study by Richard O. Baumbach, Jr., and William E. Borah, *The Second Battle of New Orleans: A History of the Vieux Carre Riverfront Expressway Controversy* (University: University of Alabama Press, 1981).

9. Arnold R. Hirsch, "New Orleans: Sunbelt in the Swamp," in *Sunbelt Cities: Politics and Growth since World War II,* ed. Richard M. Bernard and Bradley R. Rice (Austin: University of Texas Press, 1983), p. 118.

10. On Dallas see chapter 2 in this volume; Martin V. Melosi, "Dallas–Fort Worth: Marketing the Metroplex," in *Sunbelt Cities,* pp. 162–95; and Carol E. Thometz, *The Decision Makers: The Power Structure of Dallas* (Dallas, Texas: Southern Methodist University Press, 1963).

11. See Hirsch, "New Orleans"; Anthony J. Mumphrey and Pamela H. Moomau, "New Orleans: An Island in the Sunbelt," *Public Administration Quarterly* 8 (Spring 1984); and Michael P. Smith and Marlene Keller, "Managed Growth and the Politics of Uneven Development in New Orleans," in *Restructuring the City: The Political Economy of Urban Redevelopment,* Susan Fainstein et al. (New York: Longman, 1983), pp. 136–66.

12. James R. Bobo, *The New Orleans Economy: Pro Bono Publico?* (New Orleans: Division of Business and Economic Research, University of New Orleans, 1985).

13. Copelin was elected to the state legislature in 1986.

14. On the benefits and costs of stadium development in Minneapolis see Amy Klobuchar, *Uncovering the Dome* (Prospect Heights, Ill.: Waveland Press, 1986).

15. For the unitary model see Paul E. Peterson, *City Limits* (Chicago: University of Chicago Press, 1981).

16. On this point generally, see Rufus P. Browning, Dale Rogers Marshall, and David H. Tabb, *Protest Is Not Enough: The Struggle of Blacks and Hispanics for Equality in Urban Politics* (Berkeley: University of California Press, 1984).

17. Alma H. Young, "Urban Development Action Grants: The New Orleans Experience," *Public Administration Quarterly* 8 (Spring 1984): 112–29.

18. Jane S. Brooks and Deborah Weeter, "Canal Place: A Clash of Values," *Urban Land* 41 (July 1982): 3–9.

19. On Atlanta see Clarence N. Stone, *Economic Growth and Neighborhood Discontent* (Chapel Hill: University of North Carolina Press, 1976). For case studies of Atlanta, Baltimore, and five other cities see R. Scott Fosler and Renee A. Berger, eds., *Public-Private Partnership in American Cities: Seven Case Studies* (Lexington, Mass.: Lexington Books, 1982). A peak association of downtown business groups was founded in New Orleans in 1986. Jim Bob Moffett of Freeport McMoran was the main moving force in its founding. It is too early to tell if the group will have a lasting impact.

12

Structural Change and Innovation: Elites and Albuquerque Politics in the 1980s

Peter A. Lupsha

Whereas growth in Dallas was promoted and presided over by an elite business group, organized to promote development as a collective good, Albuquerque's growth has been promoted and presided over by developers and others who have particular interest in development. Peter Lupsha examines various efforts to cope with Albuquerque's phenomenal growth rate. Of particular interest are recent mayors' efforts to manage growth in a planned way consistent with a concept of the public interest. That their efforts proved short-lived is testimony to the difficulty of reining in particular interests on behalf of a collective good. It is also testimony to the difficulty of changing an informal set of arrangements through which development transactions are handled.

Lupsha directs our attention to just how limited the power of the mayor is—the short election cycle and the restricted authority leave elected officials with little capacity on their own to restructure a community's decision processes. It is hard to build an effective and durable coalition without involving those businesses that have strong particular interests in development. So, while popular support for planned growth is understandable in a city such as Albuquerque, so also is the difficulty of maintaining a regime committed to such planned growth. Lupsha thus depicts a regime of relatively freewheeling conflict, managed, not by the city's elected officials, but on an ad hoc basis by "consultant-facilitators."

What happens when a city's growth mushrooms? When new population groups from other urban environments in the United States move into a Sun Belt city? How do local elites and governmental leaders respond to such change? How do they respond to protect the long-term community interest and values? This chapter examines the case of Albuquerque, New Mexico, and the politics of urban development in that city. It looks at the questions of "who governs" and "who benefits" and how, if at all, long-term public interests and community values fare under conditions of rapid growth and development.

The origins of Albuquerque, New Mexico, lie in the settlement, some seventy years before the writing of our Declaration of Independence, of the Villa de San Francisco de Alburquerque. The name honored Saint Francis and the then duke of Alburquerque. Later, the first *r* was dropped from the current spelling, but the nickname "Duke City" remains. During those early years any growth was slow and pastoral. Indeed, the first real major growth event only occurred in 1880, and it can only be considered large in terms of the small changes that had occurred in the previous one hundred and fifty years.

In 1880 the Atchison, Topeka and Santa Fe Railroad constructed yards and a roundhouse in Albuquerque. This led to the construction of a "New Town" several miles east of the "Old Town" and brought a population of "Anglos" to the largely Hispanic and Indian community. In 1891 the city was formally incorporated under United States territorial law. Growth, however, continued to be slow and gradual.

The 1940 census witnessed a population of 35,499 in the city of Albuquerque. The economy was based primarily on the railroad, Albuquerque's location as a regional trading center, and the in-migration of "lungers"— that is, convalescent patients sent to the Southwest to recover from respiratory diseases, such as tuberculosis. World War II brought the military, its bases, and its personnel to New Mexico. For Albuquerque, this was the beginning of its long-term relationship with the military-scientific weapons community which is still a mainstay of its economic life.

By 1970 the weapons laboratories and the ancillary support and service industries had helped raise the city's population to 243,751. Ten years later, Albuquerque's growth continued to outpace the nation, with a population of 331,767 within the city's limits and another 100,000 people living in the surrounding Bernalillo County.[1] The expectation is that by 1990 some half a million people will live within the expanded (via annexation) city, and another two hundred plus thousand will reside in the adjacent area.

Even in 1980 the city, its politics, and its attitudes could be considered heavily influenced by its "Tri-cultural heritage—Indian, Hispanic and Anglo." That census showed that some 34 percent of the population was Hispanic. That percentage was falling, however, and continues to fall even more rapidly today, as this tri-cultural mix is slowly becoming more memory than reality and as new, mostly non–New Mexican, in-migrants flood into the city and state. These new in-migrants from other areas of the United States have been entering the state at a rate of some sixty-four thousand per year. The bulk of these newcomers settle in Albuquerque, Bernalillo County, and adjacent areas; and Bernalillo and neighboring Sandoval County to the north have become, in recent censuses, a single SMSA. By 1990 it is likely that Valencia County, to the south, will join this pair in a single SMSA.

Today, Albuquerque is in a period of extraordinary growth and change. It is in a phase of "popcorn development" in which new housing, businesses, and factories appear to be "popping up" on the landscape seemingly overnight, like corn kernels at the right temperature in an oiled and heated pan.

This explosive growth has overwhelmed the city's historically limited capacity to rationally lay out infrastructure planning and projects that can match these changes. Orange barrels, indicating infrastructure construction projects, are literally everywhere, and what has been labeled "the orange barrel syndrome" has led voters on more than one occasion to seek to throw the incumbents out. Indeed, some local planners believe that between now and the year 2000, conflicts and tensions over infrastructure development will become the key political issue and the key public concern.[2]

Not only has this growth brought a lot of new individual residents into the community, it has also resulted in a large number of new business and corporate residents and employers. This new business community not only brings outside capital; it also brings new values, methods, and expectations to the community. Business needs for services and interaction with the public sector result in the creation of a new class of political brokers, middlemen who link traditional political structures and elites to these corporate and business newcomers.

In terms of local politics, the issue of urban development and growth first took fire during the early 1970s, when the city manager, Herb Smith, came into direct and public confrontation with the city commission over the public control of private development and growth. While the issue was disguised in questions of policy and information control, the key was who should act to control growth and development, and how this should be done.

Smith was fired, but the resulting uproar in the community led to the abolition of the commission form of government and its replacement by a strong mayor–council system of government. The first mayor under this new form of government was a former commissioner and long-term resident named Harry Kinney, who was elected in 1974. Kinney tended to be more progrowth and conservative than Smith had been. But as a trained engineer, a nonnative product of the Sandia Base weapons lab, and an upper-middle-class Republican, while anxious to serve the traditional development and business elite, he was also anxious to reward merit and to do what he believed best for the city.

He was replaced in 1977 by David Rusk, son of former Secretary of State Dean Rusk. David Rusk, a graduate of the University of California at Berkeley, represented the high point of controlled growth and "quality" development and planning in the city's recent history. Rusk, a classic "eastern white wine and brie liberal," wanted to preserve both the multicultural values and heritage of the community and the open space and Southwestern uniqueness and big-skies vistas that made Albuquerque special. He was, however, defeated by (1) his inability to sell this program to those who wanted to maximize development profits; (2) the growing orange-barrel syndrome; and (3) the cutbacks on certain public-infrastructure maintenance programs such as the weed and litter right of way.

Rusk was replaced by the amiable Harry Kinney, who in time would also fall electoral victim of rapid growth and the orange-barrel syndrome. Both of these men represented a shifting away from the traditional friends-and-neighbors downtown Chamber of Commerce business elite and the world view of local real-estate and development interests to a much-larger vision of Albuquerque's future. While Kinney was much closer to that past than Rusk was, he too was sensitive to the growth issue, and in his second term he continued many of the programs to control unplanned growth and development that Rusk had implemented. Both men also believed in scientific management and professional administration. Under them, outside experts, professionally trained outside staff and consultants, were regularly consulted, and the new major outside corporate management was recognized as a key aspect of the city's growth future.

Whatever opportunities existed for melding this potential for controlled growth on a city-wide level and for integrating the dominant themes of a tricultural past into Albuquerque's future appear to have been overwhelmed by the very facts of rapid growth, as well as by recent changes in the city's leadership and administration. The municipal election of 1985 witnessed a throwback to the pre-Smith administrations of old. A coalition of old-time developers, downtown business interests, and "friends and neighbors" politicians, once known as the Valley Alligators, plus the tidal wave of outside Anglo newcomers, who possessed little familiarity with the city's history or past, banded together to defeat a progressive middle-class Hispanic native, whose liberal politics, in the mold of David Rusk, and whose previous independent and prochange positions as state land commissioner had earned him their suspicion. This group's candidate was Ken Schultz, a local car dealer who had come to Albuquerque from Chicago. Under him, politics and policy have shifted back in the direction of the old-time electoral patronage and cronyism that marked the city commission during the 1950s, when boomer boosterism and City Hall's nearly blind support for any and all growth tended to be the rule.

This has resulted in a badly divided and at times rancorous relationship between elements of the city council and the mayor as they squabble over issues, patronage, and internal City Hall politics, which often involves the cronyism of the rewards for electoral support. In the meantime, issues of controlling growth and guiding development and change are often avoided or simply lost, as these officials respond both to stretching ever-tightening program resources and to balancing the demands on those resources, because of the ever-present pressures and demands from developers and growth-oriented economic elites. At present in Albuquerque, it appears to many observers that money talks and that planning for development tends to be reactive. Recently, for example, seven large landowners (actually development syndicates and groups) offered to donate the land for a new ring road that would be built with state highway funds some sixteen miles west of the downtown. Public reaction from city officials or others was nonexistent. Such private largess has been silently accepted and plans are being altered that will permit these private entrepreneurs to garner large profits at minimal cost.

Another example: a wealthy entrepreneur has created an industrial and business park, creating his own zoning and infrastructure, and the city has gratefully altered its plans and zoning in the area and has accepted title to the maintenance of roads, sewers, and other established infrastructure. One local city-planning expert has analyzed that situation thus:

> Boomtown growth comes with deeper incongruities too. The crippling inconveniences of growth (spawned by licentious, rather than managed, expansion) are the symptoms of the most serious problem a city can face—known variously as selling itself short, undervaluing itself, or commiting urban self abuse.
>
> As an American Frontier town Albuquerque has always been viewed as either a place to settle in or nurture or a place to be taken, a place up for grabs. As an object of possession, Albuquerque has suffered from being sized up as both a place of vast potential value and a place that in itself, has no value at all.[3]

The southwestern Sun Belt cities possess a unique political history and culture which has facilitated "public-privatism," a politics of boomer boosterism in which government's chief role at the local level is to facilitate development, growth, investment, and profit making for the private sector. For reasons discussed elsewhere, this leads to a lower level of public-service-sector investment, a lessened publicly funded concern for social needs of the poor and minorities, and political structures and institutions that tend to defuse voting by bloc or class.[4]

The local political system in the Sun Belt Southwest tends to be dominated by local elites, coteries of economic and political notables, and, at times, by personally ambitious segments of the professional strata.[5] This latter category includes lawyers, schoolteachers, elite retirees, and "double dippers," along with neighborhood-association activists; self-selected narrow-interest activists, such as prison-reform advocates; advocates of the homeless and street people; and of course, environmentalists, among others.[6]

In Max Weber's terminology, these are citizens who tend to live "for politics," while the others noted tend to live "off politics."[7] And if this former group is not coopted over time into this latter group, its members often appear as political meteors crossing our southwestern sky. They arrive on the scene dramatically and flashily, filled with knowledge and desire garnered from prior experiences and successes elsewhere. But like meteors, they usually burn out quickly, as they move from the rarified ether of self-knowledge and rational understanding into the denser political atmosphere and come closer to the primordial political earth of "the bottom line."

The English jurist and philosopher Jeremy Bentham once wrote a cogent essay about "the harm that good men do" in their desire to establish universal right where utilitarian practical insight might better serve the situation. So, perhaps, the social analyst should not be overly concerned about the quick political demise of these heady neophytes. Instead, perhaps we should rejoice in the few political mutants who do survive the atmospheric buffeting and culture shock to bring some small fragments of innovation, creativity, and change to our local political systems.

What this means in cities such as Albuquerque is that most innovation tends to be initiated and structured by the established elites, a fact that is well documented in the literature of political science.[8] This oligarchy varies somewhat, however, with the size and nature of the particular city that one is studying. In the smaller and more insulated cities, the main-street business and commercial elite usually dominates the decisional process. In growing and changing larger cities, mixes of traditional development leaders and banking elites mix with the new corporate managers, who represent the multilocational enterprises that are constantly being added into the mix of our more dynamic, faster-growing urban centers.

In Albuquerque, main-street, local and interstate banking interests, development and real-estate investment elites, along with the new managers and corporate investors who represent outside capital and entrepreneurial interests—all come together to drive change, innovation, and growth. This mixed cadre and self-interested coalitions often play a bigger role in structuring change than do the people's elected guardians—mayor, council members, and representatives. These coalitions are, however, constrained by their need to accommodate to the system and to public power structures.

Thus, what one finds in Albuquerque and, I suspect, in a large number of fast-growing dynamic cities is the existence of what might be considered a private-political broker class. A group that often includes former city, state, and county officials and administrators who serve as "consultant-facilitators," or, better, decisional middlemen, linking the new development money, corporate development agents, and entrepreneurs to the elected and appointed political leadership and its surrounding managerial infrastructure.

The growth of this class of political brokers, who facilitate the linkages between those who seek self and corporate success and enrichment, on the one hand, with the existing elite structures and personalities, on the other hand, is a relatively recent phenomenon. These middlemen, because of their past work and association with the public sector, can make personal interventions into the public networks that represent what might be considered outside interests in a local "downhome" manner. They can assist the integration of outside capital and opportunities for profit and partnerships between locals and those outsiders who need entry to the local political system in order to attain their goals. Without the existence of these facilitating middlemen, the infusion of growth and development capital and, in turn, public infrastructure projects would occur more slowly and perhaps painfully and conflictually for the multilocational investors and the local political elites.

In almost every situation of in-migrant change, whether human, corporate, or capital, it is essential to have someone on site who can show the way, communicate, stimulate, introduce, and ease the trauma of change. These private-political brokers and middlemen serve this gatekeeper function and, as such, can help to preserve the old and valued while promoting the new. This symbiosis also places more power cards in the hands of the newcomers and the connected old elites, while the generally somnambulant two-thirds of the citizenry are picking their way through the orange barrels and the "popcorn" construction development as they regret the loss of the familiar, complain about crowded highways and new people, but accept change as inevitable and immutable.

The one set of actors on the urban political stage that does not appear to accept the role of middleman or quiescence, at least in Albuquerque and I suspect elsewhere, comprises the members of the city's professional bureaucracy. Those bureaucrats who have their advanced degrees and their national professional job orientation, perspectives, and expertise in planning, law, finance, and subdisciplines enter the game of development, structural change, and innovation, with their own values, goals, and agendas. And while these bureaucrats are not the ones who prevail in the end, they do exert a tempering and longer-range perspective on issues of growth and change than can either the elected political elites, who are made myopic by their situation and by their need to bend to campaign contributors and supporters, or the more narrowly focused middlemen and corporate and development interests, who must focus on profit as their bottom line.

What I am suggesting here is that in the Sun Belt Southwest, as exemplified by the case of Albuquerque, the questions that I raised earlier can be answered by an old but often neglected equation. Here it is not the elected officials who lead; indeed, they do their best to stay in front on the presentable and predictable, yet are made myopic by issues and timid by cross-cutting constituencies, special interests, ambition, and contributors. Nor is leadership found in the enlightened self-interests of corporate-change agents or their middlemen, for whom the bottom line is the profit that is sent to corporate centers located elsewhere. Nor does an active and enthusiastic citizenry guard the long-term public interest with its vigilance. Here in Albuquerque the coalition constantly active in limiting excessive aggrandizement toward the short-term future and its profits is composed of the professional public administrators and bureaucrats who seek to provide a voice of moderation, future orientation, and professionalism and who, more often than not, fill the vacuum and the role of public representation vacated by elected politicians for the reasons discussed earlier. A brief examination of some concrete issue areas will, I believe, further illustrate and illuminate this argument.

THE SYCAMORE HILL METROPOLITAN DEVELOPMENT PLAN

Congress passed the 1974 Community Development Act to "develop viable urban communities . . . providing decent housing . . . a suitable living environment and expanding economic opportunities for persons of low and moderate income."[9] After the passage of this law the city of Albuquerque established a number of sector-development plans. One of them covered the Sycamore Hill neighborhood, an area near the university composed of aging middle-class single-family homes, converted duplexes, and student apartments. In short, a student-elderly middle-to-working-class neighborhood. The neighborhood also contained Presbyterian Hospital, an aggressive growth-oriented facility that has a long history in the community and is connected to its elites. Presbyterian was in sound financial shape and could carry out its $19.5-million development plans and indebtedness without assistance, privately and slowly over time. It could also use the Sycamore Hill development plan and achieve its ends at much lower costs and interest rates as the centerpiece of a local, state, and federal urban-renewal project.

The hospital had gradually been acquiring private parcels of land and property, but it was quick to realize that this process could be hastened by condemnation and by city assistance in overwhelming holdouts, if the neighborhood could be declared "blighted" under the sector plan. In addition, the fiscal benefits from lower interest rates and federal grants would mean that much of the project could be funded from public resources, rather than from the hospital's funds.

With the help of its elite board members, the hospital achieved its ends. The board members not only mobilized some members of the medical community; they also provided active support for and contributions to candidates for city office. In addition, the board made use of a former city administrator as a lobbyist and middleman. Through these various efforts, some twelve blocks of housing were transformed into hospital parking lots and support buildings. The only strong opposition consisted of residents who had been rallied by members of the city's planning staff, the city's neighborhood-association professional-assistance staffs, and the arguments and data developed by city bureaucrats connected with the sector-development plan.

How did the citizens and a number of key professionals and bureaucrats on the city staff lose the Sycamore Hill battle when one would think these professionals would control many key informational and agenda-setting cards? The answer is easy. Elected officials took the decision away from these public bureaucrats and gave it to private planning consultants and outside experts for an "objective survey and decision."[10] It is common practice throughout the Sun Belt to go outside for expert assistance, even when the city has a paid professional engineering and planning staff; this has been a long-term historic fact in Albuquerque. In this way, campaign coffers can be filled, supporters can be appreciated, and conflicts between elected officials and their professional staffs can be eliminated without the obvious public appearance of favoritism.

THE COOR'S CORRIDOR PLAN

Here again the city's planning professionals were pitted against active campaign contributors, new and old elite developers, and hired middlemen, who linked elected officials to developers.[11] The issue focused on providing major arterial highways and on expanding the existing roadways to provide for major residential development on Albuquerque's west side. This area has experienced a better than 12 percent per annum growth rate over the last several years, and these highways are keystones to financial success and represent windfall profits for developers who are located at key access points.

The city council finessed the issue by passing it to the Citizen's Advisory Task Force for decision. The task force was assisted by members of the city's planning staff, who were able to argue for limited-access landscaped arterials that would help to preserve the long-term aesthetic and environmental values and landscapes of the west side. By using the citizen's group and its key members and by pitting rival development interests against one another, thus neutralizing the elected politicians, the professional planners and bureaucrats won on this one, and the longer-range interests of quality development prevailed over short-term profits and expediency.

THE RIO GRANDE BRIDGE

The west-side growth has led to the obvious need for more river crossings over the Rio Grande. The two existing ones have seven miles of burgeoning population between them. West-side residents and developers pressed the issue, and the city fathers endorsed the concept if not the suggested locations, because the logical siting runs directly through homes and acreage that belongs to the traditional community elite on the east side of the river. Shifting the location several miles upstream satisfied this group but mobilized hispanic state and county politicians whose middle-class and traditional small-farming constituents would now receive the eastern leg of the bridge. To avoid the continuing fire storm of controversy, the city council and the mayor, noting the need for state fund-assistance, tried to pass the decision on siting to the governor and the legislature. The legislature in turn tried to move the bridge further upstream, beyond the current northern bridge, thus antagonizing new interests while siting the bridge in a location that would do little to relieve the urban-transportation problems.

Some three years later there was still no bridge, although ground was broken and several sets of politicians have been elected at city, county, and state levels who have pledged themselves to the bridge, bridge funding, various locations, and twenty-four-hour-a-day construction schedules. In 1985 the matter was in the district court for the judiciary to rule on, as other political actors and units had run out of energy and alternatives. Meanwhile, the west-side traffic jams grow, all politicos say the bridge is coming, and a handful of planners note that its costs have outstripped its funded appropriation.[12]

In this case, long-term interest, planning, and logic foundered on the rocks of political pressures from various special interests. All rational argument and information founders in a fragmented multiunit political system that contains a host of narrowly focused special-interest elites, all of whom believe that it is their ox that is being gored.

Given these brief case studies, one may wonder if it is possible to restore a greater measure of public responsibility and caring to the elected public sector, thus aligning it more closely with the activities and professional management perspectives of those managers in the civil service. In Albuquerque we have had strong liberal mayors, such as David Rusk, who have seen themselves as stewards of the city's future; yet their vision and compromises often resulted in rather myopic results and in direct conflicts with the mayor's planning department. A more conservative yet thoughtful mayor, Harry Kinney, tried to walk the middle of the road, balancing managed growth against the development desires of many of his old friends and supporters. The result was often decisional avoidance on his part and a reactive attempt to cajole them into longer-range development perspectives. Where he and his administration won, it was most often due to division between rival development interests and middlemen who could be played against one another toward the end of compromise. The mayor in 1986, Ken Schultz, represents an even more laissez-faire position. As a strong supporter of boomer boosterism, he appears to see his role as simply setting the stage and providing the support mechanisms so that private developers and entrepreneurs can maximize their gains.

Unfortunately, the people's other representatives, the city council, appear to be equally acquiescent on these issues. Is this because they are elected by districts and do not have a feeling for city-wide or longer-term managed growth in the city? This likely has some effect, as do the other structural constraints that have been addressed in the literature.[13] Other factors, such as political and budgetary cycles, also have some effect on these urban leadership styles.[14] Yet, in the particular case of rapid growth and urban development, a number of additional factors constrain leadership and the taking of longer-range public-interest or community perspectives. They can be summarized as follows. First is the complexity of the issue. If there is one truth of urban governance today it is that of the complexity and interdependence of issues and their policy solutions. Whether we are talking about authorization or appropriation, urban-change-and-innovation decisions are complex and multidimensional.

Building a bridge over the Rio Grande within the city limits of Albuquerque is no longer a simple public-works decision. Rather, it involves planning and the coordination of a multitude of governmental agencies and approvals. The decision is not simply an engineering one; it involves environmental-impact statements, issues of water quality and flood control, and a variety of actors whose approvals on funding and planning are necessary before the project can be completed. This creates complexity for decision makers and opportunities for decisional opponents, who today have multiple points of decision—including veto, deflection, or delay.

Second is the diversity of issues. The days when urban decision making was limited to public works, sanitation, and public safety are long gone. Recent agendas of Albuquerque's city council, for example, include educational-leave policies, housing for the homeless, auto-emission standards, risk-management policy, funding for the arts, detention-center standards, along with zoning and development questions. The citizen city-council member is able to have only limited expertise in these matters and must answer the demands of constituents and political supporters, as well as satisfy the media, local elites, and middlemen, while staying within the budget, keeping costs down, and responding to the standards of state and federal regulations whose mission and funding may affect many of these decisions. In attempting to provide services and to manage conflict, the city council today is overwhelmed with diverse issues, from "passive smoking" to "the use of force"—all of which have their supporters and opponents. It is not surprising, therefore, that innovation and longer-range protection of the public interest often get lost.

Third is the issue of seriality. Decisions, for better or for worse, do not solve (end) problems. Rather, they often expand commitments and expectations. Thus, seriality of response can be regularized. Understanding this, urban decision makers often go out of their way to prevent issues from becoming serialized. And this can often result in decisional avoidance, or simply acquiescence to private-sector initiatives, especially when such initiatives are supported by prominent middlemen or elite interests.

Fourth is the issue of boundedness. Once a decision has been made, future decisions—such as the issue of space and flexibility in terms of optional choices—is diminished. After commitment, the range of discretionary options and alternatives becomes structured and narrowed. Past decisions can haunt present decisions and can seriously limit the range and trajectory of future decisions. After a certain point of decisional boundedness has been reached, local decision makers often find their scope of options so constrained that going along with private development concerns may appear to be the only option.

This phenomenon can be placed in bold relief by reversing the imagery and examining the flexibility of the issue. When one looks at some of the great American urban decision makers of the twentieth century, what does one find? One finds that the keys of success for almost all was the flexibility of the issue, which is created either by crisis or by access to outside funding or by both.[15] This is true not only of great mayors but also of administrators such as Robert Moses, whose coups rested primarily on the flexibility that is provided by access to money and the control over money.[16]

Fifth is the issue of proximity. Given all the constraints noted, urban decision makers often find themselves drawn to those issues that are the most immediate or that will have a quick-fix result. A key lesson of office holding is that it is often better to react than to anticipate, for the latter entails the greater risks. Thus, short-run gains, rather than long-range innovation and commitment, often become the norm.

Sixth is the issue of conflictiveness. Issues often enter the public decision-making arena only because values are in conflict. If such conflicts become polarized or rancorous, decisional avoidance is a likely outcome. In the bridge controversy, for example, the city council of Albuquerque tried to avoid decisional responsibility by passing the question of siting on to the state legislature and to the governor. Today, frequently the courts and the judicial branches of our federal system are the end points of decisional avoidance by other branches and units of government. Under conditions of conflict it is not surprising that local decision makers tend to opt for the short-range perspective rather than to risk greater losses on innovation and change.

In this chapter we have examined the issue of urban development and change, as well as some reasons for it, in the rapidly growing city of Albuquerque, New Mexico. Here we have seen that private-development elites, traditional attitudes of "boomer boosterism," and a frontier mentality have worked to limit and derail the longer-term community interest. Here middlemen have linked the old-timers with new capital and have assisted development and the smoothing of the change process with elected decision makers. We have also seen that in Albuquerque the key guardians of the public interest appear to be the professional civil servants and planners, and not the citizen's representatives, their public officials.

In addition we have attempted to show that in our process of urban pluralistic decision making, there are numerous constraints which focus the public's elected representatives away from decisions that involve change and innovation and direct them instead toward shorter-range reactive decisions which, particularly in the case of urban development under conditions of rapid growth, may direct them to abdicating their public responsibility in favor of the acceptance of private-development decisions and directions. Such actions, in the long run, only work to further constrain and limit creative public opportunities for innovation and change for the long-term community good.

It is unlikely that Albuquerque is unique among Sun Belt cities in this regard. While obviously more work needs to be done, the lessons observed here are likely to be found in other rapidly growing areas. And the function of political middlemen as linkage figures and of professional managers and civil servants as gatekeepers who are attempting to protect the longer-range community interest and values are phenomena that are likely to have much wider application and significance than a single case example can suggest.

NOTES

1. University of New Mexico, Bureau of Business and Economic Research Bulletin, "New Mexico: A Statistical Profile" (June 1983), p. 60.

2. "Albuquerque 2000," *Albuquerque Tribune,* 16 Sept. 1986, p. A-4.

3. V. B. Price, "Albuquerque: The Choices," *Albuquerque Tribune,* 20 Sept. 1986, p. A-6.

4. Peter A. Lupsha and William J. Siembieda, "The Poverty of Public Services in the Land of Plenty," in *The Rise of the Sunbelt Cities,* ed. David Perry and Alfred Watkins (Beverly Hills, Calif.: Sage Publications, 1977), pp. 161–90.

5. Ibid., p. 165.

6. Most of these activists appear to be ego-motivated and concerned with only very narrow sets of issues. They are typical, however, of the citizen-politicos who are active in the Sun Belt West.

7. Hans Gerth and C. W. Mills, eds., *From Max Weber* (New York: Oxford University Press, 1946), p. 114.

8. Dennis R. Judd, *The Politics of American Cities: Private Power and Public Policy,* 2d ed. (Boston, Mass.: Little, Brown & Co., 1984), pp. 47–59.

9. Diane Gutsky, "The Development of the Sycamore Hill Metropolitan Plan: Should Urban Institutions Plan with Their Neighbors?" (Master's thesis, University of New Mexico, Department of City Planning, June 1984); and preamble to the Community Development Act, 1974.

10. Correspondence from Mim Kantrowitz, Planning Associates, Inc., to Rex Allender, director, Metropolitan Redevelopment Department, City of Albuquerque, 30 Apr. 1981.

11. William Snyder, "The Coors Development Plan" (senior essay for Political Science Honors, University of New Mexico, Spring 1984).

12. In August 1986, ground was broken for the bridge amid protests and legal battles about the nature and location of the approaches.

13. James V. Cunningham, *Urban Leadership in the Sixties* (New York: Schenkman Publishers, 1970), pp. 28–42.

14. Peter A. Lupsha, "Constraints on Urban Leadership," in *Improving the Quality of Urban Management,* ed. W. Hawley and M. Rogers (Beverly Hills, Calif.: Sage Publications, 1974), pp. 607–24.

15. See Allan Talbot, *The Mayor's Game* (New York: Harper & Row, 1967); also Len O'Connor, *Clout: Mayor Daley and His City* (New York: Avon Publishers, 1967).

16. Robert A. Caro, *The Power Broker: Robert Moses and the Fall of New York City* (New York: Alfred A. Knopf, 1974).

13

Baltimore:
The Self-Evaluating City?

Robert P. Stoker

In this chapter, Robert Stoker looks at the much-heralded "renaissance" of Baltimore, Maryland. He describes the city's "shadow government"—the complex financial and organizational arrangements whereby the subsidy of economic-development projects is handled outside the formal structure of city government. Because these operations are not within the normal channels of democratic politics, Stoker raises the question of accountability. Specifically, How is performance judged? What restraints are there on potential abuses of power? Noting that cities, like other organizations, have little incentive to subject themselves to rigorous forms of evaluation, Stoker looks at accountability from various perspectives. He finds that development policy is particularly hard to evaluate in a formal and technically rigorous manner. Development efforts lack a clearly stated strategy, the consequences of which can be traced and measured precisely. The connection between effort and impact, Stoker points out, is oblique. Lines of causality, he reminds us, are "lengthy and indirect." Useful documentation is sparse, and much of the information that is available publicly is too promotional to be of much research value.

Political accountability is also difficult. In Baltimore the main development strategy is one of subsidizing business activities, both directly, through below-market loans, and indirectly, through providing support facilities such as the aquarium. This general strategy, in turn, involves a number of ad hoc decisions about who is to be helped and on what terms. Although the city's system of development corporations, through which subsidies are provided, is justified on managerial grounds, it is apparent that a number of basic policy judgments are being made about the use of public money and public authority. Rather than being nonpolitical, the system is one in which decisions are made under conditions of reduced public scrutiny.

Blurred public responsibility for development efforts, Stoker suggests, is itself a conflict-management strategy. Some conflicts are avoided by playing down the public character of the entities involved; and if controversy arises, it can be deflated by accentuating the private character of the development process or, alternatively, the fact that federal money is what is being used. The city's mayor has been in the enviable position of claiming credit for a general strategy of growth, while disclaiming responsibility for particular decisions and their consequences.

With recent years bringing spectacular changes in Baltimore's skyline, the city has been able to boast about its revitalized central business district and harbor area. Throughout Baltimore, ongoing programs seek to create economic and cultural attractions and to generate investment. The city, its leadership, and its development organizations have been cited as modern examples of effective urban management.[1] Despite this seeming success, the process and the content of Baltimore's development policy remain controversial. This chapter focuses upon the organizations that create and implement the city's development initiatives. Held by the popular press as worthy models of urban management, these organizations are much in need of close examination. How adequate are they as models for the governance of urban communities?

It is difficult to describe how development policy for the city of Baltimore is made. Unlike the norm in other policy domains, development policy making takes place outside of the formal organs of the city's government. A "shadow government" of civic groups, quasi-public corporations, and extragovernmental officials dominates a process that, by design, is private, fluid, flexible, and ad hoc.[2] This arrangement, which has been described as a partnership between business and government, is an amalgamation of market and state.[3]

The merit of Baltimore's development process, especially the extensive role of the shadow government, is a matter of dispute. Two conflicting views have emerged. One advocates the shadow government as an effective means for managing development policy. From this perspective, the partnership between business and government is a mutually beneficial relationship that allows the city to pursue its interest in development. The other criticizes the shadow government for its failure to be responsible to and for the diversity of interests affected by development policy. To critics, the shadow government goes too far in its accommodation of some business interests, and it seeks to avoid accountability for development decisions.

This chapter examines development policy and the organizations that create and manage it in Baltimore. Baltimore is a significant case because its development organizations form a governing arrangement that embodies certain values: namely, exclusion over participation, secrecy over openness, and management over governance. The purpose of this work is to examine the necessity and the potential for Baltimore's development organizations to engage in self-evaluation. The first step is to consider the context in which the capacity for self-evaluation is significant. Concern about evaluation and accountability may be tempered by one's view of development policy and politics. The second step is to describe Baltimore's shadow government. If accountability and the potential for self-evaluation are significant concerns, the shadow government may illustrate the potential and the problems of development organizations in this regard. The third step is to examine various means toward achieving accountability and toward nurturing the potential for self-evaluation. Each of these means is evaluated for its efficacy in Baltimore and, perhaps more significantly, for the general category of quasi-public organizations that often dominate development policy.

DEBATING THE MERIT OF THE SHADOW GOVERNMENT

The shadow government is one focus of a continuing debate between advocates and critics of Baltimore's development policies. Those who celebrate the city's recent development initiatives argue that the shadow government has contributed to the city's success by avoiding bureaucratic red tape and by creating a businesslike atmosphere that is attractive to corporate investment. In this sense, the shadow government is portrayed as a reform measure that promotes professional management and protects important development-policy initiatives from an uncertain fate in the city's bureaucracy.[4] These advocates view the revived central business district at Charles Center and the attractions of the Inner Harbor as evidence that Baltimore's development process works.[5]

Critics contend that Baltimore's development initiatives have performed unevenly, at best. Two complementary lines of criticism have developed. One alludes to "two Baltimores" and contrasts the city's apparent accomplishments with the continuing plight of its poor and minority citizens. To these critics, the frequent result of development efforts has been to attract suburban residents to the city for work or entertainment. The few opportunities that have been created for poor and minority citizens are in low-paying service jobs. A second criticism questions the image of Baltimore as a "renaissance" city. These critics examine the city (sometimes within a comparative framework) and conclude that its economic state is poor and may be getting worse. Despite evident increases in investment and growth in the tax base, economic indicators, such as average salary and unemployment rate, suggest that economically, Baltimore continues to be a troubled city.[6]

These lines of criticism converge in finding fault with the organizations that direct the city's development efforts. The shadow government serves to create and perpetuate two Baltimores by excluding poor and minority citizens from development policy making. The closed and quiet nature of decision making by the shadow government is viewed as a device to limit the influence of certain citizens, especially those who might oppose current development initiatives. Beyond this, the shadow government is ill-equipped to deal with the economic health of the city at large, concentrating instead upon the creation of a real-estate boom within designated development areas and adjacent neighborhoods. If current development activities contribute only marginally to the economic well-being of the city, could alternative strategies have accomplished more?

The dispute between advocates and critics of Baltimore's development policy has frequently centered upon which indicators of the city's economic well-being are most informative. Advocates look for investment and growth; the question is how to generate more investment, not what type of investment goals to pursue. Critics are concerned with the effects of investment upon groups within the city and the effect of investment patterns upon the city's economy: investment is no panacea; one must encourage the right kinds of investment and growth. This dispute could be dismissed as merely a reflection of concern for different constituencies. However, it may indicate a more fundamental disagreement about the nature of development policies and politics.

DEVELOPMENT POLICY AND POLITICS

The debate about the merit of the shadow government is relevant to an on-going controversy in the field of urban economic development, the center of which is Paul Peterson's *City Limits*. Peterson's analysis of the limits of city politics is a useful defense of development organizations such as Baltimore's shadow government. Peterson argues that the city's interest in economic development creates a political consensus that dominates the policy-making process.[7] The consensual nature of development politics is important for its normative implications and for the organizational foundation that it implies for development policy making; it views political participation as a liability and limits the requirements for policy-making organizations to flexibility and technical expertise.[8] To create an organizational process that is technically proficient and will protect development decisions from unreasonable citizen demands is the essence of effective policy making.

Peterson provides two reasons to limit participation in development policy making. First, citizen participation is a needless source of dissensus. The city's overriding interest in economic development precludes significant conflict over the objectives of development initiatives. Political participation is unnecessary, because it needlessly detracts from the ability of the city to accomplish its development goals. The implication of this argument is that disputes regarding development policy are motivated by selfish interests which seek to exploit the opportunities for participation that the policy-making process provides.

The nature of development issues also contributes to the need to limit citizen participation. Business matters are better carried out in small groups that have little exposure to publicity. Peterson suggests that the best way to proceeed is to limit information about development decisions until a comprehensive plan can be announced.[9] Then policy makers can build support for the decision. This implies that citizens should not participate and should not be informed as to the nature of policy deliberations until comprehensive plans have been formulated. The required secrecy is more likely to be found outside of the usual bureaucratic structures of the city's government. Quasi-public corporations appear to be appropriate to this end. From Peterson's perspective, this secrecy and lack of participation cannot compromise the public interest, because the clear and present interest of the city dominates the process and keeps development initiatives on track.

Peterson's premise—namely, that development is an overarching goal—provides more than an explanation for the creation of such development organizations as Baltimore's shadow government. His suggestion that development decisions are free from conflict defends and justifies a policy-development and -implementation process that is contrary to the norms of participation in a democratic society. Cities that are engaged in economic competition cannot afford to let fragmentation diminish their attractiveness to investors. Prudent policy makers must limit citizen participation so as to diminish the demands from unproductive sectors of the city. Organizational structures that circumvent established governmental agencies and their associated constituencies are favored for this purpose. The absence of conflict regarding the city's interest in development makes the process of exclusion and circumvention ethically palatable, even desirable.

Consistent with Peterson's line of reasoning, Baltimore's advocates view the shadow government as an apolitical means for improving the city's development potential by infusing speed, flexibility, and technical expertise into the policy-making process. This allows Baltimore to compete more successfully for corporate investment. Little concern need be given to the organization's democratic character or to accountability to the public interest, because growth and prosperity are in the city's interest, and city officials must provide tacit approval of the shadow government's activities.

Mayor William Schaefer has dismissed the notion that the organizations are political or a source of accountability problems. Referring to the city's trustees, who control a highly controversial development loan fund, the mayor has stated: "They're not independent contractors. Any time we don't like their activities, they'll stop."[10]

THE POSSIBILITY OF ABUSE

Baltimore's critics suspect that the shadow government is being abused as a source of political and economic power for well-positioned interests. The characteristic lack of discipline—either from market forces or from political accountability—frees the development organizations to pursue policies that are less effective than available alternatives would be. One critic suggests that the purpose of the shadow government is to circumvent the checks and balances established in the City Charter. The spread of corporate government in Baltimore has come at the expense of the city agencies whose status and power have been reduced. Unlike these public agencies, the shadow government frequently conducts its business outside of the public's view. The Board of Estimates—the oversite mechanism for the city's trustees—conducts private meetings, from which the public and the press are barred, when it makes important loan decisions. Decision processes such as this have led some to suggest that the shadow government is not accountable to the public.[11]

These critics apparently reject Peterson's view of development politics and base their view of the shadow government upon three claims: (1) that development-policy decisions made by the shadow government have important political consequences, (2) that development policy can be a source of intense community conflict, and (3) that the congruence of interest between the city and its business community has been exaggerated.

Peterson suggests that the transfer of power to an independent authority works best when the policy objective and the means to achieve it are clear.[12] Does the prodevelopment consensus that Peterson envisions relieve development organizations from the necessity of defining the objectives of development policy? Probably not. The literature on policy implementation suggests that significant decisions are made after the formal determination of policy objectives. These decisions cannot be avoided because of poor specification of policy objectives and the unanticipated circumstances that make it impossible for policy makers to specify a comprehensive view of their objective. Implementation analysts have noted that seeming consensus regarding policy objectives can quickly dissipate during the process of implementation.[13] Clarence Stone has suggested that the process of moving from the abstract statement of an objective to the operational language of the implementation process invariably means that the policy's objective will be redefined. Participation is regarded as a key to representation of interest, and the "low visibility" of decision making during implementation makes such participation even more crucial.[14]

The decisions that are made during the implementation process are not merely technical details. Development policy, even according to Peterson, is not always Pareto optimal—that is, both winners and losers are created as a result of development initiatives. For example, a neighborhood may be divided by an access highway to increase the convenience of city shopping and entertainment facilities for suburban residents. Development policy is fraught with externalities that affect citizens differently. The trade-offs and externalities that are implicit in a development proposal often are not clear until the program has been implemented. In Baltimore, opposition to the development of the Inner Harbor resulted when residents of neighborhoods adjacent to this valuable property realized that tax assessments were rising along with the value of their property. Some of these residents were on fixed incomes and could not afford the increased tax liability. Their choice was to sell their now-valuable homes and move from the neighborhood that had long been their residence or to seek relief from the city.

If a policy is not Pareto optimal, conflict over the policy's objective is intensified, because the point of the decision is no longer to distribute gains but to determine who gains and who loses. Such decisions constitute politics in the purest form. Viewing such decisions as the inevitable tide of neutral expert opinion was abandoned with the demise of the politics/administration dichotomy. To critics, the shadow government is not a neutral mechanism to accomplish worthy, agreed-upon objectives. It is a political arrangement that provides access and representation to some at the expense of others.

Some would object that the critic's view pays too little attention to the public's interest in business performance. Lindblom's analysis in *Politics and Markets* is relevant to this complaint. Lindblom recognizes the state's interest in business success, but the problem for the state is to distinguish between the fundamental needs of business and its more wide-ranging desires as an interest group.[15] The political participation of business confuses the boundaries between these two purposes to the advantage of business. Because the policy requirements for business success are not clear, business claims that it pursues the public interest are ambiguous. This uncertainty allows business to characterize all political activity as being motivated by public interest, regardless of its effect.[16] That business is both a public-interest group and a special-interest group is not a feature of Peterson's analysis.

For critics of Baltimore's development policy, these observations add up to an indictment of the shadow government. Organizations that create and implement development policy are engaged in significant political decision making. While the community has an interest in business success, there are limits to the congruence of the city's interest and that of its business community. The problem of governing is to develop a process that will facilitate the success of business without ignoring the city's other communities. This suggests the need for higher levels of citizen participation and for more open organizational processes than has been characteristic of the shadow government. What is needed is not simply an organization that can quickly and effectively pursue well-defined and agreed-upon goals. What is needed is an organization that is capable of considering ends as well as means. This is what Aaron Wildavsky has termed self-evaluation.[17]

THE SELF-EVALUATING CITY

The term *self-evaluation* reflects concern for an organization's ability to consider the worth of policy objectives and to devise effective means to achieve them. It is an idealized view of organizations which joins two aspects of the policy-making process: policy adoption and policy implementation. Wildavsky has said: "The ideal organization would be self-evaluating. It would continuously monitor its own activities so as to determine how well it was meeting its objectives or even whether these objectives should continue to prevail."[18] Self-evaluation transcends the management of policy initiatives to include the definition of the policy objectives. The significance of defining the objective of development policy is that it gives life to Peterson's abstract notion of the city's interest. Any ambiguities or conflicts that exist are resolved by the organizations charged with the creation and implementation of the initiative. In Baltimore, these organizations are the shadow government.

If development politics is not consensual, the organization's capacity for self-evaluation could be critical both to the organization's effectiveness and to the rights of the citizenry. How does the organization integrate the divergent views of the city's interest to establish its own policy objectives? Who should participate in these deliberations? What access to process and information is required for accountability? Are the organizations that direct development policy capable of critical self-examination and change? These questions are significant concerns for the self-evaluating city.

Wildavsky's analysis is not concerned only with what is desirable in the abstract. He also shows why organizations are reluctant to engage in self-evaluation. He observes that evaluation and organization are "somewhat contradictory" and contrasts the emphasis upon change and uncertainty that are inherent in evaluation, on the one hand, with the organization's desire for loyalty, stability, and consistency, on the other hand.[19] However, the reluctance of organizations to engage in self-evaluation does not preclude the possibility that organizations vary in the degree to which they develop an ethos favorable to evaluation. If this is so, organizations could be examined for their propensity to engage in self-evaluation.

The shadow government's potential for self-evaluation is the focus for the remainder of this work. In many ways, the organizations that dominate Baltimore's development initiatives are the polar opposite of Wildavsky's ideal. He suggests that self-evaluating organizations should nurture a diverse constituency; they should be open, truthful and explicit; and they should publicly present information about the costs and benefits of program alternatives so as to give others the opportunity to refute them.[20] The gap between this ideal and the reality of the shadow government is evident from the description that follows.

BALTIMORE'S SHADOW GOVERNMENT

The distinct characteristic of the shadow government is its synthesis of market and state. It is impossible to determine whether the "quasi-public" organizations of the shadow government are public or private concerns. This confusion is created and nurtured by the organizations themselves so as to exploit the potential to enjoy the benefits of both worlds. When financial support requires either the city's assets or public status, Baltimore's shadow government puts on its public hat and enjoys the rights and privileges available to public organizations. When the public label is not convenient, the shadow government, as well as Baltimore's development leaders, are quick to assert the organization's private character and independence.

One illustration of the convenience of this ambiguous status was the demolition of the Armistead Hotel. The Municipal Employees Credit Union, which manages the retirement investments of city employees and is directed by officials who are also city-government officials, purchased the Armistead Hotel to demolish the structure and construct a new office building on the property. The destruction of the hotel resulted in the displacement of forty residents, some of whom were sick or elderly. If the city had displaced these residents, federal and state laws would have required relocation payments totaling as much as $132,000. But because the credit union is a "private" concern, no payments were required. None were made. The role of the city in this case is ambiguous, because it supported the project with an industrial-revenue bond, backed by the city's credit, to provide low-interest financing. The city rents most of the available office space.[21]

A second illustration of the convenience of this ambiguous status is drawn from the city trustees. Because their development loans were private, the city trustees refused to enforce city policies regarding such matters as the participation of minority contractors in city projects. This policy of the trustees was eventually overruled by the Board of Estimates. One unnamed City Hall official commented: "Strange things happen in an election year."[22]

These examples illustrate how difficult it is to describe the shadow government because of its fluid nature. While organizations may be involved in several ongoing initiatives, no clear or consistent structure, no rationale for participation or role definition, exists. To describe the shadow government at any one time is only to capture a brief moment in its evolution. As a result, any description requires, first, a list of the major organizational components of the shadow government and, second, an example of their interaction. While the participation of some actors is predictable, the form and the content of the interaction vary from case to case.

The primary organizational component of the shadow government is the quasi-public corporation. In addition, governmental agencies, extragovernmental officials, and business groups are active in the shadow government. The various organizational forms of the shadow government are described below.

QUASI-PUBLIC CORPORATIONS

The shadow government's primary organizational form is the quasi-public corporation. These corporations often act in concert with other components of the shadow government, such as city agencies or extragovernmental officials. The examples described below illustrate the wide scope of the shadow government's activities. From the renewal of Charles Center to the operation of Baltimore's National Aquarium to city-wide industrial-development programs, Baltimore's corporate government is omnipresent.

Charles Center/Inner Harbor Management, Incorporated (CCIHM)

This was Baltimore's first quasi-public nonprofit development corporation; it was created in 1965 to manage the city's downtown renewal effort at Charles Center. Initially named Charles Center Management, Incorporated, this title was later changed to reflect its new status as the management corporation for the city's Inner Harbor projects. The authority of this corporation is derived from its contractual relationship with the city, under the direction of the commissioner of the Neighborhood Progress Administration, which makes the CCIHM the implementation authority for the Charles Center and Inner Harbor development plans.

Baltimore Economic Development Corporation (BEDCO)

This quasi-public corporation was created to retain and attract industrial development for Baltimore. The creation of this corporation followed the 1971 approval of a $3-million bond to finance economic development. BEDCO is intended as a comprehensive business service to assist with plant location, technical services, financing, and public regulatory agencies. Among BEDCO's many initiatives are six city-owned industrial parks, located around the city.

Market Center Development Corporation (MCDC)

Among the newest of Baltimore's quasi-public development authorities, this corporation serves as the implementation authority for the Market Center Urban Renewal District, which includes such notable areas as Lexington Market and the Howard Street commercial district. According to MCDC promotional literature, the purpose of this organization is to provide free services to developers so that they can "progress through the intricacies of government and private processes."

Baltimore Aquarium, Incorporated

This quasi-public corporation directs the Baltimore National Aquarium. The fifty-eight-member board of directors has operational control of the facility, from programmatic issues to setting fees for aquarium activities to personnel decisions. Members of the board also coordinate fund-raising activities for private and corporate sponsorship. The authority of the board is based upon a contract negotiated by the city and approved by the Board of Estimates.

BUSINESS INTEREST GROUPS

Interest groups have long played a prominent role in the shadow government. The most important of these is the Greater Baltimore Committee (GBC). This organization was formed in 1956 as an alliance of progressive business leaders who were concerned about the decline of Baltimore's central business district. The heads of Baltimore's one hundred largest firms were recruited to form its membership. Significantly, the committee created an executive director to head the Planning Council, which has its own professional staff. This staff provides expertise and continuity to the business leaders' efforts to influence the city's development policy.

CITY AGENCIES

Various organizations of the city's government interact with or sponsor the activities of shadow-government organizations. Among these are the Department of Economic and Community Development, the City Planning Commission, the Neighborhood Progress Administration, the (Mayor's) Office of Manpower Resources, the Board of Estimates, and the City Council.

Typically, the governmental agency will be involved as an oversight mechanism or as the source of the contract from which the quasi-public organization draws its authority. In some cases, the formal role of the shadow-government organization is to advise public organizations regarding development decisions. For example, the city's trustees merely recommend loan agreements to the Board of Estimates. While some observers have suggested that the mayor's domination of the board and the poor record keeping of the trustees compromise the board's ability to execute its function, the formal authority to approve loan agreements does rest there.

EXTRAGOVERNMENTAL ENTITIES

The city's trustees, who constitute one of the most controversial aspects of the shadow government, were created to finance development projects (though their organization was recently disbanded). The City Trustees for Loans and Guarantees administer a loan fund that finances city development initiatives. The trustees have a staff supported by loan fees and revenues. Proposals may be submitted by Baltimore's many quasi-public corporations for the trustee's consideration. As noted above, the final authority to make loan decisions lies with the Board of Estimates. However, the board is controlled by the mayor, who makes two appointments and has a seat for himself on the five-member board. One important source of power for the trustees is that their financial resources are more flexible than most governmental accounts. Funds are often initially designated for some specific purpose, but after they have been repaid, the money is available for other purposes. Another source of flexible funds is the return on the revolving account itself, which the trustees are empowered to invest.[23] Some federal and state officials have speculated that the fund controlled by the trustees is the largest revolving fund available to any city in the country.[24] It was estimated that the total value of the fund, when the trustees were going "out of business" in 1986, was more than $200 million.[25]

The components of Baltimore's shadow government are interesting in themselves, but the significance of these organizations can only be seen within the context of an illustration. In the following sections, two examples are presented. The first illustrates the application of Baltimore's strategy of corporate governance to the financing and operation of the National Aquarium. The example underscores the normative and practical rationale for the shadow government. The second is focused upon the Coldspring new town. This example shows the mixed blessing that speed and flexibility can be by highlighting the potential accountability problems of Baltimore's corporate government.

BALTIMORE'S SWIMMING SUCCESS

The National Aquarium in Baltimore is one of the most visible and successful attractions within the city's Inner Harbor. Since opening in August
1981, the aquarium has attracted more than seven million visitors, most
from out of state, making it the most heavily attended tourist attraction
in Maryland. Estimates of the aquarium's effect upon Maryland's economy
have suggested that directly and indirectly it has contributed $88 million
and 2,950 jobs. The city's Department of Economic and Community Development estimates that in 1984 the aquarium generated $3.3 million in state
tax receipts and $1.9 million in local tax receipts.[26] With its popular exhibits,
educational programs, and research activities, the aquarium may be the
"jewel" of Baltimore's Inner Harbor.

GOVERNING ARRANGEMENTS

The National Aquarium is operated and financed in a manner consistent with Baltimore's approach to development. The aquarium is owned by
the city of Baltimore and is operated by Baltimore Aquarium, Incorporated,
a quasi-public nonprofit corporation. Notwithstanding the usual claims of
speed, flexibility, and technical competence, this mixture of business and
government may have two other purposes: (1) to insulate the aquarium from
the city's political process and (2) to create opportunities for financial
arrangements that can take advantage of the aquarium's ambiguous public/
private status.

In an interview with the *Baltimore Sun,* Frank Gunther, Jr., who is currently the chairman of the aquarium's Foundation Board, outlined the rationale for operating the aquarium through a quasi-public corporation. His
statements echo the reformist rhetoric that frequently is used to justify the
existence of the shadow government. However, his comments also reveal the
political agenda that the creation of the quasi-public corporation may serve.
According to Gunther, "The board takes the aquarium out of the political
arena." The political system is viewed as a potential source of dissensus,
especially if the mayor who replaces Mayor Schaefer should be less
cooperative. "We couldn't have a better situation. But this aquarium will
be here for a long time. It wants to be able to move forward regardless of
who is in City Hall."[27]

These remarks indicate that the corporate government is interested in
establishing attractions that will improve the city's image, regardless of the
preferences or opinions of elected officials. Reliable partnerships are required,
because the private sector is not capable or does not wish to pay the costs
associated with creating the attractions. While Mayor Schaefer is a dependable partner, the future is uncertain. City Hall may be captured by a

candidate whose constituency demands a change in priorities. One value of corporate government, then, is that it allows the use of public resources while protecting the control of those resources from the changing winds of city politics. Because so many of its leaders are recruited from the business community, corporate government also has the effect of institutionalizing the advantaged position of business within Baltimore's development process.

DEPENDENCE UPON PUBLIC FINANCE

Political control of the aquarium is a significant concern, because the taxpayers both in the city of Baltimore and in the state of Maryland help to finance its development. Despite its success, the aquarium continues to depend upon Maryland's taxpayers for financial support. This is illustrated by the current campaign to expand the aquarium. The cost of the Pier 4 Project has been estimated at $20 million. It is hoped that the state of Maryland will fund half of the project. A $3.5-million capital-projects grant has been approved, and additional requests are expected for the 1987 session of the Maryland General Assembly. The City of Baltimore is to provide the site (a valuable waterfront property on the Inner Harbor, adjacent to the current aquarium), and the city placed a $3.5-million bond issue on the November 1986 ballot. Aquarium sources estimate that the value of the donated property plus the bond issue will represent a financial commitment by the city comparable to that requested from the state. Private contributions will underwrite the balance of the costs. In 1986 the aquarium initiated a campaign to raise $20 million from private and corporate sources.[28]

IMPLICATIONS FOR DEMOCRACY

To advocates of Baltimore's shadow government, the implications for democracy of insulating Baltimore's aquarium from city politics are not substantial. After all, the interests of the city are the same as the interests of its business community. Advocates claim that corporate management removes politics from the aquarium. But what this really means is freezing out potential political opponents, including unreliable politicians (those who have constituencies other than business), public-sector unions, and the civil service. Gunther has stated, "We did not want to get involved with a lot of problems with city employees, problems like unionization, civil service, and salary guidelines."[29] The solution is to create a governing arrangement that will effectively limit the participation of these potential troublemakers. Because the city's aquarium is not a public entity, its employees are not governed by the city's civil-service regulations, and the potential trouble is avoided.

Unquestionably the aquarium is a successful attraction, but that is not the whole of the matter. Given its dependence upon public financing, the aquarium's governing arrangement also involves the issue of democratic control of public resources. The arrangements to manage the aquarium are quite significant in their political implications. By providing resources to the aquarium, the city and the state make implicit decisions regarding the priority of this project versus others. By using such resources as the site on the Inner Harbor, the city precludes other development options. How were these decisions made? What objective of the city is served by the expansion of the aquarium? Is it right and proper that public resources should be controlled by a process that circumvents popular control?

Baltimore Aquarium illustrates that the results of corporate government are not merely greater speed, flexibility, and competence than other organizational alternatives. Corporate government also results in the creation of organizations that are public enough to garner resources yet private enough to limit popular participation. To suggest that the purpose of corporate government is mere efficiency is to belie Gunther's own claims about the significance of this governing arrangement.

BALTIMORE'S FAILED NEW TOWN

The initial award-winning plan for the development of a Coldspring new town was an ambitious attempt to draw middle-income home owners back to Baltimore. The plan called for the construction of 3,780 homes, an elementary school, a community center, retail shops, and office space. But along the way, things went wrong. After a decade of frustration, only about 10 percent of the planned housing has been constructed, while many other aspects of the plan are unfulfilled. Baltimore has several times used the deep pocket of the federal government to rescue the project from construction problems and delays. Hopeful of reviving the project, the city has undertaken a controversial and expensive buy out of the original developer's rights.

The failure to successfully develop a new town does not distinguish Baltimore. Other cities have also tried and failed.[30] What is unique about the Coldspring new town is the role played by the shadow government. Intended to bring speed and flexibility to the execution of the project, the organs of the shadow government redirected to Coldspring some federal grant funds that were intended for low- and moderate-income families, bailed out the project when construction problems threatened the developer's interest, sacrificed loans made to minority contractors, and finally bought back the rights to develop the property.

FINANCING THE NEW TOWN

From the beginning, the city's role in the development of Coldspring was extensive and involved a continuing financial commitment. Most of the resources devoted to the project came from federal funds, including more than $30 million in Community Development Block Grants and Neighborhood Development Program funds. These monies were used for site preparation, design work, relocation costs, and the laying out of physical facilities. The city also sold $11.9 million in privately insured tax-exempt bonds to provide below-market financing (7.5 percent) to home buyers.[31] General-obligation bonds totaling $5.5 million were used to finance the construction of the new town's first phase. To finance the second phase of the development, the city's trustees borrowed $7 million from a local bank. Construction loans were made by the city to the developer at below-market rates, thus subsidizing the construction costs. The city trustees also agreed to limit the interest obligation of the developer to $420,000, so that any interest charges above this amount would be paid by the city. These financial commitments are significant. However, as problems mounted, so did the demands that the Coldspring new town made upon the city's financial resources.

CITY'S FINANCIAL COSTS GROW

Construction problems created increased demands upon the city's resources when deficiencies were discovered in some homes. The developer, Newtown Corporation, a subsidiary of F. D. Rich Construction Corporation, claimed that the financial losses had resulted from redoing work by minority subcontractors. Although this was disputed, the city did underwrite the loss. That minority subcontractors were identified as the source of the problems is significant, because it links the loss to the city's policy to promote the use of minority firms. In this way, responsibility for the loss becomes the city's, not the developer's. The $1-million loss was covered by Community Development Block Grant Funds.

The city's financial losses mounted when the dispute between the developer and its minority subcontractors was left unresolved. Claims filed by the subcontractors clouded title to the property and prevented the home buyers from settling their purchases. Some had occupied their homes, paying nominal rents, pending resolution of the claims. To resolve the dispute, the city forgave $400,000 in loans to the subcontractors. The loans, which provided the working capital for three subcontractors, were provided by the city's Urban Services Agency to the Baltimore Council for Equal Business Opportunity.[32] Once again, Community Development Block Grants were used to make up the city's loss.

The use of Community Development Block Grants to cover the city's losses was controversial because it did not seem to be consistent with the stated purpose of the grants and because it precluded the possibility that the funds could be used elsewhere in the city. The funds were targeted at low- and moderate-income people. To use these funds at Coldspring implied that other projects around the city—projects more consistent with the stated purpose of the grants—might suffer. HUD (the Department of Housing and Urban Development) questioned, but eventually accepted, the city's use of the funds for Coldspring. Overlooking the opportunity cost to the city, Lawrence Daley, a city trustee, said that Baltimore citizens were not hurt by the shift in funds: "That subsidy is not city funds. That's federal grants."[33]

BUYING OUT THE DEVELOPER

The sluggish pace of development was apparently a source of frustration for city officials. However, the 1975 development agreement granted the Rich Corporation the exclusive development rights to the property until 2013. In an attempt to resurrect the project, the city decided to buy out the developer's interest.

The total cost of the buy out was set at $3.8 million, a sum that was negotiated by city officials and representatives of the developer. Of this total, $2.5 million was paid to the developer—$1.3 million for completed site work, and $1.2 million for anticipated profit that was sacrificed by the sale. The other $1.3 million was to be paid to the city trustees to settle for interest paid beyond the $420,000 ceiling negotiated with the developer. The payments were drawn from four sources: $1.9 million in city economic-development bonds, $0.5 million from repayments of UDAG loans, $0.8 million in found money from completed projects, and $0.6 million from a special revenue account from the city's Department of Housing and Community Development.[34]

The buy-out plan sparked criticism from the city council, though the council eventually approved the plan. Members of the council suggested that the financial settlement was too generous to the developer. Others questioned the need to repay the trustees for a program that they had been instrumental in creating. Still others were upset by the sources of the funds targeted for the buy out and what this would mean to other city projects.[35]

The poor development record of the Coldspring new town has caused the city to reconsider its initial plan. New proposals for the development of Coldspring have been solicited, but its future remains uncertain. Recently, the Neighborhood Progress Administration (NPA) announced that part of the new town would be redirected to commercial use. "The land south of Cold Spring Lane is going to be for economic development," according to Carl Ruskin, chief of planning and urban design for the NPA. The policy shift resulted from an unsolicited proposal to use a parcel of the land for a medical-research park and nursing-care facility.[36] Though the exact character of future development in the area remains to be seen, it is apparent that the city has determined that the original plan for Coldspring should be scrapped.

THE COSTS OF COLDSPRING

Attempts have been made to estimate the costs of the Coldspring new town by totaling the monetary value of various resources devoted to the project. These estimates are incomplete because they overlook the project's opportunity cost. On several occasions, monies that were intended for another purpose were used to bail out the new town. The monetary value of these resources is one aspect of cost. The other, often overlooked, is lost opportunity. What else might have been done with the $1.4 million in federal grants that was used to settle the dispute between the developer and the subcontractors? What alternative strategies might the city have pursued with the $3.8 million used to buy back the developer's interest? And what of the initial investment of more than $30 million? Do city leaders believe that alternative uses of this money would have been less beneficial to the city than the Coldspring development? While the city can take some solace from the fact that federal monies were frequently the source of these payments, this does not account for the lost opportunity that the city has suffered in pursuit of its failed new town.

THE POLITICS OF THE SHADOW GOVERNMENT

The oft-stated purpose of the shadow government is to infuse Baltimore's development process with speed, flexibility, and technical expertise so as to manage development initiatives more effectively. However, the political consequence of this governing arrangement is that these organizations gain access to public resources while circumventing popular control. In practicing politics, the shadow government's advocates use specific strategies to prevent significant opposition and to disarm critics. These strategies include: (1) paying symbolic homage to reformist traditions, (2) seeking funding sources that appear to be costless to the city, and (3) closely guarding information about the implications of development decisions.

The virtue of speed and flexibility is evident to any student of government. Procedures and guidelines that are intended to create accountability are too often a convenient excuse for inaction. Striking a proper balance between accomplishment and accountability is a problem that all governing arrangements must face. However, the political value of focusing upon speed and flexibility is that it creates support for this governing arrangement through symbolic reference to the goals of the reform movement. This avoids the necessity of pointing out the costs and pitfalls of the governing arrangement by focusing public attention exclusively upon its virtues. The discussion of the National Aquarium in Baltimore provides evidence that advocates present shadow-government organizations as apolitical reform measures, despite their apparent political significance.

To locate funding sources from outside Baltimore is another important practice in the politics of the shadow government, because this reduces the perceived cost of development initiatives. As a result, the public awards flexibility to those who seek to control development policy. Without financial support from outside the city, especially in the form of federal grant funds, the shadow government probably could not operate as it has. City officials are careful to assure that their most controversial actions—paying the costs of risky, ambitious ventures that go awry—do not engender significant conflict by absorbing the losses through the use of federal funds. Officials were quick to point out that the use of federal grant money made many of the subsidies provided to the Coldspring new town costless to the city. The loss is indirect and provides the satisfaction that the federal government, not the city, is paying the freight for Baltimore's development. Even less-controversial investments, such as the expansion of the aquarium, benefit from the perception that city funds are working extra hard because alternative funding sources—in this case, state tax dollars and charitable contributions—are paying a share of the cost. The political value of these creative financial arrangements, then, is to reduce the opposition to development initiatives and to provide the shadow government with the flexibility that it desires.

The secrecy and complexity of the shadow government also serve a political purpose: they mask the price of development initiatives, and even those that work have a price. In Coldspring, millions of dollars in subsidies were provided through complex arrangements whose implications did not become apparent until the project had foundered. The value of secrecy is that the risks and the negative implications of decisions can be suppressed. Typifying the closed nature of shadow-government decision making, the Board of Estimates regularly meets in executive session. Complexity contributes to secrecy by making it more difficult to connect specific actions with their consequences. Evidence of the value of complexity is provided by the poor record keeping on the part of the city's trustees, which made it almost impossible to discover who was getting what.

That the shadow government has political consequences is troubling, because these organizations are insulated from popular control. In the absence of effective oversight and public control, the city must depend upon these organizations to determine the worth of policy objectives and to devise effective means to attain them—this is the organizations' capacity for self-evaluation. But the organs of Baltimore's shadow government are unlike Wildavsky's ideal. The self-evaluating organization is open and explicit; it subjects itself to tensions that are inevitable when one invites scrutiny and criticism.[37] On the other hand, Baltimore's shadow government consists of organizations that are secretive and exclusive, organizations that seek to avoid scrutiny and to disarm critics. In the next section, I assess the possibility that development organizations such as the shadow government could engage in self-evaluation.

ACCOUNTABILITY THROUGH SELF-EVALUATION

Wildavsky's notion of the self-evaluating organization has identified two dimensions for which public organizations should be held accountable. One is the content of policy decisions. The effective organization will consider its goals and purposes in an attempt to determine whether or not these purposes should continue to direct the organization's activities. The second is the organizational implementation of programs designed to achieve the objective. The effective organization will consider evidence for and against each alternative, select the one that is most promising, and execute it. Formal evaluation is viewed as a means by which public organizations can improve their effectiveness. However, as Wildavsky suggests, in the unlikely case that an organization should choose to evaluate its activities, there are significant obstacles that make evaluation difficult in practice.[38]

Two related groups of obstacles to self-evaluation by shadow-government organizations may be identified; those that are common to development policy and those that result from the structure and practices of the shadow government itself. Obstacles that result from development policy are frequently complicated by the nature of the shadow government; these include (1) the oblique character of development policy and (2) the scale of development initiatives relative to the problem. The obstacles to self-evaluation that result from the character of the shadow government include (1) the ambiguous lines of authority; (2) the lack of a systematic collection of information, and (3) the creation of a clientele that is too homogeneous.

One of the contributions of Paul Peterson's work was his recognition that development policy is a distinct domain within the policy making of cities. While many scholars have disagreed with his characterization of the important features of this domain, most would agree that distinguishing development policy from its cohorts is useful. What Peterson has overlooked is that development policy is perhaps the most oblique of all the city's policy domains.

To engage in evaluation, an organization must be able to identify a development program as its focus. This is difficult, however, because the typical approach to development policy is oblique—that is, cities strive to create a context in which market forces will find investment attractive. This makes the lines of causality between policy actions and their consequences lengthy and indirect. Low-interest loans, tax breaks, improved services, and zoning variances are only the distant causes of development activity. This complicates the evaluation process by making it more difficult to attribute to a policy initiative the achievements that are claimed for it. The oblique character of the policy domain also belies the idea that a coherent program exists as a focus for evaluation. Development policies are likely to be formed by a disjointed series of small decisions and exemptions that are requested and granted in specific circumstances. To create special arrangements according to unspecified criteria cannot be regarded as a coherent program.

The fluid, closed nature of Baltimore's shadow government further complicates this problem. Coherent programs are difficult to identify because the process is ad hoc and secretive. The lack of clear authority to initiate programs results in an ad hoc process that makes it unlikely that consistent standards will be applied to development decisions; this is the down side of flexibility. The secretive nature of the process makes it difficult to know even if a coherent program does exist. Because there is a minimum of public participation and because the records of proceedings are confidential or cryptic, the paper trail that is generated by other types of policy organizations may not exist.

The possibility for self-evaluation also is limited by the scale of development projects in relation to the problems they seek to address. Even very large development programs may be too small to achieve statistically significant changes in aggregate measures of the city's economic health (based on city-wide data or SMSA). Analysis requires more costly and specialized information gathering, which further diminishes the prospects for evaluation. In Baltimore the organizations of the shadow government are unlikely either to gather or to provide such information. Instead, promotional information that exaggerates success and reports the tangible results of investment—how many square feet constructed, dollars invested, or people employed—is provided by corporate employees from the "marketing department."

Perhaps the most serious constraint upon the potential of the shadow government to engage in self-evaluation is its constituency. The history of development policy in Baltimore and the role of the shadow government make the association between Baltimore's business leaders and the corporate government indisputable. This has provided the shadow government with a homogeneous constituency. It also has limited the ability of these organizations to expand their view of the city's interest. As Wildavsky has observed, "Diversity creates political flexibility."[39] In the absence of diversity, it was highly unlikely that these organizations would develop an interest in self-evaluation. After all, that would defeat the purpose of this governing arrangement—that is, unless we are to believe that the purpose of the shadow government is merely to infuse the policy-making process with speed, flexibility, and technical competence.

NOTES

1. "Politics Is Not the Only Thing That Is Changing America's Big Cities," *National Journal,* 26 Nov. 1983, p. 2480; "He Digs Downtown," *Time,* 24 Aug. 1981, p. 42; "Can the Best Mayor Win?" *Esquire,* Oct. 1984, p. 57.

2. "Two Trustees and $100 Million Bank Skirt the Restrictions of City Government," *Baltimore Sun,* 13 Apr. 1980, p. A-1.

3. Katharine Lyall, "A Bicycle Built for Two: Public/Private Partnership in Baltimore's Renaissance" (Washington, D.C.: Committee for Economic Development, 1980).

4. "Schaefer Defends Use of the Trustee System," *Baltimore Sun,* 20 Apr. 1980, p. A-1 (hereafter cited as "Schaefer Defends Trustees").

5. Bernard L. Berkowitz, "Economic Development Policy Really Works: Baltimore, Maryland," in *Urban Economic Development,* ed. Richard D. Bingham and John P. Blair (Beverly Hills, Calif.: Sage Publications, 1984), p. 201.

6. "The Case for 'Two Baltimores,'" *Baltimore Sun,* 10 Aug. 1986, p. B-1.

7. Paul E. Peterson, *City Limits* (Chicago: University of Chicago Press, 1981), p. 30.

8. Ibid., p. 129.

9. Ibid., p. 132.

10. "Schaefer Defends Trustees."

11. "As Shadow Government Grows Stronger, Its Accountability to the Public Lessens," *Baltimore Sun,* 20 Apr. 1980, p. A-1 (hereafter cited as "Accountability to the Public").

12. Peterson, *City Limits,* p. 135.

13. Jeffrey L. Pressman and Aaron Wildavsky, *Implementation* (Berkeley: University of California Press, 1973), p. 6.

14. Clarence N. Stone, "Implementation of Social Programs: Two Perspectives," *Journal of Social Issues* 36, no. 4 (1980): 14.

15. Charles E. Lindblom, *Politics and Markets: The World's Political and Economic Systems* (New York: Basic Books, 1977), pp. 173–75.

16. Ibid., pp. 203–4.

17. Aaron Wildavsky, *Speaking Truth to Power: The Art and Craft of Policy Analysis* (Boston, Mass.: Little, Brown & Co., 1979), p. 212.

18. Ibid., p. 213.

19. Ibid., pp. 212–14.

20. Ibid., pp. 232–34.

21. "Displaced Armistead Tenants Got No City Relocation Help," *Baltimore Sun,* 17 Apr. 1980, p. A-7.

22. "City Broadens Minority Contractor Rule," *Baltimore Sun,* 9 June 1983, p. A-1.

23. "City Trustees Are Not Hampered by Checks Ruling Other Officials," *Baltimore Sun,* 13 Apr. 1980, p. A-8.

24. "Accountability to the Public."

25. "City Trustees Going out of Business, Schaefer Says," *Baltimore Sun,* 7 Mar. 1986, p. A-1.

26. National Aquarium in Baltimore, "Marine Mammal Exhibit Project," report contained in the aquarium's press kit, 1986 (hereafter cited as Aquarium expansion report).

27. "City-made Quasi-public Corporations Produce New Category of Public Official," *Baltimore Sun,* 19 Apr. 1980, p. A-1 (hereafter cited as Gunther interview).

28. Aquarium expansion report.

29. Gunther interview.

30. Martha Derthick, *New Towns In-Town* (Washington, D.C.: Urban Institute Press, 1972).

31. "Coldspring Due Novel Financing," *Baltimore Sun,* 31 Mar. 1978, p. A-13.

32. "City Resigns Itself to $400,000 Loss on Loans to Subcontractors," *Baltimore Sun,* 26 Oct. 1978, p. D-1.

33. "City Rescue of Coldspring Project Apparently Broke U.S. Regulations," *Baltimore Sun,* 16 Apr. 1980, p. A-1.

34. "Funds Okd to Buy Out Coldspring Developer," *Baltimore Sun,* 31 Jan. 1985, p. D-4.

35. "Council Marvels at Coldspring Terms," *Baltimore Sun,* 20 Mar. 1985, p. B-3.

36. "Jobs to Be Goal in Developing Coldspring Tract," *Baltimore Sun,* 31 Mar. 1986, p. D-1.

37. Wildavsky, *Speaking Truth to Power,* p. 234.

38. Ibid., pp. 214–20.

39. Ibid., p. 232.

CONCLUSION

14

Summing Up:
Urban Regimes, Development
Policy, and Political Arrangements

Clarence N. Stone

The opening theme of this volume was that politics matters. In describing significant struggle over both the substance of policy and the arrangements through which policy is made, case accounts have elaborated that theme. These cases suggest that while the general idea of economic growth is widely supported, the concrete measures for achieving it are often the subject of dispute.

The question of how best to pursue growth does not answer itself. The answer comes out of a community's political arrangements, broadly understood. It is therefore instructive to follow Stephen Elkin's lead and to talk about urban regimes. They are the mediating agents between the goal of economic well-being and the particular development policies pursued. Hence, regime character is itself the target of political effort.

In Elkin's formulation, as illustrated in the case of Dallas, a regime represents an accommodation between the potentially conflicting principles of the popular control of government and the private ownership of business enterprises. These potentially conflicting principles provide a structural context within which regimes form; hence there is a set of pressures that guide the working out of regime forms. At the same time, it is important to bear in mind that the reconciliation of potentially conflicting principles involves political choice and political judgment.[1] This is particularly true in the case of urban regimes, because neither the issue of how best to satisfy the principle of popular control nor the issue of how to induce private business to serve community well-being is itself the kind of question to which there is a technical answer. As the preceding chapters have made clear, there is no single form that popular control takes. Practices differ greatly. As these chapters also suggest, there is no set formula for how best to promote economic growth. There are uncertainties and trade-offs within both principles and, therefore, room for differences of judgment and for variations in practice.

This kind of open-ended conclusion is bothersome to many scholars. It should not be, however. Variations in practice can be seen as providing an opportunity to observe and then, on the basis of observation, to refine judgments. It is in that spirit, I hope, that this book will be read and future research will be conducted.

I hasten to add that variation is not a matter of chance, nor is outcome simply a matter of choice. Many conditions are not subject to control, especially at the level of the local community. Furthermore, the range of variation that occurs is not a matter of point-by-point selection. To talk about a regime is to talk about a set of complementary arrangements. Communities do not simply choose "dishes" from column A and column B. Instead, they evolve a set of arrangements. Of course, because most actors, as Norton Long has argued, operate with restricted vision of what they are about, unintended consequences may be quite extensive.[2] Still, in a sense, communities "choose" a scheme of accommodation between popular control and private ownership. Hence, political efforts are not restricted to specific policy questions; they also extend to the arrangements through which policy is made. The interconnections between development policy and political arrangements and the struggle over these interconnections are little explored territory. One aim of this book is to raise the awareness of this territory and to make a case for its further exploration.

In this wrap-up essay, the first thing I do is to offer a typology of urban regimes. The purpose of this typology is not to provide a definitive classification. Its purpose is the more modest one of illustration. The typology enables us to see that governing coalitions differ in composition and in policy orientation. The second thing I do in this chapter is to discuss various aspects of what substantively is at issue in development policy. The point of this discussion is to show that there are policy alternatives at stake in development and that the policy strategies pursued are related to the character of the prevailing coalition in various communities.

What remains for the chapter, then, is some discussion of the factors that help to shape prevailing coalitions. In this third section of the chapter, I look again at the political-economy context and attempt to show why a community's governing coalition is not necessarily identical with the coalition that wins elections in that community. Popular control is only one of the structural constraints within which regimes are formed, and popular control itself can come in more than one guise. As cities work out accommodations between the popular control of government and private ownership in business activity, I argue, it is important to remember that business enterprises themselves, individually and collectively, control important political resources. As we have seen in numerous cases throughout this volume, business is not a passive party in the struggle to shape a city's politics.[3]

What business and other actors understand is that regime character shapes policy. In some manner, a regime embodies a view of the public interest. Consequently, as business and other groups engage in fashioning a community's political arrangements, they are answering the question of how the public's interest in development will be served.

Because, as Robert Stoker's essay points out, there are no technical solutions to the problem of accountability, the public interest cannot be determined objectively. The operative understanding of what is in the interest of the community comes out of the governing coalition, the relations between its members, and their felt need for a base of public support. This is to say that power and justice are intertwined. However, this is not to suggest that the public interest is whatever those in power say it is. It is to suggest that those in power, the prevailing coalition, operate with an understanding of what the public interest is, but that view may not be universally subscribed to. In the eyes of some, power and justice may be at odds with one another. Hence struggle is to be expected.

Consider the case of Dallas. Here is a community in which development policy seemingly enjoyed support in the city's low-turnout elections. But these elections were themselves the result of efforts by economic elites to exclude "politics," that is, to restrict the channels through which popular sentiment could be expressed and to prevent public office from being used in the pursuit of patronage and particular gain. All of this was done in the name of the collective good of the whole community, but the procedures through which that collective good was determined were eventually challenged by groups that were not involved in setting the city's policy priorities.

Because policy decisions involve making an ongoing series of value judgments with which both particular and general interests are intermingled, no single group is likely to promote the good of the whole community in a way that commands universal agreement. Hence, if one thinks of democratic authority as resting ultimately on some type of informed consent,[4] then the authority to act on behalf of the community's collective interest requires broad representation. The collective good of the whole community cannot be determined reliably apart from a wide public expression of views about how various actions and inactions affect different parts of the community and about what trade-offs the citizenry is willing to make. That is part of the rationale for representation. Elements of the public may be misinformed or unduly self-centered, but the same may be said of any set of elite decision makers. No one is immune to the lure of self-interest. That is why in *Federalist* number 10, James Madison cautioned that no faction should be allowed to judge its own cause. As Stephen Elkin's chapter suggests, Dallas was an example of just that—one faction judging what kind of development it wanted in the name of the whole community.

Dallas, of course, is not an isolated example. Factional struggle, as this volume shows, is an integral part of development politics. It is important, then, to examine the nature of the "prevailing coalition," how it came to prevail, and how the character of that coalition is related to development policy. To do otherwise, to characterize the behavior of development policy makers as simply responses to the external pressures of market competition, is to undercut public debate over the appropriateness of policy and the representativeness of the group that made it. We need, then, to consider the range of development-policy regimes that are covered in this book and that are echoed in other studies, and we now turn to that task.

REGIME TYPES

The entrepreneurial regime that Elkin describes in Dallas was one in which private interests—large downtown businesses—were enabled to play a major role in guiding development policy. To facilitate comparisons with other cities and to emphasize the role that private interests play, I shall refer to this type of arrangement as a corporate regime. Typically its central concern is to promote the development interests of major downtown corporations.

With the corporate regime, as with the other two types identified here, the reader should understand that the label is something of an oversimplification. Its purpose is to identify an important central tendency. More detailed analysis would yield refinements in classification, but for present purposes, a general label will suffice.

With that qualification in mind, we can see that Dallas does not stand alone. Atlanta, as Adolph Reed and Susan Clarke separately report, falls into a somewhat similar pattern, even though the black community has gained electoral control of City Hall. Robert Stoker adds that Baltimore, under Mayor Schaefer, established a "shadow government" in which, under executive sponsorship, private interests came to play a central role in development. Jameson Doig observes that the Port of New York Authority—itself somewhat insulated from the normal pressures of electoral politics—developed important business alliances. At the same time, it was autonomous enough to pursue diverse strategies. Robert Pecorella indicates that the condition of fiscal crisis cyclically pulls New York City toward a pattern in which business enjoys a special place in development matters.

The Thirteenth Arrondissement of Paris represents quite a different "prevailing coalition." This assemblage of middle- and lower-class-neighborhood groups was committed to a progressive platform of expanded services and protected residential opportunities for diverse income levels. Again, though the pattern is more mixed and the regimes often less stable, there are counterparts elsewhere—Santa Cruz, Hartford, Berkeley, Burlington, Santa Monica, and, at times, Boston and San Francisco.[5] As Sophie Body-Gendrot's chapter indicates, these coalitions have substantial opposition to overcome, and their "prevailing" position often proves tenuous. The short-lived tenure of Albuquerque's progressive mayoral leadership, described by Peter Lupsha, is thus no surprise.

Kalamazoo represents still another situation. Here, with the aid of the referendum process, the prevailing voice has been a caretaker coalition centered in the city's small-business and home-ownership population. New Orleans, with a much-different tradition and form of politics, for a time also approximated the caretaker pattern. One can surmise from Robert Whelan's account that the New Orleans style of machine politics, combined with the political exclusion of blacks, provided small-property holders with a major role in shaping and constraining policy choices during the time that other cities were embarking on more aggressive programs of redevelopment.

None of these forms of regime is offered as a pure type, and the three types don't exhaust the kinds of coalitions we could describe. For instance, Susan Clarke indicates that the four cities she looked at display significant regime variations. The point of this brief excursion through case examples is to highlight the fact that development policies differ, and they seem to vary in line with the nature of the "prevailing coalition." As communities change politically, their development policies also undergo modification.

Different policy orientations, it seems reasonable to believe, do not reflect different technical calculations about utility maximization; instead, they reflect differences in politics. Because the development policy pursued in a community grows out of governing arrangements, policy can be expected to vary with those arrangements and to represent varying slices of what is in the interest of the community.

A CLOSER LOOK

To refer to governing arrangements or to a prevailing coalition is not to talk only about who wins elections. Although winning elections is important, governing means more than occupying a set of offices. It entails a capacity to guide and reshape various forms of interaction, to modify goals, and to alter rules of decision making. Governing, however, does not require that a group be in command of all the activities in a community, but only that it be able to recast the terms on which key social transactions occur.[6]

What we want to know about a community is not just who exercises public authority in a legal sense, but also which private actors are able to act collectively and bring concerted influence to bear. What provision is there for collective action and coordinated efforts within the governmental sector and across the private and governmental sectors? The Dallas case is especially instructive, because Elkin describes the elaborate system of achieving collective action in the private sector and how, until the 1970s, cooperation that was based in the private sector enabled a business elite to monopolize collaboration with city officials. These arrangements excluded some programs and participants—Dallas took no federal urban-renewal money and the at-large election system largely kept neighborhood and minority representation out of the city council. Infrastructure for city growth was a high priority; services for older neighborhoods and their populations were not.

Kalamazoo provides an interesting contrast. There, large- and small-property holders failed to unify into a cohesive bloc. As a result, ad hoc revolts by small-property holders succeeded in vetoing efforts to use public authority on behalf of major private investments.

The progressive coalition in the Thirteenth Arrondissement of Paris mobilized mass support behind a program of expanded services and residential opportunities. Catching private development interests at a time when they were weak, this neighborhood coalition was able to enlist governmental allies and to use the authority and resources of France's powerful governmental sector to carry out its program. Of course, such an alliance can be sustained only if it is institutionalized in some way. The election of representatives to office, who could use that position to sustain the mobilization through programmatic appeals, is one way in which it could be achieved.[7]

Whereas the caretaker coalition in Kalamazoo engaged in mass mobilization to veto governmental action, the progressive coalition in Paris used mass-mobilization techniques to press *for* governmental action. Caretaker coalitions do not face the same kind of need for institutionalization that progressive coalitions face. Caretakers can prevail by veto; progressives require sustained action. The corporate coalition in Dallas exemplifies still a different situation. It relied on an elite network to put together a partnership with local government. Its main need was to prevent challenge groups from being able to coalesce into a stable form of opposition. The city-manager plan and a politically restricted city council, along with the low-visibility arrangements that they established, served that purpose.

Let me be quick to add at this point that I am not about to embark on specifying ninety-nine hypotheses for further testing in future research. My aim is only to draw on a few of the case studies to illustrate ways in which political arrangements matter. I want now to take that argument a step further and to indicate how variations in the "prevailing coalition" can shape policy. To do that, we need to examine some major dimensions of development policy.

DIMENSIONS OF DEVELOPMENT POLICY

First, development policy is closely related to the debate over the equality/efficiency trade-off.[8] The issue has strong ideological overtones. Those on the Right tend to argue that any tilt toward equality harms economic efficiency and leaves society with decreased productivity and fewer benefits to be distributed. If there are to be subsidies, this line of reasoning runs, they should be to encourage investment, not to promote equality. A high level of investment, according to the partisans of efficiency, produces the proverbial rising tide that lifts all boats. That is the rationale for a supply-side economic policy at the national level. And there are ample local counterparts, in Dallas, Atlanta, New Orleans, Baltimore, and contemporary New York City, to draw on cases described earlier.

Those on the Left tend to argue that considerable concession can be made to equality without harming efficiency. In the terms of Robert Kuttner, it is not necessary to choose between prosperity and social justice: we can have both. Kuttner suggests that capital supply is only one determinant of growth;[9] therefore public policy need not be devoted to courting capital and subsidizing investment activities. Among even middle-of-the-road analysts of urban growth and development, some regard efforts to court capital through subsidies as ineffective, and thus call for a more balanced policy.[10]

The debate over the equality/efficiency trade-off helps us to understand the fundamental political nature of development policy. While the "supply-side" of the efficiency argument is sometimes presented as if business subsidies, combined with the avoidance of social-welfare expenditures, were a technical requirement for maximum economic growth, the issue is not that simple. Class interests are involved, and they operate against a background of uncertainty about the consequences of various policies. Kuttner observes: "Who gets what is seldom merely a technical issue."[11] In examining cross-national experiences, he makes a convincing case for his position that "a wide range of equality/efficiency bargains exists."[12] Occasional programs of social redistribution can even be defended on the grounds of efficiency. Hartford, Connecticut, for example, adopted a fuel-subsidy program in order to curtail abandonments of housing.[13] Similarly, one could argue that money that is put into education and other equality-serving forms of "human capital" promotes development, albeit indirectly, more effectively than do tax abatements and subsidized interest rates.[14]

Many of these issues are largely indeterminant. Furthermore, as Adolph Reed argues in his account of Atlanta in political transition, what one set of actors regarded as promoting development, another viewed as simply a question of group preferment. Understandings also change. In Atlanta, white business interests at one point considered requirements for minority-business participation as social experiments endangering the city's economic future. Later, they accepted these requirements as a necessary and even beneficial condition of public-private partnerships in a predominantly black city.

Put in political terms, the debate over the equality/efficiency trade-off converts into a spectrum of choices that look like this:

use of public authority and resources to further equality (e.g., fuel subsidies)	rely on free market transactions (e.g., no subsidies)	use of public authority and resources to subsidize investment (tax abatements for new business development)

In these terms, the issue is one of class equity. Is it just and fair to use public authority to promote equality? Should it be used to subsidize the investor class? Or should it be kept out of issues of allocation between classes? The use of public authority and resources to further equality is the likely choice of a progressive coalition. Progressives generally take the position that equality can be promoted without endangering economic productivity. The use of public authority and resources to subsidize investment is the likely choice of the corporate coalition. The "supply-side" argument is that maximum economic productivity comes from subsidizing investment, though a euphemism such as *encouraging* is apt to be used in place of the word *subsidy*. Furthermore, business tends to favor the use of complicated arrangements and off-budget subsidies to disguise the fact that it is being subsidized. Reliance on the free market is the likely choice of the caretaker coalition. The caretaker argument is simply that no subsidy of investment should be necessary if a truly sensible activity is envisaged. Small-property holders tend to see subsidies of any kind as unfair reallocations of what should be privately held resources. These three positions represent three different ideologies, and there is no objective standard by which one position can be deemed superior to the others.

It should be added, to avoid misunderstanding, that any given city coalition may combine features of two, or even all three, types. Ideological purity is probably rare. It depends on what particular groups make up a coalition and how directly affected each is by various measures. Dallas, for example, combines some aspects of the caretaker view with the corporate view. Dallas stayed out of the federal urban-renewal program to avoid requirements to meet progressive demands. No doubt that was a consideration in early New Orleans as well, with its obeisance to traditional racial attitudes. New Haven, by contrast, relied heavily on federal urban-renewal money and thus combined features of corporate and progressive coalitions, with corporate concerns predominant. Atlanta also used the federal urban-renewal program to pursue a corporate agenda, but it treated relocation in a way that was responsive to business and other interests within the black community.[15]

Now, let's turn to a second dimension of development, the question of the certainty that a development action will result in a net economic gain, or, in the case of equality-promoting measures, no net economic loss. At stake is a willingness to take risks. The choices thus fall on a spectrum of risk taking:

high certainty of no net economic loss (e.g., avoid large, expensive projects)	low certainty of net economic consequences (willingness to undertake new projects and services)

Here the point is that decision makers often do not really know what the net economic effects of a development action will be, particularly over the long run. For example, there is risk involved, even for a major city, in building and operating a convention center.[16] Many such ventures lose money—the World's Fair in New Orleans is a clear instance. Depending on the project, there may be several risks. If a project loses money and worsens the commercial quality or livability of an area, perhaps displacing small businesses as well, it could result in substantial costs for the city. This was a concern in Kalamazoo. There are other forms of risk too. In many cities, slum-clearance activities have led to overcrowding and to decline in adjacent areas.[17]

An active redevelopment program and extensive infrastructure expenditures can contribute to fiscal distress,[18] thereby possibly making an area less attractive for investment and almost certainly working a hardship on small-property holders and marginal home owners. That fear provided support for the caretaker coalition in Kalamazoo. While public investment and subsidies sometimes pay for themselves, they often do not. The point is that many projects are surrounded by a degree of uncertainty and the cumulative effects of development are especially hard to determine. There may be, as was the case of the New Orleans waterfront, a danger of overbuilding. Excessive density and congestion can cause an area to lose its attractiveness and may result in eventual decline—an urban counterpart to the tragedy of the commons.

The matter of risk taking is thus a political question that various community groups disagree about. Again there is no external standard that can answer the question as to what is in the best interest of the community. Ideology or special vulnerability to unwanted consequences (such as higher taxes) may incline participants one way or another in their willingness to incur risks. In practice, risk taking overlaps with the issue of class equity; each group wants to shift risks from itself to others.

Finally, let us turn to the matter of allocation of the costs and the benefits of development activities. Specifically, let us consider differences over whether these costs should be borne publicly or privately and whether these benefits are to be enjoyed publicly or privately. Again, there is some overlap with the class-equity issue in actual policies, but conceptually the issues are distinct. Because the patterns differ, we need to consider costs and benefits separately.

First, costs. Imagine this spectrum of alternatives:

tilt development costs toward the public sector (e.g., public assumption of infrastructure costs)	attempt to minimize development costs (e.g., no-growth policy in the face of costs caused by private actions)	tilt development costs toward the private sector (e.g., impact fees on private developers)

The question of the imposition of costs can be expected to divide along the cleavage between corporate and progressive coalitions, with business seeking to shift costs onto the public sector and with progressives seeking to place those costs on those who stand to make profits. The placement of costs involves numerous complexities, however. Small-property holders and people on fixed income, for example, may be squeezed out of their usual laissez-faire stance, and they may call for controls on private development in order to minimize costs that come as a side effect of growth. Furthermore, there is a connection between views on the allocation of costs and the willingness to see risks taken. The corporate coalition tends toward the position that investment can most readily be promoted by having the public assume the costs of ventures that are unlikely to yield a profit (convention centers, sports arenas, assemblage of land in rundown areas, etc.). The opposing view is that if the costs are placed on the public, then there may be no inhibition on making unwise investments. However, much depends on the particulars of the situation. Doig's account of airport control by the Port of New York Authority indicates that the ability of the Airport Operators Association to pass the cost of airport improvements on to users rather than taxpayers may have resulted in more expenditures on improved facilities.

For corporate interests and their allies, the appeal of passing costs on to the public is that the costs are dispersed rather than concentrated. If a hotel or a new auto plant is granted a tax abatement, the consequences of the foregone revenue (the costs of the special favor) are spread out over the entire taxpaying public, who must make up the difference. The political appeal of this kind of practice was exploited by machine politicians in an earlier era; corporate business finds it useful today. The counterargument to such practices is that giving a tax abatement to one business but not to another is to bestow an unfair competitive advantage. This naturally leads other businesses to demand such a break, and eventually it weakens the city's revenue base and either places a heavier burden on home owners or curtails the city's capacity to provide services.[19] The desire to protect public-revenue capacity is what often leads progressive coalitions to place the burden of development costs in the business sector.

The displacement of costs on to the public is more appealing locally if the costs can be passed on to a much larger public; hence, cities attempt to obtain state support for building sports arenas (e.g., the Superdome in New Orleans) or convention and exhibit facilities (e.g., the Georgia World Congress Center in Atlanta). As Doig shows in his account of Austin Tobin's early career, the Port of New York Authority played a major alliance-building role among local governments in seeking the protection of tax exemption for municipal bonds. Tax exemption passes a cost of development on to the United States Treasury. Similarly, the current popularity of various kinds of development bonds is attributable to the fact that they displace their costs onto the national government in the form of foregone revenue. However, they have now become a major drain on federal-revenue capacity, thereby making other forms of federal assistance harder to come by.

Let us now turn to the benefit side of the issue. Should the benefits of development policy be allocated through the public sector or the private sector? The choices can be arrayed simply:

use of development to obtain collective benefits through public policy (e.g., linkage that requires corporate developers to contribute to a city's cultural life or housing opportunities)	use of development to obtain private benefits (e.g., large profits as reward for investment, or low tax rate to maximize private choice)

Each of the types of coalition I am using for analytical purposes has a somewhat different set of aims for development policy. In the case of the progressive coalition, its members are guided by a search for goals that can most readily be pursued with the use of public authority. Progressives are concerned with communal amenities—such as historic preservation, planned growth, environmental quality, and the city as a socially and culturally diverse habitat. It would be a mistake, then, to equate the progressive coalition with a have-not population that is in revolt against a system of economic exploitation. Progressives' aims are more modest, and their goals are more diverse. Yet the values that they promote are values that call for holding in check the rapacious tendencies of profit-seeking enterprises, enterprises that are concerned mainly with short-term business opportunities in development. Progressives believe that such businesses are inattentive to the long-term consequences of their actions on the quality of community life and, progressives also argue, on the long-term attractiveness of the community as an investment site. Like Garrett Hardin,[20] progressives are willing to use public authority to curtail the destructive tendencies of rational self-interest associated with the notion of the "tragedy of the commons." Because progressives believe that a socially diverse city is a more vital city, they are willing to see public authority and resources used to encourage a wide range of residential and employment opportunities.[21] In addition, progressives are willing, in such cities as Boston, Santa Monica, and San Francisco, to use "linkage"—or requirements that investors contribute to the meeting of the community's social concerns in exchange for development opportunities.[22] Sometimes linkage takes the form of requirements that large developments devote a percentage of their costs to open space or to the arts.

Not all progressive coalitions are identical, of course. Priorities vary, and that variation is almost certainly related to the more particular composition of the coalition. With a large working-class component, Dayton shows greater concern about employment (see Clarke) than does San Francisco, with its large middle-class constituency of progressives. Minority representation in a coalition, as in Atlanta and New Orleans, is likely to heighten concern with affirmative-action requirements and minority set-asides.

The caretaker coalition is primarily interested in low taxes and a nonintrusive government. It represents a constituency that can be mobilized against progressive coalitions, and it appears to have been an element in the reversal of support for planned growth in Albuquerque. To some extent, the position is ideological.[23] But part of it is simply opposition to taxes, a position that is especially attractive to those who own property but have little economic margin. They would like to see the benefits from growth realized in the form of a low tax rate, and if low taxation cannot be maintained, they may not be all that keen about promoting growth. The corporate coalition also favors channeling the benefits of development into the private sector. Its members are primarily concerned about the interests of investors, and they try to divert efforts to garner benefits for communal amenities and social purposes. Indeed, this is the concern that encourages corporate interests to seek to insulate development activities from popular control. For this reason, in Dallas, Atlanta, and other cities, downtown business interests promote reliance on nonprofit corporations, rather than city agencies, to carry out development projects.

The corporate coalition is also eager to channel increased public revenue into the support for private investment. Hence, corporate interests have championed the use of tax-increment districts, measures whereby the increased revenue from intensified development is earmarked for expenditures on infrastructure and support facilities *in that district*. What this does is to privatize portions of the city's revenue capacity, keeping tax gains from intensified development out of the city's general budget and dedicating them to the support of private investment.

Again, it is important to see coalitions as complex, and therefore often embracing policies based on mixed principles. The political vulnerability of pure corporate regimes encourages the building of alliances. Hence, Atlanta's business community has come to accept the principle of minority-participation requirements for city-funded projects. In that sense, downtown business interests accept the allocation of development benefits to a social objective; their coalition needs lead them to do so. And as Allen Whitt shows, the inclusion of arts supporters in development coalitions also entails allocating costs and benefits in such a way as to promote a public purpose. Furthermore, Whitt indicates, drawing arts supporters into economic-development coalitions gives business interests a broader base of political support. Potential supporters of a progressive-centered coalition are thus drawn into a different alignment.

As in the earlier topics, choices about allocating costs and benefits between the public and the private sectors are political choices. Again, there is no external standard against which these choices can be judged so as to determine objectively what is in the community's interest. The policies that are pursued grow out of the prevailing coalition, the concerns and perspectives that its members bring to bear. At this stage, it should be abundantly clear that much is at stake in these choices. The politics of development is not simply a matter of choosing growth or rejecting social-welfare objectives. A complex set of considerations is at issue, and a political process is what decides them.

My use of the three types of development coalitions is only an analytical shorthand way of illustrating how policy is related to the character of the governing coalition. It is not intended to preempt concern with the full richness of development politics and the range of issues at stake. Certainly the present typology is not intended as "the" authoritative scenario of development politics. Like this volume generally, it is intended only to make the case that the politics of development is indeed worth studying, because politics matters. Positing a relationship between development policy and the "prevailing coalition" does not mean that this relationship can be captured in a few simple propositions. Because governing coalitions are complex, we would expect their relationship to development policy to be complex—decipherable but complex.

COALITIONS IN A POLITICAL-ECONOMY PERSPECTIVE

The examples of corporate, caretaker, and progressive coalitions show, first of all, that there are multiple development strategies that can be pursued, each of which may be regarded as best by some set of actors. Hence, any operational notion of the community's collective good seems to be given shape by the "prevailing coalition." Development policy is therefore not something that is calculated to serve the interest of an abstraction called "the community"; it is something that is derived through the community's politics. If there is no objective standard by which the best development strategy can be determined, we can nevertheless make judgments. But about what? While judgments can certainly be made about the substance of a development strategy, the question of what is best seems to depend greatly on the priorities appropriate for a particular community. If there is no objective standard by which these priorities can be identified, then we might train our evaluative sights on the political process through which development priorities are generated. Put another way, because actual development policy grows out of a set of political activities, it behooves us to give attention to the arrangements by which policy is made and conflict is managed. If these arrangements are flawed in some fundamental way, we cannot expect to have good policy over the long run. Development policy will reflect the weaknesses of political arrangements.

At this point, we need to examine the actual behavior of community actors, public officials in particular. What incentives, disincentives, and constraints do they respond to? In the introductory essay and in various chapters, a number of factors have been suggested.

The political-economy context should be reiterated. As Elkin has argued so cogently, development policy is made in a context of a division of labor between market and state. The market represents a substantial concentration of resources and economic activities in private hands, whereas the democratic state is based upon the principle of popular control through elections. This means that while city officials need electoral support, such support is only part of what they need. Put another way, obtaining electoral support is dependent upon being able to persuade voters that they are presiding over a viable set of governing arrangements. They need to be able to maintain order, take in revenue, borrow money, and enjoy an adequate level of economic activity. These are the multiple imperatives that Shefter talks about,[24] imperatives that are not easily met by public officials acting alone. Business elites are thus in a position to destabilize the popular support that incumbent officials have; elites can do this by withholding credit, withdrawing investment activity, and highlighting the need for business cooperation in achieving a high level of economic activity.[25] As Robert Pecorella's chapter shows, cities may go through cycles in which business power is used to check public officials and to redirect policy.

Nonbusiness groups may also affect the capacity of governing groups to meet their various imperatives. Public-safety employees, if unionized or otherwise able to act collectively, can withdraw a key support from the community's ability to maintain order. And in extraordinary circumstances such as New York City's fiscal crisis of the 1970s, union pension funds have served as a source of municipal credit. Indeed, public employees were an element in the coalition that presided over the restructuring of New York City's politics after the near bankruptcy of the municipal government. Like business interests, by their various actions, public employees may be able to lessen or enhance popular support for elected officials.

It is clear that no single group monopolizes the resources that city officials need in order to put together and maintain a workable set of governing arrangements. It is also clear that not all groups can contribute equally to a workable set of arrangements. Few groups can give or withhold credit or investment in significant amounts. Many groups are able to contribute to electoral support, but electoral support is mediated through a set of perceptions about how well the community is working. "Side payments" can be useful in influencing interpreters of these perceptions and in mobilizing or demobilizing various groups. At the same time, patronage is rarely available in the amounts that would be needed in order to sustain an army of precinct workers. Hence, few groups are able to deliver a large and dependable vote, but certainly those that are organized have a considerable advantage over those that are not. If one adds to this picture the pluralist insight that most people most of the time are indifferent about the particulars of most policy decisions, it becomes clear that putting together and maintaining a governing coalition is a task that greatly favors some groups over others.

The extent to which the nonaffluent neighborhoods are improved and housing opportunities for the poor are protected may depend on the ability of disadvantaged groups to sustain "political struggle." That is a conclusion suggested by Sophie Body-Gendrot's chapter on the Thirteenth Arrondissement of Paris.[26] Still, sustained struggles are rare. Periodic outbreaks of opposition, followed by quiescence, are more common. Challenge groups face a difficult task. To have any impact, they need to be able to maintain unity and to sustain their efforts over time. Challenge eventually seems futile unless it leads to a restructuring of political arrangements and some form of incorporation of the challenge groups into the governing coalition.[27] For this, the resources needed for electoral mobilization are not enough. Groups need to make themselves valuable to officeholders on an ongoing basis. Just as popular support is only one of several forms of resources mobilization that city officials face, so electoral mobilization is only one of several forms of resource mobilization that city officials respond to. And the ability to garner votes, as argued above, is itself not separable from other imperatives of governing.

City officials need revenue, credit, resources for side-payments, and a satisfactory level of economic activity generally. They want dependable forms of cooperation; they want to deal with those capable of contributing to, or even undertaking, large and complicated projects. Mayors, especially, want quick results and visible successes. They are on a short election cycle, with limited resources of their own. Hence they may be quite willing to substitute symbolic successes for substantive ones. Thus, while cities have only a limited capacity to influence decisions about business investment, their officials are eager to show that they are trying. Even though such practices as tax abatements and the issuance of below-market bonds may have little or no actual impact on business-investment decisions, such programs may be quite useful as symbolic stances in the garnering of popular support.[28]

The reinterpretation of New Haven under Richard Lee's mayoralty, which Heywood Sanders and I offered earlier in this volume, makes a distinction between the politics of announcement and the politics of execution. Lee's national reputation as a city rebuilder shows how important the projection of image can be. To be sure, the politics of execution takes its toll eventually, but that does not eliminate the enticement to play the politics of announcement—if anything, in the short run, it enhances it. But how do various group interests and policy considerations fit into the larger picture?

What we can say overall is that some groups, more than others, are valuable to city officials in meeting their governing responsibilities and that some groups, more than others, have strong and immediate incentives to play an active and ongoing part in making development policy. Given a similarity in these structural inducements from community to community, we would therefore expect to see considerable similarity in the development coalitions that prevail from one city to another. Banks and other financial institutions that have large trust holdings in downtown property; utilities and other businesses, including newspapers, that have a large stake in the central business district; big developers and contractors; construction unions; commercial real-estate companies; and professionals of various kinds (architects, lawyers, etc.), who gain substantial fees from development projects—all would be among those likely to hold prominent membership position in a city's development coalition.[29] They have a strong incentive to participate, and they control valuable resources, including membership in the organizational network that is likely to be at the center of a community's civic life. Some groups thus possess a superior capacity to become part of the "prevailing coalition."

Indeed, the overall impression that most observers have is one of business dominance. Although it is certainly the case that business does not get its way all of the time, it does often occupy a central place in setting and carrying out the development agenda. Moreover, in carrying out this development agenda, business seems to enjoy a considerable edge in information, thereby holding an upper hand in the bargaining process.[30] Other factors also advantage large businesses especially—in particular, the organized capacity to act, to act quickly, and to command the resources and expertise needed for big, complex development projects. In the words of Jeffrey Pressman and Aaron Wildavsky, they are often "the only show in town."[31] There is more to it than that, however. The fact of a division of labor between state and private business should not cause us to overlook the fact that business controls formidable *political* resources.

Business is, of course, not a monolithic group. Small businesses are often left out of development planning and find that their interests are hurt by vast redevelopment schemes. In Washington, D.C., for example, small businesses have come together to form the Downtown Retail Merchants Association to counter their neglect in development planning.[32] Businesses that have a direct and particular interest in development naturally have a special incentive to exert influence in city politics. Thus, in Albuquerque, when city officials embarked on a policy of managed growth, they encountered formidable opposition from developers. The Dallas example shows, however, that such interests need not be the dominant voice. Then, too, it is important to remember that not all businesses have a strong tie to a particular community. Many major businesses, especially manufacturing concerns, have a limited interest in community affairs; but, as mentioned above, banks and other financial institutions, newspapers, department stores, utilities, and various other businesses do have a large fixed stake in the central area of cities.[33] They often draw together into a downtown business association. The contrasting cases of Dallas and New Orleans indicate, however, that there is nothing automatic about forming such an association. Business interests can be organized politically in any of a number of ways.

Now let's consider the matter from the side of public officials. Jameson Doig's account of the Port of New York Authority indicates that public officials who are interested in an active program of development and seek a record of visible successes are drawn toward major business and financial interests as allies. Similarly, the case of Robert Moses suggests that activist executives are not attracted to the caretaker coalition or to an alliance with small businesses and marginal property owners.[34] These latter interests are more likely either to find their champions on city legislative bodies or to gain expression in the referendum process, as in the Kalamazoo instance.[35] For their part, city officials who are primarily concerned with small-scale patronage—with courthouse politics—may be drawn towards a friends-and-neighbors politics in which a low level of taxation keeps the boat from being rocked and keeps incumbents from being challenged. This seems to have been a factor in New Orleans until the 1960s. Overall, then, as Susan Clarke argues in her chapter, there are reasons to believe that the institutional interests of public officeholders influence development policy. When those interests are centered in large and professionalized bureaucracies that have an activist orientation, they may be drawn toward a corporate coalition.

When those interests are centered in small-scale courthouse politics, the caretaker coalition may be a more natural ally.

What sort of officeholders might be inclined toward an alliance with progressive coalitions? This alliance, perhaps more than any other, cuts across the grain of urban political economy. Generally, public officials who are inclined toward an activist stance would be expected to be drawn to those allies who have the economic and organizational resources commensurate with that stance. That may be why even black mayors, such as Maynard Jackson in Atlanta, with a strong concern for have-not constituents, are drawn toward a "supply-side" development strategy. It is much easier to bring the resources together for a trickle-down strategy than for one that is addressed directly to employment needs. Furthermore, as Robert Stoker's chapter indicates, the "supply-side" approach is subject to little public oversight. Particularly when pursued through quasi-private entities, it insulates public officials from the responsibility for adverse development impacts. At the same time, the officials can claim credit for a general policy of encouraging growth.[36]

Looking at the matter from the point of view of *governing* officials, we can see that it is not easy to base policy on a mobilization of have-nots. As Sophie Body-Gendrot's chapter on Paris suggests, successful efforts to promote a progressive agenda may require middle-class allies. The weakness of a have-not constituency as a governing base may also be a factor in the tendency for *candidates* for city office to be more progressive than they are as *incumbents* of those offices. As emphasized throughout this volume, gaining votes is only one of the imperatives that surround the running of city halls. Successful electoral coalitions do not necessarily govern.

Though unable to establish themselves widely as dominant coalitions, progressive coalitions do come to power.[37] From all indications, they require a high level of ideological commitment from public officials and a supportive constituency also disposed toward a progressive position.[38] Progressive coalitions may, however, have a built-in tendency toward instability. There appear to be troublesome contradictions in the governing coalitions of progressives—in particular, tension between the executive drive for a record of visible successes and an ideological commitment to (as well perhaps as a genuine political need for) a strong base of active citizen involvement. The Carbone regime in Hartford, for example, apparently alienated its community base by being inattentive to neighborhood-level participation in making development policy.[39] One reason this happened was that in order to generate investment activity and revenue, city officials had to engage in complicated bargaining arrangements with business interests and had to contend with opposition from the daily newspaper. Progressives appear to be faced with the necessity of fighting multifront wars, and that is not a propitious circumstance for maintaining a high level of citizen participation.

Although there are cities in which the progressive influence is substantial, in most cities a thoroughgoing progressive stance offers little hope to officeholders for a secure political future. Even where growth is rapid and investment activity is at a high-enough level to give officials a powerful bargaining hand, those businesses with palpable particular interests in development represent, as they did in Albuquerque, a potential source of opposition that is formidable. Executive-centered governing coalitions thus experience a strong tug toward some form of alliance with major business interests. Some cities—Berkeley, San Francisco, and Boston, in particular—are notable for the extent to which there are strong bases of political organization outside the business community. The Dayton case, discussed by Clarke, is also significant. But in many other cities, even cities such as Atlanta and Detroit, which have black mayors, or San Antonio and Denver, which have Latino mayors, the attraction of the corporate alliance is strong.

A survey of urban experiences thus suggests that there is a background pattern to the formation of governing coalitions. The elements are:

1. Business control of investment activity is a basic feature of all regimes.
2. Control of economic and organizational resources makes major business and financial institutions attractive as allies, especially for activist public officials.
3. Developers themselves are something of a wild card and can show up in any of several arrangements—incorporated into a general business coalition (as in Dallas) or more as free agents in deal making (as in Albuquerque).
4. As a force for passivity, the caretaker coalition is dependent on access through the city council, ward-based political organizations, or the referendum process.
5. Progressive coalitions are dependent on strong ideological commitments among key public officials and a favorable ideological predisposition among the voting public.
6. Unless public officeholders are attached to a traditional system of small-stakes patronage or are alternatively committed to a progressive ideology or perhaps a new fiscal-populism ideology, they are likely to be drawn toward an alliance with corporate interests. This is especially likely for officeholders who have a taste for activism and a pragmatic bent of mind. It seems likely that many elected executives and top-level professional administrators fall into this category.
7. Because an executive-centered, corporate-allied coalition rests on such a formidable concentration of resources, it is perhaps especially able to circumvent popular preferences and to disregard opposing interests.

8. A likely countervailing force to executive-centered coalitions that are oriented toward corporate interests is an extensive network of neighborhood, small-business, and minority-group associations actively engaged in politics. Institutions, such as Dayton's City-wide Development Corporations, can strengthen the representation of diverse interests.

Drawing on existing cases, I have made the argument that "prevailing coalitions" in development policy, especially ones that are executive centered and are allied with large business and financial interests, are likely to be somewhat unrepresentative of popular preferences and especially inattentive to various unorganized or weakly organized interests. The argument in this form is somewhat speculative. It also represents primary attention to the general structural condition in which urban regimes take shape—namely, the necessity to make an adjustment between the state (in the form of local governmental authority) and privately owned economic enterprises (increasingly in corporate form). As Susan Clarke's essay indicates, however, development policies in American cities are more varied than one would expect from this structural condition alone. To understand more refined variations in urban regimes, their politics, and their policies, we turn, then, to what future research might tell us about specifically local conditions and why they matter.

NOTES

1. Stephen Elkin, *City and Regime in the American Republic* (Chicago: University of Chicago Press, 1987).
2. "The Local Community as an Ecology of Games," *American Journal of Sociology* 64 (Nov. 1958): 251–61.
3. See also Alberta Sbragia, *The Municipal Money Chase* (Boulder, Colo.: Westview Press, 1983).
4. Chester I. Barnard, *The Functions of the Executive* (Cambridge, Mass.: Harvard University Press, 1938); and Alvin W. Gouldner, *Patterns of Industrial Bureaucracy* (New York: Free Press, 1954).
5. Rufus P. Browning, Dale Rogers Marshall, and David H. Tabb, *Protest is Not Enough* (Berkeley: University of California Press, 1984); Pierre Clavel, *The Progressive City* (New Brunswick, N.J.: Rutgers University Press, 1986); Alexander Ganz, "Where Has the Urban Crisis Gone?" *Urban Affairs Quarterly* 20 (June 1985): 449–68; and John H. Mollenkopf, *The Contested City* (Princeton, N.J.: Princeton, University Press, 1983).
6. Philip Selznick, *Leadership in Administration* (New York: Harper & Row, 1957).
7. Browning, Marshall, and Tabb, *Protest Is Not Enough.*
8. See Arthur M. Okun, *Equality and Efficiency* (Washington, D.C.: Brookings Institution, 1975).

9. Robert Kuttner, *The Economic Illusion* (Boston, Mass.: Houghton Mifflin, 1984), p. 51.

10. Katherine L. Bradbury, Anthony Downs, and Kenneth A. Small, *Urban Decline and the Future of American Cities* (Washington, D.C.: Brookings Institution, 1982).

11. Kuttner, *Economic Illusion,* p. 4.

12. Ibid, p. 3.

13. Clavel, *Progressive City,* p. 42.

14. Norton E. Long, "Can the Contemporary City Be a Significant Polity?" Paper given at the plenary session of the annual meeting of the Urban Affairs Association, Flint, Michigan, 23–26 Mar. 1983.

15. Clarence N. Stone, *Economic Growth and Neighborhood Discontent* (Chapel Hill: University of North Carolina Press, 1976).

16. Chester Hartman, *The Transformation of San Francisco* (Totowa, N.J.: Rowman & Allanheld, 1984).

17. See Christopher Silver, *Twentieth-Century Richmond* (Knoxville: University of Tennessee Press, 1984), p. 122.

18. Michael D. Kennedy, "The Fiscal Crisis of the City," in *Cities in Transformation,* ed. Michael P. Smith, Urban Affairs Annual Reviews, vol. 26 (Beverly Hills, Calif.: Sage Publications, 1984).

19. Rudolph A. Pyatt, "Life after Bloomies," *Washington Post,* 14 Mar. 1986, pp. C11–12.

20. "The Tragedy of the Commons," *Science* 162 (Dec. 1968): 1243–48.

21. Clavel, *Progressive City.*

22. Ibid.; and Ganz, "Where Has the Urban Crisis Gone?"

23. Siegrun F. Fox, "Who Opposes Public/Private Financial Partnerships for Urban Renewal?" *Journal of Urban Affairs* 7 (Winter 1985): 27–40.

24. Martin Shefter, *Political Crisis/Fiscal Crisis: The Collapse and Revival of New York City* (New York: Basic Books, 1985).

25. Todd Swanstrom, *The Crisis of Growth Politics: Cleveland, Kucinich, and the Challenge of Urban Populism* (Philadelphia: Temple University Press, 1985).

26. See also Norman I. Fainstein and Susan S. Fainstein, eds., *Urban Policy under Capitalism,* Urban Affairs Annual Reviews, vol. 22 (Beverly Hills, Calif.: Sage Publications, 1982), p. 184.

27. Note the lack of long-term success by Alinsky-style protest groups—Joan E. Lancourt, *Confront or Concede* (Lexington, Mass.: Lexington Books, 1979).

28. Bryan D. Jones and Lynn W. Bachelor, "Local Policy Discretion and the Corporate Surplus," in *Urban Economic Development,* ed. Richard D. Bingham and John P. Blair, Urban Affairs Annual Reviews, vol. 27 (Beverly Hills, Calif.: Sage Publications, 1984); B. M. Moriarty, *Industrial Location and Community Development* (Chapel Hill: University of North Carolina Press, 1980); and Swanstrom, *Crisis of Growth Politics,* esp. pp.141–50.

29. Harvey Molotch, "The City as a Growth Machine," *American Journal of Sociology* 82 (Sept. 1976): 309–31; and Robert H. Salisbury, "Urban Politics. The New Convergence of Power," *Journal of Politics* 26 (Nov. 1964): 775–97.

30. Jones and Bachelor, "Local Policy Discretion and the Corporate Surplus."

31. Jeffrey L. Pressman and Aaron Wildavsky, *Implementation,* 3d ed. (Berkeley: University of California Press, 1984), p. 28.

32. Rudolph A. Pyatt, "Keeping Small Business," *Washington Post,* 12 Nov. 1985, pp. E1–2.

33. Roger Friedland and Donald Palmer, "Park Place and Main Street," *Annual Review of Sociology* 10 (1984): 393–416.

34. Robert A. Caro, *The Power Broker* (New York: Alfred A. Knopf, 1974).

35. But see the discussion of the new fiscal populism by Terry N. Clark and Lorna C. Ferguson, *City Money* (New York: Columbia University Press, 1983).

36. See, especially, Swanstrom, *Crisis of Growth Politics,* as well as Reed in the present volume.

37. Clavel, *Progressive City.*

38. Browning, Marshall, and Tabb, *Protest Is Not Enough.*

39. Clavel, *Progressive City,* pp. 48–53.

15

Possible Directions for Future Inquiry

Clarence N. Stone

The contributors to this volume have sounded a number of common themes, but they have also written from a variety of particular perspectives. That is appropriate for the aim of this book, an aim that encourages researchers to appreciate the variety as well as the structural consistencies in urban politics. This concluding chapter on possible directions for future research reiterates that theme, and it also reaffirms that we study politics, with both its uniformities and its variations, as a fundamentally normative inquiry.

SOCIAL AND POLITICAL BASES OF REGIME VARIATION

Although the regime typology used in the preceding chapter was a helpful shorthand, the typology should not prevent future research from considering alternative and more elaborate classification schemes for relating regime to policy. Similarly, the emphasis in this volume on the political-economy context of urban regimes should not discourage research into the details of civic practices and political arrangements.

Quite the contrary, the version of regime theory that is being promoted here holds that a governing coalition reflects the particulars of time and place as well as a general structural condition. The particulars of time and place involve many elements, but especially the complex ways in which community political and civic life is organized. My comments must again be speculative. More detailed research will be necessary before anyone can talk with much confidence about the conditions that give rise to variations in regime form. Nevertheless, the case studies that are reported in this volume point to some important considerations. Simplification is unavoidable, but it may still be useful in indicating what future research would explore.

The particulars of time and place might be thought of as containing four elements.

THE SOCIOECONOMIC COMPOSITION OF THE COMMUNITY

There are many ways in which this factor might be important, but for now I want to look at only two. First is the homogeneity/heterogeneity of the community. A small and relatively homogeneous community such as Kalamazoo, Michigan, is obviously different from a highly heterogeneous metropolis like New York City. As one example of how this difference might be important politically, it seems likely that the kind of popular control that is exercised through the electoral process demonstrated in Kalamazoo is much less likely in a large and varied city in which the voting public is crosscut by numerous divisions of class, race, and ethnicity.[1]

Second is the extent to which the cityscape is populated by small property holdings versus large organizations and concentrations of economic power. Again, Kalamazoo, though it is not without large and wealthy organizations, is different from major financial centers such as New York, Atlanta, and Dallas. Small property holdings are always present, but presumably the balance point between them and large economic entities varies. The significance of the balance point between large and small economic entities has to do with their likely impact on orientation toward development. Small-property holders seem to be more inclined to take few risks, hold onto what they have, and avoid large-scale reshaping of the development environment. Their resources are inadequate for such efforts, and as Susan Clarke suggests, they may lack the resources to internalize the particular costs of coalescing around a broad program of action. Defensive battles are another matter.

Large and economically powerful organizations are quite different. They seem more inclined to be assertive in reshaping the development environment so that it will be favorable for investment opportunities. Because they have greater resources, both economic and organizational, they have a different outlook about what is at risk and what is possible.

Many other factors—for example, race and ethnicity as bonds of unity or sources of division, educational level, and home-ownership rate, to suggest a few—are likely to be important but are not pursued here. One might note by way of illustration, though, the fact that the interclass coalition in the Thirteenth Arrondissement of Paris, which is described by Sophie Body-Gendrot, was not disrupted by racial or other divisions, which are so often a factor, as she notes, in American cities.

THE DIVERSITY OF POLITICALLY ACTIVE INTERESTS

A community might be socially heterogeneous, but for various reasons that heterogeneity might not be reflected in the community's political activity. The "reform" arrangements in Dallas, described by Stephen Elkin, were created to restrict political participation. Racial exclusion in New Orleans for a time narrowed participation in that city's politics. Of course, we should also remember that the forces shaping community-level participation are not confined to the community level. Federal and state requirements and inducements, as well as broad social movements, play a significant part in activating or discouraging broader community involvement.

INSTITUTIONALIZED FORMS OF REPRESENTATION

Not only do communities differ in the extent to which a variety of groups are politically active; they also vary in the extent to which these groups enjoy a stable and independent channel of representation. Movements to incorporate previously excluded groups are likely to be successful only if representation is institutionalized in some way.[2] In Atlanta, for example, the black middle class enjoys such representation; the black lower classes do not. The weakness of organized labor and the strength of black business participation in the city's civic life give a particular tilt to representation in Atlanta. Another example of how representation can be shaped is suggested by Allen Whitt's essay. There is, he suggests, a difference between an arts community that is coopted into a business-centered development coalition and an arts community that is independently represented in a city's deliberations over development policy.

NORMS OF COOPERATION, DUTY, AND RESTRAINT
WITHIN AND AMONG VARIOUS COMMUNITY INTERESTS

The power of specific groups and the relationships between groups are likely to be shaped by the norms and traditions of the community. Norms within the business community of Dallas encouraged unity and participation, thus greatly enhancing the power of that group and enabling them to focus on their collective interests in development. New Orleans represents quite a different set of traditions, and its business community exerted relatively limited collective influence. Other contrasts can be made. Whereas the power and position of the business community in Dallas enables it to pursue a strategy of restricting "political" representation, Dayton operates with a different set of institutions and norms, bringing a variety of groups into a shared involvement in development policy.

Mixing rapid growth with a tradition of fragmented and personalized politics, Albuquerque represents something of an extreme. With weak norms of civic obligation and integrity, Albuquerque's volatile politics fits none of the regime types sketched out above—not even as a hybrid. Albuquerque doesn't fit the corporate category very well because its business community appears to be incohesive in comparison to its counterparts in Dallas, Atlanta, and Baltimore. In Albuquerque, narrow development interests contribute to an atmosphere of competition and improbity in which alliances are so unstable that planning and cooperative actions are difficult to execute. Yet, growth demands are too great for a laissez-faire caretaker regime to be established. For a time, Peter Lupsha indicates, Albuquerque moved toward a progressive regime, but in a community in which short-term opportunism was widespread, progressive mayoral leadership was unable to consolidate support for such a regime.

This brief exploration of elements in community politics is not to be taken as a grand causal statement about urban regimes. It has not attempted to make connections among the four categories of factors explored, and I doubt that these four categories exhaust the forces that are important. This exploration is intended only to show how the particulars of time and place help to form the character of urban regimes. It suggests that causation is manifold—no one overriding factor is at work; that causation is sequential—the present is shaped by the past; and that causation is cumulative—as various elements combine to contribute to a given pattern, other alternatives are increasingly difficult to realize.[3]

The line of argument here is offered only to indicate how social conditions and political arrangements might matter. In presenting this argument, I have given little attention to such specific questions as whether elections are at large or by district, where campaign funds come from, and whether leadership is executive centered or not. Such questions are not neglected on the ground that they are trivial. Quite the contrary, they are important. However, to the extent that causation is manifold, sequential, and cumulative, inquiry that attempts to isolate the universal importance of narrowly specific political structures or social variables is unlikely to be fruitful.

NORMATIVE CONSIDERATIONS

Politics is ultimately about how we conduct our lives together.[4] It is important therefore to consider *how* authority is exercised, as well as what particular policy aims it is used to further. For this reason, I see the politics of development as a testing ground for representativeness. My own preference is for arrangements that foster an inverted form of Madisonian representativeness—one in which those who have control of much property are unable to dominate those who have little or none. Such representativeness seems to me to be essential (though not sufficient by itself) to achieving that form of public fairness which we call justice.

Cities perhaps have a special claim on the need for representativeness in their governance. Many years ago, Jane Jacobs told us that the special vitality of cities comes from their diversity.[5] If cities have a "unitary" interest, it may be in protecting that diversity. They are, in any case, complex entities, engaged in a set of interrelated social experiments, many of which fall under the rubric of development or redevelopment. It is appropriate, then, that this complexity be guided by the experiences and reactions of the many rather than the few.[6]

At stake in development policy is a series of social experiments. A community learns by doing, by trial and error. It tries a policy, never certain that it will work and almost always unaware of some of its side effects. The smaller and more closed the leadership group is that conducts these experiments, the more narrow the base of correction and feedback. Or because everything in the modern city is connected to everything else to some degree, we could say that the slower and the more mediated the feedback is from those outside the inner policy circle, the weaker that feedback is in influencing future policy decisions. Presumably those whose feedback is slow and mediated in reaching decision makers are less well served than those who can provide faster and more direct feedback. If so, it matters greatly who is on the inside and on how feedback from the larger community is filtered through a city's political arrangements.

Although one may talk about development in scientific-sounding terms such as *feedback*, ultimately one must confront the fact that the city is a political community. Among other things, this means that not only does politics matter, but also that political arrangements have normative consequences. In principle, they embody an approximation of justice—some notion of how citizens ought to be related to one another.

Much could be said about this. At this point, however, I wish to offer only the simple claim that justice is not well served by policy-making arrangements under which those who form policy are insulated from segments of the population who experience the consequences of that policy. Under these conditions, social learning is impaired, and bonds of community seem sure to suffer. As urban regimes are analyzed, such normative considerations should not be ignored.

What a normatively sensitive perspective might encourage is an integrated view of evolving urban structures. Instead of fragmenting our attention by looking at discrete correlates of regime form, analysis might aim for a broad picture of how various elements of the urban community fit together in a process of change. It is possible, for example, that the scale of urban politics is changing.[7] Whereas small-property holders and local political actors once held sway, it may be that the urban arena is now one in which big organizations and concentrations of wealth predominate. If so, we should consider what such a transition means for representations. How might change of that magnitude insulate policy makers from citizens? Would it serve to organize some issues and interests into city politics and others out? A world of big organizations, each of which is attempting to control or at least regularize its environment, is undoubtedly a very complex world, but complexity is not the same as pluralism. Complexity doesn't guarantee openness and wide access; in fact, it may do just the opposite. If it is the case that large-scale organization, concentrated economic power, and command of critical masses of of technical know-how—in short, features associated with corporate business and some types of governmental agencies—are the ingredients needed in order to play the development game, then we should know how that came about and whether it can be countered in such a way as to widen representation. These are big and empirically messy questions to deal with, but if we want to understand why urban regimes take the shape that they do, they are the kinds of questions that we must face at some stage.

Although we want to be mindful of structural change, in any form, we don't want to view such change in a way that obliterates the role that individuals play in modifying and transforming structures, even though many of these changes may be unintentional.[8] Jameson Doig's chapter on Austin Tobin is a careful study of an individual and his colleagues who used opportunities bestowed by the structure of the situation while also bringing new situations into being. Individuals don't build from a structurally clean foundation, and a historically sensitive perspective can remind us of that. But it can also remind us that we are purposive and reflective creatures, capable of modifying the situations in which we find ourselves.

Research is therefore not a self-contained reward, to be gloried in purely for its own sake. As Alexis de Tocqueville cautioned, our understanding of history and causation shapes the way in which we view ourselves and affects our capacity to act as a society or a community. Tocqueville was particularly critical of those historians unable to discern the influence of individuals: "They take a nation arrived at a certain stage of its history, and they affirm that it could not but follow the track which brought it thither. It is easier to make such an assertion, than to show by what means the nation might have adopted a better course."[9]

Tocqueville argues, however, that we should not overlook humanity's capacity to think and act, "for the great object in our time is to raise the faculties of men, not to complete their prostration."[10] So, as we pursue the "determinants" of urban regimes, let us not define causal necessity in such a way as to deny the efficacy of human reflection and the possibility of adopting "a better course."[11]

CONCLUSION

We have now come full circle, from an opening discussion of where the literature on urban-development politics has been to a closing discussion of where it should go. In between, by case example and argument, the contributors to this volume have attempted to support the proposition that even in a context of economic competition among local jurisdictions, politics matters. Politics shapes policy, and it influences not only our capacity to adapt to a changing society but also our understanding of what those changes signify. The political-economy context means that development policy must attend to the fact that by and large, investment capital is privately held and mobile. There is nevertheless cause to believe that the particular arrangements of a community, informal as well as formal, fashion the form that attentiveness to investment capital takes. If so, there is reason to pursue how civic arrangements might best be designed to represent the full community they serve. I would urge this direction in the future study of the politics of development.

NOTES

1. See also Michael N. Danielson and Jameson W. Doig, *New York: The Politics of Urban Regional Development* (Berkeley: University of California Press, 1982).
2. Rufus P. Browning, Dale Rogers Marshall, and David H. Tabb, *Protest Is Not Enough* (Berkeley: University of California Press, 1984).
3. Cf. Philip Abrams, *Historical Sociology* (Ithaca, N.Y.: Cornell University Press, 1982), pp. 112–28.
4. Stephen L. Elkin, "Economic and Political Rationality," *Polity* 18 (Winter 1985): 253–71.
5. Jane Jacobs, *The Death and Life of Great American Cities* (New York: Random House, 1961).
6. See ibid., pp. 428–48, on cities and organized complexity.
7. Clarence N. Stone, "Complexity and the Changing Character of Executive Leadership," *Urban Interest* 4 (Fall 1982): 29–50.
8. Abrams, *Historical Sociology*.
9. Alexis de Tocqueville, *On Democracy, Revolution, and Society*, ed. John Stone and Stephen Mennell (Chicago: University of Chicago Press, 1980), p. 162.
10. Ibid.
11. See also Abrams, *Historical Sociology*.

About the Contributors

SOPHIE N. BODY-GENDROT teaches at the Institut d'Etudes Politiques in Paris, where she is doing research on the welfare state and on immigration and minority issues in cross-cultural perspective. A Tocqueville Scholar, she has been a visiting scholar at Columbia University and New York University. Her book, *Black Americans Today*, has not yet been translated into English, but she has published articles in American journals and in *Urban Policy under Capitalism*, edited by Norman Fainstein and Susan Fainstein, and in *The Capitalist City*, edited by Michael P. Smith and Joe Feagin.

SUSAN E. CLARKE is associate director of the Center for Public Policy Research at the University of Colorado, Boulder. She is also book review editor for *Urban Affairs Quarterly*. Her current research focus is urban economic development and interest group politics.

JAMESON W. DOIG is professor of politics and public affairs at Princeton University. He is author of *Metropolitan Transportation Politics and the New York Region*, coauthor of *The Assistant Secretaries, Men Who Govern* and *New York: The Politics of Urban Regional Development*, and editor and coauthor of *Criminal Corrections: Ideals and Realities*. His most recent publication is *Leadership and Innovation: A Biographical Perspective on Enterpreneurs in Government*, jointly edited with Erwin C. Hargrove.

STEPHEN L. ELKIN is a member of the faculty of the Department of Government and Politics at the University of Maryland. He is the author of *Politics and Land Use Planning* and *City and Regime in the American Republic*. He is also coeditor of and contributor to *The Democratic State*.

PETER A. LUPSHA is a professor of political science at the University of New Mexico. He has published numerous articles on urban politics and public policy and is currently working on a monograph on the politics of drug trafficking in Latin America.

ROBERT F. PECORELLA is an assistant professor in the Department of Government and Politics at St. John's University in New York. His work has appeared in *Polity, Public Administration Review,* and *Urban Resources.* He has recently completed a study of community elites in New York City.

ADOLPH REED, JR., is an associate professor of political science and Afro-American studies at Yale University. He is the author of *The Jesse Jackson Phenomenon* and editor of *Race, Politics, and Culture: Critical Essays on the Radicalism of the 1960s.* He served in the administration of Mayor Maynard Jackson as director of research and in other capacities. He currently holds a fellowship from the National Endowment for the Humanities.

HEYWOOD T. SANDERS is an associate professor of urban studies at Trinity University in San Antonio, Texas. He has previously written on urban-renewal and community development policy and recently completed a manuscript on the politics of urban infrastructure for the Twentieth Century Fund. He is currently researching the bureaucratic politics of federal grants under the urban-renewal program.

ROBERT P. STOKER is assistant professor of political science and faculty associate in public policy at George Washington University. His teaching and research interests include policy analysis, policy implementation, public decision making, and bureaucratic behavior. His current research is focused on the difficulties of intergovernmental policy implementation.

CLARENCE N. STONE is a member of the faculty of the Department of Government and Politics at the University of Maryland. He is the author of *Economic Growth and Neighborhood Discontent* and coauthor of *Urban Policy and Politics in a Bureaucratic Age* and author of numerous articles and papers. His current teaching and research interests are focused on power and leadership.

ROBERT K. WHELAN is an associate professor in the School of Urban and Regional Studies at the University of New Orleans. He is coauthor of *Urban Policy and Politics in a Bureaucratic Age* and author of numerous articles and papers. His major current research interest is urban economic development, focusing on the New Orleans and Montreal metropolitan areas.

J. ALLEN WHITT is associate professor in sociology and urban affairs at the University of Louisville. He is the author of *Urban Elites and Mass Transportation* and coauthor of *The Cooperative Workplace.* His major research interests are the politics of urban growth and the social and political networks among corporate elites.

Index